Envisioning Eternal Empire

ENVISIONING
Eternal Empire

Chinese Political Thought of the
Warring States Era

Yuri Pines

University of Hawai'i Press

HONOLULU

14 13 12 11 10 09   6 5 4 3 2 1

LIBRARY OF CONGRESS CATALOGING-IN-PUBLICATION DATA

Pines, Yuri.
    Envisioning eternal empire : Chinese political thought of
the Warring States era / Yuri Pines.
        p. cm.
    Includes bibliographical reference and index.
    ISBN 978-0-8248-3275-9 (hard cover : alk.paper)
    1. Political culture—China—History.   2. Political science—
China—Philosophy—History.   3. China—History—
Warring States, 403–221 B.C.   4. China—Politics and
government—To 221 B.C.   I. Title.
    JQ1516.P56 2009
    320.0931—dc22
                                        2008038712

University of Hawai'i Press books are printed on acid-free
paper and meet the guidelines for permanence and
durability of the Council on Library Resources.

Designed by University of Hawai'i Press production staff
Printed by The Maple-Vail Book Manufacturing Group

Contents

Acknowledgments

In the mid-1990s, I worked on my PhD dissertation at the Nankai University, Tianjin, under the guidance of Professor Liu Zehua 劉澤華. Already then I began contemplating how to introduce insights regarding traditional Chinese political culture of Professor Liu and his disciples, Ge Quan 葛荃, Zhang Fentian 張分田, and Zhang Rongming 張榮明, to the Western audience. It is to Liu Zehua and to Nankai friends that I owe my deepest intellectual debt, and it is to them that this book is dedicated.

My second debt is to my Western colleagues, who offered plenty of insightful comments and criticisms of the drafts of this manuscript or portions thereof and of my earlier publications. I am particularly grateful to (in alphabetic order) Michal Biran, Erica Brindley, Miranda Brown, Nicola Di Cosmo, Patricia Crone, Lothar von Falkenhausen, Carol Gluck, Paul R. Goldin, Martin Kern, Michael Nylan, Andrew Plaks, Charles Sanft, and Gideon Shelach. Many others, with whom I communicated at conferences and informal meetings and who shared with me their publications, further contributed toward maturation of my research and the completion of this book, and I am indebted to them.

While working on the manuscript, I benefited from the support of the Israeli Science Foundation (grant No. 726/02-1) and the Michael William Lipson Chair in Chinese Studies. I am particularly grateful for Agnes Gund and Daniel Shapiro Membership in the Institute for Advanced Study, Princeton NJ (2006), where extraordinarily favorable intellectual atmosphere greatly bolstered my research. And, of course, it is to my friends, most specifically Wang Yu 王宇, whom I am must thank for their multifaceted assistance during these years.

Introduction

The year 221 BCE[1] marks a momentous beginning in the political history of humankind. After a series of wars, the king of the northwestern state of Qin 秦 brought the Chinese world[2]—which for him equaled to the civilized world, "All under Heaven"—under his control. Triumphant, the king ushered in a series of ritual, administrative, and religious innovations to mark his unprecedented success, adopting the new title of "emperor" (*huangdi* 皇帝, literally "the august thearch")[3] instead of a mere "king" (*wang* 王). This was the official proclamation of a new, imperial, age in Chinese history, an age that was to last for 2,132 years under an almost uninterrupted succession of emperors, until the last child monarch, Puyi 溥儀, abdicated on February 12, 1912, in favor of the newly proclaimed Chinese Republic.

The durability of the Chinese empire defies easy explanation. Chinese emperors ruled over a vast land, with territory as diverse and population as heterogeneous as in other large continental empires, and they faced similar threats of foreign invasions, internal rebellions, and sociopolitical crises.[4] What differed in the Chinese case was not the empire's indestructibility—for it witnessed several spectacular collapses—but its almost miraculous resurrection after years of disorder. This resurrection was not merely symbolic—as it was in the case of the various self-proclaimed heirs of the Roman Empire, for instance[5]—but substantial, as far as political structure is concerned. Despite changes over the centuries in every sphere of life—from demography and topography to religion and socioeconomic structure—the basic premises of imperial rule, which were shaped in the age of the first imperial dynasties, remained largely intact. The notion of the nominally omnipotent monarch, who considered the inhabitants of All under Heaven as his subjects, presided over an ostensibly meritocratic officialdom, tolerated few, if any, instances of institutional autonomy, and pronounced his care for "the people" while denying them a role in decision-making was as valid for the Qin (秦, 221–207) and Han (漢, 206 BCE–220 CE) eras as it was for the late imperial dynasties, Ming (明, 1368–1644 CE) and Qing (清, 1644–1912). While at times de facto power relations deviated considerably

1

from this model, and various political, religious, and ethnic groups intermittently challenged the legitimacy of the ruling dynasty, none called into question these ideological foundations of the imperial political system.[6] What was the secret of this long-lived success?

Among the possible explanations for such longevity, the role of ideology appears particularly compelling. For a modern observer, the Chinese empire looks like a classical hegemonic construction in the Gramscian sense.[7] Its basic ideological premises were shared by every politically significant social group and even by its immediate neighbors; no alternative political structure was considered either legitimate or desirable; and even those rulers whose ethnic or social background must have encouraged them to be critical of the imperial polity were destined to adopt it and adapt themselves to it. Until the late nineteenth century, empire was the only conceivable polity for the inhabitants of the Chinese world.

This imperial intellectual hegemony was achieved neither through excessive coercion nor through intensive brainwashing, but rather, it can be argued, due to the unusual background to the creation of the empire. The empire was not only a military and administrative but also an intellectual construct; it was envisioned and planned long before it became a reality. Throughout the centuries of political division and sociopolitical crisis of the Chunqiu (春秋, Springs and Autumns, 770–453) and Zhanguo (戰國, Warring States, 453–221) periods, statesmen and thinkers in the Chinese world sought remedies against the ongoing turmoil. Through repeated trial and error, they developed distinctive administrative and military mechanisms that were later utilized by the empire's builders; in addition, they formulated ideals, values, and perceptions that laid the intellectual foundation for the imperial unification. These ideals, among which the unification of All under Heaven under the omnipotent monarch figured most prominently, became the building blocks of Chinese political culture, legitimating the empire long before it came into being and eventually ensuring its hegemonic position. Identifying this common legacy within the diversity of the Warring States ideologies is the main goal of this book.

My discussion focuses on three main issues in Warring States thought, each of which is present in almost every major text. In Part I, the longest section of the book, I discuss Zhanguo views of rulership—arguably, the crucial issue in Chinese political culture. I trace both the evolution of the concept of the omnipotent monarch and the different proposals on how to prevent this monarch from abusing his power. Although unanimously committed to the monarchic principle of rule, thinkers also realized that most sovereigns fell short of the ideal of a sage monarch. The preferred solution of many was to encourage the ruler to refrain from actively exercising his power and to relegate everyday tasks

to his underlings. The resultant tension between the ostensibly unlimited power of the sovereign and his sidelining in practice eventually generated endless
conflicts between the emperors and their entourages, but it also made possible
maintenance of the imperial system even under inept and mediocre rulers. The
monarch remained the ultimate symbol of unity and order, the supreme arbiter
in cases of political controversies—but usually it was his devoted officials who
actually ran the empire in his stead.

The formation of this social group of intelligent, responsible officials is
traced in Part II, which focuses on the intellectually active members of the
shi 士 stratum, the educated elite of the Warring States. I analyze the ways in
which the *shi* secured, first, their intellectual autonomy from power-holders
and, second, their position as politically indispensable public servants and as
moral guides for society. I focus on the reasons why the *shi* overwhelmingly
opted for a political career as a main avenue of self-realization and argue that
this voluntary acceptance of a government career in the ruler-centered polity
proved to be the single most important choice made by the Warring States
(and subsequent) intellectuals. It provided the rulers with a wide pool of gifted
servants, but it also created an immanent tension between the high self-esteem
of the lofty *shi* and their inferior position vis-à-vis the ruler. Prior to the imperial unification, the existence of the interstate market of talent that allowed *shi*
to shift allegiance from one court to another emboldened them, encouraging
some to defy the ruler. This oppositional stance backfired, however, bringing
about attempts to limit the autonomy of the *shi*. In the unified empire, the
descendants of the *shi*—the imperial *literati*—were mostly either subjugated or
co-opted by the rulers; but even after losing their relative autonomy, they did
not lose the pride, self-confidence, and sense of mission of their pre-imperial
predecessors. The intellectuals' political commitment proved to be one of the
most important legacies of the Warring States to the unified empire.

The final part of my discussion deals with the third component of the imperial polity, "the people," that is, the usually silent but potentially rebellious
stratum of commoners. My discussion focuses on the commoners not as objects
of monarchical munificence, but as potential political actors, whose impact on
political processes was widely recognized, albeit not necessarily welcomed. I
shall try to assess why the almost universal recognition of the people as the
foundation of the polity, whose well-being should be the ultimate goal of poli-
cymakers and whose feelings should be constantly addressed, never brought
about any meaningful attempt to allow them to directly voice their grievances
or to otherwise influence political processes. This tension between an ostensible respect for the people and their practical sidelining from political life was
capable of being maintained as long as commoners enjoyed tolerable living

conditions and a minimal degree of upward mobility. When this was not so, the desperate masses could turn to rebellion. As I show, the "people-oriented" discourse of the Warring States period contributed, if only inadvertently, to the legitimation of popular uprisings, but it also allowed the co-opting of rebels within the imperial political system, thus preventing them from challenging the foundations of the imperial rule.

In addressing three major components of the pre-imperial and imperial polity—the ruler, the intellectual elite, and the commoners—I try to locate the foundational aspects of Chinese political culture. It was the interaction among these three segments of society that determined the degree of stability of the empire, and these were the three groups frequently singled out by pre-imperial thinkers for their intellectual explorations. My selection of these topics comes at the expense of other aspects of pre-imperial political thought, including its metaphysical, cosmological, and religious foundations and the debates over proper relations between society and the state. Some of these topics have already been addressed in English studies, but others deserve further treatment.[8] Yet my study is neither a textbook, nor do I claim comprehensiveness.[9] Rather, my goal is to focus on those topics of pre-imperial political thought that bear on subsequent Chinese political culture across the centuries and that have been insufficiently addressed in the past.

Note on Methodology

Some readers may be surprised by the format of my study, especially insofar as I rarely use a single text or a putative "school of thought" as an analytical unit. In focusing on the common legacy of the Warring States thinkers, I do not gloss over their sharp disagreements, but I do not intend to reify these disagreements either, as is often done in studies focused on competing schools of thought. While classification of different texts as belonging to distinct "schools" or "scholastic lineages" (jia 家) may be a convenient heuristic device, it has obvious limitations, and these were exacerbated in many modern studies that were influenced by the twentieth-century ideological controversies, when pre-imperial debates were often interpreted as struggles between ideological "camps." This perception was taken to the absurd in the early 1970s, when radical leaders of the Cultural Revolution identified the polemics between "Confucians" (ru jia 儒家) and "Legalists" (fa jia 法家) as an eternal controversy running all the way from the Chunqiu period to the current struggle between the "two lines" in the Chinese Communist Party.[10] It was only with the ebbing of these ideological controversies that leading Chinese scholars, such as Liu Zehua, began to abandon the "competing schools" paradigm as an analytical tool.[11] The inadequacy of the "school" perspective has been also noted by several Western scholars, such as Michael Nylan and Mark Csikszentmihalyi, who argue that "all the pre-Han and early Western Han thinkers seem to have been, in essence, 'eclectics' when viewed from the much stricter normative models of later times."[12]

With this understanding in mind, I shall emulate Liu Zehua in addressing the intellectual dynamics of the Warring States not through the prism of specific schools but rather by identifying a broad perspective of a common discourse in which most contemporary thinkers and statesmen took active part. Practically, this means that my study is based not on a selective reading of a few texts attributed to major thinkers, but on my attempt to incorporate most of the extant corpus of pre-imperial literature, including both the transmitted and the archeologically discovered texts. In the preliminary stage of my research, I surveyed (first manually, then electronically) most of these texts, looking for common topics. I then tried to arrange relevant passages in a rough temporal sequence, to outline patterns of intellectual change throughout the Warring States period.[13] Having prepared the outline, I then extracted those passages that are either the most influential in terms of subsequent discourse, or the most reliable in terms of their dating (for example, those from archeologically discovered manuscripts), or alternatively the most articulate and most illustrative of the ideas discussed. The resultant picture has allowed me to highlight many previously neglected aspects of the intellectual dynamics of the Warring States.

The advantages of my approach are several. First, it highlights common concerns and common perceptions among the Warring States thinkers instead of focusing on individual differences. Second, it allows a discussion based not on highly contested interpretations of a single passage or text, but rather on a broader sample that strengthens the persuasiveness of the argument. Third, this perspective bypasses methodological challenges presented by the view that few texts have individual authors. According to this view, most forcibly proposed by Mark Lewis and supported in a modified form by William Boltz, the texts are a result of a lengthy process of accretion, during which they were "actively composed and recomposed" from smaller textual units.[14] This hypothesis, which I accept with certain modifications, makes it difficult to date precisely either the text itself or any of its component units.

It is in light of this problem of provenance and authenticity that my method becomes particularly useful. An archeological metaphor may explain its advantages. Archeologists differentiate between large-scale studies, such as regional surveys, and small-scale ones, such as specific excavations. While the latter allow for more precision, the former, due to their larger scale and comprehensiveness, can tolerate minor inaccuracies without losing their value. Such regional surveys can detect synchronic patterns as well as diachronic processes, which are invisible in the small-scale excavations of a single site, let alone a single household.[15] Mutatis mutandis, this applies in textual studies as well. An in-depth study of a single text (or, even better, of a single textual unit, such as a chapter or a paragraph) can yield remarkable results in terms of precision, but it cannot detect synchronic patterns or diachronic processes, and it is vulnerable to skeptical views of textual authenticity. By contrast, my approach allows the detection of these patterns and processes and is less vulnerable to doubts about specific passages than in-depth textual studies.

What matters to my study is not the precise date of each textual unit I use, but that all units should be written before the imperial unification and reflect the intellectual milieu of the Warring States. On this score my study may be open to criticism in light of the suppositions of certain scholars (in studies yet to be published) that the massive editorial efforts of the Han dynasty librarians such as Liu Xiang 劉向 (c. 79–8 BCE) may have distorted the content of pre-imperial texts.[16] Yet I do not believe that the evidence supports this view. Not only do visible differences in the content and vocabulary of pre-imperial texts rule out the possibility of uniform ideological "cleaning," but, more importantly, a comparison of the transmitted texts with the archeologically unearthed manuscripts also supports the authenticity of the former. Han editorial efforts focused on such aspects as unifying the language of the texts, standardizing the use of characters and grammatical particles, replacing tabooed words, and rearranging textual units within a larger text. Nowhere can we discern traces of the Han redactors having significantly modified or expurgated politically problematic statements of the Warring States' thinkers.[17] Nowadays, moreover, it is possible to confirm the pre-imperial pedigree of most of the ideas and approaches discussed in this book on the basis of archeologically discovered manuscripts, as we shall see in the following chapters. Since my conclusions are not based on a single text, but on a systematic assessment of the bulk of the extant corpus of pre-imperial literature, I believe that they can survive the challenge of radical textual skepticism.

Peculiarities of My Study

My decision to address anew the political thought of the Warring States—the single most discussed topic in the study of Chinese history—derives not only from my desire to employ new research methods and to incorporate newly excavated materials that have tremendously expanded our knowledge of political, social, and intellectual life of the pre-imperial Chinese world. A more immediate impulse was my wish to reverse the loss of interest in the political sphere of pre-imperial Chinese intellectual history in the West during the last twenty years. Initially, this loss of interest was probably a reaction against the vulgar politicization of intellectual history in the People's Republic of China in the early 1970s and also against simplistic interpretations of ancient Chinese thought as entirely this-worldly; today, however, it is spurred by a variety of new academic fashions. In distinction from their Chinese colleagues, Western scholars have been less interested in addressing political topics even when recognizing that those occupy a pivotal place in the intellectual life of the Warring States.[18]

One of the major goals of this book is to reverse this trend and refocus scholarly attention on some central aspects of Chinese political thought. Topically, my study owes greatly to Chinese scholarly approaches, especially to Liu Zehua, whose ideas of monarchism as the essential feature of Chinese political culture greatly influence my research. Methodologically, though, I am closer to Western scholars, especially insofar as textual analysis is concerned. Moreover, unlike many Chinese studies, mine is not aimed at locating the historical roots of current political malpractices, but rather at identifying the contribution of Zhanguo thinkers to the longevity of the Chinese imperial polity. I hope that my analysis will shed a new light on the legacy that the Warring States bequeathed to the age of the unified empire. Analyzed from this long-term perspective, the intellectual life of the Warring States is relevant not only for scholars of early Chinese history, but for all those who deal with traditional—and arguably also modern—Chinese political culture and for those involved in comparative analysis of traditional political ideologies worldwide.

Moving along to the way I conducted my research, I would like to call attention to my two major premises. First, my approach is historical, and I am interested not only in ideas as such, but in their emergence and evolution. Fascinated, like many others, by the continuity of Chinese civilization, I still hope as much as possible to avoid a common trap of viewing certain behavioral and intellectual patterns as "intrinsically Chinese," that is, timeless and changeless. While many of these patterns, such as the ritually based social hierarchy, ancestral worship, and the monarchic principle of rule, have a pedigree traceable to the earliest stages of stratified society on Chinese soil, this does not mean that they never changed. Especially during the Chunqiu and Zhanguo periods, as "Chinese" society witnessed unprecedented transformations, many of the previously established concepts were questioned, modified, or imbued with new meaning. Omitting these fluctuations from scholarly analysis, as is so often done, creates a skewed picture of Chinese intellectual history and inadvertently contributes to the view of the Chinese past as ossified. In contrast, I believe that the ideological life of pre-imperial China was determined not by fixed and unchangeable patterns, but primarily by reasonable choices that thinkers and statesmen made during times of crisis. It is by highlighting the background and reasons for these choices that I try to make the distinctiveness of China's political trajectory intelligible.

Second, my discussion of intellectual life is emphatically contextual. I do not consider texts to be self-contained realities. Philology is of course essential in dealing with ancient texts, and this study is based on what I hope will be accepted as meticulous philological analysis of the texts under discussion. But philology should be applied together with a historical approach and not in its stead. The texts were, after all, written by authors who were products of their times and were involved in the political and social life of their age, and the texts were directed at specific audiences with which they interacted.[19] A neglect of the sociopolitical and intellectual settings of a text, or in Paul Goldin's apt term, its "deracination,"[20] often leads to speculative attempts to find in the texts alien political or philosophical ideas (from deontology to gender equality), which in all likelihood were inconceivable to both the authors and their audience.

Relating the texts to their sociopolitical context results in a different picture from that attainable by a purely textual study. The process allows us to notice barely enunciated subtexts and even to see the importance of a thinker's sudden silence when a sensitive topic is discussed. It also enables us to qualify the self-proclaimed idealism of many thinkers by investigating the immediate political implications of their proposals. Such readings sometimes reveal that lofty statements may conceal sinister motives, while laudable moral ideals may become intolerable when translated into administrative reality. Further, it allows us to avoid ideologically biased readings of ancient texts. Instead of judging the political ideas of ancient Chinese thinkers from a modern perspective—be it in terms of class struggle, human rights, patriotism, gender equality, or democracy—we should try to understand them in their own, immediate context. What were the thinkers' goals? How did their ideas influence the political dynamics of the time? How did contemporaries assess them? Answering these questions can keep us from turning ancient Chinese thinkers into pawns in modern ideological and scholarly games.

That said, I do not deny that modern perspectives can be relevant for the analysis of ancient Chinese texts. Many of the issues faced by ancient Chinese thinkers—from the need to ensure peace to the search for a proper place for the intellectuals in society—are as relevant today as they were two millennia ago. But we must remember how different their sociopolitical setting was from our own. Their goals were neither democracy nor equality, but simply peace and stability, which the majority identified as attainable only within a universal empire. It is against this background that we can judge the achievements and failures of the Warring States intellectuals. None of them could anticipate the nature of the future imperial polity. Yet their collective vision brought about the most durable political structure in human history. How they did so is the subject of this book.

A Note on Translation

All translations in the text are mine unless indicated otherwise. For the reader's convenience, I identify, whenever relevant, the scroll (*juan* 卷, indicated by Roman numbers), chapter (*pian* 篇), and section/paragraph (*zhang* 章) of the premodern Chinese texts; they are separated by a period and are followed by the page number of the modern edition, separated by a colon. Whenever I cite recently unearthed texts, I indicate the slip number according to the sequence proposed by the original publishers; the characters are invariably written in their modern form according to the editors' or other scholars' suggestions.

PART I

The Ruler

CHAPTER 1

Ritual Figureheads

In the vastness of four seas, among multitudes of people, [all] are ruled by a single person. Even among those whose power suffices to sever the norms and whose knowledge exceeds that of their age, none will not hurry to serve—is not it due to the basic norms of ritual? . . . Insofar as [a ruler] is not as evil as Jie and Zhou[xin], and [a minister] is not as benevolent as Tang and Wu, one to whom the people flock and who is decreed by Heaven—one should preserve the separation between the ruler and the minister even at the expense of prostrating [oneself and accepting] death!

—Sima Guang

The lines cited in the epigraph come from the opening paragraphs of Sima Guang's (司馬光, 1019–1086 CE) masterpiece, *The Comprehensive Mirror to Aid the Government* (*Zizhi tongjian* 資治通鑒), arguably the most influential political-historical text of the second imperial millennium.[1] In a few sentences, Sima Guang succinctly summarizes what he considers the quintessence of Chinese political culture: first, the existence of the universal and omnipotent monarch; second, the intrinsic link between the monarch's power, the functioning of the ritual pyramid, and the preservation of the sociopolitical order in general; third, that the monarch should normally command the complete obedience of his subjects; and, finally, in certain extraordinary cases an evil ruler can—and should—be replaced. This replacement, however, as Sima Guang's narrative convincingly shows, should alter only the name of the dynasty but not the monarchical foundations of the political order. A millennium later, and writing from an entirely different perspective, the leading reformist, Liang Qichao (梁啟超, 1873–1929), may have had a similar understanding in mind when he summarized Chinese history as having a single field of "progress," that toward an ever more effective dictatorship.[2]

Many modern scholars share Sima Guang's and Liang Qichao's view of the ruler's omnipotence as a quintessential feature of Chinese political culture.

Thus when Liu Zehua, the leading current scholar of Chinese political thought, sought to summarize his twenty-odd years of studies of China's political culture, he used a term *wangquanzhuyi* 王權主義 ("monarchism") as the title of his magnum opus.[3] This term may serve as a useful departure point for my discussion. Can we indeed identify "monarchism" as a guiding principle of Chinese political culture? And if so, when and how did it emerge? Or, perhaps, was it essential to Chinese culture, just as ancestral cult and ritually based social gradations are supposed to be?[4] What are its practical implications? Was it universally endorsed by Zhanguo thinkers, and if not, what were the dissidents' alternatives? To what extent was monarchic rule religiously or philosophically stipulated, or was it primarily conceived as an administrative necessity? Were there any proposals of institutionalized limitations to the ruler's authority, and if not, how did thinkers seek to limit the abuse of power by the sovereign? These questions will be addressed in the following four chapters.

First, I outline the religious, ritual, and political background of Zhanguo views of rulership, particularly, the problematic of the Western Zhou (西周, c. 1046–1771) and Chunqiu legacy of ritually all-powerful, but politically weak, sovereigns. In Chapter 2 I trace various arguments in Zhanguo texts in favor of the ruler's exaltedness, focusing specifically on the evolution of the ideal of a True Monarch, whose power was supposed to be absolute. Yet as Zhanguo thinkers realized, most if not all of the current rulers fell well short of the idealized True Monarch, and so they had to address the situation of absolute power being concentrated in the hands of a potentially inept sovereign. Some thinkers, whose views are discussed in Chapter 3, pondered about the ways to ensure that a truly competent monarch would occupy the throne. Their failure, in turn, gave way to more sober and yet more sophisticated attempts to prevent the abuse of power by mediocre rulers. In Chapter 4, by focusing on two major late Zhanguo thinkers, Xunzi (荀子, c. 310–218) and Han Feizi (韓非子, d. 233), I show that supporters of the ruler's absolute authority simultaneously discouraged the rulers from active involvement in policy-making. The resultant contradiction between the ruler's ostensible omnipotence and the minimization of his political involvement became a source of constant tension that plagued the Chinese empire ever afterward, as I shall demonstrate in the epilogue to Chapter 4.

Religious Foundations of the Ruler's Power

In investigating early sources of the ruler's authority in China one is immediately impelled to address the cultic and ritual power of the sovereign.[5] As in many other premodern cultures, ancient Chinese rulers enjoyed sacral status due to their preferential access to the divine and their ability to mediate between the superhuman Powers and the community of the living. In the case of the Shang (商, c. 1600–1046) dynasty, for instance, it is widely agreed that the king's role as a diviner and his ability to enroll the support of the deified royal ancestors and through them of other deities, including the supreme Thearch, Di 帝, played a major role in bolstering the monarch's legitimacy. Oracle-bone records indicate that the king not only performed the divination ritual but also had a final say in interpreting the ancestors' answers. David Keightley summarizes the political impact of the king's role as the supreme diviner:

> It was the king who made fruitful harvests and victories possible by the sacrifices he offered, the rituals he performed, and the divinations he made. If, as seems likely, the divinations involved some degree of magic making or spell casting, the king's ability to actually create a good harvest or a victory by divining about it rendered him still more powerful politically.[6]

The Shang kings were not only the supreme diviners, but, in their capacity as heads of the ruling lineage, they also regulated their relatives' intercourse with ancestral spirits.[7] This system in which the lineage head was a linking chain between the living and the deceased kin was not limited to the royal lineage, but, apparently, paralleled that in other contemporary polities in which "the group leader . . . derived his authority from that of his mythical progenitor."[8] It is possible, therefore, that a system in which a single member of the community concentrated the supreme spiritual, and the adjacent secular, power, due to exclusive access to ancestral protectors, is traceable to the earliest historical stages of Chinese civilization.

The Zhou overthrow of the Shang (c. 1046) brought about significant political changes amidst overall religious continuity. The victorious Zhou rapidly extended their rule to the central and lower reaches of the Yellow River basin and beyond, dwarfing the territorial extent of the late Shang polity. Instead of the Shang system of loose alliances with other polities, early Zhou kings tried to facilitate their rule by establishing "fiefs" at strategic locations in the eastern part of their domain, either by imposing on the native population a new ruling elite drafted from the royal relatives and allies, or by granting royal recognition to local leaders. This brought about a two-tier rulership system, in which under the supreme aegis of the Zhou monarch, autonomous (and eventually independent) regional lords (zhuhou 諸侯) ruled their lands as unrivaled potentates. In what follows, I shall address both the features of spiritual power that were common to the king and the regional lords and those that were distinctive aspects of the Zhou monarch's authority.[9]

The Shang-based pontifical power of a lineage head (and, by extension, of any ruler) remained largely intact in the early Zhou period, albeit with certain modifications. Thus as the intercourse with the ancestors became increasingly ritualized and formularized, divinations lost part of their importance, remaining primarily a means of "resolving doubts," but not a source of routine political guidance; eventually the Zhou rulers lost their monopoly on performing divination.[10] Yet ritualization of the human intercourse with divine protectors by no means meant abandoning the pivotal role of the lineage head as the guarantor of the ongoing support of the spirits to their living kin. The head of the lineage presided over the sacrificial ceremony, and his presence was crucial for the ceremony's success, which would ensure ongoing ancestral assistance to the descendants.[11] In particular, Zhou kings continued to enjoy exclusive access to their dynastic progenitors and the regional lords to the founders of their state.

The power of the head of the lineage was emphasized in the course of the so-called mid–Western Zhou ritual reform, which strengthened the pedigree-based social hierarchy. In the course of this reform, sumptuary privileges were fixed, reflecting—and strengthening—the position of the heads of the trunk lineages versus the heads of branch lineages; this meant, among other things, emphasizing the superiority of the Zhou kings over the regional lords and of the lords over other nobles within their fiefs. The reform therefore solidified the position of a single leader at the apex of the ritual (that is, sociopolitical) pyramid.[12]

The impact of the Shang and Zhou religious and ritual regulations on the later evolution of Chinese political culture is enormous. The supreme and non-dispersible pontifical power of the head of the lineage meant that the kin-based religious community could not be headed by more than a single person at a given time, and the position of the head of the lineage would remain unchangeable throughout that person's life. It is not difficult to notice the conceptual foundations of monarchic rule in these religious practices. Concentration of ritual authority in the hands of a single person may have contributed decisively to the preclusion of alternative, nonmonarchic (that is, oligarchic or rotation-based) modes of rule. Even during the Chunqiu period, when such oligarchic modes of rule were practiced de facto in several states, nobody dared proposing their institutionalization; nor did this occur during the Zhanguo age when thinkers were eager to probe many novel approaches in order to cope with the ongoing crisis of the Zhou system.[13]

Kinship foundations of power were of great importance for the Zhou kings at the early stages of their rule, when many (probably most) regional lords were directly related to the dynastic founders, kings Wen and Wu, and they also were helpful for the lords, whose courts were routinely staffed by their agnates. However, it would be wrong to reduce the political system of the early Zhou to a mere extension of kinship ties. Many regional lords neither belonged to the ruling Ji 姬 clan nor were necessarily related to the Ji through intermarriage; within most of the "fiefs" significant segments of the population, including parts of the elite, did not belong to the lord's lineage. To facilitate their rule over these subjects, Zhou rulers developed a nonancestral source of religious legitimacy, which was based on their ties with celestial and terrestrial deities. Here, just as in the case of ancestral sacrifices, the rulers monopolized the cult: universal deities, particularly the most powerful and politically active deity, Heaven (*tian* 天), were worshipped exclusively by the Zhou kings, while local deities, particularly those of the "altars of soil and grain" (*sheji* 社稷) were worshipped by the regional lords only.[14] In both cases, contacts with the deity were confined to the ruler and precluded from his subjects.

To illustrate the political implications of the ruler's ritual power I shall focus on the cult of Heaven, which became an important source of authority for the Zhou monarchs. As it is well known, from the very beginning of their rule Zhou kings claimed that their overthrow of the Shang was mandated by impartial Heaven, the supreme deity in charge of political order. The Zhou dynastic founders were possessors of the sacred quality of *de* 德, which allowed them to obtain Heaven's support, and which they were bequeathing to their descendants and also to their meritorious ministers. The notion of Heaven's Decree (or Mandate, *tian ming* 天命) became the solid foundation of Zhou legitimacy.[15]

Effective as it was for justifying the overthrow of the Shang, the concept of Heaven's Decree was a double-edged sword, for it could be used in the future against the Zhou itself. To prevent another contender for power from claiming the Decree/Mandate, the Zhou kings acted swiftly to limit interactions with the supreme deity to the monarchs only. The solemn title of Son of Heaven (*tianzi* 天子), appropriated by the kings in the early generations of the Zhou rule, symbolized their quasi-kinship relations with *tian*, and these relations were further buttressed by the claim that the Zhou dynastic ancestors are present in Heaven, in the vicinity of Di, where they had apparently replaced the Shang progenitors.[16] This exclusive access of the kings to Heaven became a powerful source of royal legitimacy, which outlived not only the kings' actual power but even, as will be shown below, the very Zhou dynasty itself.

The fall of the western capital, Hao 鎬, in 771, marked the decline of Zhou royal power. By the seventh century BCE, hapless kings often became puppets of their self-proclaimed "protectors," particularly the rulers of Qi 齊 and Jin 晉. Royal representatives were sidelined from interstate meetings, and haughty regional lords routinely transgressed ritual norms by adopting royal sumptuary and sacrificial prerogatives. This, in addition to meager coverage of the Zhou royal activities in the received texts, has created an impression of complete marginalization of the royal line during the last few centuries of its existence. Some scholars have even suggested that the very notion of the Zhou symbolic centrality during that time was nothing but a post-factum creation of Han historiography.[17] Recent epigraphic discoveries call this assertion into question, lending renewed credibility to scattered accounts in the *Shiji* 史記 and *Zhanguo ce* 戰國策, according to which Zhou kings continued to maintain symbolic superiority well into the Warring States period, preserving their position at the apex of the universal ritual pyramid. Perhaps the most interesting evidence to this effect is a recently published inscription on two jade tablets made by a king of Qin 秦 soon after the final demise of the Zhou dynasty in 256 but before the imperial unification of 221. The inscription records a king's plea to the spirit of Mt. Hua 華山, which is asked to cure the king's aggravating illness. After depicting his poor physical conditions, the king of Qin states:

> The house of Zhou has now vanished,
> the standards and regulations [of sacrifices] have been scattered and lost.
> A fearful small child,
> I would like to serve Heaven and Earth,
> the four apices and the three luminaries,
> spirits and deities of mountains and rivers,
> five objects of sacrifice, former ancestors—
> but cannot obtain the [proper] way [of conducting the sacrifice].
> My sacrificial pigs are made beautiful,
> jade and silk are purified,
> but, a toddler that I am,
> I am wavering and am dull regarding [proper sacrifices] to the west and to
>   the east.[18]

This statement, made by a ruler of the state that annexed the remnants of the Zhou royal domain in 256 is, at the very least, surprising. Its explicit reverence to the Zhou, the recognition of the religious superiority of the Zhou kings, and the lament for the fall of the dynasty is at odds with the traditional image of Qin as an archvillain that brought about the Zhou downfall. Putting aside for the time being the inscription's value for understanding Qin's history and Qin-Zhou relations,[19] let us focus on the light it sheds on the status of the Zhou kings in the late Zhanguo period. While the pro-Zhou sentiments expressed in the inscription should not necessarily be taken at their face value, they do testify that the ritual prestige of the Zhou kings did not evaporate, even after the end of the dynasty. That the king of Qin, on the eve of imperial unification, still identified himself as ritually inferior to the Zhou kings suggests that the unrivaled position of the Zhou monarch as *pontifex maximus*, the supreme mediator between the divine and the human realms, remained intact throughout the eight centuries of the Zhou rule and even after the dynasty's demise.

What were the political implications of the persistent ritual power of the Zhou kings? The answer to this question is not simple. On the one hand, it is clear that ritual prestige could not compensate the Sons of Heaven for the loss of political and military prowess, especially as many of the royal ritual privileges were "usurped" by regional lords. On the other hand, the ritual superiority of the Zhou house remained its most important political asset. Not incidentally, even when the rulers of major Warring States openly discarded Zhou ritual norms and adopted the title of "king" (*wang* 王), none dared proclaim himself Son of Heaven, implicitly recognizing thereby that only one Son of Heaven could exist on Earth.[20] Textual and epigraphic evidence further suggest that occasionally Sons of Heaven were able to translate their religious prestige into political esteem and thus restore a semblance of their "universal" supremacy.[21] But in addition, the religious prowess of the Zhou kings was politically meaningful in a deeper sense. By their sheer existence as the single locus of cultic authority, the Sons of Heaven symbolized the possibility of restoration of a politically unified and stable realm, thereby adding legitimacy to the idea of political unity, as will be discussed in Chapter 2. Their symbolic significance as the ritual center of the universe contributed decisively to the remarkable survival of the Zhou house during centuries of its notorious weakness. It also explains why the final demise of the Zhou dynasty was lamented by some Zhanguo thinkers, such as those who gathered at the court of Qin circa 240 to compile the *Lüshi chunqiu* 呂氏春秋, the major pre-imperial intellectual compendium:

> Nowadays, the house of Zhou has been destroyed, [the line of] the Sons of Heaven has been severed. There is no turmoil greater than the absence of the Son of Heaven; without the Son of Heaven, the strong overcome the weak, the many lord it over the few, they use arms to harm each other having no rest.[22]

This lamentation, which curiously resembles that in the Qin royal prayer discussed earlier, is indicative of the Zhou king's political role. Centuries after the dynasty lost its ability to calm the ongoing turmoil, its mere existence perpetuated hopes for the eventual restoration of unity and stability. The power of the Zhou kings, whether religious or symbolic, remained a source of inspiration for those who hoped to see both the Heavenly realm and the world "under Heaven" well ordered and properly ruled. The very notion of the singularity of the Son of Heaven at the top of the ritual pyramid was conducive to the idea of a unified locus of political power, which, as we shall see in Chapter 2, became the major unifying thread of Zhanguo political thought.

The Chunqiu Crisis of Rulership

While the above discussion highlighted the lasting impact of the early Zhou pontifical power of the monarch, this impact certainly fell short of the expectations of the architects of the Zhou ritual system. By the sixth century BCE, the entire ritual-based sociopolitical order was on the verge of collapse, and nowhere was the crisis more evident than in the case of the declining authority of the rulers. Not only had the Zhou kings lost most of their effective power, but their erstwhile underlings, the regional lords, witnessed similar assaults on their positions by their nominal subordinates, heads of the major ministerial lineages. These parallel processes brought about endemic domestic and interstate turmoil, which came to characterize the Chunqiu age.

The declining power of the Zhou Sons of Heaven has been considered in retrospect as the major reason for, or at least a major manifestation of, the systemic disorder that was to plague the Chunqiu world,[23] but its immediate impact on contemporary political thought was limited. Although in the long run it brought about the collapse of the multistate system and resulted in continuous warfare, this result was not instantly apparent. Throughout the Chunqiu period, statesmen were actively engaged in creating a viable system of multistate relations, and it was only by the second half of the sixth century that the fiasco of these efforts was widely recognized.[24] While eventually the quest to reunify All under Heaven (*tianxia* 天下) was renewed, in the short term interstate problems were largely overshadowed by domestic crises in most Chunqiu polities. It was the decline of the regional lords' power that became a major threat for political stability.

The loss of the lords' power in the seventh and sixth centuries was a by-product of two closely related phenomena: the emergence of a system of hereditary appointments and hereditary land allotments. By the middle of the Chunqiu period, a few high-ranking aristocratic lineages virtually monopolized ministerial positions in each state, effectively preventing others from ascending to the top of the government apparatus. Land allotments (*cai yi* 采邑), which had previously been distributed to the ruler's relatives and meritorious servants, became the hereditary possessions of ministerial lineages, which then established their authority over the allotments' dwellers, who were no longer

subjected to the local lord, but to their immediate master. This meant that the
regional lords of the Chunqiu age effectively lost much of their administrative,
economic, and military power to the hereditary office-holders, who relied on
the resources of their allotments and could easily challenge their rulers.[25]

Beginning at the end of the seventh century, the situation of "weak rulers,
powerful ministers" resulted in a series of dramatic clashes between the lords
and their formal aides, clashes that were ending increasingly in the ministers'
favor. In most of the Central States (such as Jin, Qi, Wei 衛, Zheng 鄭, Lu 魯,
and Song 宋), the major ministerial lineages created coalitions that were much
more powerful than the local lords; the lords were able to partly restore their
position only in cases of friction within the ministerial alliances. Powerful ministers assassinated the lord of Jin in 607, and another one in 573; of Zheng in
566; of Qi in 548; and expelled the lords of Wei, Yan 燕, and Lu in 559, 539, and
517 respectively, to mention only a few cases.[26] Theoretically the lords remained
the legitimate leaders of their states—none of the ruling families was replaced
throughout years of turmoil—but even this advantage was of little help, as heads
of aristocratic lineages commanded absolute loyalty of their kin, retainers, and
those who dwelled in their allotments. This effectively stripped the lords of the
manpower needed to counterbalance ministerial assaults.[27]

In addition to their political, economic, and military weakness, Chunqiu regional lords were in a disadvantageous position on the intellectual front as well.
Chunqiu thinkers, whose voices we hear from the *Zuo zhuan* 左傳—the larg-
est repository of Chunqiu period history and thought[28]—belonged with a few
exceptions to major ministerial lineages. These thinkers did not combat the decline in the lords' power, but on the contrary provided ideological justifications
for this process. Their arguments can be illustrated by the following dialogue
between Lord Dao of Jin (晉悼公, r. 572–558) and his aide, Musical Master
Kuang 師曠. The discussion was prompted by unprecedented turmoil in neighboring Wei 衛, where in 559 a coalition of powerful nobles expelled Lord Xian
(衛獻公, r. 576–559 and 546–544) and replaced him with a puppet:

> The lord of Jin asked: The men of Wei expelled their ruler—is it not too
> much?
>
> [Kuang] answered: Perhaps it was their ruler who was too much [for
> them]? A good ruler rewards the good and punishes the licentious; he nour-
> ishes his people like his own children, shelters them like Heaven, bears them
> up like Earth. The people serve their ruler, they love him like their own
> parents, look up to him like the sun and moon, revere him like the deities
> and the numinous [spirits], fear him like thunder and lightning. Could they
> then expel him?[29]

Kuang begins his speech with a panegyric to the ruler, ostensibly proclaiming his divinely approved status and immunity of any kind of adverse action by his subjects. Yet following this radical dictum is a much more sophisticated argument, which sets the limits to a ruler's power:

> The ruler is the master of the deities, the hope of the people. But if he fatigues the people's lives, neglects the deities, and ignores the sacrifices, then "the hundred clans" will lose their hope, and the altars of soil and grain will have no master. What use is [such a ruler]? What can one do but expel him?[30]

The ruler's authority is not absolute but is conditioned by proper performance of his obligations to two major constituencies: the people, who require their livelihood, and the deities (here obviously referring both to terrestrial deities and to ancestral spirits) who need sacrifices. If he fails to fulfill his tasks, a ruler loses his legitimacy and is prone to regulatory intervention by the supreme deity, Heaven, whose will is executed by the ruler's aides:

> Heaven gives birth to the people and sets up the ruler to oversee and take care of them, not to make them lose their nature. As there are rulers, they are given helpers to teach them and protect them and to prevent them from exceeding [proper] measures. Hence the Son of Heaven has his lords, regional lords have ministers, ministers have collateral lineages, nobles have collateral branches, *shi* have [young] brothers and sons, commoners, artisans, merchants, lackeys, shepherds, and grooms all have close relatives and associates who help and assist them. When [the ruler] is good, he is rewarded; when he exceeds, he is corrected; when he is in distress, he is rescued; when he loses [the proper way], he is replaced.[31]

Master Kuang's argument again follows a pendulum-like trajectory. After proclaiming the sacrality of the ruler's authority (established by Heaven for the people's sake), he goes back to the proclamation of the tentative nature of the ruler's tenure. In the kin-based social system, each one has close relatives who are supposed to perform the key role of admonishing, correcting, and instructing their superior. The most interesting point is the last phrase, which ends with "when he loses [the proper way], he is replaced." Master Kuang does not specify whether replacing the ruler was the prerogative of Heaven or of the ruler's deputies/relatives, but in any case it is clear that the minister has the right to execute the will of Heaven, deities, and the people, even if this requires deposing the sovereign!

Kuang's speech is symptomatic of the Chunqiu intellectual atmosphere. While paying lip service to the sacrality of the ruler's position, the speaker presents convincing political and religious justifications for a ruler's replacement. Moreover, the right to perform this daring act is squarely granted to the ruler's relatives, who, in their capacity as ministers, are supposed to assist but also to supervise the sovereign, thereby sharing the burden of his power. This idea is echoed elsewhere in the *Zuo zhuan*. It reflects the peculiar Chunqiu situation of an intellectual hegemony of the high aristocracy, the same stratum that competed with the regional lords for power.[32] With less sophistication than Master Kuang, but with similar candor, late Chunqiu thinkers eagerly supplied philosophical, political, and moral justifications for the decline of the rulers' power and for the descent of this power to the leading ministers.

Facing a combination of political and ideological assaults on their positions, Chunqiu rulers sometimes appear as if they accepted the decline of their authority as a fait accompli. They often refrained from punishing the ministers who had assassinated earlier lords, fearing that retaliation might bring about a minister's armed revolt, with unpredictable consequences.[33] Rarely were attempts made to curb ministerial power; in most cases regional lords simply preferred to maneuver between rival noble lineages, hoping to survive on the throne in name, if not in substance. Nothing better exemplifies the regional lords' humility than an offer made in 547 by the ousted Lord Xian of Wei to Ning Xi 甯喜, the son of his former enemy, Ning Zhi 甯殖: "If you let me return [to Wei], all the administration will be in the hands of the Ning lineage, while I shall [only control the] sacrifices."[34] Here, a lord is openly suggesting that he will be satisfied with a ritual figurehead position. Although such an offer may have been too radical even for his age, it does reflect certain political tendencies of the late Chunqiu period.

Lord Xian's proposal allows us to pose an intriguing question: was there a possibility of future bifurcation between secular and spiritual power in the Chunqiu world? Could the lords (and, mutatis mutandis, the Son of Heaven) have become a sort of hereditary priesthood, with all real-life political responsibilities concentrated in the hands of aristocratic oligarchy? Such speculation is not entirely groundless, as it depicts well the actual situation within most states of the Central Plain in the late sixth century. But why, then, did none of the known statesmen and thinkers ever endorse this state of affairs and attempt to institutionalize and legitimate it?

A possible answer to this question has two parts. First, as outlined above, the unity of political and spiritual power was an ideal deeply embedded in Zhou political culture, and while certain violations could be tolerated, the complete dismissal of the centuries-old system was perhaps too radical a departure even for the most innovative thinkers. The need for a single symbolic locus of power in All under Heaven, in every state and in every lineage, mandated by the Zhou religious system, was too widely endorsed to be openly defied. Second, from a practical point of view, aristocratic oligarchy was intrinsically unstable and hence was useless as a solution to political turmoil. While in certain Chunqiu states, such as Lu and Zheng, a coalition of leading lineages could maintain the delicate balance of power for several generations, rotating leading offices and dividing the territory of the state into their private allotments, usually such arrangements depended too much on personal bonds and were too fragile to become a foundation of new order. Violent clashes between powerful aristocrats, which had almost decimated such states as Qi, Song, Lu, Wei 衛, and most importantly Jin, demonstrated the feebleness of the aristocratic oligarchy and may have discouraged its potential supporters.

This contradiction between the actual Chunqiu political situation and the dictates of political tradition and political reason brought about a kind of intellectual stalemate. Chunqiu thinkers faced a difficult dilemma with regard to the ruler's power: in their capacity as ministers, interested in their state's well-being, they had to propose restoration of effective centralized rule; but in their capacity as heads of powerful aristocratic lineages they did not fail to realize that their position would be seriously harmed if such a restoration took place. Torn between private and public commitments, Chunqiu thinkers dared not seek institutionalization of their power, but were unwilling to advocate a full restoration of the lord's authority at the expense of their lineages. The resultant standstill was broken only in the Zhanguo era, when new thinkers, members of the *shi* 士 stratum, sided decisively with the lords in their drift toward centralization. The resultant restoration of the ruler's power changed the nature of Chinese political culture for millennia to come.

CHAPTER 2

Ways of Monarchism

While the end of the Chunqiu period marks the low ebb of the rulers' fortunes, the next two centuries witnessed unprecedented resurrection of the sovereign's power in all major states. A series of profound administrative reforms brought about a new entity, which Mark Lewis has aptly named "the ruler-centered state."[1] These reforms included, among others, limitations on hereditary office-holding and its replacement with recruitment based on talent; abolition of hereditary allotments, instead of which officials henceforth received ranked salaries paid in grain, or, in rare instances, in precious metals; and replacement of the allotments' autonomy with centrally ruled "commanderies and counties" (*jun xian* 郡縣). All these steps, some of which had begun already in the late Chunqiu period but all of which matured only by the fourth century BCE, nullified the power of the hereditary aristocracy, which was now largely submerged within a new, broader, *shi* elite (see Chapter 5). Unlike the Chunqiu aristocrats, the *shi* did not possess independent sources of power and were not in a position to challenge systematically the lord's rule. These developments greatly increased the political stability in the major states: the last century of the Warring States period did not witness violent domestic turmoil on a scale comparable with the late Chunqiu age.

I shall not discuss Zhanguo reforms in greater detail here, since this task had been undertaken elsewhere,[2] but will rather focus on the interaction between Zhanguo intellectual and administrative developments. I wholeheartedly endorse Lewis's warning against a common tendency to attribute gradual and long-term reforms to a single brilliant statesman or thinker.[3] The reforms emerged largely as a series of ad hoc arrangements, spanning centuries; and although the personal contribution of certain outstanding individuals, such as Shang Yang (商鞅, d. 338), is undeniable, it would be an oversimplification to establish a direct connection between the pro-centralizing sentiments expressed in the *Shang jun shu* 商君書 and similar texts, and power arrangements in actuality. Rather than initiating reforms, Zhanguo thinkers often reacted to and rationalized extant regulations; and their major contribution to the ruler-centered state was not providing it with a direct blueprint but rather creating an intellectual atmosphere that was conducive to its emergence and development.

In what follows I shall present evidence for the ever-stronger pro-centralization and ruler-centered tendency in Zhanguo thought, but before proceeding to the detailed discussion, I would like to begin by focusing on two major sources of this general tendency. First is the impact of the ideal of the political unity as the only way to end the Warring States military turmoil. Elsewhere I have discussed extensively the emergence of this unifying thread in Zhanguo thought, which was a direct result of the breakdown of Chunqiu attempts to create a viable multistate order;[4] here, suffice it to say, not a single known thinker or statesman considered the multistate world to be either legitimate or desirable. The question was not whether or not All under Heaven should be unified, but rather how this unification would occur. For the present discussion, the most significant aspect of this pro-unification drive is the emergence of the ideal of the True Monarch (*wang zhe* 王者). The notion of the True Monarch, a person who would bring about unification of the realm, appeared in the mid-Zhanguo period and rapidly became ubiquitous in political texts.[5] While thinkers widely disagreed about the True Monarch's desired personality and his mode of rule, almost all of them endorsed the idea that a single savior-like person would bring about unity and peace.[6] This common belief in an ideal ruler as a prerequisite for unification reflects a phenomenon of "ruler-centered thought" that closely paralleled the emergence of the "ruler-centered state" of the Zhanguo age.

Second, aside from idealist expectations of the future unifier, Zhanguo "ruler-centered" ideology reflected practical considerations, namely, the increasing awareness of the pivotal importance of a ruler for proper functioning of the state. Already in the late Chunqiu period, there was a palpable correlation between the state's strength and the authority of the ruler within it; and by the fifth century this correlation had become obvious to any political observer. The parallel decline of two northern superpowers, Qi and Jin, the ruling houses of which were sidelined by unruly nobles, served as a strong warning against continuous dispersal of the lord's power. Not coincidentally, the initial drive toward centralization began precisely within those states established by the "scheming ministers" of Jin and Qi, that is, Wei 魏, Han 韓, and Zhao 趙, the successor states of Jin, and the new state of Qi, reconstituted by the "usurpers" from the Tian 田 family. Their leaders were aware of the systemic failures of their predecessor states and did their best to avoid renewed disintegration by adopting a series of reforms aimed at enhancing the ruler's authority and increasing centralization.[7] Their evident success in restoring the fortunes of their states triggered similar processes elsewhere in the Zhou world and contributed decisively to endorsement of the ruler-centered political model by most rival thinkers.

In what follows I shall systematically survey major arguments proposed by the Zhanguo "disputers of the Dao" in favor of monarchic rule. I hope to demonstrate that while the competing thinkers disagreed considerably regarding the proper mode of functioning of the monarchical system, almost nobody questioned its ultimate desirability. Moreover, as I shall show, the sheer variety of pro-monarchistic arguments and their intrinsic link with dominant philosophical, ethical, religious, and administrative ideas of the Warring States provided the future emperors of China with the most compelling ideological justifications for their unrivaled power.

The Monarch as Ritual Pinnacle

Early examples of what will later turn into "monarchistic" sentiments are discernible already in the earliest Zhanguo text, the *Lunyu* 論語, a putative collection of Confucius's (孔子, 551–479) sayings.[8] While this text was by no means written for the rulers, and its major focus is on *shi* ethics rather than on government issues, some of its ideas contributed greatly toward the restoration of the sovereign's authority. In particular, Confucius's emphasis on the ruler as the pinnacle of the ritual order was instrumental in checking the dangerous tendency of increasing infraction of the ruler's ritual prerogatives by his underlings.

In the previous discussion we noticed that the Zhou ritual system presupposed monopolization of the supreme ritual power by the sovereign, whose exalted position was manifested in exclusive sumptuary privileges both during his lifetime and in the afterlife. While these principles were never openly questioned, their actual implementation was impeded due to a process of ritual "upgrading" by the regional lords at the expense of the Zhou Son of Heaven and by the nobles at the expense of the lords. An analysis of changes in mortuary assemblages throughout the Chunqiu and the early Zhanguo periods clearly reflects a process of appropriation of the superiors' sumptuary rights by the upper echelons of hereditary nobility.[9] This process, which is attested also in contemporary texts, such as the *Zuo zhuan* and the *Lunyu*, met with mixed response on the part of Chunqiu thinkers. On the one hand, those whose voices are recorded in the *Zuo zhuan* wholeheartedly supported preservation of the ritual hierarchy as a vital means for the maintenance of the social order. On the other hand, only a few of them criticized ritual infractions committed by the fellow nobles, and none—insofar as our sources are to be trusted—defended the authority of the Son of Heaven against the arrogant regional lords.[10]

The *Lunyu* differs markedly in this respect from the *Zuo zhuan*. Confucius appears there as an unequivocal supporter of the sovereign's ritual superiority as essential for preservation of the sociopolitical order. He vehemently attacks those nobles who dared transgress ritual norms, such as the head of the Ji 季 lineage, who employed eight rows of dancers at his court and performed sacrifices to Mt. Tai 泰山, the leading Lu nobles who ordered the royal *Yong* 雍 hymn to be performed at their private ceremonies, and the late Qi statesman, Guan Zhong (管仲, d. 645), who erected a screen at the gate of his mansion in a ruler-like fashion.[11] These violations, as the *Lunyu* clarifies elsewhere, are not a minor matter, as they have clear political consequences:

> When the Way prevails under Heaven, rites, music, and punitive expeditions are initiated by the Son of Heaven; when there is no Way under Heaven, rites, music, and punitive expeditions are initiated by regional lords. If they are initiated by regional lords, few [states] will not be lost within ten generations; if they are initiated by nobles (*dafu* 大夫), few will not be lost within five generations; when retainers hold the state's [power to issue] commands, few will not be lost within three generations.[12]

This succinct statement both reflects Confucius's criticism of the current state of affairs in his homeland, Lu,[13] and provides the blueprint for proper functioning of the political order in general. Ritual and political rights are inseparable; political hierarchy should be identical with the ritual one, and the ultimate power should rest with a single person, the Son of Heaven. This idea reflects both the nascent quest for (re)unification of the realm under Heaven and also the desire to preserve a single locus of authority—a stance contrary to the prevalent political tendencies of Confucius's lifetime. This statement, just as, possibly, another famous dictum, "Let the ruler be ruler, the subject be subject, the father be father, the son be son,"[14] epitomizes Confucius's staunch support of a ruler-centered hierarchic system.

The *Lunyu*, with its ethical and *shi*-oriented focus, does not abound in pronouncements that favor the properly functioning ruler-centered ritual pyramid, but the impact of its ideas on Zhanguo ritual masters is undeniable. Those of later followers of Confucius (Ru 儒) who turned ritual expertise into their major career asset further elaborated and perfected his views about the connection between ritual and the sociopolitical order, and the texts associated with these Ru eventually became a blueprint for the future imperial ritual system. While some of the more famous ritual-political writings, such as the *Zhou li* 周禮 and the "Wang zhi" (王制, Monarch's regulations) chapter of the *Liji* 禮記, may have been produced or reworked at the beginning of the imperial era and will not be dealt with here, several earlier texts illustrate the importance of ritual thought for the elevation of the ruler's position. Of these texts I shall focus on the "Qu li" (曲禮, Minute rites) chapter of the *Liji*, which, according to Yoshimoto Michimasa's 吉本道雅 meticulous analysis should be dated to the middle or late fourth century BCE.[15] Unlike the *Zhou li* and the "Wang zhi," the "Qu li" does not focus on the functioning of political system, but rather on proper norms of social behavior among members of the elite. Nevertheless, certain portions of the text reflect the political vision of its authors, and these are of great interest for our discussion.

The "Qu li" presents the ritual system as timeless and ahistorical; neither the Zhou nor earlier dynastic regulations are ever mentioned in the text, creating an impression that the norms it promulgates are eternal and immutable. One of the most important features of these timeless regulations is the absolute superiority of the Son of Heaven. The text proclaims:

> He who rules All under Heaven is named Son of Heaven. He makes the
> regional lords to arrive at his court, distributes appointments, delivers ruling
> [power], and appoints [according to one's] achievements; he calls himself: "I,
> the lonely man."[16]

This statement, which echoes Confucius's unequivocal placing of the Son of Heaven at the apex of the *political*, and not just the ritual, pyramid is accompanied by numerous pronouncements in favor of preserving the ritual superiority of the Son of Heaven versus the regional lords. The Son of Heaven performs special sacrificial rites, and enjoys exclusive sumptuary privileges; he and his entourage employ special terms to distinguish themselves from the regional lords, and the latter are supposed to arrive at his court for ceremonial performances.[17] The text specifically stipulates that the monarch is the only one who should sacrifice to "Heaven and Earth and the four directions,"[18] implying thereby the universality of his rule. Similarly, the regional lords enjoy clear ritual superiority over the nobles in their realms, thus ensuring proper functioning of the entire ritual pyramid.

The ritualists' emphasis on a clearly pronounced hierarchical order with the Son of Heaven at its apex was not novel, of course, as it echoed the Western Zhou ritual system, but its importance in the context of the Warring States realities cannot be ignored. On the one hand, it may have contributed toward the process of ritual elevation of regional lords over the nobles of their states.[19] On the other hand, the Ru texts simultaneously undermined the regional lords' power, by promulgating a truly universal ritual and political pyramid, which would place local kings far below the True Monarch. Written during an age of the breakdown of the ritual order, when regional lords "usurped" the royal title and appropriated many of the royal ritual prerogatives, the Ru ritual texts clearly conveyed dissatisfaction with this state of affairs and powerfully reinforced the need for a unified realm with a clearly delineated ritual and political pinnacle. The "ritual reality" promulgated in the *Liji* and other Ru texts, such as the *Gongyang zhuan* 公羊傳, served to convince their audience of the desirability of a unified empire with an omnipotent monarch at its head.[20] Read in this context, the reintroduction of ancient sumptuary norms becomes a powerful political weapon in the search for political order amidst the chaos of the Warring States. Eventually, the empire builders duly incorporated many of the ideas of Zhanguo ritual masters in the imperial ritual system, which henceforth served as a solid foundation of the imperial social hierarchy. Restoration of the ritual pyramid became one of the major contributions of Confucius's followers to the emergence of the monarchical order.

The Monarch as Moral Paragon

Zhanguo thinkers who sought to bolster the ruler's position by emphasizing his ritual superiority were definitely inspired by the Western Zhou model, and similar incorporation of earlier ideas is apparent with regard to the second thread of the ruler-centered thought, namely, the concept of the sovereign as a moral paragon for the ruled. However, it is in this arena that the thinkers' creative reinterpretation of the centuries-old ideas becomes more pronounced. As we shall see, already in the early Zhanguo period, the idea of the ruler as a moral paragon brought about the emergence of a radically novel ruler-centered political model.

The notion of emulating the model of superiors—either of the ruler, or, more frequently, of meritorious ancestors—had appeared already in the Western Zhou, as is attested to in contemporary bronze inscriptions; it is echoed in the *Zuo zhuan* and other early texts.[21] Eventually, the idea of model emulation became pivotal in the ethical and political thought of Confucius, as reflected, for instance, in the following passage of the *Lunyu*:

> Ji Kangzi asked Confucius about governing: "What do you think about killing those who lack the Way in order to approach those who possess the Way?" Confucius answered: "In governing, what is the need in killing? If you desire good, the people will become good. The virtue of the superior man is wind; the virtue of the petty men is grass: the grass, when the wind blows over it, must bend."[22]

Confucius's maxim regarding the ruler's moral influence on the ruled is well known, but few readers notice that the addressee of this conversation (and of many similar pronouncements in the *Lunyu*) is not the legitimate ruler of the state of Lu, but Ji Kangzi 季康子, the notorious usurper of the lord's power.[23] Evidently, for Confucius the impact of the ruler on the ruled was not confined to a legitimate ruler, but could be exercised by any de facto leader. This observation is interesting in light of the importance of the idea of a ruler as a moral exemplar for the overall elevation of monarchy in the age immediately after Confucius's lifetime.

Mozi (墨子, c. 460–390), the second important thinker of the early Warring States period, shared Confucius's belief in the moral leadership of superiors, but he took it to the extreme. For Mozi, the ruler's influence on the people's conduct is total and complete; whatever the ruler likes—from slim waists to reckless courage to "universal love" (*jian ai* 兼愛)—will be unanimously endorsed by his subjects.[24] This notion of a ruler as exemplar becomes pivotal for Mozi's political theory, as is clarified in the "Elevating Uniformity" (or "Conforming Upwards," "Shang tong" 尚同) chapters, where Mozi presents his political ideal:

> In antiquity, when the people just arose, there were neither punishments nor [proper] administration. When we inquire into the speeches [of that period], [we see] that the people had different [concepts of] propriety. Therefore, one man had one [concept of] propriety; two men had two proprieties; ten men had ten proprieties. The more men there were, the more [concepts of] propriety appeared. Consequently, each man justified his own propriety by rejecting the propriety of others, so that human contact was based on mutual rejection. Thus within [the family] fathers and sons, elder and younger brothers fell into resentment and hatred; they were alienated and unable to unite in harmony. The hundred clans under Heaven all used water, fire, and poisonous drugs to harm each other. Even those who enjoyed extra strength were unable to work for others; surplus commodities rotted, but nobody distributed them among others; good ways were concealed, and nobody taught them to others. The disorder in All under Heaven reached the level of birds and beasts.[25]

Mozi begins his narrative with a depiction of primeval society as leading a bestial life of war of all against all. The discord was primarily moral and ideological, which probably reflects Mozi's fears of moral uncertainties. Although Mozi placed this bestial anarchistic society in the remote past, "when the people just arose," his contemporaries may have recognized the picture of generalized turmoil as all too relevant to their everyday experience. Hence the solution Mozi presented here may have appealed to his audience:

> It was clear that the disorder under Heaven derived from the absence of a ruler. Therefore, the worthiest and the most able [man] in All under Heaven was selected and established as the Son of Heaven. When the Son of Heaven had been established, he apprehended that his might was still insufficient; hence again, [he] selected the worthiest and the most able [men] under Heaven and placed them in the positions of the Three Dukes. After the Son of Heaven and the Three Dukes had been established, they apprehended that All under Heaven is vast and huge, and one or two persons could not clearly know the distinctions between the beneficial and the harmful, the true and the false regarding the people of the distinct lands; therefore, they divided it up into myriad states and established regional lords and rulers of the states.[26]

Only the establishment of the universal omnipotent ruler led humankind out of primeval chaos, which implies in turn that this would be the proper way to achieve orderly rule in Mozi's own days. Mozi's ruler shared certain common features with the Zhou kings—for example, he appointed the Three Dukes and created "myriad states"—but in most crucial aspects his reign was a clear departure from the extant models of rule. First, unlike the Zhou rulers, Mozi's monarch was established not by means of the violent overthrow of his predecessors, but through an ambiguous procedure that looks like a kind of popular election. Mozi does not specify who elected/selected the monarch, leaving this sensitive question open to interpretation; it is possible that Heaven acted as a sole Elector, but it is also possible that it was the people's action (see more in Chapter 3). Second, the choice of the ruler was not arbitrary, but reflected his proven ability, in accordance with Mozi's support of the principle of "elevating the worthy" (*shang xian* 尚賢); elsewhere in the same chapter, Mozi clarifies that the ruler was not only the most able but also the most benevolent (*ren* 仁) person on earth. Third, and most important, the power of Mozi's monarch appears to be immeasurably stronger than that of his Zhou counterparts:

> After the leaders were established, the Son of Heaven proclaimed to the hundred clans of All under Heaven: "Whenever you hear of good or bad, you must report to your superiors. You must unanimously approve whatever the superiors approve, and you must unanimously disapprove whatever the superiors disapprove. When the superiors are wrong, you must admonish them, and when the inferiors are good, you must recommend them. One

who conforms upward and does not ally with inferiors is to be rewarded by
superiors and praised by inferiors. . . . One who allies with the inferiors and
is unable to conform upwards, will be punished by superiors and destroyed
by the hundred clans."[27]

Mozi continues with a lengthy and repetitious depiction of the ideal society's structure, in which every unit is ruled by the most benevolent person, who
encourages the subjects to "conform upwards" to the supreme ruler and to in-
form him about evildoers, who "must be punished by superiors and destroyed
by the hundred clans." Features such as meritocratic appointments, close surveillance of office-holders, and, most important, unification of thought and
behavior throughout the realm mark Mozi's radically new approach to the issue
of state formation. However, Mozi's most strikingly novel aspect is his emphasis
on the concentration of power in the hands of the Son of Heaven. Being the
supreme moral exemplar and the ultimate source of uniform morality, the Son
of Heaven (and those he chooses to fill the lower levels of the state hierarchy)
becomes the pivot of the sociopolitical order. By uniformly imposing his views
and norms on his subjects, the monarch prevents transgressions and ensures
universal prosperity. The only problem with this otherwise excellent ideal is
that Mozi never specifies how to ensure that the supreme ruler remains forever
the most moral person under Heaven. To resolve the problem, Mozi resorts to
his favorite solution: he turns to Heaven as a source of inspiration:

If the hundred clans all conform upwards with the Son of Heaven but not
with Heaven itself, then the disasters are still not eradicated. Now, frequent
visitations of hurricanes and torrents are just punishments from Heaven
upon the hundred clans for not conforming upward with Heaven.[28]

Heaven, which Mozi identifies elsewhere as both the source of ultimate
morality and the politically active deity in charge of proper maintenance of
the sociopolitical order,[29] serves in a double function as both inspiring and su-
pervising the omnipotent Son of Heaven. This combination of emulation and
coercion also characterizes the relations between the Son of Heaven and his
subjects, as Mozi specifies at the end of his essay:

Hence Master Mozi said: The sage-kings of old devised the five punishments, requesting thereby to rule the people. This is the same as the unifying
thread in the skein and a main rope in a net: thereby it is possible to catch
together those among the hundred clans who do not conform upward.[30]

This resort to "the five punishments" probably reflects Mozi's sober understanding that the ruler's moral example alone is insufficient to ensure compliance of the ruled. Now, we may summarize Mozi's approach. First, the existence of the omnipotent monarch is the only way out of the beast-like turmoil under Heaven. Second, this monarch should be the most able and the most benevolent person, and his ongoing conformity with moral norms will be ensured by his emulation of the infallibly moral Heaven. Third, being the supreme moral exemplar under Heaven, the monarch should be granted limitless political power to supervise and correct his subjects, if needed, through harsh punishments. Mozi thus takes a radical step toward focusing on the ruler as the single most significant political actor, aside from Heaven; all the rest are just obedient subjects with minimal, if any, impact on maintaining the order.

Mozi's radical proposals for the ruler-centered society were not necessarily endorsed by his intellectual rivals, but his views of the ruler's importance as the supreme moral exemplar were shared by many. This notion is strongly present in the *Mengzi* 孟子, the book in which many ideas are derived from and parallel the *Lunyu*. Much more than Mozi, Mengzi (c. 379–304) was renowned as a harsh critic of contemporary rulers, whom he considered "criminals," "devourers of human flesh," and "having the proclivity to kill humans."[31] Nonetheless, his expectations for rulers as potential guarantors of moral order remained extraordinarily high. As most other contemporary thinkers, Mengzi firmly believed in the ruler's infinite ability to inspire moral behavior of his subjects, and he repeatedly raised this issue in his dialogues with regional lords. The very first of these dialogues reflects Mengzi's belief in the ruler as a moral paragon:

> Mengzi had an audience with King Hui of Liang [i.e., of Wei, 魏惠王, r. 369–319]. The king said, "Sir, you have come, not regarding a thousand of miles too far. Surely you will have something to benefit my state?"
>
> Mengzi replied: "Why must the king say "benefit"? Let there be benevolence and righteousness and that is all. The king says: 'How to benefit my state?' The nobles say, 'How to benefit my family?' *Shi* and commoners say, 'How to benefit myself?' Superiors and inferiors will compete for benefits, and the state will be endangered!"[32]

This brief exchange epitomizes Mengzi's confidence in the supreme transformative power of the ruler's values. It is the ruler who imbues his inferiors with good or bad moral values, and, accordingly, it is the ruler's sole responsibility to ensure proper moral rule. In a somewhat naïve way, Mengzi frequently stated that the ruler's morality should suffice not only to ensure his subjects' compliance, but even to turn him into a True Monarch, the unifier of All under Heaven. In a conversation with King Xuan of Qi (齊宣王, r. 319–301), whose benevolent heart impressed Mengzi, the thinker suggested:

> Treat your elders as elders, extending this to others' elders; treat your young as young, extending this to others' young, and you will hold All under Heaven in the palm of your hand! The *Odes* say: "His example affected his wife, / It reached to his brothers, / So that he could manage / His family and his state." This means that all you need is to extend this heart of yours to all others. Thus extending your compassion will suffice to protect [all those] within the four seas, but if you do not extend your compassion, you will not be able to protect even your wife and children. The ancients surpassed the others in nothing other than being good at extending their actions: that is all![33]

This statement is usually discussed in the context of Mengzi's views of "benevolent government" (*ren zheng* 仁政) and his relentless efforts to ensure moral politics, but it is useful to consider it from another angle: that of Mengzi's strong emphasis on the monarch's persona. None but the monarch is able, by the mere extension of his personal morality, to create a moral world; because of this, his impact is immeasurably higher than that of any of his subjects. That this statement does not represent a mere flattery but reflects Mengzi's convictions is suggested by another statement, which does not appear to have been directed at the ruler, but probably at Mengzi's disciples:

> Mengzi said: "It is not enough to criticize others; it is not enough to blame the government. Only the Great Man is able to rectify the wrongs in the ruler's heart. When the ruler is benevolent—everybody is benevolent; when the ruler is righteous—everybody is righteous; when the ruler is correct, everybody is correct. Just rectify the ruler and the state will be stabilized."[34]

This passage looks to be Mengzi's adaptation of Mozi's "elevating uniformity" theory. Mengzi shares Mozi's belief in the exceptional capacity of the ruler's transformative power, but he also tries to resolve the inherent weakness of Mozi's theory regarding the common situation of an inept ruler on the throne. Instead of relying on Heaven to instruct the monarch, Mengzi suggests a more effective means of rectifying the ruler: namely, the blessed impact of "a Great Man," the ruler's tutor (a task that Mengzi evidently strove to acquire for himself). Yet while Mengzi's Great Man is morally superior to the ruler, this does not permit him to replace the sovereign or ignore his power. Rather, the Great Man's task is to *serve* the ruler by instructing him and guiding him into the path of morality. The result of this instruction is supposed to be the reunification of the moral and political hierarchy and an ensuing world of "benevolent government."

Mengzi's firm insistence on the supreme power of the monarch "to make everybody correct" is crucial for his political message. While harshly criticizing contemporary rulers, Mengzi did not consider any alternative to monarchic rule; on the contrary, this mode of rule was perceived to be the only one that could eventually ensure attainment of moral goals. For Mengzi, just as for Mozi, the ruler-centered state was not only a fait accompli, but also a highly desirable situation. Because of these attitudes, Mengzi played a pivotal role in the ruler-centered discourse of the Zhanguo age. And yet his insistence on the tutorial role of the Great Man contained seeds of contradiction between moral and political power—a thread that will be discussed in greater detail in Chapter 7.

The Monarch as Divinized Sage

The emergence of the ruler-centered thought was a complex and multifaceted process. Previously, we surveyed ritual concepts and ethical ideals that contributed to this effect; now, we shall explore the impact of Zhanguo cosmological thought on the elevation of the ruler's position. The *Laozi* 老子, one of the earliest texts to combine cosmological and sociopolitical ideas, is apparently the first to use metaphysical justifications for the universal monarchy. Putting aside for the time being the controversies regarding the dating, authorship, and precise intellectual content of this text,[35] we shall focus on those aspects of the *Laozi* that contributed decisively to Zhanguo views of rulership.

The basic parameters of the *Laozi*'s approach are well known: it is based on the presupposition of a primeval and spontaneous Dao (the Way), the functioning principles of which are applicable on all levels of existence from the cosmos, down to society and the individual. A person who understands the principles of the Way and implements them in his everyday life is the Sage (*sheng ren* 聖人). We shall not focus here on these much-studied aspects of the *Laozi*'s thought, but address instead a crucial question: is the Sage of the *Laozi* the ruler or not, and if so, what are the possible implications of such an equation for views of rulership?

As we have come to expect with the *Laozi*, the text does not give an unequivocal answer to this question. Many of the *Laozi*'s maxims related to the Sage can be considered universally applicable, while certain statements, such as proposals to the Sage "to place himself last in order to become first" may very well apply to the aspiring rather than to an acting ruler.[36] But important as they are, such passages pale in comparison with what appear to be predominantly ruler-oriented statements that speak about the Sage. The Sage is supposed to properly rule by "emptying the people's hearts and filling their bellies"; he holds fast to the One (that is, to Dao) to become "a shepherd of All under Heaven," with whom "no one will contest"; he exercises his rule through nonaction and tranquility to let the people "transform themselves," "rectify themselves," and "enrich themselves"; and he is placed "above the people," although the people do not consider him "heavy."[37] All these attributes are unmistakably the ruler's, and they imply that the Sage is ultimately supposed to rule All under Heaven. This impression is further strengthened by many passages in the *Laozi* that explicitly address the ruler, advising him how to "attain All under Heaven" (*de tianxia* 得天下), how to "love the people and order the state" (*ai min zhi guo* 愛民治國), or how to stay "above the people" (*shang min* 上民), without causing commotion.[38] Actually, in these passages the *Laozi* inaugurates a new type of ruler-oriented texts, which will become fairly widespread in the second half of the Zhanguo period.[39]

The identification of the ruler and the Sage in the *Laozi* is not unequivocal, however. The text contains critical remarks about current rulers whose actions cause people to be hungry and to suffer from military atrocities. The author hopes that "kings and lords" (*wang hou* 王侯) will be able to hold fast to Dao, in which case "the myriad creatures will submit of their own accord" or "will be transformed of their own accord," but it is clear that this situation does not exist in the present.[40] Yet the text carefully avoids the potentially subversive question as to what will happen if a Sage appears during the reign of an inept ruler. Instead, the *Laozi* focuses on the ideal situation, in which the Sage *is* the ruler:

> In antiquity, these attained the One: Heaven attained the One to become pure; Earth attained the One to become tranquil; deities attained the One to become numinous; the valley attained the One to become full; [myriad creatures attained the One for their living]; lords and kings attained the One to become rectifiers of All under Heaven.[41]

This passage attributes the blessed state of affairs to unspecified antiquity, but it is clear that it refers to the normative rather than to an exceptional situation. Heaven *should be* pure; the Earth *should be* tranquil, and deities *should be* numinous. Much in the same way the rulers *should* be rectifiers of All under Heaven, and insofar as they attain the One, that is, the Way, they will become an inseparable part of the cosmic order, enabling not only "the myriad things to submit of their own accord" but even Heaven and Earth to "descend sweet dew."[42] The pivotal position of the True Monarch in the cosmic order is emphasized in what may be the single most important political statement in the *Laozi*:

> Hence the Way is great; Heaven is great; Earth is great; the Monarch is also great. Within the realm there are four things that are great, and the Monarch counts as one.[43]

The exalted position of the Monarch in the *Laozi*'s world order resembles the religious legacy of the Shang–early Zhou period, and indeed the *Laozi*'s mentioning of the king's "corresponding to Heaven" (*pei tian* 配天)[44] strengthens the apparent similarity. However, there is a major difference between the early religious views and the *Laozi*'s concept of the cosmic position of the sage ruler. In the *Laozi*, the ruler is sacred neither due to the Heaven's decree, nor as a mediator between the supreme deity and the humans, but rather as a cosmic force by himself, a counterpart of the Way, Heaven, and Earth, a pivotal part of the universe. The monarchy becomes therefore metaphysically stipulated and gains further legitimacy.

Between Sagacity and Rulership

The *Laozi*'s portrayal of a ruler as a cosmic figure and, at least potentially, as a divinized sage, left a somewhat contradictory legacy for future thinkers. Some assumed that a ruler would attain semidivine powers only insofar as he becomes a sage—presumably through a lengthy process of training and self-improvement. Others, however, held that any ruler of the unified realm would possess cosmic powers ex officio. While it was this latter view that became particularly prominent by the end of the Warring States period, we shall begin with the first one, namely, the ideas of those who encouraged the ruler to become really worthy of his elevated position. Through emulation of Heaven and Earth, the natural repositories of the Way, the ruler was supposed to become a true counterpart of the cosmic forces, attaining superhuman dimensions.

The idea that a ruler should emulate Heaven was not novel, of course; the concept had been employed long before the *Laozi*, for example, by Master Kuang (for whom it might have been just a simile) and by Mozi, who hoped to ensure thereby the continuous presence of a benevolent monarch on the throne. Later thinkers, possibly influenced by the *Laozi*, employed this ancient notion to create a new concept of rulership: by consciously emulating cosmic forces, the monarch should ensure proper fulfillment of his cosmic role. For instance, the "Mu min" (牧民, Shepherding the people) chapter of the *Guanzi*, probably dated to the mid-fourth century BCE, urges the ruler: "Be like Earth, be like Heaven, / What partiality or favoritism [have they]? Be like the moon, be like the sun, / These are the norms of the Ruler!"[45] This idea that the ruler should emulate cosmic forces to achieve the true rulership is a recurrent topic in the *Guanzi*. Another relatively early chapter of this treatise, "Ban fa" (版法, Tablets of the law), similarly recommends:

> Model yourself on Heaven: unify your virtue (*de* 德); imitate the Earth: have no favorites; form a trinity with the sun and moon and a quintuplet with the four seasons. Be happy in bestowing what you have, and [gather] the masses through diminishing [your] selfishness.[46]

These hortatory remarks should perhaps be treated primarily as rhetorical devices aimed at directing the ruler toward proper modes of behavior rather than a well-developed political theory, but even as rhetoric, frequent advice to the ruler to emulate the cosmic powers is not devoid of deeper political meaning. These statements reflect the thinkers' presumption of the cosmic role of the sovereign—if not of the reigning one, then at least of an ideal, future True Monarch. This ideal monarch should be able to influence earthly affairs in a way similar to Heaven, Earth, and other superhuman forces, and thus will have divine dimensions. This divine nature of monarchy is clearly manifest in another chapter of the *Guanzi*, the "Nei ye" (內業, Inner training). While this text is less politically oriented than most of the *Guanzi* chapters and appears too focused on self-cultivation of the adept to be read as a political manual, it nevertheless clearly promulgates cosmic—and political—potency as the most important outcome of the "inward training."[47] The crucial link between self-cultivation, grasping the cosmic forces, and attaining divine rulership is exposed in the following passages:

> Heaven prioritizes regularity, Earth prioritizes flatness, Man prioritizes quiescence. Spring and autumn, winter and summer are Heaven's seasons; mountains and ranges, rivers and valleys are Earth's resources; joy and anger, taking and giving are man's schemes. Therefore, the sage changes with the times but never transforms, follows the things but never deviates. He is able to be regular, to be quiescent, hence he is able to [remain] stable.[48]

By emulating Heaven and Earth, by preserving quiescence and regularity, the sage is able to sustain internal stability, which becomes in turn a first step toward attaining outward powers:

One whose heart is stable in his midst, his ears and eyes are sharp and clear, his four limbs are strong and durable; he can become the lodging of the essence. Essence is the essence of *qi* 氣. When *qi* obtains the Way, there is life; when there is life, there is thought; when there is thought, there is knowledge; when there is knowledge, one stops. The gestalt of the mind is that transgressive knowledge leads to a loss of vitality.

He who is able to transform a single thing is said to be divine; he who is able to change a single matter is said to be wise. Transformations do not alter *qi*; changes do not alter knowledge. Only the superior man who holds the One can do this![49]

This passage contains a curious and sudden change from passive quiescence and preserving inward stability toward active transformation of the world. By becoming "a lodging of *qi*," the common substance of the myriad things, an adept becomes viable, thoughtful, and knowledgeable. The text then explicitly recommends stopping here and not pursuing knowledge too far, to the point of self-ruin, but then it immediately shifts from accumulating knowledge toward actively implementing it. The divine knowledge will allow the adept to transform the things without losing his internal stability. He who is able to do so is the divinized "superior man," the one who "holds the One" (*zhi yi* 執 一). "Holding the One" here does not refer, *pace* Roth,[50] to the purely meditative technique of envisioning the Way, but rather to the ability to comprehend it in the way clearly reminiscent of the *Laozi* 39 passage cited above. As in the case of the *Laozi*, holding (or attaining) the One has immediate political implications:

He who holds the One without losing it is able to rule the myriad things. The superior man employs the things but is not employed by them. He who has grasped the pattern of the One is able to order his mind within, order the words coming from his mouth, and order the tasks he imposes on others: then All under Heaven is properly ordered. When the one word is obtained, All under Heaven submit; when the one word is determined, All under Heaven obey. This is told of impartiality.[51]

This passage contains the ultimate result and the goal of "inward training": attaining supreme understanding of world affairs, which turns the adept, the "superior man," into a ruler of the myriad things, and, naturally, of All under Heaven. This radical political shift shows that the "Nei ye" chapters, just like significant portions of the *Laozi*, were written not for an anonymous adept, but also for a potential ruler, the True Monarch who would be able to bring order to All under Heaven.[52] The text does not resolve, however, the political paradox of what would happen should these cosmic powers be obtained by a person who is not currently in the ruler's position. Should that "superior man" become a sovereign? And if so, how will it happen? Just like the *Laozi*, the "Nei ye" remains silent on this sensitive topic: its authors prefer to speak of the ideal and timeless sage ruler, rather than to engage in a potentially dangerous discussion of current political affairs.

The peculiarity of the "Nei ye" approach is not in its promise of universal divine powers to the adept, but rather in its strict emphasis on the elaborate, complicated way of training required to attain these powers. Most other texts that discuss the divine power of the sage ruler are less demanding. Some of the so-called "Huang-Lao" 黄老 manuscripts from Mawangdui 馬王堆, Hunan, repeatedly urge the ruler to model himself after Heaven and Earth, but the recommended processes of observing Heaven's patterns are immeasurably simpler than in the "Nei ye."[53] A further simplification of the process of attaining sagacity is observable in the *Lüshi chunqiu*. The "Da yue" (大樂 Great music) chapter, one of the loci classici of Zhanguo correlative cosmology, ends with a following passage:

> Dao is of the utmost subtlety. It cannot be shaped; it cannot be named. "Forced to give it a name, I would call it the Great One."[54] Hence the One restricts and commands, the dual follows and listens. Earlier sages rejected the dual and modeled themselves after the One; hence they were able to comprehend the nature of myriad things.[55]

We shall later return to the notion of unity versus duality and its political importance; here, suffice it to mention that the passage begins with a common topic of the *Laozi*-related texts: grasping the Way and modeling oneself after it is the path to divine knowledge. Then the text swiftly turns to the political realm.

> Hence he who can use the One to decide on governmental matters will bring joy to ruler and subjects, harmonize the distant and the near, please the black-headed people, and unify his relatives. He who can use the One to order his body will escape disasters, live a long life to the end, and keep intact his Heaven[ly nature]. He who can use the One to order his state, will eradicate wickedness and licentiousness, attract the worthy, and complete the Great Transformation. He who can use the One to order All under Heaven,

will cause heat and cold to be balanced, wind and rain timely, and become a Sage. Hence he who knows the One is enlightened; he who enlightens the dual is demented.[56]

The text presents the advantages of grasping the Way for everybody: a high minister, an average adept who seeks longevity, and then a ruler of a state and the ruler of All under Heaven. Each of them will reap benefits from holding fast to the One, but only the supreme monarch will attain true cosmic powers of influencing heat and cold, wind and rain—and only he will become a Sage. This curious twist of argument presupposes that the divine sagacity is available exclusively to rulers, and not ordinary rulers, but only to the future universal monarch. The supreme position is insufficient but is a necessary precondition for attaining the divine level.

The difference between the "Nei ye" and the "Da yue" presentations of the sage ruler is subtle but nonetheless significant. In the first case, the ruler is an entirely self-made man, whose "inward training" allows him to obtain divine powers. In the second case, it is implied that only the universal ruler, the one who is in a position of ordering All under Heaven, can attain the supreme level of sagacity. The equation between the ruler and the sage, which in earlier texts was quite subtle, in the *Lüshi chunqiu* becomes powerfully pronounced.

The "Da yue" is not the only chapter of the *Lüshi chunqiu* that appears fascinated with the superhuman powers of the future Son of Heaven, the would-be unifier. Another of its famous chapters deals with the interaction between the human and Heavenly realm. "Ben sheng" (本生, On the origins of life) starts with the following statement:

That which first gives birth is Heaven, the one who nourishes and completes is Man. He who is able to nourish what Heaven has generated without oppressing it is the Son of Heaven. When the Son of Heaven moves, it is for the sake of preserving intact Heaven[ly nature].[57]

The "Ben sheng" chapter is not a political manual, and its major focus is on a sage, who will be able to internalize the cosmos within his body, thereby obtaining longevity. This sage is not necessarily a ruler, since the text explicitly says that "above, he would not be haughty being a Son of Heaven; below, he would not be resentful in a position of an ordinary fellow: this is called a man with complete virtue (*de*)."[58] Here, as in most other texts, it is recognized that the sage and the ruler are not necessarily identical. And yet it is stated almost in passing that the Son of Heaven in the capacity of his position plays a crucial role in the cosmic order. For the authors it evidently does not matter at all whether or not the Son of Heaven is a sage. In any case it is his function "to nourish what Heaven generated."

This elevation of the Son of Heaven ex officio to the position of Heaven's counterpart appears elsewhere in the *Lüshi chunqiu*, most noteworthy in those chapters which frame the first portion of this compendium, the so-called "Monthly Ordinances" ("Yue ling" 月令), which were later incorporated into the *Liji* 禮記.[59] These chapters, which present a neat model of the seasonal activities of the Son of Heaven and of his entourage, are remarkable among other things for their warnings about the inevitable negative consequences for the violator of their prescriptions. For instance, the first month's ordinances end with the following statement:

> If at the beginning of spring you issue summer ordinances, then wind and rain will be untimely, grass and trees will early wither, and there will be great fear in the capital. If you issue autumn ordinances, then there will be great epidemics among the people, strong winds and thunderstorms will come intermittently, briars, darnel, brambles, and wormwood will grow together with the crops. If you carry out winter ordinances, floods and heavy rains will be devastating, frost and snow greatly damaging, and the crops will not mature.[60]

Such warnings are common in the texts that deal with the so-called "technical" (or esoteric) knowledge; those routinely caution a reader that a failure to implement the text's recommendations will bring about various disasters.[61] What is interesting in the case of the *Lüshi chunqiu* are the political implications of its correlative cosmology. Wrongdoings by the Son of Heaven will have negative consequences not just on personal or political level, but first of all on the cosmos itself, generating floods, droughts, epidemics, and the like. The Son of Heaven appears here as a true counterpart of Heaven, able to influence—even if negatively—natural processes. Importantly, in this case it is clear that the Son of Heaven influences the cosmos not due to his sagacity and perspicacity but *despite* his lack of these features. It is his position alone, not his personal abilities, that makes him sacred and allows him to equal the divine forces.

It is possible to conclude that the "Yue ling" authors made a radical reinterpretation of the idea expressed in the *Laozi* 25, where the True Monarch is equal to the Way, and to Heaven and Earth. While in the texts discussed above this equality is not taken for granted but results from the monarch's self-cultivation and becoming a divinized Sage, here the mere position of the Son of Heaven turns him into a cosmic figure. The renewed sacralization of the monarch in these texts became eventually a cornerstone of the idea of the monarch's sacralization in the unified empire, as will be discussed in the epilogue to Chapter 4.

The Pivot of the Sociopolitical Order

The evolution of the ruler-centered state during the Zhanguo period is well reflected in contemporary thought. While early to middle Zhanguo thinkers focused on ritual, ethical, and later cosmological justifications of monarchical power, by the second half of the Zhanguo period a new strand of pro-monarchical argument ensued: emphasis on the ruler's importance for the maintenance of the sociopolitical order. This line of reasoning was of the utmost importance for the further elevation of the ruler's position. Its proponents did not focus on the unattainable ideal of the impeccably moral or divinely sagacious ruler, but rather on the everyday contribution of the ruler—any ruler—to the well-being of the state and maintenance of the social order. These views are first heard in the late fourth-century texts, and by the end of the Zhanguo period they became all but ubiquitous.

The *Shang jun shu*, a book that is frequently considered a fountainhead of the so-called "legalist" (*fa jia* 法家) ideas, is probably the earliest text to propose a concept of the pivotal importance of the ruler's position for the state's well-being.[62] While this text largely focuses on state-society relations and not on monarchical power per se, it still contains important justifications of monarchism. These are embedded in particular in Shang Yang's evolutionary model of state formation—one of his most curious intellectual innovations:

> When Heaven and Earth were established, the people were born. At that time, the people knew their mothers but not their fathers; their way was one of attachment to relatives and of selfishness. Attachment to relatives results in particularity; selfishness results in malignity. The people multiplied, and as they were engaged in particularity and malignity, the people fell into turmoil. At that time, the people began seeking victories and forcefully contending [with each other].[63]

Shang Yang's model of primeval society slightly resembles that of Mozi, but there are major differences as well. While Mozi presupposed bestial war of all against all as result of ideological discord, Shang Yang does not deny the possibility of primeval harmony of the kin-based order. It is only due to the population pressure[64] that this initial order began disintegrating and major changes had to be introduced:

Seeking victories results in [mutual] struggle; forceful contention results in lawsuits. When there are lawsuits but no proper [norms], then nobody achieves his natural life. Therefore, the worthies established impartiality and propriety, instituted selflessness, and the people began preaching benevolence. At that time, attachment to relatives declined, and elevation of the worthy was established.[65]

The incipient stratification of society, based on "elevation of the worthy," replaced the inadequate kin-based order. However, institutional weaknesses of the new order obstructed the successful management of social turmoil resulting from a new wave of population increase. Thus was the ruler-centered state born:

In general, the benevolent are devoted to love [of benefits], while the worthy view mutual repellence as the proper Way. The people multiplied, yet lacked regulations; for a long time they viewed mutual repellence as the proper way, and hence there again was turmoil. Therefore, the sages took responsibility. They established distinctions between lands, property, men, and women. When distinctions were established but regulations were still lacking, this was unacceptable; hence they established prohibitions. When prohibitions were established but none supervised [their implementation], this was unacceptable; hence they established officials. When officials were instituted but not unified, this was unacceptable; hence they established the ruler. When the ruler was established, elevation of the worthy declined and the esteem of nobility was established.[66]

Shang Yang turns Mozi's depiction of the state formation upside down: the establishment of the ruler is not a beginning, but an outcome of a long process of increasing sociopolitical sophistication. The evolution from an egalitarian, promiscuous, kin-based order towards an incipient stratified society, and then to a mature political order based on property distinctions, prohibitions, and officials is crowned with the establishment of a ruler. Unlike in the *Mozi*, the *Shang jun shu* ruler is not established due to his being "the worthiest and the most able in All under Heaven," but because he is the sole guarantor for the proper functioning of the political order. For Shang Yang, the ruler is both an inseparable and the most important part of the state apparatus, without whom the state will disintegrate. Elsewhere, Shang Yang elaborates this idea further:

In antiquity, the people resided together and dwelled like a herd, being in turmoil; hence they were in need of superiors. Thus All under Heaven are happy having superiors, considering this orderly rule. Now, if you have a sovereign but no laws, it is as harmful as having no sovereign; if you have laws but are unable to overcome [those] who wreak havoc, it is as if you have no laws. While All under Heaven are not at rest without a ruler, they are happy to overcome his laws: therefore the entire generation is in a state of confusion. Yet to benefit the people of All under Heaven nothing is better than orderly rule, and in orderly rule nothing is more secure than to establish a ruler. The Way of establishing the ruler is nowhere broader than in relying on laws; in the task of relying on laws, nothing is more urgent than eradicating the licentious; the root of eradicating the licentious is nowhere deeper than in making punishments stern.[67]

The sophistication of Shang Yang's political thought is presented here at its best. First, the need for a social hierarchy, headed by a ruler, is the sine qua non for the proper functioning of society. Second, the ruler is the necessary but insufficient precondition of social order: he must rely on the legal system, and especially on stern punishments, which will cause his rule to be really effective. Shang Yang dismisses metaphysically based idealizations of the sage ruler whose single word will "cause All under Heaven to submit" (see the "Nei ye"), or Mozi's belief in an ideal ruler who creates the state ex nihilo. The ruler alone cannot substitute for the well-developed political system, but neither can this system act without a supreme sovereign who will keep the ultimate power in his hands. The moral or intellectual qualities of the ruler are of minor importance in comparison with his pivotal political role as the supreme administrator.

Many other thinkers shared this conviction in the indispensability of a ruler as a source of proper political order. One of its most sophisticated proponents was Shen Dao (慎到, fl. late fourth century), a thinker only small fragments of whose writings have survived the vicissitudes of history. In a major theoretical portion of these surviving fragments, Shen Dao exposes the role of the ruler in the sociopolitical order:

In antiquity, the Son of Heaven was established and esteemed not in order to benefit the single person. It is said: When All under Heaven lack the single esteemed [person], then there is no way to carry out the principles [of orderly government, li 理]; carrying out the principles is done for the sake of All under Heaven. Hence the Son of Heaven is established for the sake of All under Heaven, it is not that All under Heaven is established for the sake of the Son of Heaven; a ruler of a state is established for the sake of the state, it is not that the state is established for the sake of the ruler of the state; a head of officials is established for the sake of officials, it is not that officials are established for the sake of the head of officials. Even if the law is bad, it is better than absence of laws; thereby the hearts of the people are unified.[68]

Shen Dao presents with rare clarity his political credo. A ruler—both on the universal and lower levels—is crucial for the proper functioning of the political system; he is the real foundation of the proper order, not a beneficiary but rather a servant of the humankind. His morality is of minimal, if any, importance; as Shen Dao clearly states, poor laws are better than a lawless situation, and we may deduce that a bad ruler is better than anarchy. That the ruler's morality is marginal in comparison with his ex officio power is clarified by Shen Dao elsewhere:

When [the sage emperor] Yao 堯 was a commoner, he was not able to command his neighbors, but when he faced southward and became a king, his orders were implemented and restrictions heeded. Looking from this, [we know] that worthiness does not suffice to subdue unworthiness, but power and position suffice to bend the worthies.[69]

Yao was a paragon of morality, but it was not his virtue that turned him into a true leader, but the power of his position as a sovereign. The situation in which the political hierarchy is detached from that of morality and "worthiness" is a normative one. The ruler should focus not on cultivating his virtue but on preserving his authority intact, since otherwise not only he, but the entire society, will suffer:

When the Son of Heaven is established, he should not let the regional lords doubt [his position]; when a lord is established, he should not let nobles doubt [his position]; when a primary wife is established, she should not let concubines doubt [her position]; when a proper heir is established, he should not let minor siblings doubt [his position]. Doubts bring commotion; doubleness [of the sources of authority] brings contention, intermingling brings mutual injury; harm is from sharing, not from singularity. Hence when the ministers have double [equal] positions, the state will be in turmoil; when the ministers have double [equal] positions and the state is not in turmoil, it is because of the ruler. When you rely on the ruler, there is no turmoil, when you lose the ruler, then there is turmoil.[70]

Shen Dao further clarifies the advantages of the monarchic rule. For him, as for Mozi and Shang Yang, monarchy is the only possible way out of turmoil, which threatens to tear apart any sociopolitical system that lacks a clear hierarchy of power. It is only through unification of authority in the hands of a single person that contention and turmoil can be avoided. The statement that "doubleness means contention" became a common credo of Zhanguo thinkers, and many texts echo Shen Dao's views.[71] Later, we shall see the importance of these views for Zhanguo administrative thought; but first we shall turn to one of the latest Zhanguo texts, the "Shi jun" (恃君, Relying on a ruler) chapter of the *Lüshi chunqiu*, which summarizes earlier arguments in favor of the ruler as the pivot of the sociopolitical order:

> The nature of humans is such that their claws and teeth do not suffice to protect themselves; body and skin do not suffice to withstand heat and cold; muscles and bones do not suffice to attain benefits and escape injuries; bravery does not suffice to repel the savage and subdue the haughty. Nevertheless, [men] still master myriad things, rule birds and beasts, and subdue vicious insects, while heat and warmth, dryness and humidity can do them no harm. It is not only because humans prepare [appropriate] facilities, but also because they are able to gather into a collective. Gathering into a collective is done for the sake of mutual benefit. When benefits derive from the collective (群, *ghun), the way of the ruler (君, *kun) is established. Therefore, when the way of the ruler is established, benefits appear from the collective, and human preparations are completed.[72]

This portion of the "Shi jun" discussion closely follows Xunzi's views, discussed in Chapter 4.[73] Without forming a collective, human beings will be unable to cope with natural challenges, and without establishing a ruler, they will be unable to maintain the collective. The ruler, therefore, is essential for the proper functioning and even for the sheer survival of the humankind. Historical lessons prove this, in the authors' eyes, beyond doubt:

> In high antiquity it happened that there was no ruler. The people lived together, dwelling like a herd. They knew their mothers but no fathers, had no distinctions between relatives, elder and younger brothers, husband and wife, male and female; had no way of superiors and inferiors, of old and young; had no rites of entrance, departure, and mutual greetings; had no advantages of clothes, caps, boots, dwellings, and palaces; had no facilities such as utensils, instruments, boats, chariots, outer and inner walls, and defensive fortifications. This is the trouble of lacking a ruler.[74]

This passage adopts a negative view of primeval society akin to that of Mozi and Shang Yang, but unlike them, its authors are not preoccupied with the narrative of the state formation, but rather they focus on the gloomy condition of the rulerless humankind. Lack of a ruler means lack of appropriate technology and social institutions, which degrades human beings to the situation of beasts unable to cope with nature. The need for a monarch is therefore the most important lesson that can be deduced from history:

> From the generations of the old, multiple states were extinguished in All under Heaven, but the Way of the ruler did not decline: this is because it benefits All under Heaven. Hence those who reject the ruler are terminated; those who implement the Way of the ruler are established. What is the Way of the ruler? To benefit [others] and not to benefit [oneself].[75]

The last sentence of this passage introduces the notion of morality as imminent to the Way of the Ruler, and thus the authors try to moderate their harsh authoritarianism. This addition is important (and distinguishes the "Shi jun" authors crucially from Shen Dao and Shang Yang, whose views we surveyed above), but the crux of the argument lies elsewhere. The preservation of a ruler-centered society throughout the vicissitudes of history serves as an additional proof for the beneficent impact of the Way of the ruler on the human collective. To further support this understanding, the authors turn to "anthropological" arguments. They survey at length various "rulerless" tribes on the fringes of Chinese civilization and then summarize:

> These are the rulerless of the four directions. Their people live like elk and deer, birds and beasts: the young give orders to the old; the old fear the adults; the strong are considered the worthy, and the haughty and violent are revered. Day and night they abuse each other, leaving no time to rest, thereby exterminating their own kind. The sages profoundly investigate this trouble: hence when they consistently think of All under Heaven, nothing is better than establishing a Son of Heaven; when they consistently think of a single state, nothing is better than establishing a ruler.[76]

Empirical observations of neighboring societies prove what historical lessons above have suggested: lacking a ruler, humankind cannot maintain its normal life; human society will deteriorate into mutual strife; the benefits of civilization will be denied to a demented humanity. The ruler, by the mere power of his position, is a savior of humankind. The authors warn at the end that their support of the ruler in theory does not imply blind obedience and that the ruler should be reprimanded, if necessary, but this statement does not qualify their essential message: social order without a ruler is simply impossible. On the eve of imperial unification, the anonymous authors of the *Lüshi chunqiu* provided the future emperor with the best possible justification for the monarchic rule.

The Supreme Administrator

The last, but not least, of the pro-monarchical trends in this survey deals with the impact of monarchism on administrative thought of the Warring States. Unlike in the previous sections, I begin here with one of the latest texts under concern, namely, the "Zhi yi" (執一, "Upholding the One") chapter of the *Lüshi chunqiu*, whose authors blend ideas of Shen Dao and his ilk with the *Laozi*'s philosophical stipulations of the oneness of the Way:

> The True Monarch upholds oneness and becomes the rectifier of the myriad things. The army needs the general: thereby it is unified. The state needs the ruler: thereby it is unified. All under Heaven needs the Son of Heaven: thereby it is unified. The Son of Heaven upholds oneness, thereby unifying it [the realm]. Oneness brings orderly rule; doubleness brings chaos.[77]

This statement begins with what appears as a reference to the *Laozi* 39, but it interprets the *Laozi*'s saying in a purely administrative manner. The unity of Dao should be logically matched by administrative unity of decision-making, since any dispersal of authority means inevitable struggle and turmoil. Just as the army cannot act without a clearly defined chain of command with a supreme commander at its top, so, too, the state requires a unified command as the only way to survive in the violent competition with its neighbors. Moreover, since political unification is the only reasonable solution to ongoing warfare, it should logically culminate in the unification of power in the hands of a single person. Any alternative to this strict monarchism will have devastating effects on the entire realm.

Armed with their conviction that unified rule is the only remedy for social turmoil, Zhanguo centralizers translated it into the notion of a ruler being not simply a single locus of power but more practically a single decision-maker. The *Shang jun shu* states:

> The state is ordered through three [matters]: the first is law, the second is trustworthiness, the third is authority. The law is what ruler and ministers jointly uphold; trustworthiness is what ruler and ministers jointly establish; authority is what the ruler exclusively regulates. When the ruler of the people loses what he should preserve, he is endangered; when the ruler and the ministers cast away the law and rely on their private [views], calamity must

occur. Hence when the law is established, divisions are clarified and the law is not violated for private reasons, then there is orderly rule; when authority and regulations are decided exclusively by the ruler, then [he is] awesome; when the people trust his rewards, then successes are accomplished; and when they trust his punishments, then wickedness has no opening edge.[78]

The *Shang jun shu* author(s) translates the notion of the unified authority into administrative language. The ruler is not a single executive, but he should be a single decision-maker; this administrative singularity is a true source of his awe-inspiring power. Similar views were advocated by another major Zhanguo reformer, Shang Yang's contemporary Shen Buhai (申不害, d. 337): "He who sees independently is called clear-sighted; he who hears independently is called sharp-eared. Hence he who decides independently can become the ruler of All under Heaven."[79]

In Shen Buhai's eyes, just as exclusiveness of abilities is characteristic of the sage (whose attributes are clear-sightedness and sharpness of hearing), so, too, exclusiveness of political prerogatives is characteristic of the unifying ruler. Although the original context of the saying is unknown, it may be inferred that Shen Buhai considered the consolidation of power into a single state as a precondition for attaining the major task of unifying All under Heaven. Similar notions of the importance of preserving ultimate power in the monarch's hands are widespread in the late Warring States period texts[80] and cannot be confined to so-called Legalist thought alone. Perhaps the most interesting example of the intellectual consensus concerning the monopolization of the decision-making in the hands of one person is found in the *Mengzi*. In a rare passage, which expresses dissatisfaction with unrestricted social mobility, Mengzi advises King Xuan of Qi how to avoid making hasty promotions and demotions that will alienate hereditary ministers and the king's kin:

When the ruler promotes the able, when he has no choice [but to do so], this means he lets the humble overstep the respected and strangers overstep the kin. Can he but be cautious? When all the courtiers say that [somebody] is worthy, this is still unacceptable; when all the nobles say that [somebody] is worthy, this is still unacceptable; when all the dwellers of the capital say that [somebody] is worthy, then you must inspect him, and if he is truly worthy, employ him. When all the courtiers say that [somebody] is unacceptable, do not listen to them; when all the nobles say that [somebody] is unacceptable, do not listen to them; when all the dwellers of the capital say that [some-body] is unacceptable, then you must inspect him, and if he is really unac-ceptable, get rid of him. When all the courtiers say that [somebody] should be executed, do not listen to them; when all the nobles say that [somebody] should be executed, do not listen to them; when all the dwellers of the capital say that [somebody] should be executed, then you must inspect this, and if he really should be executed, execute him. Thus it will be said that the dwellers of the capital executed him. If you behave so, you will be then able to become father and mother of the people.[81]

Mengzi's views are often considered in terms of the importance he assigns to the people's opinion, which is indeed so (see Chapter 9 for further discussion); but it is no less important to analyze his views of the ruler's authority. The right to promote, demote, or execute any person rests, in Mengzi's opinion, squarely in the ruler's hands. The opinion of the courtiers, the nobles, and even of the general populace may be more or less important, but the ultimate decision is that of the supreme sovereign. In the final account, Mengzi's views surprisingly resemble those of the harsh authors of the "Ren fa" (任法, Relying on laws) chapter of the *Guanzi*, who stated: "Hence there are six things that the enlightened king maintains: to give life, to kill, to enrich, to impoverish, to ennoble, to depreciate. These are the six handles that the ruler maintains."[82]

The convergence between Mengzi, one of the less ruler-centered writers in Chinese political history, and the radically monarchistic Legalist writers is not incidental. Actually, not a single known text challenges the concept of the ruler's monopolization of the ultimate administrative authority. While thinkers usually urged the rulers to consult with their ministers and to heed their advice, and most texts—as discussed in Chapter 4—recommended that rulers limit their practical involvement in routine administration procedures, none proposed dispersal of the decision-making or any institutional limitations to the ruler's power. If dissenting voices ever existed, they may have been too marginal even to merit refutation from their opponents. The sheer variety and pluralism of Zhanguo political ideas makes *argumentum ex silentio* particularly meaningful in this case. It seems that the notion of the ruler's exclusiveness as the final decision-maker reflects a very broad consensus among the thinkers of the Warring States.

In the final account, this view, according to which the supreme administrative authority, just like the ritual supremacy, rests solely in the ruler's hands, may be considered one of the most far-reaching of the Zhanguo legacies. The apparent absence of dissenting voices may be puzzling indeed. After all, as we shall see in the next chapters, Zhanguo thinkers neither failed to criticize inept rulers, nor did they ignore the possible damage of the ruler's whimsical behavior on the functioning of the state apparatus. Many of them considered themselves quite capable of managing state affairs and did not hesitate justifying—or even

lauding and encouraging—opposition to the reigning sovereign. Why, then, did
none propose a kind of "constitutional monarchy" with a "council of worthies" routinely approving or disapproving the ruler's policy proposals? Why
did none dare to institutionalize their sense of moral superiority over the rulers
(for which see Chapter 7) and translate it into proper administrative regulations,
thus imposing institutional limits on the monarch? Was it a result of the thinkers' cowardice or folly, or were dissenting voices simply silenced by supporters
of the ruler's indivisible power?

I believe that the answer to these questions lies elsewhere. Zhanguo thinkers
were neither cowards, nor incapable of radical innovations. Rather, they—or at
least an overwhelming majority of them—adopted the idea of the omnipotent
sovereign, despite its evident shortcomings, as the least possible evil. Their actual
historical experience, particularly such famous precedents as the disintegration
of the Chunqiu states of Jin and Lu, where the rulers' authority had been effectively usurped by a coalition of nobles, was a powerful warning for Zhanguo thinkers. Without a supreme and universally acknowledged arbiter, there
was no possibility of maintaining proper rule and avoiding painful conflicts of
interest. Without the Unifier, there could be no unification, which meant no
peace.

In addition, another useful angle to explain the unanimous endorsement of
the monarchic principle of rule may be the peculiar situation of the Warring
States. Mark Lewis had suggestively depicted the Warring State as a military
machine,[83] and this simile (which was employed among others in the *Lüshi
chunqiu* "Zhi yi" passage cited above) is indeed useful for understanding the administrative rationale of Zhanguo states.[84] Even today it is widely accepted that
in an army, preservation of the chain of command and of the singular authority
of every commander over his unit is far more important than ensuring the best
possible commander at the top. A subordinate officer may very well surpass his
commander in intellectual abilities, but for the sake of military discipline, which
is vital for preserving the army as such, it is important that he obey commands.
Insofar as a Warring State resembled a huge war machine, the same need for
unified decision-making was obvious. For Zhanguo statesmen and thinkers,
the concept of "oneness brings orderly rule; doubleness brings chaos" required
no further explanations. By adopting strict monarchic principles of rule, these
statesmen and thinkers may have significantly impaired their own political potency, yet insofar as the ultimate goal of political order was concerned, their
sacrifice appears to have been more than justified.

CHAPTER 3

The Search for the Ideal Ruler

In Chapter 2 I noted several times the potential contradiction between the flattering image of an ideal ruler in Zhanguo texts and the negative assessments of current rulers by many thinkers. It is time now to investigate more thoroughly the impact of this implicit contradiction on Zhanguo views of rulership. We can outline two main ways in which thinkers of the Warring States tried to resolve the contradiction between the ideal and the reality: that of the optimists, who hoped to ensure that the throne would be occupied by a truly worthy person, and that of the more sober thinkers, who sought to adapt political system for an average sovereign. While neither solution was entirely satisfactory, the second proved to have more lasting appeal for imperial thinkers and statesmen.

This chapter focuses on the optimistic thinkers. I shall first briefly address their attitudes toward the possibilities of improving the monarch through educational means and then discuss in greater detail various ideas regarding the possibility of placing a worthy monarch on the throne—even if this meant violation of dynastic principles of rule. I shall try to assess why opponents of hereditary succession failed to advance their cause and why mainstream thinkers ultimately agreed to the situation of a less-than-perfect ruler occupying the throne.

Conventional Ways of Improving the Monarch

The idealized image of the True Monarch was a double-edged sword for acting sovereigns. On the one hand, it strengthened the ruler-centered order and monarchistic mindset; on the other hand, it was frequently employed as a means to criticize acting sovereigns who fell short of the ideal of impeccable morality and divine sagacity. The thinkers' unanimous awareness of the gap between the ideal and the real eventually became a source of immense tension, which is present in most, if not all, political texts of the Zhanguo period. I shall illustrate this point with a single citation from the *Mengzi*:

> Mengzi had an audience with King Xiang of Liang [i.e. of Wei, 魏襄王, r. 318–296]. Leaving the audience, he told [his entourage]: "When I observed

him, he did not look like a ruler; when I a   nim, there was nothing
awesome to be seen. Abruptly he asked m   n All under Heaven be
stabilized?' I answered: 'Stability is in unit   is able to unify it?' I answered: 'He, who has no proclivity towarc   able to unify it.'—'Who
will be able to follow him?' I answered: 'Nobody under Heaven will not follow him. [. . .] Today among the shepherds of the people there is none who
has no proclivity toward killing. If there is one who has no proclivity toward
killing, then the people of All under Heaven will crane their necks to look
at him. If this really happens, the people will go over to him like water runs
downwards: who will be able to stop this torrent?'"[1]

This brief passage contains the most important elements of Mengzi's views
of rulership. Mengzi considers the ruler as the single person who is able to
stabilize the world, and, of course, this task can be performed exclusively by a
benevolent ruler "who has no proclivity toward killing." But Mengzi emphatically denies King Xiang the right to be considered a proper candidate for this
position. Not only does he openly observe that "today among the shepherds
of the people there is none who has no proclivity toward killing," but he also
informs his unidentified interlocutors that King Xiang lacks the awe a ruler
should generate, implying that he is unfit even to his current position of a ruler
of a regional state. Eventually, Mengzi's high expectations of a ruler lead him to
question the legitimacy of acting sovereigns!

For Mengzi the contradiction between the desired and the actual ruler is
evident, and perhaps it is also evident to his audience. But how to resolve the
disparity? It is here that Zhanguo thinkers faced one of the most sensitive issues—the issue of the ruler's qualification for his office.

In discussing the ways of improving the quality of the ruler, we should distinguish between the widely acceptable, even if not necessarily efficient means
and the more efficient, but politically dangerous means. The former, on which
we shall focus first, included a broad range of remonstrance, instruction, and
correction of the erring rulers by their loyal ministers. Both the theory and
practice of remonstrance had flourished since the beginning of the Zhou dynasty if not before, yielding eventually a huge corpus of historical and theoretical texts aimed at serving as a mirror for rulers that would allow them to avoid
their predecessors' errors. Because this issue has been discussed extensively elsewhere, we will not deal with it here.[2] Another conventional means of improving the ruler, which was supposed to be even more efficient, was educating the
ruler-to-be. A variety of educational methods was employed to prevent the
emergence of particularly inept and immoral rulers and, ideally, to ensure that
only an enlightened sovereign would occupy the throne.[3]

Popular and uncontroversial though they were, educational methods, just like remonstrance, were not entirely effective, and by the middle Zhanguo period, one may discern increasing impatience regarding these ways of improving the ruler. Perhaps, as idealistic expectations of the sage ruler or a True Monarch increased, the inadequacy of ordinary means for improving the sovereign became transparent. Even such a tireless instructor of rulers as Mengzi displayed visible disappointment and lack of hope that his efforts would succeed, as is manifested in the anecdote about his meeting with King Xiang; this disappointment was widespread. Being all too well aware of stubborn or mediocre rulers who failed to heed the remonstrance and even punished their outspoken ministers, many thinkers became skeptical with regard to mild methods of improving the sovereign's quality.[4] This skepticism is explicit in a story recorded in the "Chu yu" 楚語 chapter of the *Guoyu* 國語, a collection of historical anecdotes from the Chunqiu period. The anecdote pretends to be a record of an early seventh-century BCE conversation, but its content and language clearly reflect its middle-to-late Zhanguo origin:

> King Zhuang of Chu (楚莊王, r. 613–591) dispatched Shi Men to be a tutor to the heir apparent Zhen.
>
> [Shi Men] refused saying: "I am talentless and can add nothing to him."
>
> The king said: "I am relying on your goodness to make [the heir apparent] good."
>
> [Shi Men] replied: "Goodness depends on the heir apparent; if the heir apparent seeks goodness, the good people will arrive; if he does not seek goodness, goodness will nowhere be used. Hence Yao had Danzhu, Shun had Shangjun, Qi had Wuguan, Tang had Taijia, King Wen had Guan[shu] and Cai[shu]. All these five kings possessed magnificent virtue, but also had wicked sons. It was not that they did not want goodness, but they were not able to achieve it. If the people are violating [proper norms], they can be educated; but [the aliens] Man, Rong, Yi, Di have been unsubmissive for long time, and the Central States are not able to make use of them."
>
> The king finally dispatched him to tutor the heir apparent.[5]

Shi Men's reply is unusually candid. He recalls examples of the inept sons of legendary and semilegendary paragon rulers to prove that no educational process can modify an inherently wicked person, implying in passim that the heir apparent may be comparable to the "barbarian" aliens who cannot be educated and therefore cannot be employed.[6] This harsh comparison implies not only awareness of the difficulties involved in educating the would-be ruler, but, more important, a subtle criticism of the hereditary succession. If even the best father cannot ensure that his son acts properly, then the entire system of lineal succession may not be an adequate way to ensure proper rulership. This suggestion is doubly valid if we consider the examples more closely. Yao 堯 and Shun 舜 replaced their inept sons with meritorious ministers (see below); Wuguan 五觀 of the Xia was dismissed; Taijia 太甲 of the Shang was deposed by the regent, Yi Yin 伊尹, and reappointed only after he improved his behavior; while the rebellious sons of King Wen of Zhou, Guanshu 管叔 and Caishu 蔡叔, were eradicated by their brother, the Duke of Zhou 周公. Since in at least two cases the son's ineptitude caused the end of the dynasty, Shi Men may well be hinting at this as a legitimate option.

The *Guoyu* story continues with Shi Men seeking advice from the elder Chu statesman, Shen Shushi 申叔時. Shen surveys at length proper educational means and the proper curriculum for an heir apparent, but then concludes on the same pessimistic note we have heard from Shi Men: "One who received [proper] education and does not heed it, is not a human being, how can he be let prosper? If you are charged with this responsibility, you should withdraw. If you withdraw by your own, you would be respected; otherwise you will blush for shame."[7]

Shen Shushi shared not only Shi Men's skepticism regarding the educational process (a remarkable idea, given that the *Guoyu* frequently identifies itself as an educational device!)[8] but also his harsh attitude toward a potentially inept heir. Should the heir apparent fail to follow the instructions of his tutor, he loses the right to be called a human being. And if the humanity of the would-be ruler is denied, the conclusions are unequivocal: such a ruler does not deserve his position!

The *Guoyu*'s implicit disbelief in the possibility of educating an inept ruler, echoed in such an authoritative text as the *Xunzi*,[9] contains seeds of potential subversion. Insofar as some heirs cannot be turned into worthy human beings, and insofar as even the best ruler may beget a wicked son (as the cited historical lessons confirm), then the entire hereditary basis of rulership appears significantly impaired. How then to solve the problem of attaining a proper ruler? A radical answer to this question was given by certain Zhanguo thinkers whose search for an ideal ruler brought them to the verge of questioning the very foundations of hereditary monarchy.

Replacing an Inept Ruler

Throughout most its known history, China has been ruled not by individuals, but by dynasties, the achievements of meritorious ancestors being the foundation of the reigning ruler's legitimacy. Yet the dynastic principle of rule was never considered axiomatic. The violent replacement of the Shang by the Zhou, the post-factum justification of this act through the theory of Heaven's Decree (see Chapter 1), and the retrospective invention of a similar overthrow of the Xia by the Shang—all these created a favorable climate for a would-be contender for power. The Zhou leaders were the first to realize that their Decree is not eternal, its transferability being emphasized already in the earliest portions of the *Shi jing* and the *Shu jing*.[10] Surprisingly, however, appeals to the Decree transfer were extremely rare throughout the lengthy Zhou history. Violent replacements of inept rulers occurred from the ninth century BCE on, but none of the rebels claimed possession of Heaven's Decree, and none—including the all-powerful ministerial lineages of the Chunqiu period—dared speak of replacing the ruling house.[11] Individual rulers could be expelled or murdered, but no dynasty had been overthrown by its subjects for more than six centuries since the establishment of the Zhou. Master Kuang, in a speech discussed in Chapter 1, clearly connected the fate of rulers with Heaven's approval of their activities, but even he fell short of using this argument to justify dynastic change. Thus insofar as the Western Zhou and Chunqiu periods are concerned, the theory of Heaven's Decree was insufficiently compelling to uproot the all-important hereditary principle of rule.

This principle was violated in 403, as the state of Jin was dismembered by its components, the Wei, Han, and Zhao houses, and a few years later when the powerful Tian family replaced the six-odd-centuries-old ruling house of the state of Qi. These events might have spurred a new interest in the nonhereditary transfer of power, especially as they coincided with the increasingly critical assessment of the hereditary order. As meritocratic ideas (see Chapter 5) became increasingly popular, they inevitably engendered interest in the idea of "elevating the worthy" to the very top of the government apparatus. Moreover, the very atmosphere of political reforms, which engulfed each of the contending Warring States by the fourth century BCE, allowed reassessment of some of the foundational practices of Zhou political culture, including the notion of lineal succession. Thus the fourth century became one of the most fertile in unorthodox ideas concerning the ways to ensure there was a proper sovereign on the throne. In what follows, I shall survey alternatives to the dynastic principle of rule that were presented in some texts of the period and try to explain why these alternatives were ultimately discarded by the mainstream intellectual tradition of the late Zhanguo period, and what their limitations were.

Mozi: Three Kinds of Nonlineal Succession

Mozi was not a staunch critic of hereditary succession, but his writings may serve as a useful departing point for our discussion: first, because he presents

—even if in a nascent form—all the alternatives to dynastic rule pondered by later thinkers; and, second, because his writings hint at a connection between the adoption of meritocratic principles and doubts regarding hereditary monarchy. In "Elevating the Worthy A" ("Shang xian shang" 尚賢上) chapter, Mozi states:

> Thus in antiquity when the sage kings exercised their government, they ranked [the subjects according to their] virtue and elevated the worthy. Even if a person was a peasant or an artisan, they commissioned him a high rank, increased his emoluments, assigned him [important] tasks, and empowered his orders. . . .
>
> Hence when Yao raised Shun from the northern shore of the Fu marshes and entrusted him with the government, All under Heaven was pacified. When Yu (禹, the progenitor of the Xia dynasty) raised Yi 益 from the middle of Yinfang and entrusted him with the government, the nine provinces were established. When Tang (湯, the founder of the Shang dynasty) raised Yi Yin 伊尹 from the middle of the kitchen and entrusted him with the government, his plans were fulfilled. When King Wen (of the Zhou) raised Hongyao 閎夭 and Taidian 泰顛 from the middle of the nets and entrusted them with the government, the Western Lands submitted.[12]

Mozi clearly pronounces his dissatisfaction with a pedigree-based order: only a person's talents, not his current position or family background, should matter for his promotion. But are there limits to the upward mobility advocated in "Elevating the Worthy A"? The first passage cited above falls short of proposing elevation of the worthy to the position of a ruler: insofar as appointments were made by the "sage kings of antiquity," the sage kings' position remained apparently uninfluenced by their adherence to meritocratic principle.[13] Similarly, all the historic examples in the second passage depict worthy ministers who were elevated, despite their initial obscurity, by enlightened rulers, but none of whom replaced the supreme sovereign. This is true also of a most important example cited by Mozi: that of the sage emperor Yao, who promoted his meritorious minister, Shun, from the remoteness of the "Fu marshes." As I have argued elsewhere, this passage is the earliest mention of the Yao-Shun abdication legend in the received literature.[14] Yet in this instance, the power transfer between the sage monarch and the sage minister is not complete. Shun is appointed to the highest governmental position under Yao, just like worthy ministers of later monarchs, such as Yi or Yi Yin, but there is no hint of Yao's abdication in Shun's favor, as the later legend holds.

The relations between Yao and Shun are discussed again in the second and the third parts of the "Elevating the Worthy" triplet, and this discussion may reflect an evolution in the thought of Mozi's disciples. The modified historical narrative presents the following version of Yao-Shun relations:

> In times of old, Shun cultivated land at Mt. Li, made pottery on the [Yellow] River's banks, went fishing in Lei marshes. Yao discovered him at the northern shore of the Fu marshes, raised him to [the position of] Son of Heaven, and handed him the government of All under Heaven, [thus ensuring proper] rule over the people under Heaven. Yi Zhi [Yi Yin] was a private servant of the daughter of the Xin ruler, acting as a cook. Tang discovered him, raised him to the position of his own prime minister, and handed to him the government of All under Heaven [thus ensuring proper] rule over the people under Heaven.[15]

The modification may appear at the first glance insignificant, but it has revolutionary impact. In the earlier version of "Elevating the Worthy," Shun's promotion is to the supreme ministerial position. Now Shun is elevated not merely to the head of the administration, but explicitly to the position of Son of Heaven, replacing Yao. Thus Shun is properly distinguished from Yi Yin, who is granted "only" the position of prime minister by his master, Tang. The abdication story appears here in its "classical" form: a poor and obscure person, Shun, who makes his living by tilling the soil, making pottery, and fishing, is discovered by the enlightened ruler, Yao, who then yields the throne to Shun. The ensuing proper rule over All under Heaven proves that Yao's abdication was a proper and laudable act.

Mozi thus introduces, albeit without much fanfare, the new concept of a nonhereditary transfer of power, namely, the yielding of the throne to a proper candidate. The story is never discussed again in the core chapters of the *Mozi*, which probably reflects its great sensitivity. Embedding a radical political proposal in a harmless historical narrative was a common resort of Zhanguo thinkers, and particularly of Mozi, who frequently invoked the actions of former kings to justify his radical departures from established political norms. In Chapter 2 we saw that a similarly invented tradition helped Mozi to introduce the notion of (s)electing "the worthiest and the most able [man] in All under Heaven" as Son of Heaven. Just as in the case of abdication, a story of (s)electing the supreme leader appears in the *Mozi* in passing, without further elaboration and without an attempt to explicitly relate it to the current political situation. The antihereditary topoi are present in the *Mozi* only in nascent form, but these rudimentary sentiments testify that the idea of placing the best possible ruler on the throne was not alien to Mozi's followers.

Aside from the cursorily mentioned possibilities of placing the worthy ruler on the throne through either abdication or a kind of (s)election, Mozi presents a third and much more elaborate possibility of rectifying or replacing the sovereign: Heaven's intervention. Mozi's distinctive endorsement of Heaven as a sentient and politically active deity is well known. For the matter under discussion, we shall focus on one aspect of his theory: Heaven as a supervisor of rulers. In the treatise on "Heaven's Will" ("Tian zhi" 天志), Mozi says: "I have reason to know that Heaven is really more esteemed and more knowledgeable than the Son of Heaven. It is said: 'When the Son of Heaven behaves well, Heaven can reward him; when he behaves viciously, Heaven can penalize him.'"[16]

Mozi explains elsewhere what he means by "penalizing":

> In antiquity, the vicious kings of the Three Dynasties, Jie 桀 [of the Xia], Zhou[xin 紂辛 of the Shang], You 幽 and Li 厲 [of the Western Zhou] indiscriminately hated All under Heaven, and accordingly committed crimes against it. They altered the minds of the people, leading them to blaspheme against the Supreme Thearch, mountains and rivers, deities and spirits. Heaven thought that they hated those whom Heaven loves and harmed those whom Heaven benefits; hence it increased their punishment, causing fathers and sons [of their state] to be scattered, their state and family destroyed, altars of soil and grain lost, and the calamity to reach them personally. Hence the common folk under Heaven have accordingly condemned them, transmitting this from son to grandson through myriad generations, the condemnatory bamboo strips never fading; [the people] name them "the losing rulers."[17]

Mozi clearly identified Heaven as the rectifier of rulers; the most vicious kings lose their state, family, and life. Condemnation by the people deprives them even of posthumous fame, and their destiny is intended to serve as a warning to current bad sovereigns. But do these unequivocal statements mean that Mozi wholeheartedly endorsed "revolutionary" replacement of an evil tyrant as a legitimate way of placing a worthy sovereign on the throne? The answer is not simple. Ostensibly, Mozi justifies "righteous rebellion" by the sage founders of the Shang and the Zhou against their oppressive rulers, but he is extremely cautious with this regard. In the "Fei gong xia" (非攻下, "Contra aggression C") chapter, Mozi presents lengthy narratives of the violent overthrow of the Xia and Shang tyrants; we shall focus on the later story:

When we come to the King Zhou[xin] of the Shang, Heaven did not prolong his virtue; his sacrifices were not according to the seasons. The night lasted for ten subsequent days;[18] it rained soil for ten days at [the Shang capital,] Bo; the nine caldrons moved from their place;[19] witches appeared in the dark, and ghosts sighed at night. Some women turned into men; flesh came down from Heaven like rain; thorny brambles covered up highways in the capital, yet the king became even more dissolute. A red bird holding a *gui* tablet by its beak descended on Zhou altar at Mt. Qi, proclaiming: "Heaven decrees King Wen of Zhou to attack Yin [Shang] and to take possession of its capital." Tai Dian then came to be minister to (King Wen). The River generated charts; Earth generated *chenghuang*.[20] As King Wu ascended the [Zhou] throne [after King Wen's death], he dreamt of three deities saying [on behalf of the Thearch?]: "Now that I have deeply submerged Zhou[xin] of Yin in ale-muddled virtue, go and attack him! I shall certainly let you destroy him." Then King Wu set out and attacked the mad fellow [Zhouxin], rebelling against the Shang and creating Zhou. Heaven gave King Wu the Yellow Bird Pennant. Having conquered Yin, he accepted the Thearch's gift, divided responsibilities for [worshiping] the deities; sacrificed to the ancestors of Zhou[xin], established connections with the aliens of the four borders, and none in the world dared to show disrespect. Then he continued [the Shang founder,] Tang's achievements. Thereupon King Wu put Zhou[xin] to death.[21]

Mozi's narrative is fairly interesting, not only for its possible incorporation of what appears to be early mythological materials related to the overthrow of the Shang, but also for its hidden message. While ostensibly Mozi endorses King Wu's righteous war, a careful reading of the narrative leads to a more qualified conclusion. The fantastic accumulation of portents and omens, endless stories of cosmic disasters during the reign of Zhouxin, the repeated interventions by Heaven's representatives urging kings Wen and Wu to act—all this creates an almost satiric effect. At the very least, the plausibility of the entire story looks seriously impaired. What is the aim of this inflated narrative? I believe it hints at the conclusion that only a comparable accumulation of omens and portents would justify war or rebellion in the future. Mozi turns the overthrow of Jie and Zhouxin into exceptional events, which are of limited relevance to the present. Under normal circumstances, nobody should claim that he is a new recipient of Heaven's Decree.

In retrospect, all the three possibilities of replacing an inept monarch outlined in the *Mozi* are of limited consequences for his overall political theory. The ideas of placing a worthy ruler on the throne either through (s)election or through abdication of the reigning monarch remain at the margins of Mozi's writings, while violent replacement of the vicious monarch is contradictory to Mozi's aversion to aggressive warfare and was accordingly presented as somewhat inapplicable in the present. In the final account, Mozi did not suggest any practical means for implementing his evident desire to see a benevolent and wise ruler on the throne. As we shall see, the problem of the impracticality of alternatives to hereditary succession remained one of the major barriers to promoting such ideas in Zhanguo political life.

Tang Yu zhi Dao: Moral Advantages of Yielding the Throne

Among the three possible ways outlined in the *Mozi* of placing an ideal ruler on the throne, the vague idea of "popular election" (or Heaven's selection) never gained popularity, but the notions of abdication on the one hand and "righteous rebellion" on the other became part and parcel of Zhanguo political discourse. Of these two, the idea of yielding the throne, expressed in the legend of Yao's abdication in favor of Shun (and Shun's later abdication in favor of the Xia founder, Yu 禹), became fairly widespread after the *Mozi*. From the fourth century BCE on, Yao and Shun were firmly incorporated into a line of paragon rulers of the past, and references to the abdication legend became ubiquitous in contemporary texts. Yet despite its evident popularity, the abdication legend is not discussed systematically in any of the received texts. This paradox caused Angus Graham to opine that such muted discussion may reflect the thinkers' reluctance to engage in the politically sensitive issue of questioning hereditary rule and that the extant examples of advocating the ruler's abdication are "likely to be the tip of the iceberg."[22]

Shortly after Graham's statement (and unfortunately shortly after his premature death) his insight was confirmed, for three heretofore unknown texts were published. Each of these texts (*Tang Yu zhi Dao* 唐虞之道 from Guodian; *Zi Gao* 子羔 and *Rong Cheng shi* 容成氏 published by the Shanghai Museum) is roughly datable to the second half of the fourth century BCE, and each deals extensively with the issue of abdication, expressing sentiments in favor of yielding the throne to a worthy candidate with unusual candor.[23] The *Tang Yu zhi Dao*, a brief and relatively well-preserved text of 709 characters, presents some quite unequivocal statements in support of abdication as the only means of ensuring orderly rule. The text begins with the following statement:

> The way of Tang [= Yao] and Yu [= Shun] is to abdicate and not to transmit [the throne to their heirs]. As kings, Yao and Shun benefited All under Heaven, but did not benefit from it. To abdicate and not transmit is the fullness of

sagacity. To benefit All under Heaven but not to benefit from it is the utmost of benevolence. Thus in antiquity the benevolent and sage were considered worthy to such a degree. Even when in dire straits, they were not greedy; until the end of their days, they did not seek benefits [for themselves]: they embodied benevolence! One must first rectify himself before rectifying the world; this is the completeness of the Way of the sages. Hence [the way] of Tang and Yu is [to abdicate].[24]

The first passage flatly transposes the notion of abdication from the issue of Mozi's "elevating the worthy" to a more "Confucian" idea of moral ruler-ship. Since abdication is an act of the utmost selflessness, it manifests the ruler's sagacity and benevolence, and as such allows the ruler to "rectify the world by rectifying himself" in a way that is unmistakably reminiscent of Mengzi's dictum.[25] Abdication is praiseworthy, therefore, primarily due to its ethical ap-propriateness, while its political effectiveness is derivative.

After presenting their major thesis, the authors continue with a detailed dis-cussion of the impeccable morality of the paragons Yao and Shun, whom they absolve of the suspicion that by yielding the throne, they have behaved insen-sitively toward their kin. Then the text turns to a new and surprising argument to bolster the pro-abdication position: abdication is presented as a proper way to preserve the ruler's well-being and to prolong his life:

In antiquity, the sages were capped at the age of twenty; at thirty they mar-ried, at fifty [they] orderly ruled All under Heaven; and at seventy they hand-ed over the rule. As their four limbs were exhausted, sharpness of hearing and clarity of sight weakened, they abdicated the world and delivered it to a worthy, and retired to nurture their lives. Therefore we know that they did not seek benefits [from All under Heaven].[26]

This passage is extraordinarily interesting. First, unlike most known dis-cussions of abdication, which do not abandon the Yao-Shun-Yu narrative, the authors of the *Tang Yu zhi Dao* try to establish a general pattern of abdication, elevating it to the position of a general political theory, which is only barely disguised by reference to the "sages" of "antiquity." Second, this passage is the only known attempt to outline the ideal personal conditions for the sage ruler. This ruler should not prematurely ascend the throne (the age of fifty ensures complete maturity), nor should he stay on the throne for more than twenty years. Third, the reason for the abdication is given with surprising candor: it is the ruler's physical deterioration. The text comes very near to establishing a mandatory retirement age for sovereigns![27]

The *Tang Yu zhi Dao* ends with a powerful assertion of the benefits of abdication:

> Abdication means that possessors of the supreme virtue deliver [the rule] to the worthy. When they have supreme virtue, this means that the world has the ruler, and the age is enlightened. When they entrust [the rule] to the worthy, then the people uphold [proper] teachings and are transformed by the Way. From the beginning of humankind there was nobody who was able to transform the people without abdicating.[28]

The pro-abdication sentiment is stated here with the utmost clarity. Abdication is a desirable and immediately applicable mode of political conduct, which should be regularly employed if a ruler hopes to "transform" his people in accordance with the "Way" and to reap political benefits. The final denial of the possibility of hereditary monarchy to achieve this blessed condition barely disguises the most radical attack on the principle of hereditary rule altogether.

Rong Cheng shi: An Alternative History of Power Transfers

The *Tang Yu zhi Dao* presents the most systematic discussion in favor of abdication and is the only such text that departs at times from the Yao-Shun-Yu legend. In contrast, the *Rong Cheng shi* is a purely historical text that presents its views through a lengthy narrative of dynastic changes from antiquity to the beginning of the Zhou dynasty. This relatively well-preserved text, which comprises fifty-three slips, of which thirty-seven are complete, is particularly interesting for our discussion, as it contains references to all the three possibilities of nonhereditary succession outlined by Mozi. Since I have extensively discussed abdication-related portions of this text elsewhere,[29] I shall shorten this part of discussion here, while paying more attention to the views in the *Rong Cheng shi* regarding righteous rebellion.

The *Rong Cheng shi* is unequivocal in its preference for abdication as the proper way to transfer power. The text begins with praise for legendary rulers of the past, none of whom adhered to the principle of lineal succession: ". . . [when] all [these rulers] possessed All under Heaven, they did not transmit [the throne] to their sons, but transmitted it to the worthies. Their virtue was lasting and pure, and, moreover, the superiors cared for the inferiors, unifying their will, putting arms to rest, and assigning tasks according to talents. . . ."[30]

The beginning sets the tone for the subsequent discussion. In antiquity, abdication was the only means of legitimate succession, and those days were indeed the Golden Age. The text further depicts the ideal society, in which even the weakest members are employed and cared for, and which prospered due to the selfless leadership of its kings. This is a recurrent topic in the *Rong Cheng shi*: sociopolitical idyll is invariably connected with the ruler's ability to practice abdication. After depicting the next Golden Age under the pre-Yao monarch, whose identity is unknown due to the slip's damage, the text turns to one of its major heroes, Yao:

> Yao resided between Danfu and Guanling. Yao despised amassing [riches] and acted according to the seasons. He did not encourage the people with rewards, but they exerted their efforts; he did not employ punishments and executions, but there were no thieves and bandits; he was extremely lenient, but the people submitted. Thus in the territory of one hundred *li* squared he led the people from All under Heaven, and they arrived, respectfully establishing him as Son of Heaven.[31]

The text praises Yao's political abilities, which became a common topos of depicting this Thearch, but then introduces a crucial new element into Yao's story, unknown from other texts. The passage clearly states that Yao *was established* by the people from "All under Heaven." The authors remain silent as to what happened to a pre-Yao monarch, but the text suggests that a kind of exceptional void at the top of the universal power pyramid preceded the establishment of Yao. This overt reference to the popular will as the crucial factor behind the establishment of the Son of Heaven is devoid of Mozi's ambiguity and appears to be one of the most daring statements in Chinese political thought. The issue of "the people's will" recurs in the subsequent depiction of Yao's rule:

> Yao then inspected the worthies: "Among those who tread on Earth and are covered by Heaven, those who are sincere, righteous, and trustworthy should gather between Heaven and Earth and be embraced within the four seas. He who is able to complete the [government] matters, I shall establish him as Son of Heaven." Yao taught them saying: "When you enter, I shall peep at you, to demand the worthy among you and to yield [the throne] to him." Yao yielded All under Heaven to the worthies, but the worthies from All under Heaven were unable to receive it. Heads of the myriad states all yielded their states to the worthies . . . [yielded to the] worthies [from All under Heaven],[32] but the worthies were unable to accept it. Thus all the people under Heaven considered Yao as one who is able to raise the worthies, and finally established him.[33]

Certain details of this narrative require further discussion, but the basic outline is clear enough: immediately after being established as Son of Heaven,

Yao begins searching for the worthies to whom the empire may be delivered. Initially the search is futile, but it encourages other leaders to do the same, creating a kind of abdication-based meritocratic system at the top of the government apparatus. Significantly, Yao's relentless efforts to promote the worthy are rewarded—again by "all the people under Heaven"—who "finally establish" Yao (perhaps prolonging his tenure as the Son of Heaven?). Yao is not satisfied, however, and he continues to search for a worthy candidate until he finally finds Shun. The text follows Mozi's depiction of Shun's initially humble position and then tells how Yao examined Shun's worthiness and employed him, before finally yielding the throne: "[Yao then became aged, his sight was no longer clear], his ears no longer sharp. Yao had nine sons; but he did not make his son heir. He observed Shun's worthiness and wanted to make him his heir."[34]

The story here looks like an illustration of the general principle of retirement discussed in the *Tang Yu zhi Dao*: the aged Yao must end his tenure. Yet despite his physical unfitness, Yao continues to behave prudently and selflessly. The *Rong Cheng shi* specifies that Yao had nine sons, but nonetheless chose Shun as his heir. Importantly, there are no hints that Yao's sons are inept, an argument that was often employed as a justification of Yao's transfer of power to Shun.[35] According to the *Rong Cheng shi*, Yao appointed Shun as his heir in direct continuation of earlier tradition, when "nobody transmitted [the rule] to his son, but transmitted it to the worthies."

Shun's ruling pattern largely follows that of Yao. He appoints able ministers, who put an end to natural calamities and perform other crucial tasks in ordering the society and the cosmos. A new age of prosperity follows, at the end of which ageing Shun, facing physical deterioration, promptly transfers power not to one of his seven sons, but to the worthiest of his ministers, Yu. Yu displays the necessary modesty by looking for a worthy to whom he can yield the throne and accepts the rule only when he has no other choice. Another period of prosperity follows, but it lacks the aura of cosmic harmony characteristic of earlier reigns. These signs of decline may indicate Heaven-and-Earth's dissatisfaction with the coming end of the age of yielding the throne:

> Yu had five sons, but he did not make his son heir. He observed Gao Yao's 皋陶 worthiness and wanted to make him his heir. Gao Yao then yielded five times to the worthiest in All under Heaven, and afterwards pled ill, did not leave [his house], and died. Yu then yielded to Yi 益, but then [Yu's son] Qi 啓 attacked Yi and seized power for himself. [His heirs] ruled All under Heaven for sixteen years [should be: generations], and Jie appeared.[36]

The story of the selfless transmission of power to the worthies ends almost incidentally, due to Gao Yao's early death and the decisive action taken by Yu's son, Qi, the eventual founder of the Xia dynasty. Strikingly, the topos of prosperity and orderly rule, which figured so prominently in the earlier parts of the *Rong Cheng shi*, disappears completely from the narrative of the Xia period. On the contrary, the story mentions no remarkable deeds of the dynastic founder, Qi, and moves instead directly to depict the transgressions of the infamous tyrant Jie, the last Xia ruler, under whose rule the world plummeted into deep turmoil. When Jie is overthrown by the founder of the Shang dynasty, Tang, the text again skips immediately from Tang's rule to the atrocities of the last vicious ruler of the Shang dynasty, Zhouxin. Thus while dynastic founders are not criticized directly, the authors fail to praise their deeds. Moreover, rules of Jie and Zhouxin are marked by awful atrocities, the lengthy depictions of which may serve as an indirect warning against the implementation of the principle of dynastic rule: even the virtuous founders of the dynasties may eventually beget vicious offspring.

What can be done, then, to deal with a vicious ruler in the post-abdication era? The narrative of the "righteous uprising" presented by the *Rong Cheng shi* is fairly interesting, because it departs in certain details from the known versions. I shall not deal here with the story of Tang's overthrow of Jie, since the sequence of the bamboo slips in this part is hotly contested, and the rearrangement may significantly alter the overall meaning of that section. Instead, I shall focus on a much clearer part of the text, which deals with Zhouxin and his end.

> Tang's [descendants] ruled All under Heaven for thirty-one generations, and then Zhou[xin] appeared. Zhou[xin] did not follow the Way of the former kings, behaving in the muddled way.[37] Thus he made a nine-layered terrace, placing beneath it a *yu* vessel full of charcoal. Above he placed a round wooden [beam], letting the people to walk on it; those who were able to tread on it, passed; those who failed fell down and died; those who refused his orders were fettered in the shackles. Then he created three thousand metal fetters; also he built ponds of ale, extensively delighting himself in ale, extending the night for his debauchery, and refusing to attend governmental affairs.[38]

Here the text contains significant portions of what later became a standard set of accusations against Zhouxin. Clearly, this monarch breached all the acceptable norms, lost his legitimacy, and deserved to be overthrown. However, the *Rong Cheng shi* authors do not wholeheartedly endorse the idea of rising up, even against a vicious ruler like Zhouxin:

Then nine countries rebelled: Feng, Hao, Zhou 舟, Shiyi [??], Yu, Lu 鹿, Li, Chong, and the Mixu lineage.[39] Hearing about this, King Wen said: "Even if a ruler lacks the Way, how dare the subject not serve him? Even if a father lacks the way, how dare the son not serve him? Who can rebel against the Son of Heaven?" Hearing about this, Zhou[xin] released[40] King Wen from beneath the Xia Terrace and asked him: "Can the nine countries be forced to come [and submit]?" King Wen answered: "They can." Then King Wen wearing plain [mourning] clothes and girding his loins traveled through the nine countries. Seven countries submitted, while Feng and Hao did not. King Wen then raised an army and approached Feng and Hao; he drummed thrice and approached; drummed thrice and retreated, saying: "My knowledge has many limits, but if one person lacks the Way, what is the guilt of the hundred clans?" When the people of Feng and Hao heard this, they submitted to King Wen. King Wen then, being attached to the times of old, taught the people [proper] seasonal [activities], introducing them comprehensively to the advantages of high and low, of fertile and nonfertile [terrain]; introduced [them] to the Way of Heaven and advantages of Earth, thinking how to dispel the people's maladies. So thriving was then King Wen's support of Zhou[xin]![41]

King Wen explicitly denies legitimacy of any rebellion against an acting ruler. Instead of joining and leading the rebels, he quells their activities, threatening the more stubborn of them with military action. King Wen's activities in Zhouxin's service may well indicate that even under a vicious ruler the good minister can attain certain achievements.[42] The text authors laud this conciliatory policy of King Wen; but King Wen's heir, King Wu, discontinues it.

When King Wen died, King Wu assumed the position [of the Zhou king]. King Wu said: "If my virtue is complete, I shall convince him [Zhouxin] to be replaced; alternatively I shall invade and replace him. Now, Zhou[xin] lacks the Way, muddles the hundred clans, constrains the regional lords; Heaven is going to punish him. I shall support Heaven, overawing him." Then King Wu prepared a thousand war chariots and ten thousand armored soldiers. On the *wuwu* day he marched through [the Yellow River] at Meng Ford, arriving at a location between Gong and Teng. The three armies were greatly ordered. King Wu then dispatched five hundred war chariots and three thousand armored [soldiers] to make a small meeting with the army of the regional lords at the Shepherds' Wild (Muye 牧野). Zhou[xin] was unaware of failures of his government and of his loss of the people's trust; hence he raised an army to oppose [King Wu]. Thus King Wu, wearing plain clothes and hat, declared to Heaven saying: "Zhou[xin] lacks the Way, muddles the hundred clans, constrains the regional lords; exterminates his kin and destroys his clan; he [treats] jade as earth, and ale as water. Heaven is going to punish him. I shall support Heaven, overawing him." Wearing white armor, King Wu arranged his troops at the outskirts of [Zhouxin's capital,] Yin, but Yin. . . .[43]

This part of the *Rong Cheng shi* narrative differs again from the well-known versions of the Zhou victory over the Shang. Unfortunately the last slip(s) of the text is missing,[44] which prevents us from reconstructing the narrative in its entirety, but it is clear that it gives only partial support to the notion of righteous rebellion. King Wu twice declares his intention to support Heaven in overawing (*wei* 威) rather than punishing Zhouxin, and he appears cautious with regard to military action, sending only a smaller part of his army to Muye. Ultimately, no military encounter between the opposing sides is recorded, supporting Asano Yūichi's conjecture that King Wu's goal was simply to display military might in order to convince Zhouxin to yield the throne rather than directly to overthrow him.[45] The overthrow of the Shang may, thus, be a kind of misunderstanding rather than the case of justified rebellion.

We may now summarize the political credo of the *Rong Cheng shi* authors. First, they are preoccupied with ensuring that a proper person occupies the throne: a good ruler will engender overall prosperity and peace, attaining the support of Heaven and Earth, while an evil one will bring about directly opposite results. Second, the authors unequivocally advocate application of the principle of "elevating the worthy" to the very top of the sociopolitical pyramid. Third, among the three methods of ensuring a proper ruler outlined in the *Mozi*, the *Rong Cheng shi* authors favor the second, namely, abdication. The idea of popular "establishment" of a worthy monarch, albeit outlined in the text with greater clarity than in the *Mozi*, seems to be of limited applicability unless the exceptional situation of a void at the top of the ruling apparatus exists; the idea of righteous rebellion is treated with certain skepticism, even if it is not entirely rejected. Abdication is clearly preferred as the best means of ensuring a qualified sovereign.

The preference for abdication rather than righteous rebellion in the *Rong Cheng shi* (and in other texts) is not incidental. Violent overthrow of the reigning monarch was by definition abnormal and could be employed only in exceptional cases. Voluntary yielding of the throne, in contrast, was a morally advantageous and less costly alternative. Not only could it ensure ascendancy of the best-suited rulers, but also, insofar as the ultimate decision regarding the successor's choice remained in the hands of the acting sovereign, the procedure of abdication did not infringe on the principle of the ruler's absolute power. Ultimately, therefore, abdication could be seen as the most elegant way to ensure ascension of the best possible sovereign. Its popularity is testified indirectly by a provocative question by Mengzi's disciple, Wan Zhang 萬章: "People have a saying: 'By the time of Yu, virtue had declined; [hence] he did not transfer the power to the worthiest, but to his own son.' Do you agree?"[46]

Mengzi's reply will be discussed below, but here it is important to note that the "popular saying" cited by Wan Zhang may have reflected fairly widespread antidynastic sentiments. However, it was precisely the popularity of the abdication doctrine that led to its swift collapse. Although theoretically attractive, yielding the throne to the worthies proved a woeful fiasco when translated into practical action. While it is impossible to verify the abdication gestures reportedly made by several rulers in the second half of the fourth century BCE,[47] in at least one case a real abdication did occur. In 314, King Kuai of Yan (燕王噲, r. 320–314) attempted to emulate Yao by yielding the throne to his minister, Zizhi 子之. King Kuai's motivations for this extraordinary step are not clear,[48] but the results of his decision were both unequivocal and disastrous: the state of Yan deteriorated into conflict between Zizhi and the "legitimate" heir, Ping 平, and the eventual turmoil brought about invasion and a brief occupation by the forces of neighboring Qi. Another neighboring state, Zhongshan 中山, also seized the opportunity of sending its army against Yan, declaring that yielding the throne is an outrageous act, which "goes against Heaven above and is not in conformance with the people below."[49] Although Yan reestablished its independence shortly after these events, the historical lesson had been learned: abdication is a good recipe in theory, but in actual life it may have disastrous consequences.

Mengzi: A Reluctant Supporter of Lineal Succession

While the recently discovered texts discussed above are generally critical of hereditary transmission of power, Mengzi's views are more complex. More than any other thinker, Mengzi based his hopes for the moral world on the idea that a benevolent ruler would expand his morality to humankind, and this belief may have encouraged him to pay considerable attention to the problem of placing a good ruler on the throne. Unlike most of his contemporaries, Mengzi displayed remarkable readiness to discuss even the sensitive topic of righteous rebellion and not just the issue of abdication. In one of the most famous of Mengzi's dialogues, he presents his views in a most forthright manner:

King Xuan of Qi (齊宣王, r. 319–301) asked: "Did it happen that Tang expelled Jie, while King Wu attacked Zhou[xin]?"

Mengzi replied: "This is reported in the *Traditions*."

[The king] said: "Is it permissible for a minister to murder his ruler?"

Mengzi said: "One who commits crimes against benevolence is called 'criminal'; one who commits crimes against righteousness is called 'a cruel one.' A cruel and criminal person is called 'an ordinary fellow.' I heard that an ordinary fellow Zhou[xin] was punished, but did not hear of murdering a ruler."[50]

In his reply to the king, Mengzi departs from the mode of emphasizing Zhouxin's unusual atrocities and his subsequent punishment by the almighty Heaven, as we saw in Mozi or the *Rong Cheng shi*. Instead, he refers to routine, almost universal, aberrations of Jie's and Zhouxin's conduct: their violation of the norms of benevolence and righteousness. Any reader of the *Mengzi*'s philippics against contemporary rulers will not fail to notice that they do not differ considerably from Jie and Zhouxin. What, then, is a practical conclusion to take from this analysis? Should contemporary rulers face overthrow and execution just like the past tyrants? And if so, who will decide upon such an execution? Most remarkably, Mengzi fails to mention Heaven (to which the *Mengzi* elsewhere attributes important political tasks, as we shall see below) as the major factor behind the demise of Jie and Zhouxin. Does this mean that the rebellion is a normative action against the immoral ruler? Mengzi does not raise this dangerous question in a conversation with the king,[51] but a clue to an answer may be obtained from another of his statements: "To await for King Wen and only then to rise up, is [the behavior] of common folk. As for the truly outstanding *shi*, even if there is no King Wen, they would rise up."[52]

This statement is usually interpreted as hinting at a positive moral impact of a ruler like King Wen; the term *xing* (興 "to arise," "to rise up") is interpreted as "to be moved and inspired."[53] This interpretation is not necessarily correct, however. Those who waited for King Wen to stand up were participants in his rebellion against the Shang (which was the single most important activity of King Wen). Does Mengzi imply that a truly outstanding *shi* should rise up even without a glorious leader such as King Wen? In light of the above conversation with King Xuan, this interpretation cannot easily be dismissed. Mengzi then appears as almost a revolutionary, a person who calls upon fellow *shi* to arise and put an end to Zhouxin's current counterparts!

If this interpretation is correct, Mengzi should be considered the most radical of Zhanguo thinkers in terms of his attitude toward the authority of contemporary rulers. He certainly accepts righteous rebellion as legitimate, and his fascination with the "righteous wars" launched by the founders of the Shang and Zhou further suggests his uncompromising support for the victory of the morally superb monarchs. Such radicalism evaporates, however, when we consider Mengzi's attitude toward the second way of ensuring the best possible monarch, namely, abdication.[54] Here Mengzi hesitates between endorsement of the laudable example of promoting the worthy and fear of unqualified support for yielding the throne as an alternative to the centuries-old dynastic principle of rule. On the one hand, Mengzi lauds Yao:

> As for Yao's attitude toward Shun, he ordered nine of his sons to serve [Shun], married two of his daughters to him, he provided the hundred officials, oxen and sheep, granaries and storehouses to feed Shun amidst the fields. Later he raised him and gave him the highest position. Hence it is said that kings and lords respect the worthies.[55]

This claim places Mengzi within the same current represented by Mozi and more radically by the authors of the *Tang Yu zhi Dao* or *Rong Cheng shi*, who considered the transfer of the throne from Yao to Shun a normal and desirable manifestation of "elevating the worthy." However, Mengzi, who had personally witnessed the turmoil in the state of Yan as a result of King Kuai's abdication,[56] was perfectly aware of the potential negative consequences of abdication. Hence in a series of crucial dialogues with his disciples he did his best to confine abdication to the cases of Yao and Shun only, explaining that even these instances could not have been possible without the intervention of the most powerful force—Heaven:

> Wan Zhang asked: "Did it really happen that Yao granted All under Heaven to Shun?"
> Mengzi said: "No, the Son of Heaven cannot grant anybody All under Heaven."
> "Nonetheless, Shun possessed All under Heaven. Who granted it to him?"
> [Mengzi] said: "Heaven granted it."
> "That Heaven granted it, does it mean that it earnestly ordered him so?"
> [Mengzi] said: "No, Heaven does not speak. It clarified [its intent] through conduct and through sacrifices."
> [Wan Zhang] said: "What does it mean 'clarified through conduct and through sacrifices'?"
> [Mengzi] said: "The Son of Heaven can recommend a person to Heaven, but cannot force Heaven to grant this person All under Heaven; a regional lord can recommend a person to the Son of Heaven, but cannot force the

Son of Heaven to grant this person the rank of a regional lord; a noble can recommend a person to the regional lord, but cannot force the lord to grant this person a noble rank. In the past, Yao recommended Shun to Heaven, and Heaven accepted him; he displayed Shun to the people, and the people accepted him; hence I said: 'Heaven does not speak. It clarified [its intent] through conduct and through sacrifices.'"[57]

Mengzi is visibly annoyed by Wan Zhang's preoccupation with the issue of abdication, and employs different rhetorical tactics to thwart his disciple's barely veiled attack on the hereditary principle of rule. First, Mengzi introduces Heaven's factor into power transfer to an extent unknown elsewhere in Zhanguo texts, with the major exception of the *Mozi*. Heaven is treated as an active and sentient entity, which, albeit not speaking directly with its appointees, intervenes in human affairs and determines who is appropriate to inherit the position of Son of Heaven. This invocation of Heaven, however, is a risky strategy in the age of marked decline in belief in Heaven's political potency, as exemplified in the ironic question by Wan Zhang "does it mean that it earnestly ordered [Shun to ascend the throne]?" Hence while symbolically placing Heaven at the center of his argument, Mengzi redirects the discussion from Heaven to men:

> [Wan Zhang] said: "What does it mean 'recommended to Heaven, and Heaven accepted him; displayed to the people, and the people accepted him'?"
> [Mengzi] said: "[Yao] ordered [Shun] to preside over sacrifices, and the hundred spirits accepted the offerings: this means that Heaven accepted him. He ordered [Shun] to preside over the people's affairs and the hundred clans were at peace under him: this means that the people accepted him. Heaven granted him [All under Heaven], the people granted him; hence I said: the Son of Heaven cannot grant anybody All under Heaven."[58]

Mengzi boldly proclaims the importance of the people's support. Paying due respect to Shun's ability to let the spirits enjoy his offerings, he clarifies that it is the people's acceptance of Shun as a true leader which really matters. He further explains:

> Shun acted as Yao's chancellor for twenty-eight years: it is not something that a human effort can bring about, it is Heaven. When Yao passed away, at the end of the three-year mourning, Shun escaped to the South of the River to avoid Yao's son. Yet when the lords from All under Heaven arrived at court, they did not approach Yao's son, but Shun; those who had litigations

did not approach Yao's son, but approached Shun; those who sang praises did not sing praises of Yao's son, but of Shun. Hence I said: it is Heaven. Only then did [Shun] return to the Central State and ascend the throne of the Son of Heaven. Should he live in Yao's palace and oppress Yao's son, this would mean usurpation, not the grant of Heaven. The Great Oath says: 'Heaven sees through the people's seeing, Heaven hears through the people's hearing.' It is said about this.[59]

The people appear, along with Heaven, as the second major factor behind Shun's success. Similarly, as Mengzi explains elsewhere, it is the people's action that failed Yu's appointed successor, Yi 益, and allowed Yu's son, Qi, to seize power.[60] This notion of the pivotal role of "the people," which curiously resembles much more overt statements in the *Rong Cheng shi*, may reflect the awareness of Zhanguo thinkers of the political importance of the lower strata (see Chapters 8 and 9). However, Mengzi is reluctant to turn the people into the single major factor behind power transfers, especially whenever the principle of hereditary rule is thereby endangered. To avoid the potentially subversive implications of his statements, Mengzi reinterprets the abdication legend in the way that makes Yao's posthumous yielding the throne into an exceptional event with minimal relevance to the present. The theretofore unheard of story of Shun's futile attempt to avoid Yao's son and to prevent the loss of power by Yao's family is particularly interesting.[61] This presentation of Shun's behavior indicates that the latter considered hereditary transmission of power as singularly correct.

Mengzi's attempt to prevent the abdication legend from becoming a tool to subvert the ruler-centered order is explicit in his introduction of the third crucial factor that allowed abdication to succeed in the past: the ruler's recommendation. While in the passage cited above Yao's recommendation to Heaven to appoint Shun is mentioned only briefly, in the next dialogue with Wan Zhang, which focuses on the establishment of hereditary transmission at the beginning of the Xia dynasty, the issue of recommendation becomes as crucial as Heaven's support itself. After explaining the failure of Yu's righteous minister, Yi, to inherit from his master due to the shortness of his tenure as Yu's aide, and due to the worthiness of Yu's son, Qi, Mengzi continues:

Shun, Yu, and Yi: the length of time that separated [their ministerial tenures from their enthronement], as well as the worthiness or unworthiness of their sons—all this was [arranged by] Heaven, it is not something human beings are capable of. When nobody acts, but the action is performed—this is Heaven; when nobody delivers [the power], but it arrives—this is the

Decree. For a commoner to possess All under Heaven, he must be virtuous as Shun and Yu and also have the Son of Heaven to recommend him; hence Zhongni (Confucius) did not possess All under Heaven.[62]

In this passage, Mengzi moderates the inherent radicalism of his earlier interpretation of the abdication legend. First, Heaven's support is manifested in one's longevity in tenure as well as in the aptitude of the reigning ruler's son, and not primarily in the people's action, as implied earlier. Second, recommendation by the reigning ruler suddenly becomes the most important asset of the aspiring minister, overshadowing other factors. The failure of Confucius to "possess All under Heaven" was not due to his lack of popularity among the people or lack of Heaven's support, but simply because he lacked a supportive ruler. In the final account, it is solely the acting ruler's prerogative to decide to whom to transfer power, and the idea of yielding the throne is not supposed to undermine the absolute power of the sovereign. Mengzi concludes with Confucius's alleged quote: "Tang and Yu abdicated; Xia, Yin, and Zhou transmitted [power] lineally; the meaning [or appropriateness] of their [action] is the same."[63]

Mengzi's views regarding nonhereditary means of placing a worthy ruler on the throne represent, therefore, a curious amalgam of radicalism and caution. On the one hand, he appears as the only thinker who tries to draw universally applicable conclusions from the overthrow of the Xia and the Shang, moving dangerously in the direction of legitimating rebellion by "outstanding *shi*" against an immoral tyrant. On the other hand, he explicitly distances himself from his disciple Wan Zhang, whose provocative support for abdication we noticed above, and he clarifies that dynastic succession is the entirely legitimate mode for fixing on a ruler. Like all the other thinkers, Mengzi did not present any practical alternative to the hereditary principle of rule, and his audacity—while annoying and even frightening to later rulers—remained without immediate political consequences.

Crisis of Nonhereditary Succession Options

All four texts surveyed above share a certain degree of dissatisfaction with hereditary succession as an inadequate form of ensuring that a proper ruler comes to the throne. In the earliest text, the *Mozi*, such dissatisfaction is only implicitly hinted at, while in the *Mengzi* any dissatisfaction is counterbalanced by an ostensible endorsement of the dynastic principle of rule. The most radical sentiments against hereditary rule are presented in the two recently unearthed texts, which survived vicissitudes of later editorial efforts to bring to light ideas that were eventually rejected by the mainstream intellectual tradition. These texts, coupled with some scattered historical data, such as an antidynastic "popular saying" cited by Wan Zhang and an actual attempt to implement abdication doctrine in the state of Yan, testify to what may have been an important intellectual undercurrent in the search for nonhereditary methods of putting a ruler on the throne. While it is impossible to quantify the degree of support for such ideas among the educated elite, the cumulative evidence suggests it was not negligible.

What is no less remarkable, however, is that sentiments in favor of abdication (or in the case of the *Mengzi* in favor of "revolution") are virtually absent from the late Zhanguo texts. To be sure, admiration of Yao and Shun's selflessness continues, and so does the endorsement of kings Tang, Wen, and Wu, but the political implications of these sentiments changes radically. Not only were explicit attempts to turn the early paragons' lives into guidelines for new political models discontinued, but even the unanimous adoration of their deeds gave way to a number of different assessments, some of which, as I shall demonstrate, were explicitly critical of the fact that they violated the principle of dynastic rule. By the third century BCE, a new intellectual consensus was reached which no longer favored overt assaults on the principle of lineal succession.

Why were criticisms of dynastic rule discontinued? Why did the sentiments expressed in the *Tang Yu zhi Dao* or *Rong Cheng shi* disappear from the received texts until an accidental discovery of long forgotten manuscripts at the end of the twentieth century brought them to light? Some scholars suggest that King Kuai's disastrous experience played a decisive role in the decline of pro-abdication sentiments in the late Zhanguo period.[64] This may indeed be an important turning point; but I believe the reasons for the eventual disappearance of texts like *Tang Yu zhi Dao* or *Rong Cheng shi* are deeper. Liu Baocai 劉寶才 may be more on target with his assertion that the renewed institutionalization of the Warring States after a period of profound reforms led to the reassertion of the hereditary principles of rule and the decline of the appeal of alternative modes of appointing the ruler, such as the abdication doctrine.[65] Furthermore, I think that opponents of hereditary monarchy lost their case not only because of political developments, but also due to the inherent weakness of their argumentation. Their frequent resort to historical examples at the expense of developing more analytical reasoning to bolster their views (with the potential exception of certain passages in *Tang Yu zhi Dao* and *Mengzi*) backfired. Just as Mozi, Mengzi, or the authors of the *Rong Cheng shi* manipulated history to prove their position, so did their rivals, who created alternative accounts aimed at either limiting the appeal of abdication and righteous rebellion or discrediting these modes of behavior altogether.

It is worth a reminder that in the Zhanguo age there was no unified narrative of the past; history was primarily written not by court scribes, as it was during the Chunqiu period, but by rival thinkers who routinely "used the past to serve the present."[66] The degree of manipulation of the past narratives increased enormously during the Zhanguo period, with new heroes, new events, and new interpretations of the past created by almost every contending thinker. To illustrate the point, let us briefly address the vicissitudes of the Yao-Shun legend. Already among the five versions of the story (two in the *Mozi*, and one each in the *Tang Yu zhi Dao, Rong Cheng shi,* and *Mengzi*), we may notice a significant difference between the first four and the fifth. Unlike other texts, which present Yao's abdication as normal (if not normative) behavior, Mengzi's narrative emphasizes the peculiar circumstances surrounding Shun's replacement of Yao, thus limiting the applicability of this mode of power transfer in the present. Mengzi was certainly not the only thinker who "modified" the legend to limit its political appeal; in the slightly earlier sections of the "Yao dian" 堯 典 chapter of the *Shu jing,* we may discern a similar trend. The authors of this text state that Yao sought resignation after seventy years in power (and not at the age of seventy, as suggested by the *Tang Yu zhi Dao*).[67] Needless to say, this "minor" change completely undermines the applicability of the mandatory abdication envisioned by the authors of the *Tang Yu zhi Dao.* While certain rulers could attain the age of seventy, not a single person occupied the Chinese throne (including the throne of one of the Warring States or their predecessors) for seventy years.[68] Yao's example is thus excluded from ordinary succession procedures and becomes an exceptional case with limited—if any—relevance to the present.

Mengzi and the "Yao dian" authors approved of Yao's abdication, but sought to limit its immediate relevance. Other thinkers completely reinterpreted the Yao-Shun legend, undermining the very legitimacy of the abdication. Zhuangzi (莊子, d. c. 280), for instance, introduced new figures into the legend: Xu You 許由 and other proud recluses to whom Yao (or Shun) tried to yield the throne and who refused to accept it; that these true worthies were disgusted by the offer indicated that Shun, who agreed to replace Yao, was not a real worthy, but rather a skilled manipulator, whose ostensible humbleness may be a disguise aimed at seizing the throne![69] This view is promulgated with greater clarity in several other "counternarratives" of the Yao-Shun legend, which claim that Shun actually usurped the throne of Yao, expelling or imprisoning the aged ruler.[70] Turning upside-down the old legend, Zhanguo opponents of abdication further reduced the appeal of the Yao-Shun example for contemporary politicians. While ultimately these alternative narratives were not as successful as those of *Mengzi* and "Yao dian," they sufficed to undermine the abdication doctrine, based as it was on a single example. Lacking analytical (as distinct from historical) arguments in favor of their views, the supporters of abdication failed to counter the intellectual assaults of their opponents.

Similar manipulations of historical narrative are observable, even if they are of less magnitude, in a story of "righteous rebellion." Already in the *Mozi* version we noticed sufficient accumulation of anti-Zhouxin omens to make his case absolutely exceptional. Other texts, such as the *Rong Cheng shi*, paid less attention to Heaven's portents, but stressed the exceptionality of Zhouxin's case by accumulating his crimes beyond the limits of credibility. Zhouxin, who initially was accused of "normal" cruelty, debauchery, and ineptitude, gradually became a true monster, who roasted or made mincemeat of his close aides, established ponds of ale and forests of meat, and invented particularly cruel punishments.[71] This inflation of Zhouxin's viciousness evidently served the same goal as accumulation of portents and omens in the *Mozi* story. By excessively dehumanizing Zhouxin, Zhanguo thinkers effectively limited the applicability of his overthrow in contemporary politics; after all, none of the reigning monarchs could match Zhouxin's cruelty and debauchery. Thus Mengzi's attempt to justify the overthrow of any ruler who "committed crimes against benevolence and righteousness" was sidelined by those who emphasized exceptional circumstances of the dynastic changes in the past.[72]

To demonstrate the potential of Zhanguo counternarratives to undermine conventional interpretation of history, we shall turn to one of the most radical examples of such manipulations, the "Dao Zhi" (盜跖, "Robber Zhi") chapter of the *Zhuangzi*. This chapter (or more precisely, its first part, which apparently existed as an independent textual unit) may be considered one of the most radical instances of political satire in Chinese literature (and perhaps worldwide as well).[73] The story depicts an imagined meeting between Confucius and an archvillain, Robber Zhi, whom Confucius tries to convince to become a "normal" regional lord and abandon his "robber" status. In response, Zhi not only ridicules and rebuffs Confucius, but seizes the opportunity to make a concerted assault on the entire system of values advocated by Confucius and his kind. He presents a novel vision of history according to which the sage rulers are villains who destroyed the primeval harmony of the pre-state society:

> Huang Di was unable to sustain virtue: he fought Chi You 蚩尤 at the Zhuolu fields, and the blood flowed for a hundred miles.[74] When Yao and Shun appeared, they established multitudes of ministers. [Then] Tang banished his sovereign, and King Wu killed [his ruler], Zhou[xin]. From then on, the strong oppressed the weak; the many abused the few. Since the times of Tang and Wu, everybody follows these calamitous people.[75]

Zhuangzi (or the authors of the "Dao Zhi" chapter) turns the arguments of earlier thinkers upside-down. The sages did not put an end to calamity and struggle: instead they created these miserable conditions. Their unrestrained bid for power was solely responsible for the disintegration of the primeval order into a disastrous situation of mutual strife and turmoil. And, continues Robber Zhi, this calamity was not incidental but reflected the inherent wickedness of the revered sages:

> The world esteems nobody more than Huang Di, and yet Huang Di could not preserve his virtue intact, but fought on the fields of Zhuolu so that the blood flowed for hundreds of *li*. Yao was a merciless [father], Shun was an unfilial [son], Yu was half-paralyzed, Tang banished his sovereign [Jie], King Wu attacked [his ruler] Zhou[xin].[76] All these six gentlemen are held in high esteem by the world, and yet scrutinizing them, [we see] that all of them brought confusion to their Truth and forcibly turned against their emotions and inborn nature for the sake of benefit. Their behavior is greatly shameful, indeed![77]

Zhuangzi completes his reinterpretation of history. All the esteemed paragons are rendered villains, persons of shameful behavior who are unable to preserve their true nature, sacrificing it for mere profit, and whose actual behavior is no less disgusting than that of Robber Zhi, who pronounces this tirade. These arguments are congruent with the overall assault on the ruler-centered polity in the *Zhuangzi*, the only known Zhanguo text that decisively defies the principles of monarchism.[78] Interestingly, Robber Zhi's assault on the former paragons singles out their violation of hereditary succession (either through abdication or through revolution) for the harshest criticism, while elsewhere in the text, abdicators are blamed as hypocrites.[79] Although these and similar depictions of the paragons as villains were not endorsed by mainstream Zhanguo thought, they evidently both reflected and contributed to the diminishing appeal of those political ideals that were exclusively grounded in an invocation of the paragons' behavior. Supporters of nonhereditary succession were apparently unable to defend their ideas against manipulations of their rivals, which explains the diminishing appeal of nondynastic methods of power transfer in the late Warring States period.

The success of the supporters of the hereditary transmission of power was complete. While throughout China's imperial history ideas of "righteous rebellion" and "virtuous abdication" have routinely been invoked in times of crisis to justify dynastic changes, the dynastic principle itself was never questioned again. The argumentative weakness of its opponents, the impracticality of nonhereditary means of power transfer, and the undeniable power of centuries-old tradition—all these combined to solidify the position of lineal succession as the only normative principle for determining the throne's occupant. This choice of statesmen and thinkers might have ensured a relatively high degree of stability; but it also meant giving up any hope of attaining worthy rulers. The gap between the ideal and reality was never filled.

CHAPTER 4

An Omnipotent Rubber Stamp

In the previous chapter, we outlined the rise and fall of hopes for finding a viable pattern of placing an able monarch on the throne. The ultimate fiasco of these attempts to secure an ideal sovereign did not mean, however, that the contradiction between the high expectations of the True Monarch and the low esteem of current lords was thereafter ignored. On the contrary, late Zhanguo thinkers made painstaking efforts to find a more practical solution to the inherent conflict between their ideals and gloomy reality. The solution, albeit inconclusive, was to limit the ruler's direct involvement in policy-making, thereby diminishing the potentially negative consequences of his ineptitude, while retaining the symbolic importance of his position.

To trace the ways in which this bifurcation between the symbolic and practical aspects of the ruler's power occurred, I shall focus on two major late Zhanguo thinkers: Xunzi and Han Feizi. The choice is not casual; the writings of both may be considered the apex of Zhanguo political thought, and each contributed decisively toward shaping of the imperial political culture. Both Xunzi and Han Feizi were well aware of the intellectual currents of their days, being deeply involved in ideological polemics, and each incorporated—albeit in different ways—the major achievements of their predecessors and contemporaries. Moreover, while both thinkers share many common premises and were even personally connected (Han Feizi reportedly studied under Xunzi), they differ sharply on many crucial issues, particularly the role of personal morality versus institutional arrangements for maintaining proper political order. Their similarities and differences make the two thinkers an ideal pair for comparative analysis, as together they present the significant portion of the intellectual spectrum of the late Warring States.

Xunzi: The Ruler and the Regent

Xunzi is certainly the single most important architect of the imperial political culture. A scholar who tried his best to synthesize moral guidelines of the Ru 儒 tradition with practical demands of the late Warring States politics,

Xunzi incorporated and creatively reinterpreted many ideas of his predecessors, with whom he was often engaged in fierce syn- and diachronic polemics.[1] In what follows, I outline Xunzi's monarchistic sentiments, show his awareness of the inadequacy of the current rulers, and then discuss the ways in which this thinker sought to limit the potential damage caused by the rulers' ineptitude.

The Summa of Monarchism

Xunzi's support of monarchism is so elaborate and manifold that, by itself, it can serve as an excellent summary of the arguments presented in Chapter 2. First, he unequivocally asserts that an organized state under a single ruler is the precondition for the proper functioning of the social order; hence ancient sages established them as the means to cope with the inherently bad nature of human beings.[2] Xunzi explains the blessed impact of the ruler:

> In their lives the people cannot but create collectives; when they create collectives, but there are no divisions/distinctions (fen 分),[3] there is contention; contention, and then chaos; chaos, and then separation; separation, and then weakness; when [the people] are weak, they cannot overcome things; hence they cannot obtain palaces and houses to dwell in. This is why it is said that ritual and propriety cannot be abandoned for the shortest while. . . . He who is able to employ his subjects is called the ruler. The ruler (君, *kun) is the one who is good at [making people] flock together into a collective (群, *ghun). When the way of creating the collective is correct, then the myriad things obtain what is proper [for them], the six kinds of animals obtain their longevity, all the living creatures obtain their predestined [lifespan].[4]

This passage succinctly presents Xunzi's major concept of the ruler's pivotal importance. It is the ruler whose presence makes the social pyramid work, ensuring thereby the proper functioning of the entire social order, making the human collective viable. Significantly, this function is performed by the ruler ex officio and is not linked to his moral qualities. The ruler's contribution to the social order is twofold. First, he is able to "employ his subjects," which means among other things restricting them and preventing their avarice from destroying the social fabric. Second, the ruler tops the sociopolitical pyramid, manifesting by his very existence the importance of social gradations. This role, in turn, explains Xunzi's intensive preoccupation with preserving the ritual prerogatives of the sovereign and maintaining his distinct sumptuary privileges. The ruler's garments, food, dwelling, and even specific appellations—all these manifest his unparalleled exaltedness.[5] Perhaps the most radical manifestation of this exaltedness is Xunzi's justification for the Ru demand that the ruler be mourned whole three years—a period appropriate for a father:

> Why does the ruler's mourning continue for three years? I say: the ruler is the master of orderly governance, the origin of the patterns of refined culture, the utmost of [proper] feelings and appearance, so when the people lead each other turning him into the most eminent—what is unacceptable about this? The *Poems* say: "Joyful is the prince, [he is] the father and mother of the people." That prince, he deserves the definition of "father and mother" to be taken for granted. The father can give life [to the child], but not nourish him; the mother can feed him, but cannot educate him; the ruler not only can feed him, but also can educate him: are not three years [of mourning him] too short after all?[6]

This passage elevates the ruler to a position of equality, and even subtly assumed superiority, with the parents—a marked departure from a more family-oriented "mainstream Confucian" tradition.[7] The ruler's ritual exaltedness is the acceptable price paid for his social contribution and for his ability to ensure the people's livelihood and to educate them. While his ability to educate refers to the ruler's moral qualities, and will be addressed below, we shall first focus on the ruler as "the master of orderly governance." The political contribution of the sovereign is indeed a major topic in Xunzi's ruler-oriented discussions. The ruler is the guarantor of political order, and this order is attainable only insofar as the monarchic principle of rule is maintained:

> A ruler is the preeminent person of the state; a father is the preeminent of the house. When there is a single eminent figure, there is orderly rule; when there are two—there is calamity. From antiquity until present days, it has never happened that when two preeminent figures struggled for power, they could survive for long.[8]

The task of ensuring orderly rule, just like the task of maintaining the social hierarchy, is attainable by any ruler; but the highest goal—unification of All under Heaven—is attainable only by the True Monarch:

> To preserve the Way and virtue complete, to be the highest and the most esteemed, to enhance the principles of refined culture, to unify All under Heaven, to put in order even the smallest things, to cause everyone under Heaven to comply and follow him—this is the task of the Heavenly Mon-

arch. . . . If All under Heaven is not unified, and the regional lords customar-
ily rebel—then the Son of Heaven is not the [appropriate] man.[9]

Here Xunzi introduces another crucial aspect of his ruler-oriented discussions: the impact of the monarch's competence on his performance. While
any ruler contributes decisively toward sociopolitical order, it is only the True
("Heavenly" or "sage") Monarch who is able to achieve the truly universal
tranquility. Nothing will remain outside his blessed impact:

> When a sage monarch is above, he apportions dutiful actions below. Then
> the *shi* and the nobles do not behave wantonly; the hundred officials are not
> insolent in their affairs; the multitudes and the hundred clans are without
> odd and licentious habits; there are no crimes of theft and robbery; none
> dares to oppose his superiors.[10]

Every social group, from officials down to commoners, will be held in check
by the morally impeccable sage monarch. This monarch engenders absolute
compliance and order, eliminates the deviant customs or habits (*su* 俗) of the
populace, and ensures universal adherence to the norms of morality, thereby
diminishing the need for a punitive system.[11] These attainments are based on
the ruler being a source of moral inspiration for his subjects:

> The sovereign is the singing master of the people; the superior is the stan-
> dard for the inferiors. When [the people] listen to the singing master, they
> respond; when they see the standard, they move; when the singing master is
> silent, the people cannot respond; when the standard is obscure, the people
> cannot move. Without reacting and moving, there will be no existence for
> the superiors and inferiors; it is as if there were no superiors at all! Nothing
> can be as inauspicious as that. Thus, the superior is the root for inferiors;
> when the superior is clear, then inferiors are ordered; when the superior is
> sincere, then inferiors are honest; when the superior is public-minded and
> upright, then inferiors are easily rectifiable.[12]

In a way that is reminiscent of both Mozi and Mengzi, Xunzi assumes that
the ruler is a source of inspiration and emulation for his subjects and that he encourages a nearly mechanical compliance with his will. This compliance is not
given to any ruler, however, but only to a sage monarch. An inept sovereign may
mislead society into awful turmoil "as if there are no superiors at all." Later we
shall address the issue of the ruler's possible transgressions; but first we should
ask whether or not the compliance with the ruler's will proposed by Xunzi is

truly universal. Does it pertain exclusively to the lower strata or also to the elite? The quoted passage mentions that, among others under the sage monarch, "*shi* and the nobles do not behave wantonly," and this issue is reiterated elsewhere:

> The Son of Heaven is the most respectable in terms of his power and position and has no rivals under Heaven.... His morality is pure; his knowledge and kindness are extremely clear. He faces southwards and makes All under Heaven obedient. Among all the people, there is none who does not politely hold his hands following him, thereby being compliantly transformed. There are no recluses under Heaven, the goodness of no one is neglected; the one who unites with him is good, the one who differs from him is bad.[13]

This passage introduces another dimension to the moral and cultural authority of the True Monarch: he is not just a moral exemplar and a teacher for his subjects in general, but he is in particular responsible for mending the ways of the elite. Not only "there are no recluses under Heaven" (that is, nobody has the right to withdraw from public office—see Chapter 6), but in addition "the one who unites with him is good, the one who differs from him is bad." This is one of the most radical pronouncements in Zhanguo texts, which directly reminds us of Mozi's "conforming upwards" principle. Effectively, it means the cessation of intellectual autonomy among the educated elite. In Chapter 5 we shall see that the monopoly of fixing what is right and what is wrong was one of the primary assets of the *shi* stratum, as advocated, among others, by Xunzi himself. That the thinker was willing to yield this asset in favor of the sage monarch reveals the depth of Xunzi's commitment to the ideal of the omnipotent ruler.

All the aspects of the ruler's superiority outlined above—social, ritual, political, and moral—reflect Xunzi's creative appropriation of the views of earlier monarchistic-minded thinkers and appear at first glance as Xunzi's ultimate adoption of an extreme monarchism. Indeed, insofar as the ruler's will is the measure of correctness, and insofar as the ruler's very existence guarantees the persistence of the sociopolitical order, the monarch is supposed to be both infallible and indispensable. These pronouncements turn the *Xunzi* into a summa of Zhanguo monarchistic arguments. Yet as we shall see, behind the idealized vision of the monarchy, Xunzi conceals a much more sober estimate of contemporary rulers.

Between the Ideal and Reality

Xunzi is sometimes labeled as an "authoritarian-minded" thinker and such accusations are certainly connected to many of his pronouncements cited above.[14] Yet a closer look at his text shows that many of those pronouncements focus on the ideal ruler—the True Monarch, the would-be unifier (or one of his early predecessors, such as the sage dynastic founders of the Zhou and the Shang)—and not on current regional lords. With regard to acting rulers, Xunzi displays a sober attitude, reminding his audience that a ruler's power is not derived exclusively from his position, but first from his compliance with the norms of morality:

> The ruler is the fountainhead of the people; when the fountainhead is clear, the stream is clear; when the fountainhead is muddy, the stream is muddy. Hence when the owner of the altars of soil and grain is unable to care for the people and is unable to benefit the people, but demands the people to feel intimate and care for him, he is unable to get this.[15]

This passage introduces the notion of reciprocity in the ruler's relations with his subjects. While they are supposed to provide for him and are willing to brave death for his sake, this is not done blindly, but in exchange for the ruler's care and moral guidance:

> Thus when a benevolent person is above, the hundred clans esteem him as Thearch, feel proximity to him as to their parents, are glad to go to the deadly battle for him—and all this for no other reason that whatever he approves is truly admirable, whatever he attains is truly great, and those whom he benefits are truly numerous.[16]

The ideal situation of a benevolent ruler who induces total compliance is, unfortunately, quite at odds with current gloomy conditions:

> In our generation this is not so: [the rulers] increase levies in *dao* and *bu* coins to steal [the people's] wealth; double the taxes on fields and meadows to steal [the people's] food; impose merciless customs on passes and markets to make [the people's] occupations difficult. Moreover, [the rulers] also condemn and accuse, spy out and cheat, make schemes to uproot [their enemies] in order to overturn each other, thereby exhausting and exterminating [the people]. The hundred clans clearly understand [the rulers'] filthiness and violence and are going to imperil them. Hence when some ministers murder their rulers, when inferiors kill their superiors, when [the people] are timid about defending the walls, turn back on their obligations, and are not ready to die in [the rulers'] service—it is for no other reason than the ruler had chosen this himself. The *Poems* say: "No word is unanswered, no virtue is unresponded to"—it is said about that.[17]

The harshness of Xunzi's pronouncement cannot be ignored. Not only are current rulers almost universally condemned, but the conclusion seems even more ominous. A ruler who behaves improperly, violating the life of his subjects and displaying cruelty and avarice, loses his right to rule; he bears the sole responsibility for his future dethronement; and "while he was enfeoffed as a regional lord and is named 'a ruler,' he does not differ from an ordinary fellow and a robber."[18] This saying directly reminds us of those of Mengzi and appears to place Xunzi among the radical supporters of "righteous rebellion."

A more careful reading of the *Xunzi*, however, leads to a different conclusion. While Xunzi accepted in principle the righteousness of the Shang and Zhou founders who overthrew the tyrants Jie and Zhouxin, he was much less enthusiastic than Mengzi in applying these patterns to modern circumstances. Nowhere does Xunzi make any statement that may be interpreted as a justification of rebellious action by contemporary subjects; on the contrary, he explicitly recommends that a minister who lives under a cruel tyrant preserve his life by avoiding confrontation.[19] Rebellion is not an option for Xunzi and his followers; its mention is intended to serve as a warning to rulers and not as a guideline for subjects. It is only under truly exceptional circumstances that the overthrow of the ruling dynasty can be justified, as Xunzi explains in his defense of the deeds of kings Tang and Wu:

> The vulgar people say: "Jie and Zhou[xin] possessed all under Heaven, while Tang and Wu usurped and robbed it." This is not so. Indeed, Jie and Zhou[xin] happened to inherit the regalia of All under Heaven; they indeed personally possessed the regalia[20] of All under Heaven—but it is untrue that All under Heaven was possessed by Jie and Zhou[xin].[21]

Xunzi explains at length that the tyrants of the Xia and Shang dynasties had lost the reins of power long before being overthrown by kings Tang and Wu and that the disintegration of their realms had denied them legitimacy as Sons of Heaven. Moreover, their exceptional folly and ineptitude were matched by the even more miraculous abilities and virtue of those contending for power, Tang and Wu, who happened to be true sages:

> The Son of Heaven is only he who is [a truly appropriate] person. All under Heaven is extremely heavy: only the strongest can bear it; it is extremely large: only the smartest can divide it; it is extremely populous: only the wisest can harmonize it. Hence one who is not a sage cannot become a [True] Monarch. When a sage has internalized the Way, accomplishing its beauty, he will hold the scale and the weight of All under Heaven.[22]

The very success of Tang and Wu serves as post facto proof of their exceptional worthiness; a less sagacious contender would never have accomplished the task of establishing a new dynasty.[23] This accumulation of good qualities by the dynastic founders was mirrored in turn by the utmost wickedness of the last rulers of the Xia and the Shang:

> As for Jie and Zhou[xin]: Their thought was extremely dangerous; their desires extremely benighted; their behavior extremely calamitous. Their relatives were estranged from them; the worthies despised them; the people resented them. Despite being the descendants of Yu and Tang, they had nobody to support them; they dissected Bigan, arrested Jizi;[24] they were personally killed and their state overthrown; they were greatly punished by All under Heaven, and those in later generations who talk of wickedness refer to their [case]. This is the way of not providing for your wife and children.[25]

Having explained the preconditions for a legitimate dynastic overthrow, Xunzi summarizes his points:

> Hence the worthiest inherit [all within the] four seas; those are Tang and Wu. The extremely unworthy cannot provide for their wife and children: those are Jie and Zhou[xin]. Now, the vulgar people of the age say that Jie and Zhou[xin] possessed All under Heaven and had Tang and Wu as their servants—is it not too excessive?[26]

Xunzi's overall argument here is akin to that pronounced thirteen centuries later by Sima Guang (who was obviously influenced by Xunzi's thought):[27] under truly exceptional circumstances, when a morally impeccable leader acts under a monster who has already lost the reins of power, a rebellion may be justified; but normally, this is not an option. Certainly, this is not the way to replace an ordinarily inept ruler with a moral one. Xunzi also rejects the idea of abdication as an alternate means of ensuring the ruler's quality. After a long refutation of what he considers untrue claims about Yao and Shun's abdication, Xunzi concludes:

> Hence the sayings "Yao and Shun abdicated" are empty words, transmitted by mean people, theories from the remote outskirts of those who have no idea of defiance and compliance [and of alterations between] the large and the petty, between the attained and the unattained; it is impossible [to discuss] with [these people] the great patterns of All under Heaven.[28]

Having denied the applicability of abdication and having severely limited that of righteous rebellion, Xunzi cannot but turn back to the basic question: how to bridge the gulf between the idealized True King, which Xunzi promotes throughout his writings, and actual mediocre or inept rulers? Ideally, of course, the ruler's quality can be improved through self-rectification. Xunzi explicitly recommends:

> "May I ask of ruling the state?"—I answer: "I have heard of self-cultivation, but never heard of ruling the state. The ruler is the standard, the people are its reflection; when the standard is upright, the reflection is upright. The ruler is a plate, the people are water: when the plate is round, the water is round. . . . Hence it is said: I have heard of self-cultivation, but never heard of ruling the state."[29]

Self-cultivation appears to be the most appropriate way to improve the sovereign's quality, but Xunzi does not trust this solution entirely. Education and self-cultivation were essential for "superior men"—these were preconditions for entering the elite—but for rulers, whose position was determined exclusively by the right of birth, it was naïve to expect universal dedication to moral cultivation. Xunzi may have tacitly acknowledged this problem in his discussion of Yao's inept son, Zhu 朱, who was unable to benefit from his father's "educational transformation" (*jiaohua* 教化).[30] In the *Xunzi*, accordingly, we find neither the *Mengzi*-like dialogues in which the thinker tries to convince rulers to improve their ways, nor even the proclamations according to which "educating the ruler" is the thinker's most honorable task. Instead, Xunzi searches for more practical, if subtle, ways to ensure that the sovereign's ineptitude will not destroy the polity.

The Passive Sovereign

Xunzi's endorsement of the dynastic principle and his limited expectations regarding the ruler's moral cultivation effectively meant that he accepted the situation in which mediocre rulers might occupy the throne. How, then, did one ensure proper functioning of the state, which, as we have learned, depends crucially on the monarch? Xunzi's solution is subtle but brilliant: the ruler will preserve the façade of his omnipotence, while relegating actual powers to his aides, especially to the morally upright Ru, who will perform everyday political tasks in the ruler's stead.

The idea of a worthy aide as the architect of the ruler's success has certainly been one of the best-attested concepts in Chinese thought from the very beginning of the Zhou period, if not earlier. Stories of worthy ministers who aided

the founder kings of Zhou, as well as of their later counterparts who were instrumental in the successes of various Chunqiu and Zhanguo rulers, circulated
throughout the Zhou world, and the pair of "a clear-sighted ruler and a worthy
minister" (*ming jun, xian chen* 明君賢臣) remained the paradigmatic recipe for
political success throughout Chinese history.[31] The novelty in Xunzi's approach
is twofold: first, he emphasizes ministerial power to a degree almost unheard of
in earlier texts, and second, he encourages the ruler to choose appropriate aides
and then to leave active political life, allowing his worthy ministers to lead the
state.

Xunzi's admiration of the "superior man" (*junzi* 君子) and his flattering
image of the elite members will be discussed in detail in Chapter 5; here one
example will suffice. The chapter "Wang zhi" (王制, King's regulations) contains the following panegyric of the superior man:

> Heaven and Earth are the beginning of life; ritual and propriety are the
> beginning of orderly rule; the superior man is the beginning of ritual and
> propriety. He acts according to them, practices them, accumulates them, and
> brings them to the perfection—this is the superior man.[32] Hence Heaven
> and Earth give birth to the superior man, while the superior man patterns
> Heaven and Earth. The superior man stands in trinity with Heaven and
> Earth, regulates the myriad things; he is the father and mother of the people.
> Without the superior man, Heaven and Earth will not be patterned, ritual
> and propriety not regulated; above there will be no ruler and teacher, below
> no father and son; this is called "utmost calamity."[33]

In this passage, the superior man is assigned with the tasks and features that
are usually characteristic of the ruler: being the organizer of Heaven and Earth,
"father and mother" of the people, and regulator of ritual and propriety and of
myriad things are common ruler's attributes.[34] By depicting the superior man
in these ruler-related terms, Xunzi clearly hints at the crucial role morally upright individuals play in maintaining sociopolitical order. Therefore, acquiring a
superior man becomes the ruler's most important task:

> Hence when the ruler wants to ensure peace and joy, the best is to turn to
> the people; when he wants to subdue the people, the best is to turn to ad-
> ministration; when he wants to improve the administration and beautify the
> state, the best is to search for [proper] men. He who is able to accumulate
> and attain them, his dynasty will not be cut off. . . . If these people are em-
> ployed in great [position], the world will be unified and the regional lords
> subjugated; if employed in petty position, the [ruler's] power will overawe

neighboring enemies; and if the ruler is unable to employ them but [at least] can prevent them from leaving the state, until the end of his life the state will meet no troubles.[35]

It is not difficult to observe a significant change of emphasis between the earlier quoted passages in which the ruler appears as a sole creator of the political order and this statement, which confines the ruler's activities almost exclusively to looking for truly capable aides. Indeed, Xunzi argues: "The enlightened sovereign urgently seeks proper people, while the benighted one urgently seeks his power [of authority]."[36] After acquiring a good aide, the ruler delegates to him routine administrative undertakings and himself dwells in a blessed state of nonaction:

> Thus the enlightened sovereign endorses the guiding principles, while the benighted ruler endorses the details. When the ruler endorses the principle, one hundred affairs are [arranged] in their details; when the ruler endorses details, one hundred affairs are disordered. The ruler selects one chancellor (*xiang* 相), arranges one law, clarifies one principle in order to cover everything, to illuminate everything, and to observe the completion [of the affairs]. The chancellor selects and orders heads of the hundred officials, attends to the guiding principles of the hundred affairs, and thereby refines the divisions between the hundred clerks at court, measures their achievements, discusses their rewards, and presents their achievements at the year end to the ruler. When they act correctly, they are approved; otherwise they are dismissed. Hence the ruler works hard in looking for [proper officials] and is at rest when employing them.[37]

This passage introduces a second crucial topic in Xunzi's discussion of the ruler: the ideal of ruler's quiescence as the best way of managing state affairs. This idea is intrinsically linked with the concept of nonaction (or in Slingerland's eloquent translation "effortless action," *wu-wei* 無爲), which became particularly popular after the second half of the Zhanguo period. While the general evolution and philosophical background of the *wu-wei* ideal had been discussed elsewhere, it is important to note here the appeal of this idea with regard to rulers.[38] One of the earlier proponents of the application of this idea to the functioning of the sovereign was Shen Buhai, who argued:

> The mirror reflects the essence [of things] effortlessly, but beauty and ugliness manifest themselves; the scale reflects the balance effortlessly, but light and heavy discover themselves. The way of relying on others is to embody

public spirit and be without affairs: [when the ruler] is without affairs, All under Heaven arrives itself to the utmost [order].[39]

Shen Buhai's insistence on the ruler's minimal action was not just echoing the *Laozi*'s advocacy of acting effortlessly and being without affairs, but had a deeper administrative rationale behind it. The ruler was supposed to preserve the essentials, "the levers" (of rewards and punishments, *bing* 柄), while the "constant" affairs were to be performed by officials under his overall supervision. For Shen Buhai, just as for Shen Dao, who proposed similar arrangements, this was a rational way of adjusting the ruler's capabilities to the vastness of his task.[40] Xunzi apparently inherited the views of his predecessors, but with Xunzi the ruler's nonaction (or, more precisely, noninterference in everyday administrative tasks) becomes even more complete. Unlike Shen Buhai and later Han Feizi (discussed below), who considered ministers as potential enemies of the sovereign, Xunzi believed that if good aides are selected, they will be reliable servants of the ruler; hence the ruler has to minimize even his supervisory functions, entrusting those to the worthy chancellor.

Xunzi's arrangement appears, at first glance, as an elegant solution to the delicate problem of a ruler's potential unfitness to perform his duties. Since the ruler's aides are supposed to be the best men in the country, selected for their superb moral and intellectual qualities, entrusting them with administrative tasks will benefit the government and will permit relaxation for the ruler. This relaxation was probably considered a bonus for the sovereign, reflecting the popularity of the idea of nonaction in late Zhanguo thought, and the possibility of ruling in a relaxed manner is a recurrent topic in Xunzi's discussions of orderly government.[41] Moreover, Xunzi reminds the ruler that entrusting officials is the only way to overcome the limitations of one's personal abilities: a single person will never be able to comprehend the multitude of government affairs; hence "the sovereign cannot act independently; ministers, chancellors and aides are the cane and the stick of the sovereign."[42] But the question may be asked: what will remain of the ruler's power after the entire corpus of his tasks has been relegated to his subordinates?

The answer is that not much power will remain in the ruler's hands. After selecting a good aide, the ruler is supposed to refrain from interfering in everyday administration, which in turn means that his input in government policy will be minimal. Some passages in the *Xunzi* may disclose the author's hopes for an ideal state of affairs in which a capable minister rules the state in the name of a supportive sovereign but without any interference from the monarch. Such an ideal pair were the Duke of Zhou, the single most admirable statesman in Xunzi's eyes, and King Cheng (周成王, r. c. 1042–1021), the duke's nephew, the early years of whose rule passed under the duke's regency:

> This is the efficacy of the Great Ru: when King Wu died and King Cheng was young, the Duke of Zhou supported King Cheng, continued King Wu's [enterprise] to make All under Heaven submissive, hating [the idea] that All under Heaven would rebel against the Zhou. He held the regalia of the Son of Heaven, maintained the affairs of All under Heaven, being at ease as if it was his fixed possession, but All under Heaven did not consider him greedy. He killed [his rebellious elder brother] Guanshu, emptied the Yin [Shang] capital, but All under Heaven did not consider him cruel. He ruled uniformly All under Heaven, establishing seventy-one states, of which fifty-three were occupied by the [members of the royal] Ji clan, but All under Heaven did not consider him partial. He taught and instructed King Cheng, clarifying for him the Way so he would be able to follow the steps of kings Wen and Wu. When the Duke of Zhou returned to the Zhou [capital], he gave back the regalia to King Cheng, while All under Heaven did not cease serving the Zhou; then the Duke of Zhou faced north [as due to a subject] and attended the court. . . . All under Heaven were at peace like a single person: only the Sage can attain this. This is the efficacy of the Great Ru![43]

Xunzi's praise of the Duke of Zhou is somewhat effusive: not only is the duke absolved of any suspicion regarding his intentions when he seized the royal regalia, but his actions are also justified in terms of supreme dynastic interests, which defy the usual norms of behavior. Such adoration of a major ministerial paragon in Chinese history is not surprising by itself, but what is interesting for our discussion is the treatment of the legitimate ruler, King Cheng. During the seven years of the Duke of Zhou's regency, King Cheng appears to be a nullity, a shadowy occupant of the throne (who even lacks the royal regalia), a person without any observable impact on the affairs of the state. Are these Xunzi's true expectations of a monarch? Does his idealization of the Duke of Zhou, "the Greatest Ru," reflect his hope for a similar regent-like power for himself and for other "Great Ru"? Is an ideal ruler-minister couple one in which the ruler shrinks to become a ritual figurehead, similar to some Chunqiu lords under the thumb of their nominal aides?[44]

One would search in vain for unequivocal answers to these questions in the *Xunzi*. The issues at stake were too sensitive to be treated openly, and I am not sure whether the questions themselves were ever conceptualized in the way I propose them. However, certain passages in the *Xunzi* contain clues that support my feeling that the ultimate hope of this thinker was to preserve a symbolic ruler—one who is clever enough to choose proper aides and noninterfering enough to let these aides lead the country in his stead. One such clue appears in Xunzi's polemics against those supporters of the abdication, who, like the authors of the *Tang Yu zhi Dao* and *Rong Cheng shi* cited in Chapter 3, claimed that the rulers of the past abdicated due to their advanced age and its accompanying physical deterioration:

> [Some] say: "[Yao and Shun] became old, deteriorated, and then abdicated." This is also not true. As for blood, breath, and muscle power, these could deteriorate, but as for understanding and thought, they did not deteriorate. . . . The Son of Heaven is the one whose power is the heaviest, and whose body is the most relaxed; his heart is the most pleased, and his will has nothing to complain about; his body does not work, as he is the most respected.
>
> As for his garments, they comprise five colors mixed with assorted colors, enriched by embroidery and adorned with jade and pearls. As for his food, he has the most of the great *lao*,[45] and rare tastes are prepared for him; they are most fragrant and delicious when delivered. The drum is beaten when he eats; Yong melody is played when [the remnants] are removed for the five sacrifices; those who hold sacrificial vessels are awaiting in the western kitchen. Whenever he holds an audience, a protecting curtain is erected; when he turns his back to the screen and comes up, the regional lords hasten beneath the hall [as the audience ends]. When he leaves the inner door, shamans perform sacrifices; when he leaves the outer gate, an ancestral intendant performs sacrifices. When he rides the great *luo* chariot, a mat is placed to nourish his ease, at the sides a fragrant flower is burned to nourish his sense of smell; in front of him there are ornamented yokes to nourish his eyes. Sounds of bells are harmonized: they play Wu and Xiang [melodies] while [the chariot] moves slowly, and Shao and Huo when it moves quickly—to nourish his ears. The Three Dukes hold the shaft end and grasp the inner reins; the regional lords grasp the wheel, encircle the chariot, or lead the horses; the great states' lords are standing in the rear followed by their nobles; the small states' lords and their grandees stand behind them. Various *shi* wearing armor are standing in a row of honor; the commoners run off and hide, daring not gaze upon him.
>
> When at rest, [the Son of Heaven] is like a great deity, when moving he is like the Heavenly Thearch. What can be better than that to uphold the old and nourish the deteriorated? Old age is rest; what rest can be more tranquil and enjoyable than this? Hence it is said: the regional lords can retire due to the old age; the Son of Heaven cannot retire due to the old age.[46]

This lengthy discussion of the Son of Heaven's dolce vita is more revealing than is observable at first glance. In distinction from the *Tang Yu zhi Dao* authors, who argued that only a mature and physically able ruler would be suitable at the throne, Xunzi maintains that the physical conditions of the monarch are negligible for his overall performance. The Son of Heaven's life appears as a purely ritual enterprise, where even a potentially significant affair, such as a court audience or a royal outing, is ritualized to a degree that prevents any independent action by the monarch. The Son of Heaven in Xunzi's eyes is not supposed to make harsh decisions, work through the night on emergent problems, lead his armies, or inspect in person the remote areas of his realm. Rather, his functions are purely ceremonial: he is provided with the best possible treatment, is surrounded by the highest, but subservient dignitaries, and enjoys the utmost pleasures, but he *is not supposed to act* in a political sphere. Ritualization of the Son of Heaven's activities eventually results in his depersonalization—the mere possibility of his acting autonomously and actively is seriously impaired. The statement "the Son of Heaven is the one whose power is the heaviest, and whose body is the most relaxed" may well reflect Xunzi's general view of the proper mode of the king's behavior.[47]

What, then, are Xunzi's views of rulership? I think we may discern in his proposals three divergent models of a ruler. First there is the figure of an idealized True Monarch, the omnipotent ruler, whose moral example will lead the masses into compliance and whose superb abilities and impeccable morality will make him uniquely capable of managing the affairs of All under Heaven. Second, there is the average ruler, for whom Xunzi suggests a simpler solution: he should find good aides and entrust them with the reins of power. Such a ruler is supposed to be intelligent enough to select worthy ministers, but thereafter his functions will be largely ceremonial. Finally, a third category is implied in certain passages: the figurehead rulers, minors or senile elders, whose physical (and potentially even mental) limitations will not damage the state and the monarch as long as all affairs are carried out either by a powerful surrogate or, at the very least, in strict accordance with ritual norms.

The coexistence of distinct, at times contradictory, models in the same book does not imply the author's negligence; nor should the work be attributed to multiple authors. While some difference in emphasis may derive from different audiences, whom Xunzi addressed, or from changes in his views over time,[48] I believe that the three models reflect the thinker's deep understanding of the inherent problems of rulership. As it was demonstrated above, Xunzi inherited the pro-monarchical ideas of earlier thinkers, especially the premises that any dispersal of authority would be disastrous, and any institutionalized limitations on the sovereign's power would exacerbate internal calamities in the state.

Simultaneously, however, Xunzi was well aware of the weaknesses of unlimited autocracy and of the potential inadequacy of rulers—the only office-holders who owed their position not to their skills but exclusively to their pedigree. His ensuing combination of different models of rule was a highly original attempt to create a modus operandi for every kind of ruler: the highly qualified, those with average qualifications, and the least qualified.[49] In each case the ruler's interaction with his immediate entourage and the populace at large will change in accordance with his abilities, preserving the form of monarchic rule but altering the content.

We shall return later to the impact of Xunzi's views on later imperial political culture, but first we shall check whether his solution for the problem of an inept sovereign was peculiar to this thinker or shared by his contemporaries. To answer this question we shall focus on the ideas of one of the most famous of Xunzi's disciples, Han Feizi, arguably the most ruler-oriented writer in the history of Chinese political thought.

Han Feizi: Depersonalization of the Omnipotence

Han Feizi, Xunzi's disciple and intellectual rival, matches the sophistication of his master, but differs from him at certain crucial points. Of major importance for our discussion are two issues: the role of personal morality in government affairs and the nature of ruler-minister relations. With regard to the first, Han Feizi dismisses the idea that the state can rely on the morality of its leaders and even less so on the morality of the masses. Only perfectly maintained institutions and strict impartial laws will ensure massive compliance and proper functioning of the society. Second, Han Feizi emphatically denies the possibility of long-term cooperation between the ruler and his entourage. In a society driven by self-interest, the ruler must beware of his aides rather than trust them. While Han Feizi recognizes in principle the possibility of truly loyal ministers, just as Xunzi recognizes the possibility of treacherous ones, their basic views on ruler-minister relations remain diametrically opposite.[50]

Aside from these two major differences, Xunzi and Han Feizi diverge also with regard to how practical their theories are. While Xunzi may rightly be considered China's greatest political theorist, Han Feizi focuses much more on pragmatic issues that face the ruler, rather than on theoretical constructions. Although at times Han Feizi displays considerable theoretical sophistication, his overall concern is how to deal with actual challenges to the ruler's authority, and practical advice to the rulers occupies a much more prominent place in his work than in the *Xunzi*.[51] Paul Goldin has even observed that Han

Feizi lacks any truly compelling political theory whatsoever and that "his sole purpose is to expound his doctrine of self-interest and to apprise his readers of the dangers of ignoring it."[52] While I concur with much of Goldin's astute analysis, I believe that Han Feizi was nonetheless committed to the higher goal of a universally beneficent orderly rule and that this commitment—however subtle—clashed with his cynical analysis, causing much tension in his views of rulership.

Safeguarding the Ruler's Power

Han Feizi's theoretical views are largely concentrated in the first two *juan* of the received text, particularly the "Yang quan" (揚權, Extolling the authority) chapter. Here, Han Feizi directly links the unifying power of the sovereign with that of the Way:

> The Way is great and formless, Virtue (De 德) embeds its pattern and is all-reaching; as it arrives at all the living, it makes use of them after delibera-tions: the myriad things all prosper, but they are not tranquil together with it. The Way is not involved in everyday matters; it investigates them and then decrees their destiny, giving them time for life and death.
>
> Surveying the names of different matters we should uniformly penetrate their substance. Hence it is said: The Way is not identical to the myriad things; Virtue is not identical to *yin* and *yang*; weight is not identical to light and heavy; rope is not identical to exiting and entering; harmony is not identical to dry and wet, the ruler is not identical to the ministers. All these six derive from the Way. The Way has no pair; for that reason it is named "the One." Hence the enlightened ruler values the independent appearance of the Way. The ruler and the ministers have different ways: [the ruler] checks his [underlings] according to the names: the ruler embraces the name (*ming* 名), the minister employs its form (*xing* 形); when the form and the name match each other, the superior and the inferior are in harmony.[53]

Han Feizi's equation of the ruler to the Way is not exceptional, as it echoes some of the post-*Laozi* texts surveyed in Chapter 2, and, as we shall see later, it allows the author to promote his particular concept of the ruler's quiescence. In the text above, the simile of the Way is employed to buttress the singularity of monarchical power; but the topic is not explored in the later parts of the chap-ter. For Han Feizi—and perhaps for most of his audience—the exalted position of the ruler had become axiomatic and did not require further elaboration. Han Feizi effectively employed this axiom in his polemics against different op-ponents, such as those thinkers who advocated either the abdication doctrine or the idea of righteous rebellion. In the chapter on "Loyalty and Filiality" ("Zhong xiao," 忠孝) Han Feizi states:

> All under Heaven affirms the Way of filiality and fraternity, of loyalty and compliance, but they are unable to investigate the Way of filiality and fraternity, of loyalty and compliance, and to implement it precisely; hence All under Heaven are in chaos. Everybody affirms the Way of Yao and Shun, and models himself accordingly: hence some murder their rulers and some behave hypocritically toward their fathers.
>
> Yao and Shun, [kings] Tang and Wu: each of them opposed the propriety of ruler and minister, wreaking havoc in the teachings for future generations. Yao was a ruler who turned his minister into a ruler; Shun was a minister who turned his ruler into a minister; Tang and Wu were ministers who murdered their masters and defamed their bodies; but All under Heaven praise them: therefore until now All under Heaven has been lacking orderly rule. After all he who is called a clear-sighted ruler is the one who is able to nurture his ministers; he who is called a worthy minister is the one who is able to clarify laws and regulations, to put in order offices and positions, and to support his ruler. Now Yao considered himself clear-sighted but was unable to feed Shun,[54] Shun considered himself worthy but was unable to support Yao, Tang and Wu considered themselves righteous but murdered their rulers and superiors: this means that the clear-sighted ruler should constantly give, while a worthy minister, constantly take. Hence until now there are sons who take their father's house, and ministers who take their ruler's state. When a father yields to a son, and a ruler yields to a minister, this is not the Way of fixing the positions and unifying the teaching.[55]

Han Feizi comes to the logical conclusion of Xunzi's premise that maintaining the ruler's position is of pivotal importance for preservation of the moral social order based on "filiality, fraternity, loyalty, and compliance." If the ruler is the apex of this order, then any assault on his position is deplorable, and the hereditary monarchy itself is also sacrosanct. Han Feizi dismisses both devices proposed by his predecessors to place the best possible monarch on the throne: each of these devices (abdication or rebellion) undermines the very foundations of the monarchical institution and, mutatis mutandis, of the social order in general. Logically, preservation of the ruler's supreme authority becomes the most important task of a thinker and a statesman, and this is indeed what Han Feizi focuses on throughout most of his chapters.

It is with regard to safeguarding the ruler's power that Han Feizi makes his most outstanding contribution to Zhanguo political thought. No other thinker—not even Shang Yang and Shen Buhai, whose views Han Feizi incorporated—ever identified themselves so squarely with preserving the ruler's interests. Nor did any known thinker dare to pronounce Han Feizi's harsh statements against the ruler's entourage, identifying each one within the ruler's reach as potentially a mortal enemy of the monarch. Among a ruler's enemies, the harshest and most threatening are, precisely, the ministers, those men whom Xunzi admired, but whom Han Feizi compared to hungry tigers, who are ready to devour the sovereign unless he is able to overawe them into submissiveness.[56] In his "Extolling the Authority" chapter, Han Feizi explains:

> The Yellow Thearch (Huang Di 黃帝) said: "A hundred battles a day are fought between the superior and his underlings." The underlings conceal their private [interests], trying to test their superior; the superior employs norms and measures to restrict the underlings. Hence when norms and measures are established, they are the sovereign's treasure; when the cliques and cabals are formed, they are the minister's treasure. If the minister does not murder his ruler, this is because the cliques and cabals are not formed. Hence when the superior loses half-inches and inches, the underlings find yards and double-yards. The ruler who possesses the capital does not enlarge secondary cities;[57] the minister who possesses the Way does not esteem his kin; the ruler who possesses the Way does not esteem his ministers.[58]

This is an amazing saying: the minister is, by his nature, deceitful and murderous, and his failure to murder the sovereign is simply a sign of insufficient preparations, not of an unwillingness to do so. Han Feizi's obsession with the issue of regicide and usurpation is quite odd given the rarity of such events during his lifetime; probably by scaring the ruler, he hoped to elicit the sovereign's trust.[59] His warnings are not restricted to the ministers alone: the ruler should be afraid of any person around him. His wife, his beloved concubine, his elder son and heir—all of them hope for his premature death because that may secure their position. The threat comes also from the ruler's brothers and cousins, from uncles and bedfellows, from dwarfs and clowns who entertain him, from dancers in his court, and, of course from the talkative *shi* who connive with foreign powers to imperil his state. The ruler should trust no one; every single person should be suspected; and minimal negligence can cost a ruler his life and his power.[60]

Han Feizi's paranoid ruler, who strongly resembles the dictator from Gabriel Garcia Marquez's *Autumn of the Patriarch*, is, however, not doomed. While he should not trust his advisors, he must be able to outmaneuver them and even to utilize them in his service. Han Feizi states, with his usual candor:

A minister brings to the rulers' market [his ability] to exhaust his force to the point of death; a ruler brings to the ministers' market [his ability] to bestow ranks and emoluments. Ruler-minister relations are based not on the intimacy of father and child, but on calculation [of benefits]. When the ruler possesses the Way, the ministers exert their force, and the treachery is not born; when he lacks the Way, the ministers above impede the ruler's clear-sightedness, and below accomplish their private [interests].[61]

How then does the ruler outplay his ministers? On the one hand, this task demands the utmost perspicacity. Han Feizi, following Shen Buhai, ostensibly addresses the "enlightened/clear-sighted ruler" (ming jun 明君), who will not be misled by ministerial tricks but will sternly supervise his underlings, avoiding the pitfalls of personal feelings, will never disclose his emotions, and will strictly preserve the utmost power of authority—rewards and punishments—in his own hands.[62] On the other hand, Han Feizi does not overly trust the ruler's intellectual abilities as sufficient for the proper maintaining of the ruler's position. Instead, the sovereign should rely primarily on "the Way": namely, perfect legal and administrative mechanisms:

> If the sovereign personally inspects his hundred officials, the whole day will not be enough; his power will not suffice. Moreover, when the superior uses his eyesight, the underlings embellish the look; when he uses his hearing, the underlings embellish the sound; when he uses his contemplation, the underlings multiply the words. The former kings considered these three [methods] as insufficient: hence they cast away personal abilities and relied on laws and [administrative] methods examining rewards and punishments. The former kings preserved the principles [of rule]; hence the laws were clearly understood and not violated. They ruled single-handedly within the seas; [hence] the clever and astute were unable to employ their trickery; the malicious and impetuous were unable to expose their flattery; the vicious and evil had nothing to rely upon. At the distance of one thousand li, none dared to deviate from their words; and those in the corridors of power dared not conceal the good and embellish the evil. Among the multitudes at the court, those who gathered and those who stayed alone did not overstep each other.[63] Hence there was more than enough daytime to achieve proper order: it was because the superior properly relied on the power of his authority.[64]

Han Feizi echoes Xunzi and earlier thinkers who warned the ruler of the impossibility of personally maintaining the affairs of the state, but their reasons for this inability differ radically. Xunzi argued that the sovereign's problem lies in the natural limitations of humans to grasp enormous quantities of information; hence he recommended that the ruler rely on his underlings. For Han Feizi, those very underlings are the problem: it is their malicious machinations that will deprive the ruler of access to reliable information. Hence the solution is not empowering the ruler's aides but outmaneuvering them. Impartial laws, a proper combination of checks and double-checks of ministerial actions, strict surveillance of the relation between "names" and "forms" (that is, between the tasks assigned to a minister and his actual performance), all these are the sine qua non for proper rule. Employing these methods and fully utilizing his monopoly over rewards and punishments, the ruler will be able to secure his position and moreover attain his political goals despite the potential machinations and malpractices of his subordinates.

The Invisible Ruler

Han Feizi is aware of the possibility that a perfect system such as he is seeking would serve a tyrant, an ultimately bad ruler who would utilize his unlimited power to achieve his sinister aims, bringing calamity and destruction on himself and his subjects. However, for Han Feizi this is a regrettable but unavoidable price for the proper social order under an ordinary sovereign. A realist, Han does not expect a truly enlightened sovereign to reign frequently, but similarly, monsters like Jie and Zhouxin are also exceptions. Hence when defending Shen Dao's thesis regarding the advantages of the ruler's reliance on the power of authority (*shi* 勢) rather than on personal morality, Han Feizi concedes the possibility of occasional inappropriateness of institutional solutions, but he then clarifies this:

> Yao, Shun, Jie, and Zhou[xin] appear once in one thousand generations; they are like a living creature whose shoulders are behind his heels. Generations of rulers cannot be cut in the middle, and when I talk of power of the authority, I mean the average. The average is he who does not reach Yao and Shun above, but also does not behave like Jie and Zhou[xin] below. When one embraces the law and acts according to the power of his authority, then there is orderly rule; when one turns his back on laws and on the power of authority, there is calamity. Now, if we abandon authority, turn back to law and wait for Yao and Shun, so that when Yao and Shun arrive there will be order, then in a thousand generations, one will be well ruled. If we endorse the law and locate ourselves within the power of authority, and then await Jie and Zhou[xin] so that when they arrive there will be calamity, then in a thousand generations, one will be calamitous. So, to have one orderly generation among thousand calamitous ones or to have one calamitous generation

among thousand orderly ones—this is like galloping [in opposite directions] on the thoroughbreds Ji and Er: the distance between them will be great![65]

Han Feizi's position is clear enough: impartial laws and regulations that allow the ruler to utilize his power to the utmost are preferable to the naïve expectations for a moral True Monarch. But there is more. By explicitly stating that his major concern is with *average* rulers, Han Feizi qualifies his pronouncements in favor of "enlightened" sovereigns. While the adjective *ming* 明 frequently means not merely clear-sighted but "numinous," which is an epithet of deities, for Han Feizi the descriptor is applicable to an average monarch. Indeed, advocacy of proper institutional arrangements that will allow the ruler who is not exceptionally intelligent and sagacious to secure his position is a recurrent topic in the *Han Feizi*. Remarkably, while Han Feizi's solution is primarily institutional and is not based on a sage minister, it still bears a strong similarity to that of Xunzi insofar as the ruler's nonaction is concerned. Han Feizi's advocacy of *wu-wei* becomes at time quite pervasive, and it even attains certain utopian dimensions, which are unusual to this thinker:

> In antiquity, those who preserved the Great Body watched Heaven and Earth, observed rivers and seas, relied on mountain valleys. As for whatever is illuminated by the Sun and Moon, influenced by the four seasons, covered by clouds and moved by the wind—they neither wore out the heart by knowledge, nor wore out themselves through private [desires]. They entrusted orderly rule and calamity to laws and techniques [of rule], delegated [the questions] of truth and falsity to rewards and punishments; made light and heavy follow scales and weights. They did not go against the Heaven's pattern, did not harm their disposition and nature.[66]

In this rare invocation of unspecified antiquity, Han Feizi presents an ideal rule as a curious mixture of the sage ruler's following both natural and human-made laws. This abidance by the norms of the Great Body (the Way) allowed them to achieve blessed tranquility:

> Hence at the age of the perfect peace, laws were like morning dew: simple and not scattered; hearts were without resentment, mouths without superfluous words. Hence horses and chariots were not exhausted by lengthy roads; banners were not mixed in disorderly fashion at great marshes; the myriad people did not lose their predestined life at the hands of robbers and military men; thoroughbreds did not impair their longevity under flags and standards; bravos were neither incising their names on maps and documents

nor recording their merits on [bronze] *pan* and *yu* [vessels]; and the wooden planks for the yearly records remained blank. Hence it is said: there is nothing more beneficial than simplicity; no good fortune continues longer than peace.[67]

The idyllic situation depicted by Han Feizi testifies once more to the popularity of the nonaction ideal among Zhanguo thinkers, and, just as in the case of Xunzi, it appears also as an attempt to lure the ruler into adopting Han Feizi's design for orderly rule. Utopian depictions, however, are rare in the text; Han Feizi employs a variety of different arguments in favor of the ruler's quiescence. Some of those arguments are particularly sophisticated philosophically, such as those in the chapter "The Way of the Sovereign" ("Zhu Dao" 主道):

> The Way is the beginning of the myriad things, the norm [distinguishing between] the true and the false. Hence the enlightened ruler preserves the beginning to comprehend the origins of myriad things; orders the norms to comprehend the edges of success and failure. Hence empty and tranquil he is awaiting the orders,[68] ordering the names to name themselves, and ordering the affairs to stabilize themselves. Empty—and hence he comprehends the substance of reality; tranquil—and hence he comprehends correctness of action. He who talks, gives names himself; he who acts, creates forms himself; when forms and names unite, the ruler has nothing to do about them and let them return to their substance.[69]

Han Feizi's recommendations to the ruler to emulate the Way and preserve tranquility are reminiscent of similar passages in several other late Zhanguo texts, which are sometimes associated with the so-called "Huang-Lao" 黃老 tradition;[70] and the ultimate impact of the *Laozi*—at least on the level of the thinker's vocabulary—is also observable here. However, Han Feizi quickly abandons pure philosophical speculation for more practical stipulations for the ruler's quiescence:

> Hence it is said: the ruler does not reveal his desires, since should he do so, the minister will carve and embellish them;[71] he does not reveal his views, since should he do so, the minister will use them to present his different [opinion]. . . . The way of the enlightened sovereign is to let the knowledgeable to exhaust completely their contemplations—then the ruler relies on them to decide on the matters and is not depleted of knowledge; to let the worthy utilize[72] their talents—then the ruler relies on them, assigns tasks, and is not depleted of abilities. When there is success—the ruler possesses a

worthy [name], when there is failure—the minister bears the responsibility: thus the ruler is not depleted of his [good] name. Hence, being unworthy, he is the Master of the worthies; being unknowledgeable, he is the corrector of the knowledgeable. The minister works, while the ruler possesses the achievements: this is called the foundations of the worthy sovereign.[73]

The ruler will benefit twice from preserving secrecy and nullifying his desires. First, he avoids the traps of scheming ministers; second, he is able to manipulate them and achieve glory and fame. The promise of the undeserved fame serves here to lure the ruler into adopting Han Feizi's views. Hinting at the possibility that the sovereign, albeit unworthy and unknowledgeable, will become the teacher and corrector of his worthy subjects, Han Feizi again discloses his ultimately low expectations of the monarch's morality and wisdom. All important in their capacity as the apex of sociopolitical order, the rulers are also human beings—and quite often, inept human beings. It is the goal of the perfect administrative system, envisioned by the author, to allow these mediocre sovereigns to perform their tasks without endangering themselves and (as implicitly hinted at but never explicitly stated) without overburdening their subjects.

The results envisioned by Han Feizi—a perfectly functioning administrative machine which preserves the authority of even a mediocre ruler—appear to be a convincing solution to the situation of potentially inept monarchs, but this solution is not free from internal contradictions. First, the most apparent problem is that impartial laws and regulations are still supposed to be maintained by human beings—the cunning and scheming officials whom Han Feizi detests. Inasmuch as the ruler can trust none of his aides, it is not at all clear how the regulations will work. Second, what about the ruler? What will remain of his power after he is absolutely submerged by laws and regulations and is not supposed to express his desires or even to demonstrate his feelings? Is it not possible that Han Feizi's omnipotent sovereign turns into a slave of his office?

The question is not an idle one. The more we read Han Feizi's recommendations regarding the ruler's secrecy, impartiality, lack of emotion, and lack of interference into everyday affairs, the more we feel that the sovereign is not just invisible but becomes to a certain degree a nullity, a non-persona. He is constantly urged to be public-minded (*gong* 公), which means he must abandon his right to express private opinions, and he is not supposed to let his personal feelings (*si* 私) influence his policy-making.[74] All this amounts to a complete depersonalization of the ruler and his transformation into an instrument of power—an instrument of his personal power, to be sure—but still without any possibility of exercising his true will or of having personal input in policy-

making. Just like his teacher, Xunzi, Han Feizi promulgates the vision of the
ruler, whose symbolic presence is important but whose personal impact should
be reduced to the minimum.

A Ministerial Trap?

The discussion has suggested that the master and his disciple, Xunzi and Han
Feizi, appear much closer to each other than first impressions led us to believe.
Both argue that monarchical rule is the foundation of the sociopolitical order,
and hence the power of the monarch should be theoretically limitless; both
support the dynastic principle of rule and disqualify alternative modes of plac-
ing a worthy sovereign on the throne. They diverge on the issue of the True
Monarch, of whom Xunzi, in contradistinction to Han Feizi, has high expectations, but their practical advice to a mediocre ruler is surprisingly similar.
Although Xunzi recommends delegation of power to the ministers, while Han
Feizi dislikes this idea, in the final account both thinkers envision monarchs
who are not supposed to act independently or interfere in everyday affairs.
The price for their omnipotence is refraining from exercising their limitless
power!

The ultimate convergence of two ostensibly antithetical approaches is not
incidental. Reading late Zhanguo texts, we find time and again similar advocacy of the ruler's impartiality, lack of emotion, and refraining from action as the
quintessence of political wisdom. For instance, the "Relying on Laws" chapter
of the *Guanzi* explicitly recommends that the ruler not rely on his personal
knowledge or on his personal likes and dislikes, but instead emulate the impartial Way and attain the blessed state of nonaction; the ruler is explicitly required
to follow the Law. Almost every major late Zhanguo text, from the *Guanzi* to
the *Lüshi chunqiu*, from Shen Buhai's fragments to the Mawangdui "Huang-
Lao" silk manuscripts, advocates the ruler's impartiality and lack of whimsical
intervention in the affairs of his state.[75] Different texts supply different ratio-
nalizations for the nullification of the ruler's personality: either the need to
comply with the cosmic Way, or the advantages of following impersonal human
Law; either moral imperatives, or the need to preserve power against scheming ministers. Some recommend that the ruler trust his ministers, while others
warn him of their plots; some advocate secrecy, and others demand that the
ruler behave as a moral exemplar, but none of the contending thinkers seems to
support the notion of an active ruler who undertakes everyday administrative
tasks and personally intervenes in the affairs of his ministers.

What are the reasons for such a consensus among the rival thinkers? Two
possible explanations come to mind. First, it is quite probable that many if not

most of these thinkers genuinely believed that a ruler who is overly engaged in routine government affairs would exhaust himself; the rational division of labor between the leader and the led was therefore both acceptable and desirable. But a different, more sinister explanation also comes to mind: these thinkers may simply have hoped to preserve actual power in the hand of their social stratum, that is, in the hands of ministers, while relegating the ruler to the position of theoretically omnipotent but practically negligible figurehead. By enslaving him to legal, ritual, or moral demands, the thinkers were effectively neutralizing the monarch. The monarch retained his symbolical position but was not expected to exercise his will directly. In this fashion the thinkers hoped to ensure that even an inept ruler would not cause unreasonable damage to his state. If we place their ideas in a different cultural context, we would conclude that the ruler was supposed to be the Almighty God, while the ministers were to be his priests and prophets, the mediators between his inscrutable will and everyday life.[76]

Eloquent as it may seem, the idea of neutralizing the ruler by raising him to a superhuman height was not free of contradictions. At the end of Chapter 2, I mentioned that none of the Zhanguo (or later) thinkers dared to suggest institutional limitations on the sovereign's power. Instead, they opted to constrict the ruler through the art of persuasion, convincing him to restrain himself and minimize his activities for the sake of the state and himself. The problem was that the art of persuasion had its limits. While many rulers could easily be satisfied with their theoretically superhuman power and enjoy the good life as a ritual figurehead, some had more far-reaching plans and less quiescent personality. Such rulers wanted to rule, not just to reign, and the conflict between their institutionally justified quest for effective power and the prevalent mood of their courtiers was therefore imminent. This conflict indeed ensued upon the establishment of the first imperial dynasty, the Qin.

Epilogue: The First Emperor and His Aftermath

The imperial unification of 221 was the most astounding event in Chinese history. Although for more than a century the state of Qin had steadily increased its military and economic prowess, inflicting dreadful defeats on its enemies and gradually annexing their lands, few expected that all of the six "hero-states" of the east would be wiped out within ten years of rapid campaigns. The amazing success of the unification and the apparent lack of large-scale organized resistance to Qin rule boosted the self-confidence of the king of Qin and of his entourage. Proudly proclaiming his successes as surpassing those of the thearchs and kings of the past, the Qin monarch adopted a new title—emperor (*huangdi*

皇帝, literally "august thearch"; hereafter I shall use both titles interchangeably)—inaugurating thereby a new era in Chinese history.

The immensity of the First Emperor's success may explain his hubris, for which he was frequently censured in later generations. This ruler had indeed all the reasons to identify himself as a savior who had miraculously put an end to the immanent warfare and turmoil of the Warring States, bringing peace and tranquility to humankind. Qin imperial proclamations, inscribed on steles placed at the top of sacred mountains, reflect the degree to which the August Thearch had incorporated the discourse of the Zhanguo masters (*zi* 子) in molding his self-image.[77] Thus, he repeatedly addresses the universal quest for peace and stability, reminding his subjects that "warfare will never rise again," that he has "brought peace to All under Heaven," and that the "black-headed people are at peace, never needing to take up arms." "He has wiped out the powerful and unruly, rescuing the black-headed people, bringing stability to the four corners of the empire"; by "uniting All under Heaven, he put an end to harm and disaster, and then forever he put aside arms," the result of which is the "Great Peace" (*tai ping* 太平).[78] Making All under Heaven one family (*yi jia tianxia* 壹家天下), unifying everything within "the six directions" (*liu he* 六合) and "four extremities" (*si ji* 四極), the emperor fulfilled the long-term aspirations of the Zhanguo thinkers and apparently attained the goal of "stability in unity."[79]

A second major topos of the inscriptions is the social and political order that the August Thearch has brought. "The distinctions between noble and mean are clarified, men and women embody compliance"; the Thearch "unified and led in concord fathers and sons"; and henceforth "the honored and the humble, the noble and the mean will never exceed their position and rank." This social stability is matched by personal security: "six relatives guard each other, so that ultimately there are no bandits and robbers."[80] Political order under the "clear laws" (*ming fa* 明法) of Qin has ensued: "Office holders respect their divisions, and each knows what to do"; "all respect measures and rules." Furthermore, the August Thearch has ordered the terrestrial realm: he "tore down and destroyed inner and outer city walls; broke through and opened river embankments, leveled and removed dangerous obstacles, so that the topography is now fixed."[81] This results in universal affluence and prosperity: "Men find joy in their fields; women cultivate their work." The Thearch "enriches the black-headed people," so that "all live their full life and there is none who does not achieve his ambitions." Even "horses and oxen" receive the emperor's favor.[82] In Martynov's eloquent definition, these declarations turn the thinkers' utopia (literally: "no-place") into the emperor's "entopia" (literally: "in this place").[83]

The First Emperor has not forgotten his responsibility to be a moral exemplar for his subjects. He proudly proclaims himself as "sage, knowledgeable, benevolent, and righteous," declaring that he "radiates and glorifies his teachings and instructions, so that his percepts and principles reach all around" and "prohibits and stops the lewd and licentious."[84] The people have been transformed accordingly: "None is not committed to honesty and goodness"; "men and women are pure and sincere." The emperor's "greatly orderly rule cleansed the customs, and All under Heaven received his influence."[85]

Having appropriated all the qualities of the True Monarch and having performed the Monarch's tasks, the First Emperor naturally considered himself the embodiment of this messianic figure. His self-divinization (to use Michael Puett's words) was expressed immediately after the unification when he adopted a new title, the August Thearch, with its overt sacral connotation. The next logical step was self-proclamation as a sage, a title that theretofore had been applied in Zhanguo discourse only to former paragons but never to a living ruler. The emperor plainly declares that he "embodies sagehood" (gong sheng 躬聖),[86] and he enjoys the new title so much that he mentions it no less than ten times in seven imperial inscriptions. By doing so, the August Thearch squarely proclaims to his entourage that henceforth the ideal and reality are unified. The sage and the monarch have become a single person![87]

By audaciously appropriating the posture of the True Monarch, the First Emperor created an unprecedented political situation. The Masters' practical recommendations to the sovereign, surveyed above, were designed for an average monarch, who was supposed to rely on his underlings and delegate to them everyday administrative tasks. But inasmuch as this monarch was a sage, it was entirely legitimate for him to rule actively and to intervene in policy-making—which the First Emperor most eagerly did. Accordingly, in his inscriptions the emperor proclaims that he "is not remiss in rulership, rising early in the morning and resting late at night," "is not idle in inspecting and listening," and "uniformly listens to the myriad affairs."[88] We do not know whether the emperor was actually examining daily the documents he dealt with, not going to rest until a certain weight was reached,[89] but the imperial proclamations and constant tours of inspection to the most remote corners of the new realm all suggest that he was not content with a passive figurehead role. The "Great Sage" of Qin wanted to rule and not just to reign.

The new figure of the emperor, the embodiment of the True Monarch of whom Zhanguo thinkers dreamed, was the single most important contribution of Qin's August Thearch to posterity.[90] Yet the First Emperor's radical attempt to actualize a centuries-old ideal met with considerable resentment. While the history of Qin is too marred by later biased interpretations and accusations to permit us a reliable reconstruction of the contemporary court atmosphere, the extant evidence overwhelmingly points to ministerial resentment with the emperor's policy.[91] What is clear is that the emperor's hubris became one of the major accusations raised by Han and later thinkers against the Qin, and it was thereafter routinely mentioned as one of the primary reasons for the swift fall of the Qin dynasty shortly after the death of its founder.[92] Faced with this overwhelming criticism of their predecessor, Han and later emperors could not adopt his policy unchanged, but neither were they willing to reject the Qin legacy in toto. The result of these contradictory assessments of the past was a complex process of adoption and adaptation of Qin's model to the newly emerging empire that stabilized in the early Han period.

Han and later emperors resolutely adopted certain basic parameters of the First Emperor's self-posture. They preserved the sacred title of "August Thearch" and much of the Qin imperial vocabulary. Most important, the identification of the ruler and the sage became an essential feature of the Chinese emperor's image. The word "sage" (*sheng* 聖) became a common adjective, akin to "imperial," and was employed with regard to both dead and living emperors.[93] However, these and other superlatives, which became routine attributes of the monarchy, were not necessarily taken any longer at their face value. Unlike the case of Qin, where at least some genuine belief in the emperor's sacredness may have existed, in the later dynasties this became primarily, again adopting Martynov's words, "a yardstick" of a desired utopia, but one largely detached from its original meaning.[94] Emperors routinely entrusted their ministers with political affairs and frequently displayed commendable humility, claiming a lack of ability and requesting advice of their aides. Most Chinese monarchs were aware of the Qin precedent and consciously tried to distance themselves from the intemperate First Emperor.

This coexistence of the ostensible humility and putative sagacity of the emperors created complex dynamics in the rulers' relations with their aides. While many rulers acquiesced in exercising primarily symbolic and highly ritualized leadership, yielding the reins of power to their courtiers in exchange for a privileged life and unparalleled respect, others were not willing to act as a ritual rubber stamp. These activist rulers, especially but not exclusively dynastic founders and their immediate heirs, did not give up the desire to influence the affairs of All under Heaven. Yet their attempts to translate their presumed sagacity and infallibility into actual power led them into conflicts with stubborn courtiers, who definitely preferred an inactive monarch. The resultant tension was not easily resolvable. A subtle differentiation between the political *yang* (the sovereign's sagacity and omnipotence) and *yin* (common awareness of the emperor's being a less than a perfect human being) was not necessarily clear to everybody. The courtiers could combat an obtrusive emperor with moral admonitions and references to the past precedents, but as the monarch's inactivity was never actually institutionalized, courtiers more often than not simply chose to obstruct imperial initiatives by subtle or active noncompliance. The results could be tragic, ranging from a gloomy stalemate, as depicted in the immortal *1587: A Year of No Significance* by Ray Huang, to the vicissitudes of the Cultural Revolution, launched by Mao Zedong (毛澤東, 1893–1976 CE) in part to avoid the role of the "living ancestor," thrust upon him by party leaders.[95] In retrospect, it may be asserted that the Chinese political system was quite allergic to sages on the throne, in sharp contrast to most of the Zhanguo thinkers' declarations!

Does this mean that the efforts of the Zhanguo thinkers to establish an effective ruler-centered political system had failed? Not necessarily. If we assess the achievements and failures of the Chinese imperial system not in terms of the idealized type embedded in the True Monarch, but in terms of other premodern and modern political systems, the results appear quite impressive. Under normal circumstances, the imperial system allowed significant ministerial input in decision-making, while preserving for the emperor a function as the supreme arbiter in case of controversies. While it was difficult to accommodate exceptionally gifted or exceptionally wicked monarchs, the imperial system, in accordance with Han Feizi's vision, fitted well average and mediocre rulers, who, after all, were the rule and not an exception, given the dominant principle of lineal succession. The very ability of this system to survive for more than two millennia, adapting itself to peasant-emperors, general-emperors, and nomad-emperors among others, testifies to its extraordinary success.

PART II

Shi: The Intellectual

CHAPTER 5

The Rise of the *Shi*

The heart of the ancient benevolent persons . . . was neither to be delighted in things nor to feel sorry for themselves. At the loftiness of [imperial] temples and halls, they worried for their people, in the remoteness of rivers and lakes they worried for their ruler. Hence entering [the court], they worried; and leaving it, also worried: so when did they enjoy? It must be said: they were the first to worry the worries of All under Heaven, and the last to enjoy its joys. Oh! Without these persons, where could I find my place?
　　—Fan Zongyan

This epigraph, taken from the "Inscription of the Yueyang Tower" ("Yue-yang Lou ji" 岳陽樓記) by Fan Zhongyan (范仲淹, 989–1052 CE), contains arguably the most famous lines by this leading intellectual of the Northern Song dynasty (北宋, 960–1126).[1] Fan, one of the pivotal figures of the Northern Song intellectual revival, succinctly summarized certain basic features of the self-image of the Chinese elite. Dedicated to one's lofty ideals to the point of self-denial, being public-spirited and politically involved (worrying about the people and about the ruler), and having a sense of collective identity, a notion reflected in Fan's desire to "find his place" among his admirable predecessors—all these were characteristic of the superior men's self-ideal from the Zhanguo period on.

Among the superior men's features outlined by Fan Zhongyan, two—self-confident idealism and political involvement—will stand at the center of this part of the book. In Chapter 5 I show how the rise of the *shi* stratum from the lower segment of the hereditary aristocracy to the ruling elite changed the self-image of the intellectually active *shi* and how these intellectuals succeeded in defining their position as the moral leaders of the society. In Chapter 6 I analyze various attitudes the *shi* had toward political involvement, showing that despite frequently proclaimed antagonism toward the filthy career-oriented life, the imperative to serve the ruler—whether for egoistic or for idealistic reasons—remained a major guideline for the Zhanguo *shi*. In Chapter 7 I show how the tension between the lofty self-image of the *shi* and their actual position as the ruler's servants endangered political stability and how late Zhanguo thinkers began proposing to curb *shi* autonomy. In the epilogue to chapter 7, I shall focus on the implementation of these proposals shortly after the imperial unification and on how in these new conditions the descendants of the Zhanguo *shi*, the imperial literati, achieved a tense and yet sustainable coexistence with the imperial power-holders.[2]

We shall begin our discussion of the self-image of Zhanguo *shi* with a citation from one of the latest texts of the Warring States period. Writing on the eve of the imperial unification, the *Lüshi chunqiu* authors dedicated the following praise to *shi* who attained the Way:

> Those who have attained the Way . . . consider Heaven as ultimate standard, virtue as a behavioral norm, the Way as their ancestor. They endlessly change together with things; their essence fills Heaven and Earth and is boundless, their spirit covers the universe and is inexhaustible. Nobody knows their beginning, nobody knows their end, nobody knows their gate, nobody knows their limit, nobody knows their source. Nothing is exterior to their greatness, nothing is interior to their smallness: this is called the most esteemed. As for these *shi*, the Five Thearchs could not obtain them as friends, the Three Kings could not obtain them as teachers; only when they cast aside their Thearchs' and kings' airs could they approach and be able to attain them.[3]

This passage displays some of the common topoi of the *shi*-related discourse of the late Zhanguo period. Extraordinary pride, firm belief in their abilities to grasp the essentials of the True Way, and a haughty stand toward the rulers, even the best of whom must "cast aside their Thearchs' and kings' airs" to "approach and attain" the worthy *shi*, became part and parcel of the *shi* image as reflected in many other texts. In this chapter I shall trace the evolution of this self-image and try to identify the social and intellectual processes that contributed to its emergence. In particular I shall focus on two achievements of pre-imperial Chinese intellectuals: their ability to convince the rulers of their indispensability for the state's well-being and their attainment of intellectual autonomy from and superiority over power-holders. Having attained both goals, some *shi* began thinking of themselves in almost superhuman terms, as the passage above reveals.

When I speak of the intellectually active members of the *shi* stratum, I should remind readers that the term *shi* is not entirely coterminous with the modern Occidental "intellectual" and that its semantic field is much broader.

In different contexts, *shi* can refer to a warrior, a husband, a retainer, or a petty official. In English it has been rendered as "gentleman," "scholar," "scholar-official," "officer," "man of service," and "knight," among others. As none of these terms can accurately convey the broad semantic field of the term *shi*, I prefer to transliterate rather than to translate, although whenever I deal with intellectually active *shi*, the term "intellectuals" may be applicable, at least for heuristic purposes. But before we deal with these intellectuals, it may be useful to begin with a brief analysis of the changing content of the term *shi* from the Chunqiu period, when it referred to a well-defined but politically insignificant social stratum, to the Zhanguo period *shi* as a loose appellation of both acting and aspiring elite members.

In his pioneer study conducted almost half a century ago, Hsu Cho-yun traced the rise of the *shi* from Zhanguo and Han textual sources, showing how these originally marginal sociopolitical players advanced into the heart of the Warring States political apparatus.[4] Today, Hsu's analysis may be updated and fine-tuned thanks to recently obtained archeological data, which is particularly valuable for assessing changes in the elite composition from the Chunqiu to the Zhanguo period. Lothar von Falkenhausen's systematic study of Chu graves shows that during the Chunqiu period there was a clearly pronounced distinction between the graves of higher and medium-ranked nobility on the one hand and of what may be called a "sub-elite" (which tentatively may be identified as the *shi* stratum) on the other. Graves of the elite and sub-elite were distinguished in almost every principal status-defining component, such as sets of bronze vessels, funerary jades, horse-and-chariot items, and weapons. This marked difference disappeared, however, during the Zhanguo period, at least insofar as the Chu metropolitan area is concerned. By then, similar assemblages of ritual vessels (or, more often, their ceramic *mingqi* 明器 imitations) are observable in the tombs of all members of the former middle and lower elite and the sub-elite, blurring the differences between those strata. Similar trends are observable also with regard to the Central Plain graves, although there a systematic study of the kind undertaken by Falkenhausen for the state of Chu is still lacking.[5] It seems, therefore, that between the late Chunqiu and the middle Zhanguo period, deep changes occurred in the composition of the elite, which may tentatively be identified as a decrease in the internal stratification of the elite and a broadening of its social base.

Rereading textual data in light of archeologically observable phenomena allows further insights regarding the rise of the *shi*. A huge gap between the *shi* and the higher nobility is duly observable in the texts from the Chunqiu period, specifically in the *Zuo zhuan*. During that period, *shi* were primarily minor siblings of nobles, and they constituted the lowest stratum of hereditary aristocracy. As such, they were largely excluded from political processes in their states. The highest positions in the state hierarchy were firmly occupied by leading members of a few noble lineages, who effectively prevented outsiders from entering the inner circle of power-holders. *Shi* made their living largely as retainers and stewards of the noble lineages, and only under truly exceptional circumstances could they gain national prominence.[6] Moreover, since *shi* lacked hereditary allotments, they were not allowed to establish ancestral temples, which meant that they were ritually impaired. Their debasement in ritual matters is clearly reflected in the *Chunqiu* (春秋, Springs and Autumns) *Annals* of the state of Lu, which never mentions a *shi* (or a commoner) by his name, indicating the low status of this stratum.[7]

Perhaps the most important aspect of the *shi* marginalization in the Chunqiu period was not their actual low position but an adverse intellectual atmosphere that strongly inhibited their advancement. Insofar as the *Zuo zhuan* reflects the Chunqiu intellectual milieu, it seems that the idea of "elevating the worthy" (*shang xian* 尚賢) with regard to the *shi* was no part of contemporary discourse. In a few recorded references to social standing of the *shi*, some of the eminent Chunqiu thinkers, such as Yan Ying (晏嬰, c. 580–520), are cited as opposing to the entrance of humble men "from the remote outskirts" into the lord's service and as advocating a social system in which *shi* "will not overflow" the nobles.[8] Significantly, none of the Chunqiu *shi* is ever referred to in the *Zuo zhuan* as a superior man (*junzi* 君子), despite the prevalent interpretation of this term as pertaining to a person's moral and intellectual abilities and not simply to his pedigree (see below). Insofar as Chunqiu nobles—whose voices are recorded in the *Zuo zhuan*—are concerned, *shi* were not supposed to join the upper echelons of power.

The opposition of the nobles notwithstanding, by the end of the Chunqiu period the rise of the *shi* had become an increasingly widespread phenomenon. As the high nobility was decimated in the bloody internecine feuds, some of the regional lords found it expedient to appoint the more subservient and less threatening *shi* to fill gaps in the ranks of high officials. Other *shi* benefited from the ascendancy of their patrons, the extraordinarily powerful nobles, particularly the heads of the Zhao, Wei, Han, and Tian lineages, who by the fifth century BCE had turned their allotments into fully independent polities. After becoming regional lords, these leaders continued to staff their governments with *shi*, allowing members of this stratum to rise to the top of power pyramid. Concomitantly, the expansion of the government apparatus in the wake of the administrative and military reforms of the Warring States period created new employment opportunities for the *shi*.[9] While details of these processes (or indeed details of fifth-century BCE history generally) are not clear due to a dearth of reliable sources, the general trend of the rise of the *shi* during this century is undeniable. The archeologically distinguishable merging of the higher and lower elite, observed by Falkenhausen, is thus duly reflected in the middle to late Zhanguo texts, which routinely employ the term *shi* as a common appellation for members of the elite.

This said, we should also notice that the increasing social mobility of the Warring States period blurred the clearly pronounced boundaries of the *shi* stratum. When Zhanguo texts speak of the *shi,* they may refer to a great variety of persons, including ranked officials but also aspiring members of the elite; sometimes the texts hint at a common social background and sometimes at common behavioral norms. This heterogeneity of the *shi* should be taken into account to avoid a simplistic equation of *shi* with "schoolmen" or "officials"; nor should we assume a uniform ideology or behavioral mode for all the *shi*. Yet insofar as intellectually active members of the *shi* stratum are concerned, we can discern clear traces of a group consciousness among them. In what follows, I shall primarily focus on this intellectual group and on its increasing ideological assertiveness.

"Elevating the Worthy"

The rise of the *shi* was one of the most important developments of the preimperial period, not only socially, but also ideologically, for it brought about a reconceptualization of the nature of elite status. Intellectually active *shi*, of whom Confucius is the first known spokesman, promoted new concepts of elite membership that largely dissociated it from pedigree. Their views had a long-term revolutionary impact on the composition of the upper classes in Chinese society. Although a person's birth remained forever significant for his career, his abilities were supposed to play a far more prominent role; and this understanding influenced elite behavior enormously throughout the imperial millennia.

Absorption of the notion of "elevating the worthy" into political discourse was an outcome of a relatively lengthy process. Its seeds are observable in the Chunqiu period ethical reinterpretation of the term "superior man"—a common designation of an elite member. While its connotations of pedigree remained clear (and as a result the *Zuo zhuan* never applies this designation to a *shi*), the term was nevertheless increasingly imbued with ethical content. Only the noble who behaved properly and prudently deserved his elevated position; otherwise he could be designated a "petty man" (*xiao ren* 小人), which indicated that he was unworthy of noble status. In an age of frequent downfalls of powerful ministerial lineages, this emphasis on the personal qualities of "superior men" provided contemporary aristocrats with a convenient explanation for the ever-accelerating downward mobility of members of their stratum.[10]

Confucius and members of his entourage were the first known thinkers to employ this "ethicization" of the concept of *junzi* for the sake of their stratum. In the *Lunyu*, this term has much less pronounced hereditary connotations and is instead primarily a designation of benevolent, perspicacious, and courageous men; it is readily applicable to the *shi*. But if *shi* can be "superior men," then should they be eligible for the appropriate social standing and political power? The *Lunyu* does not provide an unequivocal answer to this question, which probably reflects the self-restraint of Confucius and his disciples in an age when elevation of the *shi* was still uncommon. While many of Confucius's sayings disclose his high aspirations, and his recommendation to promote "the upright" persons is conducive to the upward mobility of the *shi*, he does not speak explicitly of *shi* as peers of the aristocracy.[11] At the very least, the text contains no direct endorsement of the concept of social mobility, which is prominent in later writings.[12]

While the *Lunyu* is less politically radical than later texts, it played a crucial role in shaping the self-image of the newly rising elite. This is the first text in which the term *shi* itself becomes an object of inquiry, and it is treated in a way similar to the term *junzi*—namely, primarily as an ethical, not a hereditary, designation. Time and again Confucius is asked by his disciples who can be designated *shi*, and the answers strongly resemble his discussions of superior men. *Shi* are "people with aspirations" (*zhi* 志), and these aspirations, just as those of the Master himself, are directed at the Way, namely, toward the ideal of moral and political order. A *shi* is a person who "has a sense of shame" in his conduct and "will not disgrace his ruler's orders when dispatched to the four directions"; minimally, he is a person who is renowned for his filiality and fraternal behavior or at least is a trustworthy and resolute man. A *shi* is "decisive, kind, and gentle" with friends and relatives. And, most importantly, he is a person wholly dedicated to his high mission: "A *shi* who is addicted to leisure is not worthy of being considered *shi*."[13]

What, then, is the mission of a *shi*? A clue may be gathered from the following dialogue:

Zilu (子路, 542–480) asked about the superior man.
> The Master said: "Rectify yourself to be reverent."
> [Zilu] asked: "Is that all?"
> [The Master] said: "Rectify yourself to bring peace to others."
> [Zilu] asked: "Is that all?"
> [The Master] said: "Rectify yourself to bring peace to the hundred clans.

To rectify yourself thereby bringing peace to the hundred clans: even Yao and Shun considered this difficult!"[14]

The ultimate goal of rectification is therefore political: to bring peace to the hundred clans, presumably by restoring a kind of ideal rule akin to that of Yao and Shun. This goal, however, is extraordinarily difficult, almost unattainable: even the ancient paragons could not easily accomplish it. The mission of a *shi*/superior man is therefore a heavy burden. Confucius's disciples shared the Master's view: thus, Zizhang (子張, 503–?) defines a *shi* as a person who "sacrifices his life when facing danger, thinks of righteousness when facing [possible] gains,"[15] while Zengzi (曾子, 502–435) speaks of the tasks of a *shi* in the following way: "A *shi* cannot but be strong and resolute, as his task is heavy and his way is long. He considers benevolence as his task—is not it heavy? He stops only after death—is not [his way] long?"[16]

Zengzi's definition, one of the classical *shi*-related statements in pre-imperial literature, reflects the strong sense of self-respect of members of the newly rising stratum, who accepted their mission to improve governance above and public mores below, and who considered themselves spiritual leaders of the society. These feelings, which were apparently shared by most if not all of Confucius's disciples, were indicative of the coming new era of *shi* dominance in both social and intellectual life.

While the *Lunyu* contributed decisively toward shaping the self-image of intellectually active *shi*, a second major Zhanguo text, the *Mozi*, added another dimension to *shi* assertiveness that helped supply ideological justifications for their ascendancy. Unlike the *Lunyu*, the *Mozi* appears free of hesitations or self-restraint insofar as the social standing of the *shi* is concerned. Mozi proudly proclaims that the *shi* are indispensable for the state's well-being: "When the state has plenty of worthy and good *shi*, its orderly rule is abundant; when it has few worthy and good *shi*, its orderly rule is meager; hence the task of the Grandees is to multiply worthies and that is all."[17]

In the "Elevating the Worthy" chapters, from which the passage above was cited, Mozi proposes a detailed list of measures aimed at attracting and promoting the "worthy and good *shi*." We shall return to these proposals in Chapter 6; here I shall focus on Mozi's unambiguous support for social mobility. After depicting the implementation of "elevating the worthy" policy by the sage kings of antiquity, according to which "neither the officials were perpetually esteemed, nor the people forever base,"[18] Mozi specifies its blessed results:

Thus at that time, even among those ministers who enjoyed rich emoluments and respected position, none was irreverent and reckless, and each be-

haved accordingly; even among peasants and artisans, each was encouraged
to enhance his aspirations. So, *shi* are those who become aides, chancellors,
and heads of officials. He who attains *shi*, his plans meet with no difficulties,
his body is not exhausted, his fame is established and achievements are accomplished; his beauty is manifest and ugliness will not come into being: it
is all thanks to attaining *shi*.[19]

Mozi is unequivocal: even among the low strata of peasants and artisans
some people may contribute to the state's well-being; accordingly, there should
be no limitations at all on social mobility, and one's position should reflect
exclusively one's worthiness and righteousness. Simultaneously, those who occupy high positions should beware of downward mobility. In Mozi's idealized
system, nobody remains secure in his position. Hence, he explains, ancient sages,
in promoting the able and the worthy:

> ... did not align themselves with uncles and brothers, were impartial toward
> rich and noble, and did not cherish the beautiful-looking. They raised and
> promoted the worthy, enriched and ennobled them, making them officials
> and leaders; they deposed and degraded the unworthy, dispossessed and de-
> moted them, making them laborers and servants.[20]

The implications for the nobles are clear enough: they are no longer supposed to be secure in their position in a society where personal abilities alone
determine a person's future. What is astonishing is that Mozi's attack on the
centuries-old order apparently went unopposed, without traceable attempts to
defend the pedigree-based social order. It is possible that the voices of the opponents of social mobility were simply silenced after the rise of the *shi* became
a fait accompli, but even if this is the case, the fact that none of these voices
is discernible in either received or archeologically discovered texts is remarkable. Thus, even if Mozi's remark that "*shi* and superior men from All under
Heaven, wherever they dwell and whenever they talk, all [support] elevating the
worthy"[21] exaggerates the support for his views, it does reflect a clear change
in the intellectual atmosphere from the time of the *Zuo zhuan*. "Elevating the
worthy" had become the paradigmatic rule of political life, and aristocrats qui-
etly yielded their power and hereditary rights.

After the middle Warring States period, it appears that many if not most
rulers had firmly internalized the notion of the indispensability of the "worthy and good *shi*" for their state's well-being. *Shi*, who lacked an independent
power base, were less threatening than the potentially unruly nobles, while their
expertise in military and administrative issues was much needed in an age of

profound sociopolitical change. As the advantages of attracting *shi* became clear
to the rulers, a new atmosphere of competition for attaining the best of the *shi*
ensued. Zhanguo and later texts vividly depict how this competition caused
some of the rulers to go to extremes of politeness and generosity in order to attract worthies.[22] Although these stories should inevitably be read *cum grano salis*,
the overall change in attitude toward the employment of *shi* from the middle
Zhanguo period onward is undeniable.

Anecdotes aside, the idea of "elevating the worthy" and, more importantly,
the end of the pedigree-based social order became a reality in most of the
Warring States. Although members of the ruling lineage and sons of meritorious officials continued to enjoy easier access to lucrative offices, the overall
composition of the ruling elite changed profoundly. The most decisive change
occurred in the state of Qin, which introduced new principles of promotion
based on military merits and high tax yields, bringing about unprecedented
social mobility, which is reflected in Qin epigraphic sources.[23] Elsewhere, as in
the state of Chu, the change may have been much less profound, but the overall trends were similar to those of Qin.[24] While certain thinkers continued to
criticize the principle of "elevating the worthy"—either because of the negative social consequences of unrestrained competition between the "worthies"
or because of the vagueness of the definition of "worthiness"—none suggested
reestablishment of the pedigree-based social order.[25] The bloodless *shi* revolution was completed both in ideology and in praxis.

"Possessors of the Way"

The endorsement of the principle of "elevating the worthy" since the middle
Zhanguo period and the rise of the *shi* to the top of the government apparatus fueled the pride of the *shi*, but even more important in this regard was the
ability of the leading *shi* to affirm their intellectual superiority. By the middle
Zhanguo period, leading *shi* intellectuals—and by extension the *shi* stratum as
the whole—succeeded in identifying themselves as "possessors of the Way,"
namely, as the intellectual and moral leaders of the society. The Way (Dao, a
term I use here as a generic designation of proper moral, sociopolitical, or
cosmic principles, essential to the well-being of the state and a single person)[26]
became an exclusive asset of the *shi*, enabling them not only to preserve their
autonomy vis-à-vis power-holders, but even at times to claim moral superiority
over the rulers.

Some aspects of the *shi* appropriation of the Way are still unclear and may
remain so unless new data change our perceptions, but it is possible to outline
the basic parameters of this process.[27] In the Chunqiu period, there appears to

have been no independent locus of intellectual authority beyond the courts. Ideological leadership was in the hands of the aristocratic ministers whose voices dominate the *Zuo zhuan* narrative; if any *shi* prior to Confucius was intellectually active, our sources remain silent with this regard. By the Zhanguo period, this situation changed drastically. The *shi* thinkers owed their authority not to their exalted position (which they frequently lacked) but to their intellectual expertise, namely, their access to the Way. For reasons currently inexplicable, hereditary aristocrats made no traceable attempt to combat *shi* intellectual authority or to preserve control of ideological discussions in their own hands. Possibly, the sheer depth of the crisis of the Chunqiu sociopolitical order created such an urgent need for immediate remedies that even the advice of *shi* thinkers was welcome.

Several ideological devices allowed the *shi* masters (*zi* 子) to affirm their intellectual authority. First was their appropriation of the past, especially but not exclusively of its quasi-canonical heritage, the *Poems* and the *Documents* associated with the sage kings of the Shang and Zhou dynasties. Early masters, such as Confucius and Mozi, embedded many of their proposals in claims that they were the true transmitters of the ancients' wisdom, although already in Mozi's case we can see clear departures from the ancient models (as discussed in Chapters 2 and 3). Later thinkers modified and enriched the tradition of "using the past to serve the present": they introduced a variety of new "sage kings" of antiquity, modified extant narratives of the past, and probably also created new "canonical" chapters of the *Documents*.[28] Remarkably, court scribes, who were the most prominent guardians of the past throughout the Chunqiu period, had all but disappeared from the Zhanguo landscape, leaving compilation of the narratives about the past firmly in the hands of competing thinkers. "The Way of the former kings" was henceforth firmly appropriated by its self-proposed interpreters, the *shi* Masters.[29]

By the middle Zhanguo period, conflicting narratives of the past diminished the appeal of the "Way of the sage kings": this way was simply too much contested and manipulated by rival thinkers to be considered fully compelling.[30] Eventually new strands of argumentation ensued, of which those based on cosmological stipulations of the political order are particularly interesting for our discussion. Insofar as the *Laozi* may be considered the earliest proponent of these views, it is useful to review its approach from the point of view of securing the intellectual autonomy of the *shi*. The *Laozi*, which discusses extensively the Way amidst frequent complaints about its effusive nature and inscrutability, dissociates this concept from the legacy of the former kings and places it on a cosmic level. Once it has been detached from the ancient power-holders, the Way becomes an object of inquiry and possible attainment by any person, including, of course, the author of the *Laozi*. In the "Nei ye" chapter of the *Guanzi* (discussed in Chapter 2), we observe this process with far greater clarity: any adept may be able, through proper "inner training," to achieve the cosmic power of a Dao-holder. Neither ruler nor courtiers have any advantage in attaining the Way over an ordinary *shi*. While the "Nei ye" may be exceptional in its specifications of the methods of attaining the Way, its authors' conviction in the ultimate attainability of Dao by an adept was shared by many other thinkers.[31]

It is not my intention here to survey all the possible ways in which thinkers claimed exclusive access to the Way; what is important for us is the consensus among them that the Way was attainable outside the ruler's court. Although many thinkers continued to yearn for a sage monarch, whose administrative power would be matched by intellectual and moral superiority, practically, as we have noted in Part I, the *shi* masters overwhelmingly denied the right of the current rulers to be considered sages. Effectively, this meant that at least temporarily the Way would reside among the Masters alone, who posed themselves as possessors of vital intellectual expertise. In Chapter 7 we shall see that this implicit denigration of the court eventually brought about anti-*shi* reaction that climaxed shortly after the imperial unification in Li Si's "biblioclasm" of 213, but throughout most of the Zhanguo age the superiority of the *shi* Masters over the rulers in terms of access to the Way was not questioned. Intellectually active *shi* attained their intellectual/moral autonomy of and superiority to the throne with almost unbelievable ease.

To demonstrate how this sense of autonomy and of superiority determined the *shi* discourse of the middle Zhanguo period, I shall briefly focus on three major thinkers: Mengzi, Zhuangzi, and Xunzi. The first of these, Mengzi, was chosen because by comparing his sayings to those of his paragon, Confucius, we may discern the degree of change that occurred in the *shi* self-view throughout the first half of the Zhanguo period. As is well known, the *Lunyu* and the *Mengzi* share many similarities in ideology and style, which are conducive to highlighting their different emphases. Among these, the distinct stance of Confucius and Mengzi vis-à-vis rulers is particularly illuminating. Although the *Lunyu* contains a few anecdotes about Confucius's dissatisfaction with insufficiently polite treatment by his superiors, this topic remains marginal there,[32] but in the *Mengzi* it occupies a pivotal place. Mengzi's staunch adherence to the norms of ruler-minister etiquette caused him to leave repeatedly those rulers who failed to treat him with due respect. Mengzi's demarches became a topic of constant discussion with his disciples, and in one of these discussions Mengzi raised the notion of the near equality between the ruler and his advisor with the utmost clarity:

Zengzi said: "The richness of Jin and Chu cannot be matched; [but] while they have their riches, I have my benevolence; while they have their ranks, I have my righteousness: so am I lesser than they?" Could Zengzi say anything inappropriate? There may be a certain Way there. There are three matters that command respect under Heaven: first is rank, second is age; third is virtue. At court, rank is supreme; in the village community, age; but in supporting the generation and prolonging the people's [life], nothing is comparable to virtue. How would a possessor of one of these behave arrogantly toward a possessor of the second? Hence the ruler who has great plans must have a minister who cannot be summoned; if he wants to make plans together [with the minister], he must approach the minister.[33]

Mengzi outlines here three parallel hierarchies: a political-administrative one, with the ruler at its apex; a social one (confined to small communities), which prizes age; and a moral hierarchy in which he and his like occupy the leading position. While politically inferior to the ruler, outstanding *shi* are morally superior to the sovereign, and their relations should be therefore based on mutual respect, which diminishes hierarchic distinctions. Putting aside the implications of this view on ruler-minister relations (for which see Chapter 7), we can immediately note that Mengzi's (and Zengzi's) sayings reflect the much greater pride and self-confidence of the *shi* than was observable in the *Lunyu*. This difference is reflected not only in Mengzi's proud stance vis-à-vis rulers, but also in the treatment of the term *shi* in the text. Unlike the *Lunyu*, in the *Mengzi* nobody asks "who is a *shi*"; instead the master and his disciples compete in making flattering proclamations about *shi*. Mengzi states: "Only a *shi* is able to preserve a stable heart without stable livelihood"; elsewhere he cites a saying: "A *shi* with high aspirations will never forget [that he may end] in a ditch, a brave *shi* will never forget [that he may] lose his head."[34] One of Mengzi's disciples cites another saying: "[as for] *shi* with abundant virtue, rulers were unable to turn them into subjects, fathers were unable to turn them into sons"; while another disciple claims that a *shi* should not accept a regional lord's unofficial patronage.[35] All these statements, while containing an element of bravado, create the sense of a proud community, united by common behavioral norms, the members of which did not feel inferior to rulers.

The idea that the moral/intellectual hierarchy parallels the political one and is independent of it is inherent in the *Mengzi*, and this notion bolsters the pride of the thinker and his entourage. Nowhere is this pride as explicit as in the ideal of the Great Man, proposed as an alternative to those contemporaries who compromised their integrity for the sake of career:

To consider compliance as correctness is the way of spouses and concubines. [The Great Man] lives in the broad lodging of All under Heaven, occupies a proper position in All under Heaven, follows the great Way of All under Heaven. When his aspirations are fulfilled—he follows [the Way] together with the people; when they are not—he follows his Way alone. Wealth and high status cannot tempt him, poverty and low status cannot move him, awesomeness and military might cannot subdue him—this is called the "Great Man."[36]

Mengzi presents the Great Man as an entirely self-sufficient person, a proud counterpart of the ruler above and the people below. Being internally empowered by firm attachment to the Way, he is able to defy whatever external challenges are presented by those who want either to entice or overawe him. The Great Man is almost superhuman: he is not a minor actor on the sociopolitical scene, but a creator of his own moral universe, to which he can retreat from the inadequate outside world. This moral universe, as Mengzi clarifies elsewhere, is not desolate, but rather is inhabited by aspiring Great Men—the *shi*:

> Mengzi told to Wan Zhang: "Good *shi* of a village should befriend good *shi* of the village; good *shi* of a state should befriend good *shi* of the state; good *shi* of All under Heaven should befriend good *shi* of All under Heaven. If befriending good *shi* of All under Heaven is still insufficient, then you still can debate with the ancients. Recite their *Poems*, read their *Documents*: is it possible that then you will not understand these people? Thus when you discuss their generation, this is as if you befriend them."[37]

The picture of a community of friends who share aspirations and educational background (which allows them also to debate with "the ancients") supplements logically the notion of a self-sufficient Great Man. This synchronic and diachronic community, being apparently independent of the state and its hierarchy, may have been particularly appealing to critically minded people like Wan Zhang, who once defined the lords of his time as "robbers."[38] Morally upright *shi* may have found relief in such a self-sufficient community, probably even an escape from the predicament of serving morally inferior rulers.

Mengzi's firm belief in the internal power of a *shi* who attained the Way is echoed in later texts, such as those associated with Xunzi and Zhuangzi, on which I shall focus here.[39] It is almost a truism to say that these two thinkers are intellectual opposites. They sharply disagreed with regard to almost any pivotal question, such as the nature of organized society, the attainability of truth, the desirability of state institutions, and, of course, the proper conduct of a *shi*.

Nonetheless, in the books associated with both of them we find many interesting parallels with regard to the social standing of the intellectuals who attained the Way. These superb individuals are depicted in both books as infinitely superior to power-holders. For instance, the *Zhuangzi* contains abundant anecdotes about proud "men of the Way" (*Dao ren* 道人), who defied social norms and ridiculed the rulers. Among these men we find lofty recluses who treated the sage monarchs disdainfully, displaying an overwhelming sense of superiority over earthly sovereigns. For instance, the "Xiao yao you" (逍遙游, Free and easy wandering) chapter contains a following anecdote about Yao's futile attempt to yield his throne to the worthy recluse Xu You:

> Yao yielded All under Heaven to Xu You, saying: "If torches are not extinguished after the sun and moon have already come out, would it not be difficult for them to [remain the source] of light? Irrigating while the seasonal rains are falling—is it not a waste of labor? If you are established [as the ruler], All under Heaven would be well ordered. Insofar as I am impersonating [the ruler], I am aware of my failings. I beg to deliver All under Heaven into your hands."[40]

Yao accepts as given Xu You's superiority; his only desire is to reconcile the moral and political hierarchy by placing Xu You on the throne. The recluse, however, dismisses Yao's offer:

> Xu You said: "You govern the world, and the world is already well governed. Now if I take your place, will I be doing it for a name? But name is only the guest of reality—should I become a guest? When the tailorbird builds its nest in the deep woods, it needs no more than one branch. When the mole drinks at the river, it takes no more than a bellyful. Go home and forget the matter, my lord. I have no use for the rulership of All under Heaven! Even if a cook [at the sacrifice] does not run his kitchen properly, the impersonator of the dead and the invocator will not leap over the wine casks and sacrificial stands and go take his place."[41]

Xu You's statement contains two explanations for his refusal. Hailing self-sufficiency and disdainfully rejecting the futile search for name/fame (*ming* 名), as well as praising Yao's rule, Xu You ostensibly behaves in accordance with the conventional morality that demands the ritual yielding (*li rang* 禮讓) of superior men. But on a subtler level, Xu You displays his contempt of Yao, who is compared to a humble cook, while Xu You, the moral recluse, is compared to the ritually important impersonator and invocator. The political power and its holder appear as immeasurably inferior to the true power of the Way. Zhuangzi clarifies this elsewhere, when praising the "divine people" (*shen ren* 神人, another kind of "men of the Way"):

> These men, with their virtue, will embrace the myriad things and make them one. The age pleas for calamity: who should exhaust himself to become engaged with All under Heaven? [As for] these men: nothing can harm them. Though flood waters pile up to the sky, they will not drown; though a great drought melts metal and stone and scorches the earth and hills, they will not feel hot. From their dust and dregs alone one could mould a Yao or a Shun: how would they engage with things?[42]

Zhuangzi uses his glorification of the "divine men" for a double purpose: he asserts their infinite exaltedness and ridicules the imperative of political involvement. The second issue will be discussed in Chapter 6; here we shall focus on the unrivalled superiority of the divine men. The *Zhuangzi* takes this notion far beyong the *Mengzi*. The divine men stand not only above the masses and above the rulers but also above Nature itself, being unmoved by floods and drought. They dwarf not just average rulers, but even the paragons, Yao and Shun, who amount to no more than "dust and dregs" of these men. While their Way, as the Way of recluses and other "men of the Way" mentioned throughout the *Zhuangzi*, differs markedly from that of Mengzi's Great Man, their standing vis-à-vis the world remains similar.

When we turn to Xunzi, conventional wisdom may suggest that he will not engage in unrestrained praise of the superior *shi* to any extent comparable with Mengzi and Zhuangzi. Not only is Xunzi's thought ostensibly much more ruler-oriented than that of his predecessors, but he is also fairly critical of intellectual pluralism and of haughty *shi* in general. In his polemic "Contra the Twelve Masters" ("Fei shi'er zi" 非十二子), Xunzi criticized his ideological rivals for abandoning the Way of the Former Kings, which, in his eyes, should be the supreme criterion of truth and falsehood of the proposed doctrine. He had further proposed that sage kings forbid "licentious affairs, licentious hearts, and licentious doctrines."[43] In Chapter 7 we shall see that Xunzi's views contributed in no small measure to the assault on the intellectual autonomy of the *shi* that peaked under Xunzi's disciple, Li Si. And yet despite Xunzi's dislike of intellectual pluralism, he remained a staunch believer in the superiority and intellectual independence of the outstanding *shi*, or, more precisely, of those *shi* who follow the True Way: the Way of Confucius and Xunzi. Unless the world is ruled by a sage True Monarch, possession of the Way, with its attendant responsibility and glory, remains firmly an asset of these superior men, as Xunzi clarifies in the pivotal "Ru xiao" chapter (儒效, The effectiveness of the Ru):

> Hence the superior man is noble without rank, rich without emoluments, trustworthy without words, awesome without anger. He lives in poverty but is glorious, dwells alone but is joyful—is it not that he accumulated the essence of the most respectable, the richest, the most important and the sternest? . . . Hence the superior man is devoted to internal cultivation and yields externally, devotes himself to accumulating virtue in his body and dwells in it to comply with the Way. Thus, his nobility and fame arise like the sun and moon, All under Heaven respond to him as to thunderbolt. Hence it is said: the superior man is obscure, and yet is luminous; he is mysterious and yet is brightly clear; he speaks of yielding and yet overcomes. The *Poems* say: "The crane cries at the nine marshes, its voice is heard in Heaven." It is said of this.[44]

This flattering depiction of the superior man, who is self-sufficient and independent of external factors, clearly resembles both the *Mengzi* and *Zhuangzi*: as in the former text, the superior man is primarily a political animal; and as in the *Zhuangzi*, he acquires certain superhuman (or, more precisely, ruler-like) dimensions that allow him to rival the impact of sun, moon, and thunderbolts. The superior man (or, as he is rendered elsewhere, the Great Ru or the Great Man) appears as both autonomous of and immeasurably superior to his surrounding:

> This Great Ru, even when he is obscure in an impoverished lane in a leaking house and has not enough territory to place an awl, kings and dukes are unable to contest his fame; when he has a territory of a hundred *li* squared, none of the states of one thousand *li* squared can contest his superiority. He beats down violent states, orders and unifies All under Heaven, and nobody is able to overturn him—this is the sign of a Great Ru. . . . When he succeeds, he unifies All under Heaven; when he fails, he establishes alone his noble fame. Heaven is unable to kill it; Earth is unable to bury it; Jie and [Robber] Zhi are unable to tarnish it: only the Great Ru can establish it like this.[45]

This panegyric to the Great Ru again surpasses that of Mengzi and approaches Zhuangzi-like dimensions. The Great Ru not only stands aloof from society, but is partly independent even of Heaven and Earth, which cannot destroy his name/fame (*ming*). Not only is he independent, but he is also superior to

power-holders: if given the slightest chance, just a tiny territory of one hundred
li squared, the Great Ru will subdue the regional lords. Even if this chance is
not given, Xunzi assures us that the Great Ru will still beat kings and dukes at
least insofar as the contest for fame is concerned: his moral superiority is taken
for granted. Thus, despite his advocacy of a harsh, ruler-centered system, Xunzi
remains an enthusiastic supporter of the exaltedness of outstanding *shi*. Differing radically from Zhuangzi, and at times from Mengzi with regard to the
proper self-fulfillment of an intellectual, Xunzi nonetheless shares their conviction in the infinite superiority of the best of the *shi* over the rest of society. This
superiority reflects the fact that the superior men/Great Ru have exclusively
acquired the Way, which gains them the position of being moral (and ultimately
political) leaders of the human world.

Inflation of Self-esteem

Neither Zhuangzi nor Xunzi considered an average *shi* as superior to the rest
of the society; this exaltedness was confined to the most intelligent and brilliant representatives of this stratum.[46] However, for some of the intellectually
active *shi*, it was their stratum as a whole that possessed the Way. Many late
Zhanguo texts, such as *Zhanguo ce*, *Lüshi chunqiu*, and the like, extol the exceptional capabilities of the *shi* and promote a vision of the *shi* as "the most
esteemed" (see, for example, the passage cited on p. 116). These texts reflect an
atmosphere of escalating self-confidence and pride among intellectually active
shi, some of whom began harboring extraordinarily high aspirations. Thus, the
Mozi tells of a certain Wu Lu 吳慮, from the southern outskirts of the Lu capital, who "made pottery in winter and plowed in summer, comparing himself
to Shun."[47] Did this anonymous Wu Lu expect that a modern Yao would find
him and elevate him to the rulership? Such an assertion seems plausible in light
of several Shun-related references in contemporary texts.[48] Other *shi* did not
even bother to wait for a new Yao to proclaim their superiority. A *Zhanguo ce*
anecdote tells us:

> King Xuan of Qi (齊宣王, r. 319–301) had an audience with Yan Chu,
> saying: "Chu, come forward!" [Yan] Chu also said: "King, come forward!"
> King Xuan was displeased; his courtiers said: "The king is the ruler; Chu is
> a subject. Is it acceptable that when the king says 'Chu, come forward!' you
> also say: 'King, come forward!'?"
>   [Yan] Chu answered: "I come forward out of admiration for power (*shi*
> 勢); the king comes forward to hasten toward a *shi* 士. Is not it better to let
> the king hasten toward a *shi* rather than to let me hasten toward power?"

The king's face changed to the color of anger, and he said: "Is the king esteemed or a *shi* esteemed?"

[Yan Chu] answered: "A *shi* is esteemed, the king is not."

The king said: "Can you explain this?"

[Yan] Chu answered: "I can. Once, Qin attacked Qi, issuing an order: 'He who dares to collect firewood at less than fifty steps from Liuxia Ji's tomb will be punished by death without pardon.' Another order said: 'He who attains the head of the king of Qi will be enfeoffed as a lord of ten thousand households and granted one thousand *yi* of gold.' Looking from that, the head of a living king is less worthy than a tomb of a dead *shi*."

The king remained silent and displeased.[49]

The story continues on a more serious note, as Yan Chu explains to the angry courtiers that a good king must do whatever he can to attract bright *shi*, as this is the only way for him to survive in fierce interstate competition and to attain a good name. "Yao transferred [the power] to Shun; Shun to Yu; King Cheng of Zhou relied on the Duke of Zhou, and generations hail them as enlightened rulers: from this it is clear that a *shi* is more esteemed."[50] Enlightened in this way, King Xuan finally acts as a true talent-seeker:

King Xuan said: "Alas! How could I presume to insult the superior man—I brought this malady on myself! Only now, as I have heard the words of the superior man, I realize how mean my behavior was. I beg you to accept me as your disciple. Moreover, Master Yan will spend time with me, eat only a great *lao*, go out only riding a chariot, with beautiful concubines and garments."[51]

Yan Chu rejects this generous offer, claiming, in Zhuangzi-like fashion, that he prefers a simple, self-sustaining life without the dangers of the court; but even before the refusal, Yan Chu has attained his goal. The king is convinced to respect *shi* and to spare nothing in order to attract them. Remarkably, to impress his potential patron Yan Chu has proposed neither political nor military stratagems, nor even discussed the mysteries of prolonging one's life, as many sage advisors did: he has merely ridiculed the king and praised the *shi*—which have sufficed to ensure his potential employment! Historically unreliable as it is, the anecdote is indicative of the atmosphere that some of the *shi* intellectuals wanted to generate at court: the atmosphere of utmost respect to the members of their stratum, which should bring about career proposals. Insofar as the *Zhanguo ce* contains "educational materials" for peripatetic advisors to take to the competing courts, its anecdotes, of which the above is just a single example, may reflect hopes and attitudes of a significant segment of the educated elite of the Zhanguo age.[52]

In Chapter 7 we shall see that the haughty behavior of Yan Chu and his like eventually backfired, giving rise to anti-*shi* polemics in such texts as the *Han Feizi*, but there is little doubt that this haughtiness was a relatively widespread phenomenon in the late Warring States period. The *Lüshi chunqiu*, the last major pre-imperial compilation, with which we began this chapter, may serve as an excellent mirror of the self-ideal of late Zhanguo *shi*. This text, prepared jointly by thinkers of different intellectual affiliations, who gathered on the eve of imperial unification at the court of the rising power of Qin under the auspices of the almighty prime minister, Lü Buwei (呂不偉, d. 235), was devised as a summa of Zhanguo intellectual developments. Its authors frequently disagree on political, philosophical, and moral issues, but they have certain beliefs in common. Among these, the insistence on elevating the *shi* is so pervasive in the *Lüshi chunqiu* that the entire text may well be read as a promotion campaign by Lü Buwei's "guests." The text abounds with stories of wise rulers who attracted *shi* and benefited enormously from their services and of those who failed to do so, bringing disaster on themselves.[53] Frequent references to "*shi* who possess the Way" (*you Dao zhi shi* 有道之士) convey a feeling that the authors considered the True Way as a kind of a common possession of the worthy members of their stratum. Repeatedly hailing impoverished, but upright, "plain-clothed" (*buyi* 布衣) *shi*, the authors proclaimed their membership in a morally dignified and incorruptible elite. The following passage illustrates their views:

> *Shi* are the men who, when acting in accord with [proper] patterns, do not escape the difficulties; when facing the troubles, forget the profits; they cast aside life to follow righteousness and consider death as returning home. If there are such men, the ruler of a state will not be able to befriend them, the Son of Heaven will not be able to make them servants. At best, stabilization of All under Heaven, or, second to it, stabilization of a single state must come from these men. Hence a ruler who wants to attain great achievements and fame cannot but devote himself to searching for these men. A worthy sovereign works hard looking for [proper] men and rests maintaining affairs.[54]

This passage is plain and unsophisticated, as are many other similar ones scattered throughout the *Lüshi chunqiu*. First, it hails the high morality of the *shi*, who prefer righteousness to gains and even to life. Second, it hails their loftiness: the mere ruler of a state would be unable to befriend them and the Son of Heaven would fail to turn them into servants.[55] Then the authors go to the most important part of their message: they advise the ruler to acquire the services of these lofty *shi* as the one necessary precondition for overall success. With these servants, the ruler will rest—presumably because the worthy aides will maintain affairs in his stead.

Each of these topics—lauding the morality of the *shi* and their loftiness, as well as repeated advice that the ruler attract these possessors of the Way to his service—recur throughout the *Lüshi chunqiu*. There are no limits to the authors' pride in their social stratum, in its ideals and in its masters. The "Dang ran" 當 染 chapter, for instance, specifically praises the two most popular spiritual leaders of the *shi*: Confucius and Mozi:

> These two *shi* [that is, Confucius and Mozi] lacked ranks and positions to illuminate themselves among the people; they lacked awards and emoluments to benefit the people; but one who speaks of the most glorious under Heaven must refer to these two *shi*. They died long ago, but their followers are ever multiplying, their disciples are ever increasing, filling All under Heaven. Kings, lords, and grandees follow them and make them resplendent, sending beloved sons and younger brothers to learn from them; there has not been a moment that [such behavior] ceased.[56]

This praise for the two most outstanding early Zhanguo thinkers makes specific the idea of *shi* loftiness that we encountered in the writings of Mengzi and Xunzi. The moral superiority of Confucius and Mozi has allowed them to prosper posthumously despite their lacking ranks and emoluments in their lives; their fame dwarfs that of kings and lords; and the true social hierarchy is indeed that in which the possessors of the True Way occupy the supreme position:

> *Shi* who possess the Way can really be haughty toward the sovereign, while inept sovereigns are also haughty toward the *shi* who possess the Way. If every day they behave haughtily toward each other, how will they attain each other? . . . A worthy sovereign should behave differently: although a *shi* behaves haughtily, he should treat him ever more politely; how then will a *shi* be able not to come to him? One to whom the *shi* come, All under Heaven follows him, he becomes a Thearch. The Thearch (*ttek-s) is he who is called upon (*s-tek) by All under Heaven. A monarch (*wang) is he who is gone (*wang-q) to by All under Heaven.[57]

This statement reflects one of the peaks of *shi* pride: their spokesmen proclaim that a *shi* has the right to behave haughtily toward the sovereign, while the ruler should not behave in a similar fashion, but on the contrary, he should continue to treat his advisor "who possesses the Way" all the more politely! This proclamation may be considered a logical outgrowth of the statements from Mengzi, Zhuangzi, and Xunzi that are cited above: if a *shi* surpasses the ruler in morality and ability, why, then, should not the sovereign treat the *shi* as a superior? But behind the façade of self-praise and immeasurable pride, we can discern a different subtext. The authors' anxious remark: "[H]ow will they [the ruler and a *shi*] attain each other?" is indicative of their hope for appointment at court. Just as in an anecdote of Yan Chu, the proud stance is meant primarily to enhance the value of the *shi* in the rulers' market, and the insistence on independence and autonomy cloaks a desire to attain a good position in the ruler's service.

The intrinsic link between the infinite pride and the search for employment is characteristic of the *Lüshi chunqiu*. It sheds a new light on the repeated proclamations of the *shi* loftiness throughout the text. Can they not all be read as a veiled bargaining for a better position? And if the answer is positive, how does this reflect on the entire *shi*-centered discourse surveyed in this chapter? How does the quest for autonomy mesh with the desire for a court career? Is the relentless search for employment peculiar to the *Lüshi chunqiu* authors, or does it reflect—as do most topoi of this compendium—a kind of an intellectual consensus on the eve of the imperial unification? These questions are the focus of the next chapter, at the end of which we shall return to the issue of the intellectual autonomy of the *shi* and its limitations.

CHAPTER 6

To Serve or Not to Serve

We have seen that the increasing self-confidence of Zhanguo *shi* was intrinsically linked to their rise to the top of the government apparatus. But how much were the *shi* dependent on this apparatus? As a departure point for our discussion we may take two Mengzi's statements. On the one hand, he claimed: "[F]or a *shi* to lose his position is like for the regional lord to lose his state," and "[S]ervice (*shi* 仕) for a *shi* is like tilling for a peasant,"[1] thus identifying a government career as the only appropriate mode of existence for the *shi*. On the other hand, Mengzi also stated: "The superior man has three joys, and ruling All under Heaven is not among them,"[2] implying that even the best of careers—ruling the world—is not the true peak of a superior man's aspirations. How are these statements related to each other? To what extent do they reflect *shi* attitudes toward government service? To answer these questions I shall first address the socioeconomic background of *shi* relations with the government and then survey various approaches toward that service, covering the entire spectrum of attitudes, from shameless career-seekers to proud recluses who disdained any involvement with filthy power-holders. I hope to show that behind the variety of conflicting approaches, we may discern a common thread of the imperative to political involvement, which decisively shaped the career patterns of the Zhanguo *shi*, and, to a significant extent, of their descendants—the imperial literati.

Shi and the State: Socioeconomic Background

For many scholars the linkage between the *shi* and government service seems axiomatic. Not only is it suggested by the semantic closeness of the terms *shi* 士 and "to serve" (*shi* 仕, which is frequently interchangeable with another *shi* 事, meaning [government] affairs), but it is supported also by the earliest textual references to *shi* careers. In the Chunqiu period, *shi* lacked independent sources of wealth, such as hereditary allotments, and had to support themselves by serving their superiors. The *shi* personages who are mentioned in the *Zuo zhuan* invariably appear as either petty officials or, more frequently, as the "household servants" (*jia chen* 家臣) of major aristocratic lineages, for whom they performed administrative, ritual, and military tasks. If some early *shi* made their living in ways other than serving the regional lords and the nobles, they remain unknown to us.

The employment patterns of the Zhanguo *shi* are more complex and heterogeneous than those of their Chunqiu predecessors. Especially in the late Zhanguo period, when several states, such as Qin, established new recruitment procedures in which military merit or cash payments could be traded for rank and even for positions in the administration, the social boundaries of the *shi* stratum became blurred. Contemporary texts mention *shi* both in a same compound with nobles (*dafu* 大夫) and with commoners (*shu min* 庶民), which clearly reflects the social fluidity of the *shi*. Inevitably, this expanding stratum comprised people who did not uniformly pursue official careers. While many *shi* were eventually incorporated into the expanding state administration, others were engaged in different activities, becoming, for instance, specialists in technical and occult matters (physicians, diviners, magicians). Some sources mention *shi* who were craftsmen, merchants, and even farmers. Other *shi* sought the patronage of rulers and powerful courtiers, becoming their retainers (literally, "guests," *binke* 賓客); among this group we meet the "assassin-retainers" whose biographies were eventually collected by Sima Qian.[3]

Having observed the diverse employment patterns of the Zhanguo *shi*, we now turn to the intellectually active members of this stratum and ask whether new employment opportunities diminished the importance of service in determining their livelihoods. The clearest affirmative answer is proposed by Mark Lewis. In his seminal *Writing and Authority in Early China*, Lewis argues that Zhanguo "schoolmen" (he refrains from using the term *shi*) were economically independent of the state and could make their living not only as administrators but as teachers, technical/occult masters, or retainers of a powerful patron. This economic independence was, according to Lewis, essential to the ensuing intellectual autonomy of the *shi* Masters and their disciples, which allowed the emergence of a "permanent and inevitable opposition" between these Masters and the state.[4]

There are many laudable aspects in Lewis's analysis, which is superior to earlier simplistic identifications of the *shi* as mere administrators, but Lewis goes too far in the opposite direction of dissociating the *shi* and the state. Probably my disagreement with him has something to do with definitions of both "schoolmen" and "state." As for the first, there is no evidence for a separate social stratum of "schoolmen" in the Zhanguo age: masters and disciples alike identified themselves as *shi*, and their career pattern should be analyzed within this broader social context. Second, the "state," *pace* Lewis, is not necessarily identical with the reigning regime and even less so with the administrative machine run by this regime. Lewis considers any employment of a "schoolman" that is not administrative (that is, employment as a ruler's personal advisor or a "guest") as "independent of the state," and any criticism of the current political situation as being an anti-state stance.[5] This perspective, I believe, is misleading. Insofar as we speak of the state in its broader meaning, as the ruler-centered system of political power, the notion of the "schoolmen's" independence largely evaporates.

Scholars and other *shi* who were patronized by a ruler or by a powerful courtier may have been independent of an individual court, for they could shift their allegiances to a different one (see Chapter 7), but they were not independent of the system of power relations that I call "the state." Not only was the ruler's patronage a direct extension of his power as the de jure owner of the state, but even the so-called private courts, famous for their support of *shi*, were largely entangled in the state-ordered web of power. Such famous patrons of the *shi* as Tian Wen (田文, a.k.a. Lord Mengchang 孟嘗君, d. 279), Huang Xie (黃歇, Lord Chunshen 春申君, d. 238), and Lü Buwei were at times in opposition to their king, but they were not "independent." Their power, wealth, their very ability to attract *shi* derived primarily from their proximity to the court, either as members of the royal lineage or as high executives; serving such people was very much "serving the state" insofar as we mean an individual's involvement with political power.[6]

But putting patronage aside, let us focus on other possibilities as to how a *shi* could make his living outside the state service. One activity, raised by Lewis, was as a teacher. While I shall not deal here with a position of a village teacher, as few if any would argue that the income or status from this job were compatible with those of officials, another possibility, making a living as a "schoolmen's" master, deserves greater attention. Lewis argues that as schoolmen paid a kind of tuition fee, this could provide the master with living expenses, thus ensuring his economic independence. This observation, based largely on anecdotal data about Confucius and his disciples, may be correct, but it does not provide the full picture. Which disciples were rich enough to support their master? How substantial was their support? What was their source of income? All these questions bring us back to the issue of wealth and political power in the Zhanguo world.

In traditional China the two major sources of individual enrichment aside from a political career were land accumulation and trade or trade-related industrial activities, such as salt and iron production. For the first of the two, the situation in the Zhanguo period differed markedly from that of imperial China. While scholars continuously debate the origins of private landownership, it is clear that even if it emerged in the pre-imperial period, its social and economic impact at that time was marginal. Liu Zehua has noted with great insight that while transfers of land were common in pre-imperial China, there is no evidence of a land market in that period; lands were either grabbed, or exchanged, or granted by the ruler to his meritorious servants, and they could be alienated at any moment. Insofar as large plots of land are concerned, the evidence overwhelmingly suggests that their possession was intrinsically linked to an owner's position within the state-approved social hierarchy. No wealthy landowner beyond the fringes of this hierarchy is known, and it may be plausibly assumed that this stratum as a whole emerged independent of the state only during the early Han period.[7] Thus we will only search in vain for private landowners among the *shi* or among their patrons and supporters.

An alternative, and more prominent, method of private wealth accumulation was to engage in trade and related industrial activities. Biographies of wealthy merchants, gathered by Sima Qian, as well as scattered references in other texts, indicate that the burgeoning economies of the Warring States allowed certain individuals to make huge fortunes. It is notoriously difficult, however, to deduce from these anecdotes more about socioeconomical position of merchants as a whole in Zhanguo society. As both texts and epigraphic evidence clearly suggest that the state was actively intervening in commercial and industrial activities, it is unlikely that an independent stratum of wealthy merchants with a distinctive "class consciousness" could have emerged then. It is even less likely that merchants as a group were engaged in patronage of high-minded *shi*, and in any case, there is no evidence of this.[8]

If there were no substantial sources of income independent of the state, then it is clear that most patrons and disciples of the masters had to be involved in the state-sponsored power relations web and that the masters' independence of the state was largely illusory. The degree of their economic dependence is further indicated by the stories of the immense poverty of those *shi* left outside state service and the patronage system. These *shi* reportedly "ate neither in the morning, nor in the evening, starving to the point of being unable to exit the gate," lived "in an impoverished lane in a leaking house," lacked enough clothes and food, and were reduced to the most miserable existence.[9] Poverty was so much associated with the lack of a government post that by itself it became a kind of hallmark of true *shi,* who proudly called themselves "plain-clothed" (*buyi* 布衣), a term firmly associated with low income.[10] Thus while the existence of non-state career patterns for *shi* is undeniable, their impact on the basic sustenance of the *shi* should not be exaggerated.

Our discussion of the economic attractiveness of a government position in comparison with other activities can be usefully ended with an anecdote about

Lü Buwei, a wealthy merchant who made an astute investment by supporting the future King Zhuangxiang of Qin (秦莊襄王, 249–247) when the latter was still a hostage prince held at the capital of Qin's rival, Zhao:

> A man of Puyang, Lü Buwei, traded in Handan. He observed that a prince-hostage from Qin differed from other people, and returning home told his father:
>   "How much can you gain from tilling the soil?"
>   [The father] answered: "Tenfold [profit]."
>   "And what is the gain from pearls and jade?"
>   [The father] answered: "Hundredfold."
>   "And what is the gain from installing a ruler of the state?"
>   [The father] answered: "Immeasurable."
>   Lü Buwei said: "Now, you painfully exert your force in the fields and do not get even warm clothes and extra food, but by establishing the ruler of a state, blessings can be bequeathed to future generations. I intend to go and serve him [a Qin hostage]."[11]

Anecdotal though it is, the story is indicative of the relatively low esteem of agricultural and commercial activities in comparison with a political career. Lü Buwei's "investment" and his eventual success were extraordinary, and we are in no position to estimate whether if an average *shi* shifted from commerce to politics it would be as profitable. But the evidence suggests that this would be a wise choice. Han Feizi mentions: "When the district governor dies, his descendants for generations go on riding in carriages; hence the people respect this position."[12] At least in comparison with agriculture, which, according to Lü Buwei, did not suffice to ensure "warm clothes and extra food," the advantages of holding office are clear.

Aside from the economic impetus to serve, status considerations were an equally powerful factor in attracting *shi* to government office. The office was the source not only of a stable income, but also of high prestige. Entering service meant receiving a rank in the state hierarchy; and this in turn entitled a person to a series of sumptuary privileges that encompassed many spheres of life, from mortuary arrangements to garments, dwelling, and even food. While details of the Zhanguo rank systems and the related sumptuary privileges cannot be clarified at present, there can be no doubt that office and rank meant a lot in that society.[13] Moreover, government service could bring fame/name (*ming*) to a *shi*, and while the desire for fame as a guiding force for one's action is unquantifiable, its strong impact on Zhanguo career patterns is suggested by endless references in almost every received text to name-seeking.

Riches and Fame: Career-Seekers

It is not surprising that many, probably most, Zhanguo *shi* sought careers primarily for economic and social reasons. This motivation is well attested in contemporary texts. Mozi, for instance, had very practical recommendations to the ruler who wanted to attract the best *shi*:

> So, what is the method of multiplying the worthies? Master Mozi says: "If, for instance, you want to multiply in your state the *shi* who are good archers and chariot-drivers, you must enrich them, honor them, respect them, and praise them—then it will be possible to attain and multiply in the state those *shi* who are good at archery and chariot-driving. How much more should this be done with respect to the worthy and good *shi* who abound in virtuous conduct, are well versed in speaking, and are well versed in methods of the Way: they are the treasure of the state and the assistants to the altars of soil and grain. They must also be enriched, honored, respected, and praised: then it will be possible to attain and multiply in the state worthy and good *shi*.[14]

Mozi's suggestions are simple: like other specialists in different fields, "worthy and good *shi*" are interested in praise and emoluments, and to attract them the ruler should generously subsidize them. Strikingly, despite their advertised abilities, *shi* appear here as uniformly motivated by a quest for riches and fame. Mozi may have been aware that his views demean the worthies' motives, but probably he considered the policy of "enriching, honoring, respecting, and praising" as too efficient to be abandoned for the sake of the *shi* image. Elsewhere, however, he felt compelled to qualify his views:

> Thus in antiquity when the sage kings exercised their rule, they arranged [the subjects according to their] virtue and elevated the worthy. Even if a person was a peasant or an artisan, they commissioned him a high rank, increased his emoluments, assigned him [important] tasks, and empowered his orders, saying: "If the rank and the position are not high, the people will not respect him; if emoluments are not generous, the people will not trust him; if his administrative orders are not decisive, the people will not be in awe of him." They delivered these three to the worthies not as a prize to the worthies, but because they wished the affairs to be completed.[15]

Mozi supplies here a more sophisticated justification for enriching and empowering *shi*: these measures are needed not just to attract the worthies but also to clarify to the general populace that these persons of humble origin are really entitled to lead the people. Plausible as it is, this justification does not deny personal interest of the *shi* in riches and ranks; rather it provides an additional reason to satisfy their desires. This sober estimate of *shi* inclinations is certainly not exceptional to Mozi. It was generally shared by the major *genii* of Zhanguo administrative thought, such as Shang Yang, Shen Buhai, Han Feizi, and the authors of several *Guanzi* chapters. The very emphasis of these thinkers on the overall importance of rewards and punishments as two major "levers" of government was based on their belief that the *shi*, just like the general populace, are motivated primarily by self-interest. Many Zhanguo thinkers and statesmen took for granted that the *shi* were as greedy as any "petty man." This understanding could occasionally become a useful political asset, as is evident from the following *Zhanguo ce* anecdote:

> The *shi* of All under Heaven joined in a vertical alliance,[16] meeting in Zhao to attack Qin. Lord of Ying, the Qin chancellor, said: "There is nothing to worry about. Today I beg to undo [their plans]. The *shi* of All under Heaven do not resent Qin, they just seek riches and honor for themselves. My king, have you seen your dogs? Some are asleep, some are awake, some are walking, some are standing, and they do not fight each other. But if you throw them a bone, they will easily rise and bite each other: why?—because of their predisposition to fight.[17]

Fan Sui (范雎, d. 255), Lord of Ying 應侯, himself a prominent *shi* who rose to the supreme power in the court of Qin from initial obscurity,[18] spoke rudely of his fellow *shi,* but his rudeness did not appall either the king or the anecdote's authors. A verification added at the end of the anecdote hails Fan Sui's perspicacity: a bribe-bearing envoy he dispatched succeeded in dismantling the anti-Qin coalition. Putting aside the interesting—and rare—comparison of *shi* to hungry dogs, we may conclude that the basic estimate of the authors is identical to that of Mozi: *shi* "just seek riches and honor for themselves."

The *Zhanguo ce,* with its candor, is a precious repository of a frequently hidden side of the noble self-image of the *shi.* In addition to anecdotes that praise the high morality and loftiness of the *shi*, the collection also includes stories that disclose less frequently celebrated aspects of the Zhanguo intellectual atmosphere. Of particular interest are those stories that focus on the "peripatetic persuaders" (*you shui* 游說), the exceptionally active career-seekers, who traveled from one court to another in search of employment. The first in the series of anecdotes about the paragon of this group, Su Qin (蘇秦, d. 284), is revealing. It tells how at the beginning of his career, Su Qin arrived at the state of Qin, where he attempted to persuade King Hui (秦惠王, r. 337–311) to adopt a more assertive military policy with the aim "to annex the regional lords' [states], to swallow the world, to declare yourself Thearch, and to bring about orderly rule." Yet the king rejected the advice, refused to employ Su Qin, and left the latter in dire straits:

> Su Qin submitted over ten documents to the king of Qin, but his stratagems were not employed. His sable fur coat was worn out, one hundred catties of gold wasted completely, his provisions depleted; he left Qin and returned home. Skinny and exhausted, he dragged his feet, bearing his books in a bag on a shoulder pole. Haggard and fatigued, with black circles around his eyes, his appearance was that of disgrace. When he arrived home, his wife did not stop weaving, his sister-in-law did not cook for him, his parents did not talk to him. Su Qin sighed and said: "My wife does not consider me her husband, my sister-in-law does not consider me her brother-in-law, my parents do not consider me their son: all this is the fault of Qin."[19]

Determined to avenge his humiliation, Su Qin studied hard, working at night and keeping awake by pricking himself with an awl till blood came. He said to himself: "Is there a persuader who is unable to make the ruler part from his gold, jade, silk, and brocade, and receive the honors of high minister and chancellor?" And Su Qin did indeed succeed in attaining his goals. He became an architect of the anti-Qin alliance, achieving the highest position simultaneously in several states and acquiring fabulous riches. The authors of the anecdote praise him:

> Su Qin was after all a mere *shi* from poor circumstances, dwelling in a mud cave with mulberry branches and a bending lintel instead of a door. Yet leaning on the dashboard and holding the reins, he traveled across All under Heaven, spoke to kings and regional lords, and confounded their aides; nobody under Heaven was a match for him.[20]

The anecdote ends with a story of Su Qin's triumphal return home where his parents, wife, and sister-in-law treat him with the utmost respect and awe. Su Qin exclaims:

> Alas! When one is poor and humble, parents do not treat him as a son; when one is rich and noble, relatives are afraid of him. When a man lives in this world, how can he ignore the power of his rank and the affluence of his wealth?[21]

The historical veracity of this anecdote need not concern us here, nor shall we focus on its obvious self-contradictions (if Su Qin was so poor at the dawn of his career, where did he get the hundred catties of gold, a sable fur coat, and provisions to spend in Qin?). What is important is the moral lesson conveyed. For Su Qin, the content of the proposed policy matters very little: hence throughout most of his life he has struggled against the state that he wanted to benefit at the dawn of his career. Su Qin concerns himself with nothing but personal welfare. The authors praise this self-interest: this is the way of the world, they say; even family values pale in comparison with career considerations, and the aim of a *shi* is to attain glory and riches. Far from being scolded for his intellectual duplicity, Su Qin is hailed as a true model *shi*!

The candor of the *Zhanguo ce* surpasses most, if not all, contemporary texts, but the differences are often ones of degree rather than of content. The more moral-leaning *Lüshi chunqiu* echoes the *Zhanguo ce* in speaking of career, with its material pleasures, as the single noble goal of *shi* cultivation. Thus while encouraging diligent learning, its authors tell the following story:

> Ning Yue was a man from the outskirts of Zhongmou; he was bitter at the labor of tilling and sowing and said to his friend: "How can I escape this bitterness?" His friend replied: "The best is to learn. After learning for thirty years, you will fulfill [your goals]." Ning Yue said: "I pledge to make it within fifteen years. When others are to rest, I shall not dare to rest; when others are asleep, I shall not dare to sleep." He learned for fifteen years and became the teacher of Lord Wei of Zhou.[22]

Ning Yue 甯越, an important thinker from the early Zhanguo period,[23] began his career just to avoid the hard and unrewarding toil of a peasant, but this motive is not considered shameful by the *Lüshi chunqiu* authors, in whose eyes the only exceptional feature of Ning Yue's conduct is his diligence and ultimate success. Career aspirations for the sake of riches and glory were legitimate, and even normative—at least for some Zhanguo *shi*.

The importance of these anecdotes cannot be underestimated. The sinister motives of the respected *shi* that are presented here with the utmost clarity are sure to have been just the tip of the iceberg. Since public figures usually prefer to disguise their personal interests behind a façade of noble intentions, few are expected to be as candid as Su Qin or Ning Yue; but many doubtless follow their path however little they may reflect on it. The outspokenness of the *Zhanguo ce* and similar texts suggests that egoistic office-seeking was not only fairly widespread, but was gaining intellectual legitimacy. In this context, we may assess more properly the challenges faced by those thinkers like Confucius and his followers who sought to ennoble *shi* interests with moral imperatives and the preservation of personal integrity.

Service as a Mission: Confucius and Mengzi

Confucius, the earliest known intellectual leader of the *shi*, is also the person who shaped decisively their approach to holding office. While endorsing the quest for office, which was essential for *shi* livelihood, he imbued it with a novel meaning, that of a noble moral mission, an essential part of one's attachment to the Way. Confucius clarifies:

> Riches and honors are what every man desires; but if they cannot be attained in accordance with the Way, do not accept them. Poverty and base status are what every man detests. But if they cannot be avoided in accordance with the Way, do not avoid them.[24]

In Confucius's eyes, service has economic, social, and moral aspects. The quest for riches and honor, which is associated with holding the office, is entirely legitimate and acceptable, but it should be subordinate to the moral imperatives of the Way. Insofar as one can satisfy personal interests while behaving morally, this is fine; but if the two goals are unattainable simultaneously, morality should prevail. This statement, radically echoed by Mengzi, who claimed that he would "choose righteousness at the expense of life,"[25] may be considered the quintessence of the "Confucian" approach with regard to the moral dilemmas of political service.

It is well known that Confucius considered the Way, "hearing of which in the morning, one can [without regret] die in the evening," as the highest moral criterion for a superior man's action and that this adherence to the Way often led him into conflicts with power-holders.[26] It is less frequently noted, however, that adherence to the Way was intrinsically linked to service, which was instrumental in realizing the thinker's goals. Confucius promised: "[O]ne who would employ me will attain results within a year, and [the tasks] will be completed within three years," and he was willing to serve even politically dubious figures insofar as this could allow revival of the "Zhou in the east"; his disciples echoed his hopes.[27] To realize his intentions, Confucius wandered throughout the Zhou world in search for appropriate appointment. He was anxious that his name would not be remembered when he passed away, and once he confessed that he was waiting for a good price to "sell his beautiful gem"—his talents.[28] He similarly directed his disciples toward office-holding, and discussions about proper behavior while serving a lord occupy significant portion of the dialogues in the *Lunyu*.[29] Furthermore, Confucius identified "bringing peace to the hundred clans" as the ultimate goal of self-cultivation, and this goal was unattainable outside government service.[30] Zixia (子夏, 507–?), one of the leading disciples, summarized the Master's message: "When serving, if you have extra force, go and learn; when learning, if you have extra force, go and serve."[31]

Confucius's interpretation of political action as a vehicle for obtaining moral goals had two profound impacts on *shi* behavior. On the one hand, it generated a moral commitment to serve, further strengthening the *shi* attachment to the state. On the other hand, the Master decisively distanced himself and his followers from shameless career-seekers, whom he viewed with explicit contempt.[32] This, in turn, created the problem of distinguishing between a "superior man," for whom political service was an act of moral self-realization, and an unscrupulous "petty man" (*xiao ren* 小人), who dreamt only of riches and glory. To avoid any suspicions about his integrity, a superior man had to scrutinize his deeds while at court and to resign whenever he felt that his service was no longer consistent with the Way. Confucius himself set an example for the future lofty *shi* by repeatedly resigning from courts where he had earlier sought a position, creating an almost endless chain of appointments and resignations (or of unfulfilled appointments). Confucius's ultimate failure to realize himself may explain certain tragic notes in the *Lunyu* and his lamentations about being "unrecognized."[33]

The conflict between finding an appropriate government position and compromising one's ideal by serving unworthy rulers became a source of immense tension, which permeates the thought of Confucius and his followers. There was no (and probably could not be) easy resolution of this conflict; no strict rules of "do" and "do not" could be applicable to the ever-changing political situation. Confucius sounds frustrated at times; sometimes he hints at self-cultivation as almost a self-contained goal that should not necessarily be linked to the government career; a superior man may enjoy learning for the sake of learning.[34] This notion of potential self-realization outside the government eventually gave rise to a powerful tide of refusals to serve, which we shall survey below; but Confucius himself never supported such a radical interpretation of his reservations. For him, resignations were always temporary; and learning and training, while pleasant by themselves, were not the goal but a means to influence a larger world. Hence in the final account Confucius strongly urges his disciples to serve—but only when the conditions allow:

> Xian asked about shame. The Master answered: "When the Way prevails in the state, eat its grains [that is, serve]; when the state lacks the Way, to eat its grains is shameful."[35]

The Master said . . . Qu Boyu was a superior man. When the Way prevailed in the state, he served; when it lacked the Way, he could roll up [his principles] and keep them near to his heart.[36]

The Master said: "Be sincere, trustworthy, and love learning; follow the good Way unto death. Do not enter the imperiled state; do not dwell in a calamitous state. When the Way prevails under Heaven, show yourself; when there is no Way, hide yourself. When the Way prevails in the state, it is shameful to be poor and base there; when the state lacks the Way, it is shameful to be rich and noble there."[37]

All the three statements have much in common. Each suggests that an individual's acceptance or rejection of the office should be determined by external circumstances, namely, by the state's adherence to the Way. Insofar as the Way prevails, to hold an office is not only acceptable but is mandatory: being base and poor in such conditions is shameful. But it is equally shameful to serve when the state lacks the Way: in these conditions a *shi* should either travel to another location or "keep his principles close to his heart." A superior man who follows Confucius's advice should behave flexibly, constantly adapting himself to changing circumstances and never forgetting the priority of moral ideals over other considerations. This art of adaptation, the knowledge of when to retreat and when to advance, became the hallmark of Confucius's thought, causing Mengzi to praise Confucius as the most "timely" of all sages.[38]

Mengzi, with whose contradictory statements we opened this chapter, not only inherited the complex legacy of Confucius but elaborated it, creating probably the most sophisticated theory of office-holding in Chinese intellectual history. Mengzi proclaims that Confucius is his model,[39] and indeed the career patterns of both thinkers were quite similar. Like his paragon, Mengzi traveled throughout the Zhou world seeking an appointment; at times he was successful enough to serve at the court of Qi, one of the most powerful states of his time. Armed with an unwavering belief in the supremacy of his moral mission, Mengzi relentlessly preached to power-holders and to fellow *shi,* hoping to bring about establishment of the moral Way. However, Mengzi's enthusiasm notwithstanding, the thinker also repeatedly had to resign from his positions, leaving those courts where he had previously tried to promote his moral vision. This inherent contradiction between pursuing employment and later retreating from it fueled repeated discussions between Mengzi, his disciples, and his opponents, in the course of which Mengzi outlined some of his basic premises regarding the holding of office:

Chenzi asked: "Under what conditions did the superior men of old times serve?"

Mengzi replied: "Three [conditions] caused them to approach [the ruler] and three to abandon him. If [the ruler] welcomed them with the utmost respect and ritual politeness, saying that he was going to implement their words, they approached him. When polite appearances were still kept, but the words were not implemented, they left him. Second, even if he was not going to implement their words, but welcomed them with the utmost respect and ritual politeness, they approached him; when polite appearances faded, they left him. When they ate neither in the morning nor in the evening, starving so as to be unable to leave their compound, and the ruler, hearing this, said: "At large, I am unable to implement their Way and am also unable to follow their words, but if I let them die of starvation in my lands, it will be shameful to me," sending them provisions, they accepted them, just to avoid death.[40]

The three reasons to hold an office outlined by Mengzi may serve as a useful guide for his own behavior. Ideally, a superior man should serve the ruler in order to implement his Way, but if this is not immediately possible, one can stay in the vicinity of the ruler in exchange for the latter's respect and politeness. Finally, if he is in desperate economic condition, a superior man may accept the ruler's financial support as a matter of survival. What is remarkable, however, is that while discussing the conditions to serve, Mengzi felt it necessary to outline immediately the conditions for resignation. The proximity of the two is ominous; after Confucius, the ability to resign was considered, no less than the ability to serve, as a hallmark of the superior man.

Mengzi's discussions of service-related issues with his disciples reflect an immense tension between the moral commitment to serve and the fear of resembling shameless career-seekers. Two questions haunt Mengzi: when to serve and when to resign. Mengzi does his best to outline a proper course of action for a *shi*, but eventually he admits that there can be no single correct course; a number of equally legitimate possibilities exist. Mengzi describes these possibilities with the help of historical examples of the past sages. Boyi 伯夷, a proud recluse, refused to serve unworthy rulers and compromise his integrity. On the opposite side, however, we find Liuxia Hui 柳下惠, who would humbly accept any office, and Yi Yin 伊尹, an advisor to King Tang, the founder of the Shang dynasty, who, pitying the common folk deprived of worthy rule, "undertook the heaviest task of All under Heaven," endlessly seeking office to fulfill his duty.

Mengzi considers each of these sages worthy of emulation, although he is slightly critical of Boyi's extreme purity and of Liuxia Hui's apparent lack of self-respect. However, his true hero is Confucius, one who knew "when to hurry, and when to wait, when to stay and when to serve"—a person who combined the advantages of earlier sages, surpassing them all.[41] Confucius, as Mengzi explains, was so deeply attached to government service that after three months without an office he had to be consoled, and yet he repeatedly resigned. Mengzi explains the reasons behind the Master's resignations and behind his own reluctance to serve: "The ancients always desired to serve but hated to do it not in accordance with their Way. To approach [the ruler] not in accordance with the Way is like 'cutting holes' [for men and women to meet each other secretly instead of becoming properly engaged]."[42]

Going back to the three conditions of service outlined in Mengzi's answer to Chenzi, we may notice the importance of economic factors. Unlike Confucius, who claims that "a superior man thinks of the Way and not of food,"[43] Mengzi recognizes the material dependence of the *shi* on a ruler. This recognition, as well as Mengzi's willingness to accept the rulers' patronage, at times angered his more purist supporters, causing him to explain the rules of economic intercourse with the ruler. Mengzi argues that insofar as accepting the gifts does not compromise the thinker's integrity and sense of self-respect, it is tolerable. If one is serving out of economic despair, one should accept only minor positions; richer gifts and general patronage are acceptable only when the ruler and a thinker "share the same Way" (in which case even accepting All under Heaven, as Shun received from Yao, would not be considered exorbitant).[44]

While the purists attacked Mengzi's recognition of the economic dependence of the *shi* and his willingness to receive the rulers' support, others criticized Mengzi's extreme gestures of protest against those rulers whose treatment was insufficiently polite in his eyes. As this topic was discussed in Chapter 5, I prefer to focus on the last of Mengzi's imperatives: to serve the ruler provided he promises to implement the thinker's Way, or, more precisely, the Way of benevolence (*ren* 仁) and righteousness (*yi* 義). Mengzi personally hoped to attain precisely this kind of relationship with the lords and conversed with them at length in an attempt to "rectify" their hearts. These attempts, however, proved to be as futile as those of Confucius. Mengzi's wanderings across the Zhou world always ended with resignations: he left the court of King Xiang of Wei, whom he thought lacked the aura of a ruler, and that of King Xuan of Qi, after the king ignored his advice.[45] After resignation from Qi, where the thinker held probably the most significant position in his life, Mengzi exclaimed in despair:

Once in five hundred years, a True Monarch is certain to arise; while in the interim there certainly will be some who determine the destiny of the generation.[46] From the [establishment of the] Zhou, there have been already seven centuries; judging from this count, the [expected coming of the Monarch] has already passed; but if we analyze the timely [conditions], it is still possible. Yet Heaven does not want to order All under Heaven; should it want to order All under Heaven, who will cast me aside in our generation?[47]

Speaking from the depth of his heart Mengzi reveals his belief in the messianic potential of the soon-to-come True Monarch and of his surrogate, the one who is able "to determine the generation's destiny," that is, Mengzi himself. The ultimate fiasco of the thinker's efforts was therefore painful not only economically, but morally, as it crushed his lifetime aspirations, and possibly religiously, insofar as Mengzi truly hoped for Heaven's help. It is probably against this background that Mengzi began uttering such notes of despair as his surprising statement, cited at the beginning of this chapter, that ruling All under Heaven is not one of the joys of the superior man. Elsewhere, Mengzi states:

> He who fully realizes his heart, can comprehend his [inborn] nature, he who comprehends [his] nature, can comprehend Heaven. Preserve your heart and nourish your nature to serve Heaven thereby. Unwavering whether facing a short or lengthy life, rectify yourself and await [the decreed end]: thus you will establish your destiny.[48]

Mengzi further exclaims: "The myriad things are within me. I turn toward myself and [attain] integrity. There is no joy greater than that."[49]

These sayings exemplify a crucial "turning inward" in Mengzi's thought. Leaving aside for the time being its philosophical significance, let us focus on its political implications. If a thinker who has dedicated most of his life to wandering among the competing courts and persuading the rulers and their aides suddenly declares that he will just "preserve his heart/mind and nourish his nature," enjoying mostly "turning toward oneself," does it mean that he has abandoned his political aspirations? Does it mean that the attainment of internal completeness, or integrity (*cheng* 誠), is equal to bringing peace and orderly rule to All under Heaven? Did Mengzi lose hope in the possibility of changing the world and turn instead toward changing the self?

The notion of despair that is observable in these passages of the *Mengzi*, just as in those of the *Lunyu* mentioned above, became one of the characteristics of the lofty *shi*. Not all of them arrived at the conclusion that maintaining one's integrity was indeed the greatest joy; but it was a widespread conviction that when facing unfavorable times, a *shi* must concentrate on cultivating the self, awaiting a turn for the better in his destiny. The terms "destiny" (*ming* 命), "times" (*shi* 時), and "encountering" (the opportunity, that is, to serve the enlightened monarch, *yu* 遇) became ubiquitous in *shi* texts and later were firmly incorporated into the literary works of the imperial literati.[50] The entire notion of self-cultivation gradually became linked with the expectation of a predestined meeting with a clear-sighted sovereign, who would recognize one's worth. A short text unearthed in Guodian, *Qiong da yi shi* (窮達以時, Failure and success depend on the times),[51] summarizes these feelings:

> There is Heaven, there is man; Heaven and man differ. Investigating differences between Heaven and Man, we know how to act. If he is an appropriate man, but the times are not appropriate, then even if he is worthy, he will not be able to act. But if he attained his age, what difficulties would face him? Shun cultivated land at Mt. Li, made pottery on the [Yellow] River's banks, and then rose to become the Son of Heaven—this is because he encountered Yao. . . .[52]

Clarifying from the beginning that human ability to act in the world is determined by an external force, Heaven, the text provides historical examples that prove this observation. Shun's example is paradigmatic: a farmer and pottery maker turns into the Son of Heaven due to the grace of meeting Yao. This is indeed the pattern: the text sketches the careers of once obscure, poor *shi*, whose good destiny brought them to the attention of enlightened sovereigns, which propelled them to the top of political power. In contrast, those who were not predestined to prosper met a cruel fate, as, for example, did Wu Zixu (伍子胥, d. 484), an advisor of King Fuchai of Wu (吳王夫差, r. 495–473), whose loyalty remained unrecognized and who was ordered to commit suicide. A *shi*, whatever his abilities, cannot determine success or failure of his lifelong mission: this depends on external, Heavenly, forces:

> To encounter or not to encounter—this is determined by Heaven. One acts not for the sake of success, hence in failure one is not resentful. One studies not for the sake of name, hence nobody knows one, but one is not regretful. . . . Failure and success depend on the times; obscurity and clarity will not recur; hence the superior man is sincere in turning toward himself.[53]

The authors' message is clear: one cannot determine one's own success or failure, but one should continuously cultivate oneself in hopes of having the opportunity. Self-cultivation is intrinsic to the superior man and should not depend on external circumstances. "Turning toward oneself" becomes a temporary solution for the frustrating situation in which a *shi* cannot realize his aspirations due to adverse "times."[54]

Eloquent as it is, the proposal to "turn toward oneself" does not appear as a convincing resolution of the tension between the high aspirations of the *shi* and gloomy reality. The authors' focus on the careers of former paragon ministers discloses their deep attachment to political service and their frustration that adverse circumstances do not allow the *shi* to realize their aspirations. The attraction of the government career appears in the *Qiong da yi shi* and in similar texts as too powerful to overcome through mere invocation of the notion of self-cultivation. Being simultaneously committed to government service as a means of moral self-realization and distracted from it out of fear of compromising one's ideals, the lofty *shi* continued to suffer from a sense of frustration for generations to come.

Abandoning Office: A Recluse Ideal

Thus far we have focused on two groups of *shi*: shameless career-seekers, and lofty moralists who considered career as a means of self-fulfillment. Both groups shared deep commitment to the government service, although the moralists' desire to subordinate this service to higher goals created immense tension in their relations with power-holders. Yet in the immensely rich intellectual landscape of the Warring States, there was a third group: those *shi* who were so appalled by unworthy courts and benighted sovereigns that they pondered the idea of complete disengagement from the political career. This mood gave rise to the phenomenon of reclusion, which came to have a paramount impact on Chinese political tradition.

The phenomenon of reclusion, or, more precisely, of refusal to hold government office, has been extensively discussed in several recent important studies, among which that of Aat Vervoorn is especially valuable for analyzing the pre-imperial antecedents of this phenomenon.[55] I shall try to avoid insofar as possible repeating Vervoorn's insights, focusing instead on a single question: how can the idea of reclusion be related to the general commitment to office-seeking, whether for egoistic or idealistic reasons, depicted above? More precisely, did "reclusion" (or "eremitism" in Vervoorn's terminology) pose an alternative to the political-oriented career pattern, or was it a part of this pattern?

To answer this, it may be useful to distinguish between two major types of "disengagement."[56] One form was promulgated by those *shi* who were inspired by Confucius's ideals of prioritizing the Way over service; this led to a retreat from government service as a form of protest against power-holders. In this case "hiding" in the world was a temporary measure, since if the Way should prevail, the "hidden hero" would reappear. An alternative approach was that of thinkers like Zhuangzi, who rejected government service in toto as an undeserving way of life. This rejectionist view is particularly interesting for our discussion, for it contains the most significant protest against dependence on the state.

The first type of disengagement is conceptually indistinguishable from that of moral resignation. Since a superior man was supposed to resign in order to prove his integrity, it was expected that some would give up the idea of finding an appropriate employee, at least for the time being. While most thinkers were constantly moving across the Zhou world in search of an office, some concluded that the search was futile and that preservation of one's integrity demanded complete disengagement from the outside filthiness. For such rejectionists, Boyi and Shuqi 叔齊, a pair of upright brothers who refused to serve the righteous King Wu of Zhou out of protest against his overthrow of the legitimate sovereign, Zhouxin, became the model. Starving themselves to death, according to some of the versions of the legend, in order "not to eat the grains of Zhou," the brothers apparently manifested the extreme version of Confucius's dictum: "when the state lacks the Way, to eat its grains is shameful."[57] Mengzi admired Boyi, although he distanced himself from Boyi's extreme purism. However, it was not Mengzi, but rather some of his disciples who turned Boyi and men like him into a source of inspiration.

In Chapter 5 we noted a marked increase in *shi* self-confidence and pride between the lifetime of Confucius and that of Mengzi. This process was paralleled by an increasingly critical attitude toward political involvement among some of the lofty *shi*. Confucius's disciples, most explicitly Zilu, were at times critical of some of the Master's moves, but they never opposed the idea of engagement with rulers as such.[58] In Mengzi's case, he had to withstand radical criticism from those who considered the very willingness to accept a regional lord's patronage as compromising to a thinker's integrity. Wan Zhang, one of Mengzi's leading disciples, visibly irritated his master when he claimed that since all current lords were "robbers" (*yu* 禦), it was immoral to be engaged with them.[59] This was not just the view of one dissenting disciple. The increasing number of lofty *shi* became frustrated with endless futile travels among the courts, coming to the conclusion that serving *any* ruler in the current world was morally wrong. Disengagement from service was the only means of preserving one's integrity. Instead of seeking employment and then resigning, they advocated simply boycotting the courts!

The purist total rejection of political involvement was an outgrowth of Confucius's dictum to give the Way priority over office, but it challenged another dictum, that of implementing the Way in the social realm. This explains the complex attitude of the more "orthodox" of Confucius's followers toward the purists, as is clear from the following dialogue in the *Mengzi.*

> Kuang Zhang said: "Is not Chen Zhongzi a truly upright *shi?* He lived in Wuling, having nothing to eat for three days; his ears lost hearing, eyes lost eyesight. There was a plum near the well, half-eaten by insects; he crawled to eat it, and it was only after swallowing three pieces that his ears regained hearing and eyes eyesight."
>
> Mengzi said: "Among the *shi* in the state of Qi, I would raise a thumb for Zhongzi. Nonetheless, can one call Zhongzi truly upright? To live like Zhongzi is possible only if one were an earthworm. An earthworm eats dry soil above, drinks from the yellow springs below. As for Zhongzi, was his house built by Boyi or was it built by Robber Zhi? Was the grain he ate sown by Boyi or by Robber Zhi? This is impossible to know."[60]

Mengzi's reply, and his further criticism of Zhongzi's insufficiently filial behavior, shows his uneasiness when confronted with the position of extreme morality. Chen Zhongzi 陳仲子, a member of the Qi ruling lineage, opposed the unjust emoluments of his elder brother and refused to enjoy them himself, making living instead by weaving sandals together with his wife. His purity was indisputable, but in Mengzi's eyes he went too far. In the world of human beings complete purity is unattainable, for the very nature of economic intercourse brings everybody into contact with people whose decency is unverifiable. In this situation insistence à la Boyi on not eating the "contaminated" grains of unjust rulers is simply not feasible.[61] But we should notice also that Mengzi's criticism of Chen Zhongzi is incomparably milder than his diatribes against those contemporary politicians who profane moral principles for the sake of power, wealth, and status; nor can it be compared with Xunzi's harsh criticism of Chen as a "robber" who undeservedly "stole" a good name.[62]

The radicalism of the purists who quit government careers annoyed Mengzi (as it reportedly annoyed Confucius's disciples and later Xunzi),[63] but its impact on the overall pattern of *shi* relations with power-holders remained limited. Refusal to serve was just another method of protest, which did not differ conceptually from righteous resignations and did not challenge the principle of political involvement.[64] The real challenge came from another group of disengaging thinkers, those who questioned in principle the idea of self-fulfillment as government officials.

The origin of an anti-political trend in Zhanguo thought (which is sometimes, quite problematically, labeled as "Daoism") is a much disputed topic. While the traditional approach tends to trace this concept primarily to the

Laozi and the *Zhuangzi*, modern skeptical scholars have begun questioning this view, doubting in particular the traditional account of the early origins of the *Laozi*. Accordingly, they have introduced new figures into the history of "Daoist" or "individualist" thought, most notably Yang Zhu (楊朱, fourth century), whose position was inflated to such an extent that many Western scholars routinely employ the term "Yangism" to depict this thinker's putative legacy. It is not my intention here to join these polemics. While I assume that the dating of the *Laozi* precedes that of the *Zhuangzi* and that Yang Zhu's contribution to the history of Chinese thought is largely unverifiable, these matters are of limited importance to the following discussion. With regard to criticism of intellectuals' becoming politically involved, there is no doubt that the *Laozi* and *Zhuangzi*, no matter who wrote them, are the most important representatives of this trend among Zhanguo texts.[65]

The *Laozi*, which eventually became a master text for the opponents of political involvement, was not necessarily conceived as an anti-political treatise; on the contrary, as I argued in Chapter 2, it may be regarded as one of the earliest ruler-oriented texts in China's intellectual history. Nonetheless, at least two of the concepts of the *Laozi* were conducive to the idea of withdrawal from official service. First, the ideas of minimalism, spontaneity, and "effortless action" placed the *Laozi* markedly outside the common trend of fervently seeking an appointment—either for personal and ideological matters. Instead of traveling among the courts in search for an office, it advised attaining power through the force of retreat:

> Rivers and seas can become kings of the hundred valleys because they excel in placing themselves beneath them; hence they are able to become kings of the hundred valleys. Hence when the sage wants to be above the people, he must speak about himself as being beneath them; when he wants to lead the people, he must place himself behind them. Thus the sage is located above, but the people do not consider him heavy, is placed at front and is not harmed; therefore All under Heaven endorse him and are not tired of him. Since he does not struggle, none under Heaven struggles with him.[66]

What the *Laozi* recommends here is certainly not withdrawal from the public life, but just a distinct way to achieve one's goals: pretending to be humble and noncontesting, the sage will attain power with ease where his rivals have failed. Insofar as this idea justifies resignation from office at all, it is supportive of what we may call a "feigned resignation," the ostensible rejection of office in order to attain a better offer in the future. This was certainly an interpretation of the *Laozi*'s message by some Zhanguo *shi* (see below), but it would be grossly unfair to reduce the advice of this book's authors to sheer manipulation of public opinion.

The *Laozi* contains a second, more important concept that questions the desirability of holding office, namely, the principle of personal well-being. The text is probably the first to treat the body or the self (*shen* 身) as a legitimate focus of concern.[67] In marked distinction to the *Lunyu*, which explicitly recommends a *shi* "sacrifice the body in order to accomplish benevolence," and Mengzi's counsel "to sacrifice oneself for the sake of Dao,"[68] the *Laozi* recommends preserving the body: by grasping the Way, the adept will meet no danger until the end of his life and will escape numerous disasters. Hence the sage "retreats from his body, and the body advances; treats it as external, and the body is preserved."[69]

In the newly approved set of priorities, preserving the body has greater importance other attainments. The *Laozi* rhetorically asks: "What is closer to you: body or name?" and the answer is clear. The search for fame and reputation pales in comparison with preserving one's life; to attain longevity one should "know what is sufficient" and "when to stop," which may well be interpreted as limiting political involvement.[70] As it is usual with the *Laozi*, more than one conclusion may be drawn from the text; for instance, if these passages are directed at the ruler, their implications are different from the case when they are directed at a *shi*. Yet for the purposes of the current discussion, the important reading of these passages is that which assumes that preservation of the body legitimizes sacrificing one's career.[71]

Uncertainties aside, the idea of retreat from political career for the sake of self-preservation is explicitly promulgated in several other texts. It became firmly associated with Yang Zhu, whose selfish refusal to sacrifice a single hair of his body for the sake of All under Heaven so appalled Mengzi that he accused his rival of advocating a beast-like state without rulers.[72] Sober apprehension of the dangers associated with a political career made many *shi* refuse to forfeit their most precious belonging—life—for the sake of fame and power. A "madman of Chu," Jie Yu 接輿, who reportedly startled Confucius by singing about the dangers of political involvement, may be representative of this trend.[73] Self-preservation, an ideal that resonated well with the Confucian dictum of the filial obligation to keep the body intact, became a legitimate source of concern for office-holders in the turbulent Zhanguo age.[74] One *Zhanguo ce* anecdote tells how a traveling scholar, Cai Ze (蔡澤, fl. 250), convinced the all-powerful prime minister of Qin, Fan Sui, to yield his position by pointing at the mounting personal dangers for the gifted statesman. Fan Sui initially tried to rebuff Cai Ze, saying: "For a superior man to die in order to attain fame is propriety; even dead I shall have nothing to regret—why should I avoid it?"[75] Fan was quickly overwhelmed, however, by Cai's appeal to the advantages of timely retreat. The anecdote, whatever its veracity, is indicative of the importance of the issue of preserving the self in Zhanguo discourse and possibly in Zhanguo political praxis.

Of all known texts, the *Zhuangzi* is certainly the most explicit in its opposition to a political career, which it criticizes from several distinct angles. First of all, it claims that serving the government endangers one's life and should be avoided for the sake of mere self-preservation. A series of anecdotes scattered throughout the chapter "Ren jian shi" (人間事, Among the people) and in the "Outer" and "Miscellaneous" chapters of the *Zhuangzi*[76] repeatedly point out the dangers of political involvement and advocate disengagement from office-holding. Zhuangzi's views are succinctly summarized in one of the most famous of his anecdotes:

> Zhuangzi was fishing on the banks of the Pu River. The king of Chu dispatched two nobles to announce him: "I would like to bother you with the affairs of my realm."
>
> Zhuangzi held on to his fishing pole and said, without turning his head: "I heard that there is a sacred tortoise in Chu that has been dead for three thousand years. The king keeps it wrapped in cloth and boxed, and stores it in the ancestral temple. Now would this tortoise rather be dead and have its bones preserved and honored, or would it rather be alive and dragging its tail in the mud?"
>
> Two nobles said: "It would rather be alive and dragging its tail in the mud."
>
> Zhuangzi said: "Go away! I also prefer to drag my tail in the mud."[77]

The anecdote's message is clear enough: the advantages of office-holding in terms of riches and fame cannot compensate for the dangers inherent in court life; the mere calculation of gains and losses undermines the reasonability of seeking a political career. But service does not just threaten one's life; it is also completely futile in terms of moral self-realization. Lofty goals are unattainable at the courts of rulers, and the hopes of influencing sovereigns are as ridiculous as the attempts of a praying mantis to stop a carriage with its arms.[78] Furthermore, taking office in the immoral world is not just dangerous and naïve, but is also intrinsically immoral. Insofar as rulers—even the best of them—are mere "bandits," any involvement with power-holders means serving monsters. The "Robber Zhi" anecdote, mentioned on pages 79–80, shows Confucius humiliating himself in front of the frightening robber, who greets the Master while eating a lunch of human liver. Confucius humbly presents himself and then proposes to carve out a state for the robber, thereby turning him into a respectable ruler. Robber Zhi replies by bitterly criticizing Confucius as a petty profit-seeker who deserves to be named "Robber Qiu."[79] The leitmotif of this anecdote, namely, the immorality of rulers and the "righteous *shi*" who continue to serve them, is repeated elsewhere in the *Zhuangzi*: "He who steals a belt buckle is executed; he who steals a state becomes a regional lord; 'benevolence' and 'righteousness' are placed at the regional lords' gates."[80] And again:

> In recent generations, those executed lie heaped together, cangue bearers tread on each other's heels, those mutilated are watching each other, while Ru and Mo[zi's followers] have recently begun to crawl in between the shackles and fetters, waving their arms. So excessive are they in their shamelessness and brazenness![81]

Zhuangzi overturns the Ru imperative for morally driven political involvement: in truth, office-holding is utterly dishonest. Those who fulfill their Way by seeking positions at the rulers' courts effectively legitimize and participate in criminal regimes, their lofty moral principles notwithstanding. Thus seeking a political career is dangerous, imprudent, and immoral. Being a staunch critic of organized society and the state, Zhuangzi (and other contributors to the eponymous book) resolutely rejects the imperative of engagement with the state.

The iconoclastic stance of the *Zhuangzi* is well known, but does the text propose practical alternatives to political service? To my mind, the answer is negative. Economically speaking, the *Zhuangzi* does not present any attractive alternative to service or patronage. Its heroes—cripples, convicted criminals, odd creatures, fishermen, and other types at the margins of human society—are impressive in their ability to realize with the utmost fullness their Way, but their examples are unlikely to attract those who can reach official positions. An anecdote about Zhuangzi being in dire straits and seeking a subsidy from a local potentate reflects the degree of a *shi* dependence on power-holders, proud proclamations notwithstanding.[82]

Furthermore, does the alternative, apolitical morality promulgated by Zhuangzi really challenge the system of cooptation of lofty *shi* into the government? Again, the answer appears to be negative. While Zhuangzi is ostensibly opposed to political involvement, this opposition is tentative. Proud recluses, like Xu You (see Chapter 5), can prove their moral superiority only insofar as an office (or the position of a ruler) is offered to them, an offer which they have to decline. But this means that the very act of disengagement from the political world is meaningful only insofar as engagement is considered normative. By proudly proclaiming the superiority of refusal to serve, Zhuangzi may have inadvertently strengthened the very social system that he criticizes so harshly. Moreover, if the refusal to serve is the highest proof of one's attainment of the Way, then an ironical situation ensues: the more a person proclaims his disengagement, the more worthy of the office he is considered. Ultimately, the stance of a recluse becomes an excellent avenue to a government career!

This possibility of a feigned disengagement was not unnoticed by Zhanguo *shi*. The lofty Yan Chu, whose story was told in Chapter 5, and who so impressed King Xuan of Qi that the king wanted to become Yan's disciple, declined the offer and left court, but a cynical reader may ask what his reasons were for coming to an audience in the first place. Is not it possible that the final refusal was just another move to increase Yan Chu's prestige—and ultimately his price? These questions may be posed with regard to many other righteous rejectionists. The *Lüshi chunqiu* in particular abounds with stories that simultaneously praise disengagement and yet urge rulers to look for recluses and acquire them as the most precious *shi*. At one point the authors recommend:

> In our age, one who looks for *shi* who have attained the Way must do this between the four seas, amidst mountain valleys, at lonely and secluded locations, and thus he will be lucky to obtain them. After attaining these [*shi*], which of your desires would remain unattainable? Which action will not be accomplished?[83]

A cynical reader may ask again why these lofty *shi* who could save the generation have escaped to such remote locations, but this question was not raised by the *Lüshi chunqiu* authors, whose admiration for recluses coexists with their hopes to attain office. Nowhere is this linkage as clear as in the chapter "Gui sheng" (貴生, Esteeming the life), which contains several anecdotes from the "Rang wang" (讓王, Yielding the monarchical position) chapter of the *Zhuangzi*.[84] It is interesting to compare the different ending of one of these anecdotes, which deals with Yan He 顏闔 of Lu, who stubbornly refused to receive the gifts of the lord of Lu, fleeing from his home village to avoid contact with the lord. The *Zhuangzi* anecdote ends by praising him: "One like Yan He, he really despised riches and honor."[85] The "Gui sheng" version ends on an entirely different note:

> Hence one like Yan He did not despise riches and honor [as such], but he despised them because he saw his life as [more] important. The rulers of our age frequently rely on riches and honor to behave haughtily toward men

who have obtained the Way: hence they are unable to recognize each other. Is it not a pity?[86]

A sudden twist of argument not only qualifies Yan He's disdain for riches and honor, proclaimed in the *Zhuangzi*, but, more important, it introduces a crucially new element into the Yan He story. The "Gui sheng" authors use the story of Yan He's escape to criticize the lord of Lu for his insufficient respect of worthies. The authors' cry: "Is it not a pity?" with regard to the disengagement of worthy *shi* from rulers appears to come from the depth of their hearts. The yearning for the office was apparently too powerful among Lü Buwei's "guests" to be concealed even behind a respectable topic of self-preservation!

This unashamed self-promotion of the "recluses" did not remain entirely unnoticed. Xunzi, one of the most perceptive Zhanguo thinkers, bitterly complains:

> In the past, those who were called "reclusive *shi*" were people of high virtue, who were able to preserve quietude, cultivated uprightness, understood destiny, and manifested correctness. Today, those who are called "reclusive *shi*" lack abilities, but speak of themselves as able; lack knowledge, but speak of themselves as knowledgeable; are insatiably profit-minded, but pretend to have no desires. They behave hypocritically, maliciously, and vilely, but forcefully speak lofty words of sincerity and honesty. They turn the uncustomary into their custom, behave frivolously and opinionatedly.[87]

This diatribe, which reminds us unmistakably of the *Zhuangzi* attacks on hypocritical Ru and Mozi's followers,[88] reflects the easiness with which the lofty ideals of the recluses degraded into yet another avenue to power and fame. Xunzi carefully distinguishes between the respectable recluses of the past and the current "feigned recluses," who conceal sinister behavior behind lofty words, and he singles out his contemporaries for harsh criticism. A critical attitude toward hypocritical "purists" is evident from other texts. A *Zhanguo ce* anecdote tells of a Qi thinker, Tian Pian 田骈, whose proclaimed refusal to serve was ridiculed by a fellow countryman:

> "My neighbor's woman claims not to be married to him. For thirty years it has gone on like that, and they have seven sons. If they are unmarried, let it be so, but their marriage is exceptionally substantial. Now, you pledge not to serve, but you are nourished by a thousand bushels and have one hundred attendants. If you do not serve, let it be so, but your wealth is exceptionally substantial." —Master Tian excused himself.[89]

The anecdote, just like Xunzi's and *Lüshi chunqiu* passages cited above, clarify the degree to which the ideal of withdrawal from service was incorporated into the prevalent ruler-centered intellectual atmosphere. A powerful combination of economic factors with moral imperatives created such strong an attachment of *shi* to the loci of power that neither brilliant thinkers like Zhuangzi nor their eloquent theories could really challenge it. For some, the office was a source of fame and riches; for others, it was a mission; and yet for others, such as Mozi, Shang Yang, or Han Feizi, it was simply the natural occupation of a *shi*. Facing this overwhelming attractiveness of government service, the dissenting thinkers, like Zhuangzi and his ilk, failed to provide a substantially compelling alternative. Although refusal to serve remained associated for generations to come with moral loftiness, more often than not it served as a disguise for seeking a better appointment.[90] Eventually, the disdain of Zhuangzi and others for a government career was incorporated into the general model of a politically involved intellectual and served to buttress the normality of political engagement, even when glorifying disengagement.

Epilogue: Service and "Psychosis"

The imperative to serve bolstered by both egoistic and idealistic concerns firmly attached the intellectuals to the state. This attachment was adaptable enough to survive the vicissitudes of history and remained the single most powerful factor in the lives of the imperial literati for the next millennia. From the early imperial period, as private landownership came into being, with its inevitable consequences—including the class of large landowners—it was possible to attain a sufficient economic livelihood outside state service. Nonetheless, either in a search for prestige or out of genuine moral commitment, the imperial literati continued to seek service, engaging themselves anew with power-holders, their frequent frustrations notwithstanding. In retrospect, this appears as a single most important choice of China's educated elite. By lending their intellectual and moral prestige to the state in exchange for the ability to influence political affairs, the Zhanguo *shi* and their imperial offspring became a particularly powerful stratum that combined spiritual and political authority to an extent barely known elsewhere. By doing so, they both immensely enhanced the prestige of the state apparatus and also made possible a much higher input of their ideology into everyday sociopolitical life than it was possible for most intellectuals elsewhere on the globe.

Being engaged with the state was definitely a source of power for the literati, but it was also a source of predicament. By willingly becoming imperial servants in a ruler-centered polity, intellectuals accepted bonds of dependence on the sovereign, which led to their eventually yielding much of their intellectual and personal freedom. Bitterly assessing this predicament from a post-Maoist and post-Tiananmen perspective, Liu Zehua considers it the source of endless frustrations, or even "psychosis" (*jingshen bing* 精神病), that marred the life of *shi* under imperial rule.[91] In this work I shall not endeavor to analyze the correctness of his assessment with regard to the imperial literati. For the present discussion, what is important to note is that during the Warring States period, the dominant mood of *shi* was not one of frustration and psychosis. In Chapter 7 I shall try to show that despite their economic dependence on power-holders, the *shi* were sufficiently autonomous to adopt a posture of pride and self-confidence rather than one of servility. Yet the inevitable contradiction between the proud self-image of the *shi* and their position as a lord's servants resulted in immense tension in Zhanguo politics, eventually bringing about a major reappraisal of *shi* relations with the throne in the age of the unified empire.

CHAPTER 7

Shi and the Rulers

In Chapters 5 and 6 I focused on two major developments that shaped the *shi* image and behavior during the Zhanguo period. First was their growing pride and feeling of indispensability as possessors of the Way and the rulers' guides; second was their ever-stronger attachment to official careers bolstered by their economic dependence on the government and their self-imposed imperative to serve at the rulers' courts. These coexistent trends created a peculiar situation in which *shi* intellectuals considered themselves superior to the rulers morally, but at the same time were obliged to behave as the rulers' servants. The resultant tension became particularly acute with regard to those *shi* who attained high ministerial position. They desperately searched for ways to serve the ruler loyally while preserving their role as independent political actors.

In this chapter I shall trace the impact of this tension on Zhanguo views of ruler-minister relations. I shall analyze different ways in which ministers tried to preserve their position as autonomous political actors in a ruler-centered political system and their justifications for occasional defiance of the sovereign's orders or abandonment of their master. I shall show that the peculiar situation of an interstate market of talent, which allowed ministers to shift their allegiance from one court to another, emboldened them to conceptualize ruler-minister relations in reciprocal rather than hierarchical terms. This ministerial boldness eventually backfired, however, as it endangered the stability of the government apparatus. The resultant ideological counterassault on ministerial power and, more generally, on *shi* autonomy in general foreshadowed vast changes in the position of the *shi* after the imperial unification and their final subjugation to the ruler-based order.

Conditioned Loyalty

Tension between rulers and ministers is one of the persistent features of Chinese political culture, their origins being traceable to the earliest surviving political texts, such as the "Shao gao" 召誥 and "Jun Shi" 君奭 documents of the *Shu jing*.[1] How would a minister preserve his autonomy in the ruler-centered order? And how to prevent this autonomy from becoming a destabilizing force? Is it possible for a minister to remain loyal and yet to disobey the sovereign? Answers to these questions fluctuated considerably throughout the centuries, reflecting shifts in the balance of power between the rulers and their aides. For instance, during the Chunqiu period, at the heyday of ministerial power, leading aristocrats conceptualized ruler-minister relations in the way that both reflected and further enhanced their power. Considering themselves as shareholders in the state administration, proud hereditary ministers treated their lord as a mere primus inter pares rather than as an omnipotent sovereign. They claimed that their true loyalty was given to the "altars of soil and grain" (*sheji* 社稷, that is, to the state),[2] and not to the ruler personally. Thus Chunqiu ministers could defy the ruler in the name of "the altars" and even—as indicated in the speech of Master Kuang, cited in Chapter 1—claim the right to correct and if necessary replace an erring sovereign. The political discourse of the Chunqiu period perpetuated, therefore, a situation in which the ministers acted as the ruler's peers rather than his subjects.[3]

As we have seen in Chapters 1 and 2, the exceptional ministerial power of the Chunqiu period eventually backfired, contributing directly to the overall deterioration of political stability. With the formation of the new, ruler-centered entities of the Warring States period, the ministers lost their hereditary positions and were no longer considered "masters of the people" who owed allegiance to "the altars" rather than to the ruler.[4] Nonetheless, this did not mean dispensing with a minister's autonomous stance. Proud Zhanguo *shi* were not willing to become obedient tools of the ruler, as Confucius explicitly stated.[5] Rather, they reconceptualized their obligations to the rulers in a novel way, which preserved their autonomy. Confucius was apparently the first to propose a new focus of ministerial loyalty: "He who is called 'a great minister' is the one who serves the ruler according to the Way, and when it is impossible, stops [serving]."[6]

The idea of the Way as the supreme focus of allegiance was intrinsically linked with Confucius's assertion that one should serve the government only insofar as by doing so, one promotes his moral principles. From the ministers' point of view, it was a brilliant device, allowing them to preserve autonomy vis-à-vis the sovereign. Insofar as Zhanguo *shi* maintained their position as possessors/transmitters of the Way, they could always invoke this highest authority to justify defiance of the ruler's orders or cessation of service. As mentioned in Chapter 6, Confucius himself set a precedent for "following the Way" at the expense of serving regional lords, leaving those who did not heed his advice. This mode of behavior became paradigmatic for high-minded *shi*, especially from among Confucius's followers. Mengzi in particular repeatedly promulgated the superiority of the Way over the rulers. As we have already discussed, Mengzi conditioned his loyalty to the ruler on the ruler's endorsement of Mengzi's moral principles. It is worth noting that Mengzi justified not just resignation from the court of a morally impaired monarch, but also shifting allegiance to another lord, including to the adversary of his former master. In this context he hailed Yi Yin, who "five times approached Tang and five times approached Jie," when seeking the path of benevolence.[7] That Yi Yin intermittently served two bitter rivals was not disgraceful insofar as he did not compromise his own moral credo. As we shall see below, this legitimation of shifting allegiances became one of the most powerful intellectual assets of the Zhanguo *shi* and a major challenge to the ruler-centered political order.

The impact of Confucius's and Mengzi's ideas on the Zhanguo *shi* is obvious. Thus while Mozi himself never promulgated the idea of "following the Way" at the expense of the ruler, this topos was firmly incorporated by his disciples in the collection of Mozi-related anecdotes gathered in chapters 46 to 50 of the eponymous text.[8] The same topos dominates many of the stories of recluses and purists, like Boyi, who defied rulers in the name of their lofty ideals, as discussed in Chapter 6. The anonymous tradition, cited by Xunzi, "follow the Way, do not follow the ruler," evidently expressed a widely shared belief of the lofty-minded *shi*.[9]

From the point of view of ministers, and perhaps of the *shi* in general, the idea of the Way as a focus of one's allegiance was most laudable. Insofar as ideological expertise—namely, the definition of the Way—was firmly monopolized by the *shi*, it allowed any minister to navigate individually, guided by his own moral principles and by his understanding of the state's interests. For those the *shi* served, the consequences were mixed. On the one hand, it was certainly advantageous to have intelligent servants rather than subservient yes-men, and insofar as the rulers tacitly recognized the intellectual superiority of their underlings, granting them a certain freedom of action was highly desirable. But on the other hand, there was a distinct possibility either that an overzealous adept of the Way would undermine the ruler's authority to the point of endangering the political stability, or that a shrewd manipulator would employ lofty principles to pursue his sinister goals. The rulers had to be convinced that "the Way" of their ministers would not harm their interests. As we shall see, it was only after Xunzi succeeded to address these fears of the rulers that the notion of "following the Way" could be incorporated into ministerial ethics of the imperial age.

Subordination of ruler-minister relations to the Way, that is, to ideological considerations, was not the only device employed by Zhanguo ministers to ensure their autonomous stance vis-à-vis the rulers. More representative in terms of political *mores* of the Warring States was the widespread demand that rulers respect the dignity of their aides. This demand reflected a dominant view, which interpreted ruler-minister ties as personal rather than institutional. This personalization may be a Chunqiu period legacy, for it was a time when most *shi* were employed on a contractual basis as retainers ("household servants," *jia chen* 家臣) of powerful nobles. Yet while Chunqiu *shi* were in an unequivocally inferior position to their masters, whom they had to follow without wavering after the lifelong contract was concluded, their Zhanguo heirs emphasized reciprocity rather than obedience in their relations with the superiors. This reciprocity reflected the unprecedented flexibility of the Zhanguo retainers (called "guests," *binke*) in selecting or leaving an employer.[10] As we shall see below, this freedom of employment dramatically bolstered the self-confidence of Zhanguo *shi* and shaped decisively the ruler-minister relations of that age, and especially the ministerial discourse.

The conceptualization of ruler-minister relations as more reciprocal than hierarchical is duly reflected in the writings of Confucius's followers. Confucius himself is cited as saying: "A ruler employs ministers according to etiquette (*li* 禮); ministers serve the ruler loyally (*zhong* 忠)."[11] This description implies that ministerial loyalty was not unconditional, but was traded in exchange for the ruler's polite treatment. A similar, yet much more intensive preoccupation with the ruler's politeness characterizes Mengzi, whose views have been discussed in Chapters 5 and 6. Many more *shi*, some of them not necessarily identified with Confucius, enthusiastically endorsed the idea that they should serve a ruler only insofar as he treated them respectfully. Among numerous anecdotes that promote this ideology, one of the most revealing is a story of a famous assassin-retainer, Yu Rang 豫讓, who spared no efforts to avenge his late master, Zhi Bo (知伯, d. 453). When asked why he did not profess a similar loyalty toward his previous masters, heads of the Fan 范 and the Zhonghang 中行 lineages, Yu Rang reportedly answered: "When I served the Fan and Zhonghang lineages, they treated me as a commoner, and I repaid them as a commoner. Zhi Bo treated me as a *shi* of the state, and I repaid him as the *shi* of the state."[12]

Yu Rang made it clear that a servant's loyalty was not an obvious obligation towards his master, but rather discretionary behavior given in exchange for respectful, polite treatment. Only the ruler who recognized the worth of his retainers or ministers could expect devotion in return; as Yu Rang stated elsewhere: "A *shi* dies for the sake of the one who profoundly understands him."[13] This emphasis on profound understanding (*zhi ji* 知己, literally "to understand the other as you understand yourself") is further indication of the increasing demand for reciprocity in ruler-minister relations.[14] Mere respect was not enough; the *shi* expected a sort of spiritual affinity with their masters; they wanted to be the master's friend!

The widespread simile of "friends" (*you* 友) for ruler–minister relations is yet another remarkable manifestation of the haughtiness of *shi* discourse during the Warring States era. Among the many similes for ruler–minister ties employed in Chinese political discourse from the Western Zhou period on (heart/mind and limbs or organs of senses, father/son, husband/wife, and the like), this was the only one that de-emphasized the hierarchical dimension of these relations.[15] For instance, authors of the *Collected Sayings* (*Yu cong* 語叢), a collection of brief and ideologically significant statements discovered in Guodian, frequently employed the friendship simile to de-emphasize the hierarchical nature of the ruler–minister relations:[16]

> Friendship is the way of ruler and minister.[17]
>
> Father is both a relative and is revered. Elder and younger brother are [connected] by the way of relatives. Friends (*you*) and ruler and ministers are not relatives. Although revered they are not relatives.[18]
>
> Ruler and minister are [like] friends; [they] select [each other].[19]

These statements do not just reflect the markedly nonhierarchical mindset of their authors, but they have another important dimension: they serve as a justification for the potential shift of allegiance from one ruler to another. This conclusion is articulated in the following statement from the *Collected Sayings*:

> A father is not hated. The ruler is like a father: he is not hated. He is like a flag for the three armies—he [represents] correctness. Yet he differs from the father: when ruler and minister are unable to respect each other, you can sever [these relations]; when you dislike [the ruler], you may leave him; when he acts improperly/unrighteously towards you, do not accept it.[20]

This saying clarifies not only that the minister's obligations to a ruler are inferior to kinship duties, and that the ruler–minister relations resemble those of friends, but it also draws a clear conclusion: ruler–minister ties are reciprocal and can be severed with fascinating ease. A minister is free in selecting a ruler and should be free in his choice whether to serve the ruler or to leave him. Whenever he feels that the ruler mistreats him, whenever the ruler violates the minister's notion of propriety (*yi* 義), whenever a minister is not satisfied with his position and "cannot stay together" with the ruler, he may abandon the sovereign. The minister enjoys, accordingly, truly remarkable autonomy, and his dependence on the throne is completely obliterated. Once again we see how the political discourse of the Zhanguo period strengthened the minister's bargaining power vis-à-vis the ruler, allowing a *shi* in a ruler's service to preserve his autonomy and self-respect.

The Market of Talent and *Shi* Haughtiness

The radically pro-ministerial conceptualization of the ruler-minister relations in most Zhanguo texts may be puzzling. After all, Zhanguo ministers did not match the political power of their Chunqiu predecessors, for whom defiance of the ruler's orders was a common matter. Is it possible that the lofty pronouncements in favor of the minister's dignity and integrity were just a veneer behind which ministerial obedience and servility were hidden? Not necessarily. Although they lacked the political, economic, and military power of Chunqiu aristocrats, the *shi* of the Warring States had one great advantage over their predecessors: unprecedented employment flexibility. Unlike Chunqiu ministers, who generally served only in their natal states, Zhanguo "peripatetic advisors" routinely crossed boundaries in search of better employment. This freedom to find a new master radically emboldened the Zhanguo ministers.

The world of the Warring States can be compared to a huge market of talent, in which a gifted person could seek employment at any of the competing courts. This distinctive freedom of crossing boundaries was, as Mark Lewis has insightfully noted, completely at odds with the general trend of the Warring States to limit the geographical mobility of their population. While the rulers did their best to control the movement of average subjects, they apparently excluded *shi* from this harsh control, accepting as normal a situation in which a *shi* "served Qin in morning and Chu in evening" (*zhao Qin mu Chu* 朝秦暮楚).[21] Therefore, for a *shi*, resignation from an inhospitable court did not mean the end of his career but rather a return to the rulers' market with a renewed chance to find a better employer. Han Feizi aptly summarizes:

> A minister brings to the rulers' market [his ability] to exhaust his force to the point of death; a ruler brings to the ministers' market [his ability] to bestow ranks and emoluments. Ruler-minister relations are based not on the intimacy of father and child, but on calculation [of benefits].[22]

Han Feizi uses the market metaphor to undermine the idea that ruler-minister relations are based on either ideological or spiritual affinity; rather, he argues, they are moved by sheer self-interest. Later we shall return to this claim; but first let us analyze the impact of this "market of talent" on ruler-minister ties. In a situation of acute competition between rival courts, if the demand for gifted statesmen exceeded the supply, the *shi* were in an excellent bargaining position. Rulers dared not offend them and would tolerate even the harsh criticisms of Mengzi and the affronts of people like Yan Chu (see Chapter 5), since a disgruntled *shi* leaving an inhospitable court could constitute a severe brain drain that benefited the lord's rivals. A following dialogue from the *Mengzi* portrays a ruler's plight:

> Mengzi said to King Xuan of Qi: "If a ruler treats his subjects as his hands and feet, they will treat him as their belly and heart. If he treats them as his horses and hounds, they will treat him as a mere fellow. If he treats them as mud and weeds, they will treat him as a mortal enemy."
>
> The king said: "Ritual requires of a minister to wear mourning for his ruler. How in these circumstances will it be possible to wear mourning?"
>
> [Mengzi] said: "The ruler should follow [the minister's] remonstrance, heed his advice, and benefit the people below. If [the minister] has a reason to leave the country, the ruler should send someone to conduct him beyond the border, and somebody to prepare the way ahead. Only if after three years abroad [the minister] does not return, the ruler may take over his fields and dwellings. This is called 'the three courtesies.' If the ruler behaves so, then it is the minister's duty to wear mourning for him. Today the remonstrance is not followed, advice is not heeded, the people below see no benefits. When a minister has a reason to leave, the ruler has him arrested and put in chains, makes things difficult for him in the state he is going to, and confiscates his fields and dwellings the day he leaves. This is what is meant by 'mortal enemy.' What mourning is there for a mortal enemy?"[23]

This exchange is not only illuminating with regard to Mengzi's audacity vis-à-vis the ruler, but it is also revealing with regard to the connection between ministerial boldness and employment flexibility. Mengzi clearly implies that a minister has no fixed obligations toward a ruler: their relations are based on a quid pro quo, and the ruler cannot expect a better attitude than the one he displays toward his aide. Moreover, the minister, in Mengzi's eyes, has an inalienable right to leave the ruler and go to another state; with remarkable chutzpah, Mengzi even demands that the ruler respect the right of the minister to leave the court for a rival state and yet still preserve his emoluments!

We do not know whether King Xuan of Qi accepted Mengzi's arguments, but if he, as the anecdote's authors want us to believe, tolerated Mengzi's affront, this may have been precisely because he feared that a harsh reaction would cause Mengzi (and other ministers) to shift allegiance to the king's rivals. This atmosphere of tolerance bolstered ever haughtier pronouncements of

Mengzi and his kind. Some *shi* were no longer satisfied with reciprocity. They demanded a higher position: that of the ruler's teachers rather than his friends. This demand is explicit in the following anecdote from the *Mengzi*:

> Lord Mu [of Lu] went several times to visit Zisi, asking him: "In antiquity, how did [the rulers] of a one-thousand-chariot [that is, small] state manage to befriend *shi*?" Zisi did not like that, answering: "Men of antiquity had a saying, 'talk of service'; did they say 'talk of friendship'?" As Zisi did not like [the lord's question], why did he not answer: "Judging by position, you are the ruler, and I am the minister—how dare I befriend a ruler? Judging by virtue (*de* 德), you serve me—how can you befriend me?"[24]

Mengzi outlined here the essence of the problem that faced Zhanguo *shi*. In the parallel systems of moral and administrative hierarchies, promulgated by Mengzi himself and enthusiastically endorsed by many of his contemporaries, an intellectual had to serve the ruler, whom he considered morally inferior. Mengzi's last sentence, which postulates the inadequacy of the ruler's *de*, thus creates a potentially explosive situation. As Mengzi and his disciples knew perfectly, among other semantic fields of the term *de*, one of the most important was that connected to charismatic power, or, in other words, the very right to rule.[25] Thus if a minister had superior *de*, and if the ruler was supposed to "serve" (*shi* 事) him, this effectively meant that the sovereign and his underling should shift their positions!

This view of a minister as potentially a ruler's teacher rather than his friend is echoed in a few other Zhanguo texts, some of which we surveyed in Chapter 5 in discussing the self-esteem of the Zhanguo *shi*.[26] Amazingly, even some rulers appear to have internalized this discourse and acquiesced with the supposedly inferior position. This is suggested by a remarkable piece of epigraphic evidence: the inscription on the King Cuo of Zhongshan 中山王䝮-*da ding*. This inscription commemorates a successful military expedition carried out by a minister of Zhongshan named Zhou 𧊒 against the state of Yan in 316 or 315, in the aftermath of the infamous abdication of King Kuai in favor of his minister, Zizhi (see Chapter 3). In the inscription King Cuo hails Zhou's achievements, saying among other things:

> Heaven sent down a gracious decree to my state, [therefore we] have this loyal servant, Zhou, [who] is able to be acquiescent and obedient, and always is guided by benevolence. Reverently compliant with Heaven's virtue, he thereby assists me, the Lonely Man, on the left and the right. He made me understand the responsibility of the altars of soil and grain and the propri-

eties of servant and master. From dawn to dusk he does not slacken in guiding me, the Lonely Man, toward goodness.[27]

The king spares no superlatives in depicting Zhou, and even states that Zhou's assistance is tantamount to his receipt of Heaven's Decree (*tian ming* 天命). He seemingly has adopted the view that a righteous minister should be the ruler's teacher; hence he emphasizes that Zhou "led and guided" him. It is worth noting that this inscription was not a piece of *shi* propaganda, but was cast on a vessel placed in the king's tomb, where its message was directed at the king's ancestors, not the general public. If this is so, the inscription may well reflect the king's genuine sentiments. Even Mengzi could not demand more of the ruler![28]

It is ironical that this panegyric to Zhou appears in a text that bitterly criticizes King Kuai of Yan, whose similar "respect of the worthy" led him to yield the throne to Zizhi. For me, it seems that the kings of both Yan and Zhongshan were profoundly engulfed in the pro-*shi* discourse that placed a minister in the position as the ruler's master. To a certain extent the Zizhi affair may well be regarded an offshoot of this discourse, and it is not impossible to imagine a similar transfer of power taking place in the state of Zhongshan, whose king believed in his minister's moral and intellectual superiority. The overwhelmingly pro-ministerial political discourse of the Warring States period contained, therefore, the seeds of potential usurpation.

This assertion is not a mere speculation. As we noted in Chapter 3, in the middle Zhanguo period, certain radical *shi* began contemplating the idea of a worthy minister replacing, not just "instructing," the ruler. The question: "Why Confucius did not become the Son of Heaven," allegedly asked by a follower of Confucius, Gongmeng Yi 公盟義, and echoed in a muted form in the *Mengzi*, may reflect these suggestions of unifying the moral and political hierarchy under a worthy *shi*.[29] While eventually this dangerous topic was dropped from political discourse, being transformed during the Han dynasty into the ideal of a "textual," "plain-clothed king" (*su wang* 素王),[30] its emergence was indicative of the potential transformation of the *shi* pride into politically destabilizing force.

The combination of haughty pronouncements, the muted hopes of some *shi* to replace the rulers, and also probably the impact of King Kuai/Zizhi affair—all these may have contributed to the gradual re-evaluation of ruler-minister relations during the second half of the Warring States period. Eventually the sweeping enthusiasm of the *shi* to pose as the rulers' equals or superiors backfired. As more Zhanguo thinkers began realizing the potentially destabilizing impact of the unchecked elevation of *shi*, they began pondering ways to restore stability, which effectively meant restoring the ruler's authority over his haughty ministers and over the *shi* in general.

The Anti-*Shi* Reaction

The peculiar employment flexibility of the *shi* in the Zhanguo market of talent had doubly negative consequences for political stability. First, as demonstrated above, it allowed proliferation of the radically pro-ministerial discourse that became potentially detrimental to the ruler's authority. Second, it generated deep mistrust between the ruler and his entourage. When a trusted aide of today could become the deceitful subject of tomorrow, no ruler could feel secure. To aggravate matters, movement of *shi* among the courts was frequently motivated by economic rather than moral considerations. As we have seen in Chapter 6, *pace* lofty pronouncements, most Zhanguo *shi* sought wealth and power, patterning themselves not after Boyi, but after Su Qin, who succeeded in serving several rulers simultaneously, each of whom had good reason to suspect that Su was conspiring with his rivals.[31] In the world dominated by professional turncoats, *shi* freedom of movement became a major destabilizing force. Zhanguo "market of talent" eventually blurred the distinction between friends and foes.

Considering this, we should not be surprised that the prevalent atmosphere at the courts of the Warring States was neither one of ruler-minister friendship nor one of teacher-disciple relations but one of mutual distrust and deception. Zhanguo texts repeatedly tell of unfortunate ministers who failed to prove their fidelity to the masters and encountered suspicion and slander.[32] Other stories tell about naïve rulers who relied on treacherous aides, endangering their states or their position. This background explains a reaction against the dominant pro-ministerial discourse in the second half of the Zhanguo period.

Anti-ministerial and anti-*shi* discourse was threefold. First came an assault on *shi* occupational autonomy, particularly on their right to move to competing courts. Shang Yang, one of the earliest representatives of this trend, singled out talkative "peripatetic" (*you* 游) *shi* as one of the major maladies of the state, calling them persons who distract the commoners from agricultural and military activities, gain fame in illicit ways, are unproductive, and possibly conspire with foreign powers.[33] For Shang Yang the very existence of a social group outside strictly centralized state control was highly undesirable. Incorporating the *shi* into the state administration would put an end to their negative impact on the public mores and to their potential subversiveness.

The second line of anti-*shi* discourse focused on the unreliability of those *shi* who were employed by the courts, high-ranking ministers and petty officials alike. This line of argumentation is identified most with Shang Yang's contemporary Shen Buhai, who called upon the ruler to rein in his officials. Shen Buhai singled out the potential treachery of the ministers and the dangers of usurpation as the most immediate threat on the sovereign's power:

> Now the reason why a ruler builds lofty inner walls and outer walls, looks carefully to the barring of doors and gates, is [to prepare against] the coming of invaders and bandits. But one who murders the ruler and takes his state does not necessarily climb over difficult walls and batter in barred doors and gates. [He may be one of the ministers, who] by limiting what the ruler sees and restricting what the ruler hears, seizes his government and monopolizes his commands, possesses his people and takes his state.[34]

Shen Buhai emphatically argued that the court was inhabited by dangerous foes and not by friends of the sovereign. As argued in Chapter 4, these claims seem inflated, given the paucity of actual usurpations throughout the Warring States period, but these (or Han Feizi's) invectives against ministerial treachery may have reflected the atmosphere of increasing mistrust at late Zhanguo courts and probably further exacerbated it. Moreover, the very exposure of public servants not as morally upright individuals but as treacherous and profit-seeking conspirators may have profoundly influenced the overall pattern of relations between the rulers and the *shi*. If no *shi* can be trusted, whatever their lofty pronouncements, then the only way for a ruler to maintain his power will be through an efficient system of surveillance and control over his aides. This system duly materialized by the end of the Warring States period.

We still lack reliable materials about life in Zhanguo courts, but insofar as the lower levels of officialdom were concerned, they were clearly put under extremely tight control. Chu and Qin administrative documents from Baoshan 包山 and Shuihudi 睡虎地 reveal the deep mistrust of the state for its servants. A belief in the inherent greediness and selfishness of the average office-holding *shi* may well have been on the mind of those who demanded no less than four signatures to register grain coming into a granary and of those who defined any misreporting of grain transactions as theft.[35] While the idea of the moral education of officials was not dismissed, as testified by such texts as *Wei li zhi Dao* (為吏之道, The Way of being an official) from Shuihudi,[36] general administrative practices of the Warring States reflect that the power-holders had little belief in the morality of their underlings.

The third and eventually the most consequential assault on the *shi* focused on their intellectual and not just their occupational autonomy. The ideal society envisioned by many these thinkers was one in which the *shi* would be obedient tools of the state and not independent players. This vision is already implicitly present in the "Elevating Uniformity"/"Conforming Upwards" chapters of the *Mozi,* and it is reflected, albeit with different emphases, in such texts as *Shang jun shu* and *Han Feizi.* Its clearest exposition is in the "Relying on Law" chapter of the *Guanzi:*

> Ruler and minister are Heaven-and-Earth positions; the people are the image of multiple things. Each occupies his position awaiting thus for the ruler's orders: will then the ministers and the hundred clans use their heart to establish selfish [interests]? Hence when one respectfully implements the ruler's orders, even if he is hurt and defeated, he is not to be punished; while if one implements what the ruler did not order, even if he succeeds he must be punished by death. Thereby the inferiors will serve the superiors as an echo responds to a sound, and ministers will serve the sovereign as a shadow follows the body. Thus when the superiors order and the inferiors respond, when the sovereign acts and the ministers follow [him]—this is the Way of orderly rule.[37]

The authors present their views with the utmost clarity: in an orderly ruler-centered state independent actions by underlings are undesirable and punishable. The inherent selfishness of the *shi,* presupposed in this text, annuls whatever benefits the state can reap from their talents and abilities unless these are harnessed to the state machine. The authors consider overall restriction of the *shi* as the most laudable goal, the desirability of which is indisputable. Rejecting Confucius's dictum that "a superior man is not a tool," they envision the *shi* as instruments in the ruler's hands.[38] Only thus can political order be attained.

Among the staunchest opponents of *shi* autonomy, Han Feizi occupies a special position. This cynical and astute observer of contemporary mores, who opined that any minister is a potential usurper, turned the tables on the lofty *shi,* mercilessly exposing their selfish manipulations. Among other things, Han Feizi ridiculed prevalent notions of loyalty, which focused on a devotion to the Way or on personal fidelity to a ruler-friend. The paragons who embodied these ideals, Han Feizi argues, were utterly useless to the state and to the ruler:

> Now if we take Yu Rang who was a minister of Zhi Bo, above he failed to convince his master to employ the patterns of clear laws, techniques, rules, and methods to avoid the disturbances of troubles and misfortune; below, he failed to command his multitudes in order to protect [Zhi Bo's] state. Yet

when [Zhao] Xiangzi killed Zhi Bo, Yu Rang branded his face, cut his nose, and deformed his appearance in order to kill Xiangzi and avenge Zhi Bo.[39] Although he thus mutilated and sacrificed himself for the sake of his master's reputation, in reality this was as useless for Zhi Bo as a fringe of an autumn hair. This [behavior] is what I discard, but the rulers of our age consider this loyalty and elevate it. In the past there were Boyi and Shuqi. King Wu [of Zhou] yielded All under Heaven [to them], but they refused to accept it; both men starved themselves to death at Shouyang hill.[40] Ministers like these neither fear heavy punishment, nor are they moved by handsome rewards; penalties cannot restrain them, rewards cannot encourage them: these are called useless servants. I [try to] diminish and dismiss them, while the rulers of the age multiply them and seek [their service].[41]

Loyalty that is not directed at serving the state is a false loyalty. A prudent ruler is not in need of ministers like Boyi or Shuqi, who followed their Way disregarding the state, or of those like Yu Rang, whose fidelity was traded in exchange for spiritual affinity with the master. Such notions of loyalty are useless or even harmful to state interests. Han Feizi favors loyalty that is political: it is aimed at benefiting the state and the ruler personally:

> Thus one who has a loyal minister has no worry of rival states abroad, has no anxiety of calamitous ministers at home; he enjoys lasting peace in All under Heaven, and his name is handed down to posterity. This is what is called "a loyal minister."[42]

The loyalty promoted by Han Feizi is coterminous with serving the state; it is defined by practical results and is possible only within the state apparatus. It cannot serve as justification for either resignation or defiance of the ruler's orders; even if (as Han Feizi painfully learned from his own tragic experience) a loyal minister falls victim to a ruler's mistrust, these are simply regrettable lapses of the system. Under no condition is it permissible to disobey the sovereign. Being loyal is laudable, but it gives a minister no extra rights.[43]

Han Feizi's desire to locate the notion of loyalty within institutionalized political obligations and detach it from vague concepts of the Way and friendship is part of his more general assault on the intellectual autonomy of the *shi*. Following his teacher Xunzi (of whom see below), but not constrained by the Ru legacy of an intellectual's autonomy, Han Feizi systematically attacked various aspects of contemporary discourse that he found did not serve state interests. Thus, for instance, he ended his criticism of the ideals of abdication and of righteous rebellion with the following conclusion:

Thus the minister should not praise the worthiness of Yao and Shun, should not extol the punitive expeditions of Tang and Wu, should not talk of the loftiness of zealous *shi*. [Only] he who with the utmost force preserves the law and focuses wholeheartedly on serving the ruler is the loyal minister.[44]

Here the very right of an official (or of any *shi*) to be engaged in a potentially subversive discourse is denied. Astutely realizing that such discourse may encourage dissent and potentially lead to opposition between a minister and the ruler, Han Feizi plainly proposes to halt any dangerous discussions. Elsewhere, he supplements these recommendations to a minister with similar advice to the ruler:

Now, when the ruler listens to [a certain] learning, if he approves of its doctrine, he should promulgate it among the officials and employ its adepts; if he disapproves of its doctrine, he should dismiss its adepts and cut off its ends.[45]

This proposal amounts to nationalization of intellectual activity. It shrewdly makes use of the claims made by competing thinkers that they possess the most efficient prescriptions for curing the state's maladies. Han Feizi does not deny in principle that such solutions may indeed be found in the thinkers' proposals, but he denies the *shi* the right to develop and elaborate any such proposals independently of the state. Specifically, this stricture is directed against the system of the ruler's patronage of the *shi* that flourished throughout the Zhanguo period, which allowed competing thinkers to benefit from the state resources without being directly engaged in the state apparatus. Han Feizi leaves them no illusions: intellectuals can pursue their ideas only insofar as they are part of the state-ordained system of power, otherwise their "ends will be cut off." Elsewhere, Han Feizi concludes:

Accordingly, in the country of an enlightened ruler there are no texts written in books and on bamboo strips, but the law is the teaching; there are no "speeches" of the former kings, but officials are the teachers; there is no private wielding of swords, but beheading [enemies] is the valor.[46]

Han Feizi's recommendations were echoed almost verbatim by his fellow student and nemesis, Li Si, who eagerly implemented the policy of "turning officials into teachers" in 213 BCE, as we will discuss below. But before we turn to the first attempt to abolish the autonomy of the *shi*, it is appropriate to note the inherent problematic of Han Feizi's suggestions. Being a *shi*, an advisor, and an aspiring minister, Han Feizi proposed radical limitations on the freedom of action of members of his own stratum. These proposals could gain him popularity at courts (as reportedly he succeeded—posthumously—at the court of Qin), but they could not be endorsed by most *shi*, except perhaps for those who were firmly entrenched in government service. Thus when Han Feizi's ideas triumphed for a short while under Qin imperial rule, this caused much dissatisfaction among the intellectually active *shi* and eventually created intolerable conflict between the state and the educated elite. Although he correctly outlined the dangers of *shi* independence, Han Feizi failed to propose an appropriate way to restore stability to the intellectuals' ties with the throne.

Xunzi: Ministerial Ethics for the Imperial Age

We shall now go back to Han Feizi's and Li Si's teacher, Xunzi, a thinker whose views were not greatly heeded during his lifetime but who contributed enormously toward the modus vivendi between the *shi* and rulers from the time of the Han dynasty forward.[47] Living at the end of the Warring States period, Xunzi encountered a much chillier atmosphere than that enjoyed by Mengzi. The diminishing enthusiasm of contemporary rulers for "worthy *shi*" can be illustrated by a blatant question that King Zhao of Qin (秦昭王, r. 306–250) asked Xunzi: "Are Ru useless to the state?"[48] The markedly defensive stance Xunzi adopted in response contrasts sharply with Mengzi's haughty pronouncements. The changed political atmosphere caused Xunzi to seek a middle way that would increase the usefulness of the *shi* (especially the Ru), without abandoning the Ru's sense of self-respect.

Xunzi resolutely supports the notion of the intellectual autonomy of a Great Ru, whose proud attachment to the Way allows him to dwarf immoral rulers. Such pronouncements as "after cultivating your will and mind, you can despise riches and nobility" and "when your Way and propriety are great, you can belittle kings and lords"[49] clearly echo Mengzi and his like. However, Xunzi's support of the intellectual autonomy of the *shi*—one of the major foundations of their power vis-à-vis the rulers—is somewhat equivocal. First, he denies it completely to those living under a True Monarch (see Chapter 4). Second, even under an average ruler, intellectual autonomy should be limited to the Ru, and not include their rivals. In sharp distinction to Mengzi, for whom fierce polemics are mostly an intellectual enterprise, Xunzi envisions state intervention to put an end to subversive ideologies. In his major polemical essay "Contra the Twelve Masters" Xunzi postulates:

Hence labor that is not in accord with the people's task is called "illicit undertakings"; knowledge that is not in accord with the standards of the former kings is called "illicit knowledge"; versatile theories that are profitable but are not in accord with ritual and propriety are called "illicit theories." Sage kings prohibited these "three illicits."[50]

Xunzi's implicit appeal to state power to put an end to "illicit theories" is revealing. While it is possible that he envisioned such intervention as legitimate only in a state ruled by a True Monarch, or at least by the Great Ru, the very willingness to involve administrative means to put an end to ideological deviations is indicative of Xunzi's fatigue with the endless intellectual divisions of his age. Not incidentally, among the positive results of the superior man's employment, Xunzi promises cessation of disruptive talks by opponents of the Ru.[51] The desire to employ the state machine in ideological controversies reflects Xunzi's identification of intellectual pluralism with political anarchy and his resoluteness to combat such anarchy, even if taking action against it inevitably undermines the autonomy of the *shi.*

Xunzi's equivocal position characterizes not only his approach to the question of *shi* autonomy, but also his attitude toward the proper mode of relations between the *shi* and the ruler. Again, certain similarities between Xunzi and his ideological predecessors, Confucius and Mengzi, are apparent. Xunzi wholeheartedly supports the right of a minister to defy a ruler's orders and considers this the purest manifestation of loyalty. In his "Chen Dao" (臣道, The Way of the minister) chapter, where he creates a blueprint for ministerial ethics of later ages, Xunzi clarifies:

> He who obeys the orders and benefits the ruler is called compliant; he who obeys the orders and does not benefit the ruler is called servile; he who contradicts the orders and benefits the ruler is called loyal; he who contradicts the orders and does not benefit the ruler is called an usurper. He who cares not for the ruler's glory or disgrace, cares not for the success or failure of the state, but just blandishes and flatters the ruler in order to grasp emoluments and nurture ties [with the sovereign] is called the state's villain.[52]

In a world that lacks a True Monarch, the ruler's orders are not sacrosanct; they can—and should—be defied if the major precondition is preserved: that is, if the defiance is made in order to "benefit the ruler." Xunzi explicates different courses of action for a loyal subject who opposes a ruler's orders in order to serve the highest interests of the ruler and the state: from resigning to "stealing the ruler's power and opposing the ruler's undertakings in order to relieve the danger of the state and to eradicate the ruler's disgrace."[53] Ministers who act in this way are called "remonstrating, contesting, supportive, and assisting" and are hailed by the thinker:

Thus remonstrating, contesting, supportive, and assisting ministers are the ministers of the altars of soil and grain, the ruler's treasure. The enlightened ruler respects and treats them generously, while the benighted sovereign and the suspicious ruler consider them personal enemies. Hence he whom the enlightened ruler rewards, the benighted ruler penalizes; he whom the benighted ruler rewards, the enlightened ruler executes. Yi Yin and Jizi may be called remonstrating; Bigan and [Wu] Zixu can be called contesting; Lord Pingyuan of Zhao can be called supporting; Lord Xinling of Wei can be called assisting. The tradition says: "Follow the Way, do not follow the ruler"—it is told of these cases.[54]

An enlightened ruler does not need submissive yes-men or empty flatterers; rather, he must appreciate contesting and critically minded servants. Of the examples cited by Xunzi, the most interesting is the last one, Lord Xinling 信陵君 or Prince Wuji 無忌, a royal sibling from the state of Wei who defied his king's orders, stole the royal army, and attacked the powerful state of Qin, presumably out of concern for the state of Wei. Xunzi hails Wuji's defiance as a manifestation of true loyalty, since his actions ultimately benefited the state and the king of Wei. Defiance and nonconformism were thus welcome, provided they bring about positive results.

His unequivocal support of the right to disobey the ruler, including his invocation of Confucius's dictum "Follow the Way, do not follow the ruler" appears to place Xunzi squarely within the *shi*-oriented discourse of Confucius and Mengzi. The situation is not so simple, however. First, Xunzi is eager to clarify that one cannot defy the ruler's orders just for the sake of personal morality, but only with the ultimate goal of benefiting the ruler and the altars of soil and grain, and thus preserving the Way. The criterion of loyalty remains, therefore, in political realm. Remarkably, Xunzi designates a loyal minister as both a "minister of the altars" (*sheji zhi chen* 社稷之臣) and "the ruler's treasure" (*jun zhi bao* 君之寶). In contrast to the Chunqiu period, Xunzi treats the ruler and the state/altars as identical, and makes serving them properly precisely the fulfillment of one's Way, that is the Way of the ruler-centered political order.[55] Thus loyalty to one's principles, to the Way, means loyalty to the state, which by definition means loyalty to the ruler. In a few sentences Xunzi succeeds in synthesizing previous concepts of loyalty in a way that preserves the minister's dignity, does not endanger political stability, and benefits the ruler personally.

Xunzi's departure from earlier *shi*-oriented traditions is distinguishable not only in his unequivocal identification of the Way with serving the ruler and the state, but also in his dropping of the notion of ruler-minister friendship. Xunzi accepts the possibility of resignation, but only for political reasons and because of personal offenses. But probably the most remarkable yielding to the ruler's interests is Xunzi's consistent evasion of discussing the possibility of crossing boundaries as a way to protest against the ruler. Although Xunzi never explicitly rejects this possibility (after all he personally shifted allegiance more than once), he ominously eliminates it from the minister's legitimate modes of action. He says:

> In serving a sage ruler, be attentive and compliant without remonstrance and arguments. In serving an average ruler, remonstrate and argue without flattery and servility. In serving a violent ruler, you should mend his deficiencies without ostensibly opposing him. When encountering a calamitous age, living in poverty in a violent state and having nowhere to escape, you should praise [the ruler's] fine character, hail his goodness, avoid [exposing] his badness, conceal his mistakes; speak of his advantages and do not mention his shortcomings—turning this into your habit. The *Poems* say: "When the state has the Great Decree, do not tell it to others, just preserve your body." It is told about this.[56]

There are four possible ways to interact with a ruler, but none of them includes the most evident act for a Zhangguo minister, namely, leaving to go to another state. By speaking of conditions in which "there is nowhere to escape," Xunzi apparently envisions a possible unified empire that effectively monopolizes the former market of talent putting an end to free boundary crossing by members of the elite. By eliminating this possibility in advance, Xunzi further contributes to the ruler's power: a critical minister without the ability to leave can not defy the sovereign with Mengzi's haughtiness. Xunzi thus inadvertently gives up a minister's most powerful means of preserving his independence and makes a crucial step toward redefining a minister as a ruler's critical servant, but not his friend or his teacher.

Epilogue: *Shi* under the Imperial Monopoly

Lü Buwei's "guests" who gathered at the court of Qin around the year 240 to prepare what they hoped would become a blueprint for the future empire, the *Lüshi chunqiu*, did their best to convince their patron, and through him the king of Qin, as to the indispensability of upright *shi* and the need to respect their independence. Their hopes were dashed, however. The imperial unification of 221 brought about a major transformation in *shi* relations with the throne; it became, in Li Si's words, an "autumn for the traveling persuaders."[57] The global market of talent suddenly disappeared, giving way to a solid state monopoly on riches and glory. *Shi* had to adapt to totally new conditions.

As is well known, Qin imperial relations with the *shi* were marked by escalating conflict that peaked in the infamous biblioclasm of 213 and the execution of the "technical masters" (or, possibly, other scholars) a year later. I shall not discuss the much-debated topic of the historicity of these events, but accept for the time being Martin Kern's insightful analysis, according to which the book burning was not directed at suppressing traditional culture, but rather at establishing a new Qin canon, while simultaneously suppressing "private learning" (*si xue* 私學).[58] In my eyes, this state-sponsored assault on private learning marks a watershed in *shi* relations with the throne. To clarify this point it is useful to address the famous memorandum of Li Si that initiated the biblioclasm. The trigger for Li Si's attack were political controversies regarding the degree of centralization, but after rebuffing his opponents as "supporters of the past who negated the present," Li Si turned to a more substantial issue:

> In the past, All under Heaven was scattered and disordered and unable to unify. Hence regional lords rose together, and all the *Speeches* talked about the past to harm the present, adorning empty words to wreak havoc in facts. Everybody liked his private learning, using it to negate whatever the rulers established.[59]

In the opening of his memorandum, Li Si identified ideological pluralism, spurred by private learning, with the political disorder of the divided All under Heaven. This topos was not exceptional for Li Si, for several late Zhanguo texts had hinted as much, albeit in a much milder form.[60] But Li Si went one step further, suggesting that private learning was not only divisive but also subversive:

> Now that you have annexed All under Heaven, you have separated black and white and have fixed the single respectable. But [adherents of] private learning continue to reject among themselves the teaching of the Law. When they hear of orders, each discusses them according to his [private] learning; when entering [at court], negates them in heart; when exiting—discusses them at lanes and alleys. They oppose the sovereign to attain reputation, accept the unusual as lofty, and lead the multitudes to slander. If they are not banned,

the sovereign's power will collapse above and cliques will be formed below. It is advantageous to prohibit them.[61]

Having identified two major maladies brought on by private learning—divisiveness and potential subversion—Li Si makes his radical suggestion to eliminate copies of the *Poems, Documents,* and *Speeches of the Hundred Schools*[62] from private collections, explicitly excluding, however, those in the possession of the court erudites (*bo shi* 博士). After enumerating the books to be burned and those to be spared, Li Si concludes: "And those who want to study laws and ordinances, let them take an official as a teacher!"[63]

Li Si's final recommendation, as well as his sparing of the erudites' collections, indicates the deep motives behind his drastic measures. The suppression of private learning was not primarily an ideological act—Li Si did not suggest any reprisals against his ideological opponents at court—but rather an institutional measure. Much like Han Feizi, Li Si considered the nationalization of learning as the only way to establish proper relations between the *shi* and the finally solidified ruler-centered policy. The perfectly ordered state of Qin, in which "everyone understands what to do, and tasks are without doubts and uncertainties"[64] could not possibly tolerate an unruly stratum of scholars, whose very existence was intrinsically linked to the chaotic legacy of the past. The suppression of private learning was an inevitable outcome of this outlook.

"Burning the books and executing the scholars" was just one step toward the nationalization of talents. Qin rulers intended not only to frighten dissenting *shi* but also to incorporate this stratum within the officialdom. This policy is not only hinted at in Li Si's proposals to equate officials and teachers and in Han Feizi's views discussed above, but it is also suggested by the very nature of the Qin administrative machine. We cannot precisely estimate the scope of this machine, but epigraphic evidence suggests that it was impressive, to put it mildly. A hyperactive bureaucracy, which intervened in the everyday lives of peasants, checking the weight of the oxen, investigating the number of rat holes in the granaries, delivering written reports about spoilt iron tools, and tracing fugitive debtors into the remotest corners of the empire, required a huge number of personnel.[65] This personnel had to be educated—literacy was essential for coping with an official's tasks—and also, preferably, morally cultivated.[66] It was natural to incorporate educated and cultivated *shi* into this officialdom, and this was apparently Qin policy. If, as Leonard Perelomov suggests, at the same time Qin was actively incorporating even the village elders into its administrative machine, then the possibility that the empire's architects envisioned a total merge of the elite and officialdom becomes even more plausible.[67]

What was the *shi* reaction to this policy? Many of them, as Jia Yi (賈誼, c. 200–168) remarked, "docilely bowed before [the emperor's] wind."[68] Some, the court erudites, for instance, may have even been delighted with a situation that wiped out their potential competitors. But for many others the suppression was too harsh and too rapid to be tolerated. Even if we put aside the anti-Qin propaganda of later periods, we can find clear instances of *shi* opposition to the regime. In particular, the decision of Kong Jia 孔甲, a descendant of Confucius in the ninth generation, together with other Ru, to join the rebellious peasant Chen She (陳涉, d. 208), becoming Chen's erudite, is noteworthy.[69] Other independent-minded *shi* likewise flocked to the camps of various anti-Qin rebels, vividly expressing their dissatisfaction with the policy Li Si had crafted.

The Han dynasty, which inherited the Qin, learned the lesson. It did not try to turn all educated persons into officials, and it tolerated a certain degree of intellectual autonomy, while at the same time keeping the major "levers" of social (and ultimately economic) advancement in the court's hands. The recommendation-*cum*-examination system, which originated in the early Han period and was continuously modified and adjusted until it became the major avenue of personal advancement in the late imperial China, turned out to be an ideal compromise between the elite and the state. It preserved to a considerable degree the dignity and self-respect for the literati, while efficiently channeling their incorporation into the system of state service. As in many other respects, Han both abandoned the harsh model of Qin and inherited its basic guiding principle—that of maintaining a single source of wealth and fame for the members of the educated elite.[70]

The complexity of relations between the elite and the throne in imperial China defies an easy summary, and in what follows I shall confine myself to a few observations regarding the impact of the Zhanguo modes of *shi* behavior on the imperial educated elite. One of the most notable continuities between pre-imperial and imperial intellectuals is their ongoing attachment to the state. As I mentioned at the close of Chapter 6, while the imperial literati were less dependent on the throne economically than their Zhanguo predecessors, they did not disengage en masse from the state unless under duress. A combination of economic, social, and ideological factors continued to encourage the most brilliant members of the educated elite to seek their fortune near the throne, endless complaints about the court's filthiness and moral degradation notwithstanding. This, in addition to the empire's firm monopoly on the avenues to prestige and power (except during periods of political turmoil), radically limited the literati's choices and thus reduced their autonomy. Because they lacked the privilege of their Zhanguo predecessors to freely "choose the tree"[71] and switch allegiance from one patron to another, the literati had to adopt a less haughty stance than that promoted by Mengzi or by the *Lüshi chunqiu* authors. In marked distinction to pre-imperial times, their language, rites, and general mode of court behavior all highlighted their dependent and inferior position. While the lamentations of some modern commentators about the literati's putative servility are probably exaggerated, an overall decline in the intellectuals' position vis-à-vis the rulers is undeniable.[72]

Dependent though they were, the imperial literati largely succeeded in preserving their dignity and self-esteem throughout the imperial millennia. Here again the importance of the Zhanguo heritage cannot be underestimated. The very depth of the literati cultural attachment to the legacy of their pre-imperial predecessors ensured that the *shi* pride would not easily evaporate, humiliations and oppression notwithstanding. The idea of "following the Way and not the ruler" was never abandoned, even though its more radical implications, such as affronts to sovereigns, were actively discouraged. Nonetheless, throughout the centuries, leading intellectual figures repeatedly braved harsh penalties in order to prove their true attachment to the heritage of the past.[73]

The ability of the literati to defy rulers despite their overall dependence on the power-holders reflected not just a memory of the proud stance of Zhanguo *shi* but also another legacy of the pre-imperial age: a common belief in the indispensability of intellectuals for the preservation of the state's well-being. The Zhanguo idea of "elevating the worthy and selecting the able" became integral to Chinese political culture and became the intellectuals' most important asset. Rulers and the general populace alike accepted the concept of the educated elite acting as mediator between the throne and commoners, and the ensuing prestige this brought to the literati allowed many members of this stratum to maintain their dignity and even, occasionally, to promote their ideals despite disadvantageous political situations. In the final account, the Zhanguo legacy of politically engaged intellectuals appears to me to be less tragic than some modern scholars perceive it. While the literati did lose their independence, the social prestige, self-respect, and considerable political impact that ensued may have been a worthy compensation.

PART III

The People

CHAPTER 8

Ruling for the People

Thousands of years before Thomas Jefferson or Abraham Lincoln, a
Chinese poet wrote that, quote, "the people should be cherished . . .
the people are the root of a country . . . the root firm, the country is
tranquil." Today the people of Asia have made their desire for freedom
clear—and that their countries will only be tranquil when they are
led by governments of, by, and for the people.

—President George W. Bush

W hen President George W. Bush chose to cite the lines of the epigraph from
"The Song of Five Sons" ("Wu zi zhi ge" 五子之歌)—a forged chapter of
the so-called "old text" (*gu wen* 古文) *Book of Documents*—on the eve of his
visit to the People's Republic of China in November 2005, he made a clever
choice.[1] The idea that "the people are the root" (or the foundation) of the
country (*min ben* 民本), that the ruler bears responsibility for their livelihood,
and that forsaking this responsibility may result in grave consequences for the
monarch, was one of the most common convictions of pre-imperial and imperial thinkers and statesmen. This conviction was "rediscovered" in the early
twentieth century by reformists and revolutionaries, most significantly Liang
Qichao, in their search for traditional Chinese parallels for Western democratic
principles. Thereafter, and especially in recent decades, Chinese scholars have
elevated the "people as foundation" concept as a central principle of Chinese
political culture. A lively debate continues with regard to the relevance of this
concept to modern Western democratic notions, such as the people's sovereignty. It should be noticed, however, that *pace* President Bush, most scholars
follow Liang Qichao's assertion that the *min ben* idea was supportive rather than
subversive of the monarchic order and was not conceived as an alternative to
the ruler-centered polity.[2]

Modern usages of "the people as foundation" concept aside, Chapters 8
and 9 will focus on the place of "people-oriented" thought (that is, thought
that considers "the people" as the most important component of the polity,

and for whose sake the government exists) in pre-imperial discourse. The very broadness of this topic, which relates to almost all aspects of economic, administrative, educational, and military policies, in addition to philosophical issues such as the problem of human nature, is such that a comprehensive discussion would require a full monograph.[3] My goals here are more modest; I focus primarily on the thinkers' views as to the political role of commoners, who are usually, albeit not exclusively, referred to as "the people." In this chapter I trace the origins of the "people as foundation" concept, relating it to the kin-based cohesiveness of the tiny polities of the Western Zhou period and to the political activism of certain segments of the lower strata in the Chunqiu period. In Chapter 9 I demonstrate the ongoing importance of the *min ben* idea in the Warring States period and then analyze thinkers' views regarding the political role of commoners. In particular, I address the seemingly paradoxical coexistence of a strongly pronounced belief in the "people's" political importance yet a nearly unanimous aversion to commoners' intervening in political processes. The latent tension between the declared respect for the people as the polity's raison d'etre and their simultaneous exclusion from policy-making may have eventually contributed to the phenomenon of popular uprisings that plagued imperial China. In the epilogue to Chapter 9 I shall try to show how people-oriented discourse not only legitimated these rebellions but also provided the means for incorporating the rebels into the imperial political system, which prevented them from challenging the foundations of the imperial sociopolitical order.

The discussion of the "people as foundation" concept can be conveniently opened with the following paradigmatic statement by Mengzi:

> The people are the most esteemed; the altars of soil and grain follow them, and the ruler is the lightest. Hence one who attains [the support of] the multitudes, becomes Son of Heaven; one who attains [the support of] the Son of Heaven, becomes a regional lord; one who attains [the support of] the regional lord, becomes a noble.[4]

This statement, which assigns the people an extraordinarily important political role, may serve as a suitable departure point for our discussion. The conviction that the people are the most important component of the polity is not exceptional to Mengzi, but, as I shall show below, reflects a common thread of thought among Zhou period thinkers. In this chapter I shall focus on the early stage of the evolution of this idea, outlining sociopolitical reasons for its early emergence. In particular, I suggest that the legacy of communal cohesiveness among kinship groups and later the actual experience of capital-dwelling commoners participating actively in the political life of the Chunqiu states contributed decisively to elite awareness of the commoners' importance.

Lineage Cohesiveness and Ruling "for the People"

The belief in the exceptional political importance of "the people" is traceable to the earliest layers of the Chinese political tradition. A statement from the "Tai shi" (泰誓, The great oath), a putatively early Zhou document cited in the *Mengzi*, says: "Heaven sees through the people's seeing, Heaven hears through the people's hearing."[5] Another statement from the "Tai shi" cited in the *Zuo zhuan*, presents what may be a conclusion drawn from that statement: "Heaven inevitably follows the people's desires."[6]

The precise dating of the original "Tai shi" is unverifiable, but there is little doubt that both these assertions reflect authentic Western Zhou views. Many of the early Zhou documents of the *Shu jing* display a similar belief regarding the relationship between the people and Heaven. This interrelationship is twofold. On the simplest level, the people serve as a barometer of Heaven's intent, a kind of *vox Dei*: "the awesomeness and intentions of Heaven are discernible from the people's feelings."[7] On the more substantial level, Heaven's intervention in human affairs is motivated primarily by its concern for the people. A ruler's oppressiveness, neglect of the people's needs, and other kinds of misbehavior can cause Heaven to replace the transgressing monarch. Thus malpractice and abuses by Jie, the last Xia king, caused Heaven to pick the Shang founder, Tang, as a new "master of the people" (*min zhu* 民主). Similarly, the cruelty of Zhouxin caused Heaven, which pitied "the people of the four corners" (*si fang min* 四方民), to replace again its "primary son" (*yuan zi* 元子). The new incumbent, King Wen, was able to care for the "small people" (*xiao min* 小民), which made him specifically deserving of Heaven's support. "Protecting the people" (*bao min* 保民) was accordingly identified as one of the major tasks of Zhou government, insofar as the new leaders wanted to escape the miserable fate of the Xia and the Shang.[8]

Many doubts have been raised with regard to the dating and authenticity of each of the *Shu jing* documents, but whatever their dates, it is highly unlikely that their ideology postdates the Western Zhou period.[9] Aside from major declarations about the interconnection between the people's sentiments and Heaven's Decree, there is plenty of evidence that the miserable conditions of the people were a source of major concern for early Zhou statesmen.[10] For the purposes of our discussion, the most interesting issue is not just the sympathy that early Zhou texts express toward commoners, but the authors' explicit belief that Heaven establishes the ruler specifically for the sake of the people. This assertion is present in the clearest form in a lost document, cited in the *Mengzi*: "Heaven, having sent down the people below, created for them a ruler and a Master just in order that the latter help the Thearch in loving [the people]."[11]

This identification of the people as the ultimate end of Heaven's establishment of the ruler is extraordinarily important not only because of its classical provenance, which itself ensured its lasting impact on Chinese political culture, but also due to its amazing earliness. What are the reasons for this? Why did the Western Zhou ideologists, who invariably belonged to the high aristocracy, identify "the people" as the most important component of the sociopolitical order? Was it just one impact of the lessons learned from the demise of the Shang, as the authors of the *Shu jing* chapters want us to believe?[12] Without ruling out this possibility, I would like to suggest that the origins of people-oriented thought should be searched for elsewhere.

To contextualize the emergence of people-oriented thought in the early Zhou period, it is useful to consider, first, who "the people" in contemporary texts were. Of course, as with most terms of political discourse, "the people" (*min* 民) is not a terminologically precise concept, and its semantic field may at times comprise the entire population—that is, all of the ruler's subjects, nobles and commoners alike—or only commoners.[13] In most cases, however, I believe, that the term *min* refers primarily to the politically active segment of commoners, who, in the early Zhou period, were largely coterminous with members of the Zhou clan. Actually, in several *Shi jing* odes, *min* is clearly an exclusive self-appellation of the Zhou clansmen. Thus in a phrase "she who gave birth to the people at the beginning was Jiang Yuan,"[14] "the people" referred to are the descendants of Jiang Yuan's 姜嫄 son, the Zhou forefather, Hou Ji 后稷. Similarly, when the "Mian" 綿 ode depicts the history of "the people," it deals exclusively with the Zhou clan. This equation is persistent in the early parts of the *Shi jing*, strengthening my assumption that "the people" referred to in the *Shu jing* documents discussed above are primarily Zhou clansmen.[15]

The importance of clan (and later lineage) cohesiveness for engendering people-oriented thought cannot be underestimated.[16] Any noble lineage of Zhou times was composed primarily of unranked commoners, who ensured the lineage's economic and military power and whose well-being was directly linked to that of the lineage head. In such a relatively small social unit, communal ties based on common descent moderated internal rank-based gradation, creating a sense of solidarity that transcended social boundaries. If this assertion is correct, then repeated references to the fate of commoners in early Zhou texts were not just political rhetoric but a genuine conviction that reflected common social practices of that age. The ruler was not merely a symbolic "father and mother of the people" (*min zhi fumu* 民之父母),[17] but a real head of their clan/lineage, and his care for his kinsmen was indeed akin to parental treatment. In that case early Zhou people-oriented thought was a by-product of the era's lineage-oriented consciousness. What is remarkable, though, is that this ideological commitment to the well-being of commoners remained intact in the markedly different sociopolitical circumstances of the Chunqiu and Zhanguo periods.

Chunqiu Capital Dwellers

The notion of the political importance of the people that we encountered in Western Zhou texts became overwhelming in the Chunqiu period. The *Zuo zhuan* and the later *Guoyu* abound with statements about the pivotal role of "the people" for the polity's survival and about the ruler's obligation to care for them. The *Zuo zhuan* in particular is considered a true repository of people-oriented ideology.[18] One of its clear manifestations is a frequently cited concept of the people as "masters of the deities" (*shen zhi zhu* 神之主), according to which the people's sentiments are the decisive factor that ensures divine support for the ruler. For instance, in the year 706 the *Zuo zhuan* records a speech by Ji Liang 季梁, an officer from the tiny state of Sui 隨, who disillusioned his ruler of the possibility that the deities would continue to support the state of Sui merely in return for appropriate offerings:

> The people are masters of the deities. Therefore, sage kings accomplished the people's affairs first, and then attended to the deities.... Devote your efforts to the three [agricultural] seasons, improve the five teachings, let [the people] treat appropriately the nine grades of relatives, and then perform sacrifices. Under such conditions people will be peaceful, and the deities will bestow good fortune, so that activities will be successfully completed. Nowadays, however, each person has his own intentions, and the spirits and deities lack their master. Though your [sacrifices] are lavish, what good fortune can be achieved in this way?[19]

Ji Liang rejects the ancient quid pro quo formula according to which divine support would be received in exchange for lavish offerings. Instead, he suggests that the ruler improves the people's well-being, since their sentiments will determine the deities' response to the ruler's pleas. This approach radicalizes the *vox populi–vox Dei* idea of the *Shu jing*: the people determine the behavior of the deities and are not merely a barometer measuring divine approval or disapproval of a given policy. Ensuring a proper economic and moral life for the people becomes accordingly a true precondition for perpetuating divine support and ultimately for the polity's survival. This view is cited in numerous other speeches in the *Zuo zhuan*.[20]

Who were "the people" whom Ji Liang and other speakers considered "masters of the deities"? Were they coterminous with the members of the ruling lineage? In the case of a tiny statelet of Sui, or of other similarly small polities, the size of which did not differ considerably from that of a large-scale (trunk) lineage, the answer may be affirmative.[21] In such polities the deities, especially the ancestral spirits of the ruling lineage, would be particularly attentive to their living kin. But an equation between the people and kinsmen, while appropriate in this case, is not necessarily relevant for all cases of people-oriented thought recorded in the *Zuo zhuan*. Why, otherwise, were the rulers of larger polities such as Chu and Jin, which contained dozens of noble lineages, still urged by their aides to focus on the people's needs as the primary focus of political concern? What other factors, beyond mere lineage cohesiveness, turned their attention to the problems of commoners?

The answer to this question lies, from my viewpoint, in a peculiar social group, the capital dwellers (*guo ren* 國人), who played an extraordinarily active role in Chunqiu politics.[22] This group of people comprised most of the male inhabitants of the capital, including petty nobles (*shi*) and unranked commoners. Some of these capital dwellers were farmers whose plots were located outside the walls, but the group also included the nobles' retainers and merchants and artisans. These people were a major source of manpower for the ruler's armies, and as such they were exceptionally significant. Although they could not match the chariot-riding professionals of aristocratic descent, infantry soldiers recruited from among the capital dwellers were of huge importance not just as auxiliaries, but as the last-ditch (or, more properly, last-wall) defenders of the capital during times of siege.[23] The degree of martial spirit among capital dwellers was therefore an important component of the polity's overall military prowess. The narrator of the *Zuo zhuan* and its protagonists repeatedly identify dissatisfaction of "the people" (meaning primarily capital dwellers) with their ruler and the resulted unwillingness to fight as the major reason for the inglorious demise of such important polities as Wei 衛, Liang 梁, and Guo 虢, among others.[24] Accordingly, many statesmen argued that the people's living conditions directly influenced the state's military prowess. This idea is clearly stated in the following speech by a Chu statesman, Shen Shushi 申叔時:

When the people's lives are plentiful and virtue is correct; when they are employed in whatever is beneficial and their tasks are regulated; when the seasons are followed and products come to fruition, then superiors and inferiors are harmonious, no undertaking is deviant, each demand is addressed and each one knows the standards. Hence the *Poems* say: "You have established the multitudes of our people, everyone follows your standards." [In this way] the deities deliver good fortune, the seasons are without natural disasters, the people's lives are bountiful and plenteous, they are harmoniously unified in attending upon their superiors. Everyone exerts his force to follow the superiors' orders, sacrificing their lives to stand in place of the [combat's] victims. Thereby military victory is attainable.[25]

Shen Shushi's speech exemplifies a common assessment in the *Zuo zhuan* of the people's military role. First, unless the people obey their superiors' commands and are willing to brave death, no victory is possible. Second, the people will not obey unconditionally, but will only do so in exchange for proper treatment in times of peace. Third, the deities will also respond to good rule by providing further assistance to the upright ruler, but their importance is obviously secondary to that of the people. The conclusion is clear: assuring a plentiful livelihood for his subjects becomes the ruler's primary obligation and a major precondition for victory.

The military importance of Chunqiu capital dwellers pales in comparison with the military role of Zhanguo commoners, discussed in Chapter 9. Politically, however, Chunqiu *guo ren* were by far the most active commoner-based group in Chinese history. Their activism derived from their proximity to their ruler, which, at times of domestic turmoil, became an important political asset. When battles were waged on the streets of the capital, aristocrats had no particular advantage, and military intervention by capital dwellers could be decisive. Already in 841, the *guo ren* reportedly had participated in a rebellion within the Zhou royal capital, ousting an oppressive King Li (周厲王, r. 878–841).[26] In the Chunqiu period such interventions became routine: I have identified in the *Zuo zhuan* no less than twenty-five cases in which capital dwellers actively influenced the outcome of internal struggles, such as succession conflicts or inter- and intralineage feuds.[27] In the middle to late Chunqiu period the *guo ren* appear as the most important political force in many states.

Chunqiu statesmen and thinkers did not fail to apprehend the impact of capital dwellers on political struggles. Shen Shushi's recommendation to attract the commoners economically was heeded both by regional lords and by their rivals from among the leading ministers. The contenders for power frequently adopted overtly "populist" measures to attain the people's support: cutting taxes; cancelling old debts; supporting widows, orphans, and the needy; behaving frugally; and the like. Thus Prince Bao 公子鮑 of Song distributed grain to the starving population during a famine, securing thereby the capital dwellers' assistance in a coup against his elder brother, Lord Zhao (宋昭公, r. 620–611) in 611. Similar steps ensured the survival of the Han 罕 lineage in the state of Zheng and the Yue 樂 lineage in the state of Song during the tensest period of interlineage feuds in those states. Probably the most famous example of a scheming minister employing populist measures was the policy adopted by the Tian family in the state of Qi. The Tian leaders used a double system of measures and weights so that they lent the people more grain than the people had to repay. This policy, which reportedly caused the people to "sing and dance" in praise of the Tian, allowed them not only to overcome rival lineages, but ultimately to usurp the power in their state.[28] The consistent efforts of the Tian leaders to secure support from the commoners indicate that the importance of the lower strata was not merely a rhetoric device of moralizing statesmen but a political reality.

In addition to eliciting economic benefits from the lord or from his rivals, capital dwellers sometimes intervened directly in policy-making. Their opinion was influential enough to determine the course of affairs between states or to influence certain promotions and demotions.[29] There were even certain arrangements that institutionalized the input of capital dwellers in policy-making. In cases of exceptional emergency, such as disastrous defeats, domestic turmoil, or just before a fateful decision such as relocation of the capital, rulers assembled capital dwellers, apologized for "humiliating the altars," or performed a religiously significant alliance ceremony (meng 盟) to reconfirm their ties with the populace.[30] This kind of a "people's assembly" encouraged certain scholars to suggest that capital dwellers were "citizens" rather than mere "subjects" and even to assert that Chunqiu polities bore strong similarities to the ancient Greek city-states.[31] This comparison is inaccurate, however, since in the Chunqui polities, unlike in the Greek poleis, the people's assemblies were an extraordinary ad hoc measure and not a normal political institution. Nonetheless, their existence, even if marginal, allows us to pose an intriguing question: why were these nascent participatory modes of policy-making discontinued in later periods and what was their impact, if any, on Zhanguo and later political models?

To answer this question it is useful to assess the attitudes of Chunqiu thinkers toward the political involvement of commoners. The picture obtained from the Zuo zhuan is rather ambivalent, as can be demonstrated from a series of anecdotes about the leading Zheng minister, Zichan (子產, d. 522). Zichan, an exceptionally gifted statesman and a paragon minister in the eyes of later thinkers, rose to power in 543 after a lengthy period of internal feuds in his state, in which capital dwellers were particularly active. This background explains Zichan's exceptional attentiveness to the concerns of the lower strata and his occasional tolerance of their dissenting voices.[32] A famous anecdote tells that the Zheng people were assembling at the *xiao* (校, often translated "schools," but probably meaning a kind of community club) to debate and criticize government actions. Zichan's colleague, Ran Ming 然明, suggested demolishing these places of dissent, but was rebuffed by Zichan:

> Why do you suggest that? The people at morning and dusk retreat and meet together in order to debate the goodness or badness of the power-holder. If I implement whatever they consider good and correct whatever they consider bad—then they are my teachers. Why should I demolish [the clubs]? I have heard of being loyal and good to decrease resentment, not of overawing [the people] to obstruct resentment. Would it not quickly stop in this way? It is like obstructing the river: when it overwhelms the dam, more people will be hurt and I will not be able to save them: is not it better to allow small breaches to direct it? Is not it better that I listen [to criticisms] to make them my medicine?[33]

The story itself may be apocryphal, but that is of minor importance for us: Zichan is clearly portrayed here as a tolerant leader who recognizes the value of public opinion and is willing to mend his ways accordingly. This "democratic" impression, however, is contradicted by another anecdote, told about events that happened a few years later. The Zheng capital dwellers resented Zichan's tax reforms and openly reviled him. Zichan was not impressed, however:

> What is bad about it? If this benefits the altars of soil and grain, I shall follow [this policy] in life and death. Moreover, I heard that the good do not change their measures, hence they are able to succeed. The people cannot be followed, measures cannot be altered. The poem says: "When there is no transgression in ritual and propriety, one should not care for the talk of others." I shall not change [my policy].[34]

The message of this anecdote directly contradicts the prior one: the people are not clever enough, and their opinions should not become a guideline for political action. A leader should make decisions alone, in accordance with his understanding and not with the public mood. The contradiction between the two anecdotes may well reflect Zichan's complex personality. The *Zuo zhuan* tells how at times this leader recognized the importance of the commoners' sentiments and even reestablished a former aristocratic lineage to satisfy public demand. On other occasions, however, when Zichan was confident in his policy, he ignored public opinion or even directly rejected it. Significantly, the *Zuo zhuan* narrator usually demonstrates Zichan's perspicacity by telling how his unpopular policies succeeded.[35] It seems, therefore, that the text as a whole tends to view intervention in political life by the masses rather negatively. If this assumption is correct, this makes the scattered accounts in the *Zuo zhuan* about political activities of capital dwellers all the more significant.

In addition to the Zichan-related anecdotes there are several other speeches in the *Zuo zhuan* that discuss the need to allow the multitudes to have their say on political matters. The paradigmatic one is that by Master Kuang, a large portion of which was cited in Chapter 1. After attributing the downfall of Lord Xian of Wei to his neglect of the people, Kuang outlines the way in which the ruler could have avoided this miserable end:

> From the king down, every one has a father and elder brothers, sons and younger brothers to assist and scrutinize his way of management. Scribes compile documents, blind musicians compose poems, [musical] masters chant admonitions and remonstrance, nobles correct and instruct, *shi* pass on remarks, commoners criticize, traveling merchants [voice their opinion] in the markets, and the hundred artisans contribute [=remonstrate] through their skills. Hence the *Xia Documents* say: "The herald with his wooden-clappered bell goes about the roads, officials correct each other, while artisans would take up their means of remonstrance." This happened in the first month at the beginning of spring, [so that people could] remonstrate [with the ruler] for losing the constant [norms].[36]

Master Kuang outlines here an interesting sort of highly ritualized universal remonstrance system. Not only do professional scribes and music masters (such as Kuang himself) have the right and the duty to criticize the ruler's transgressions, but all social strata, including commoners (but, of course, excluding slaves), should participate in a yearly remonstrance ritual. This ritual reminds us strongly of the earlier age of lineage cohesiveness and may well reflect vestiges of early communal rites, of which Master Kuang, in his capacity as a blind musician and preserver of oral tradition, may have been aware.[37] If so, the speech is even more remarkable, for it outlines the maximum legitimate political participation by commoners. A yearly remonstrance was this maximum; other political action—such as "assisting," "scrutinizing"—and if needed "replacing"—the sovereign were the exclusive right of his closest aides, preferably his kin (see the rest of the speech on pp. 21–22). Commoners were supposed to join a chorus of voices aimed at correcting the ruler's behavior, but they were not to become active political players.

To summarize, the *Zuo zhuan* presents a picture of an extraordinarily active stratum of capital-dwelling commoners, but it also shows the limitations of their political participation. The involvement of capital dwellers in policy-making may have been tolerated, but it was not a desirable factor in the political life of Chunqiu states. Unlike the Greek *poleis*, Chunqiu "city-states" (insofar as this term can be applied to some of the contemporaneous polities) never developed institutionalized means for consulting the opinion of the lower strata. Only under exceptional duress was the "people's assembly" gathered, which indicates that the very involvement of the people in policy-making was a symptom of deep crisis. Being associated with political turmoil, popular political participation remained characteristic of the overall systemic disorder of the Chunqiu age, rather than a hallmark of political correctness.

Interestingly, neither in the *Zuo zhuan* nor in contemporary or later texts do we ever hear of demands by the lower strata to increase their political leverage. This is not just a result of commoners remaining voiceless in our sources. If such demands existed, it may plausibly be assumed that they would have been addressed—even if not endorsed—by those statesmen and thinkers who displayed remarkable concern for the needs of the lower strata. The numerous "people-oriented" speeches in the *Zuo zhuan* and *Guoyu*, of which we cited that by Shen Shushi, repeatedly address the economic concerns of commoners and their need for peace and justice in litigations, but they never speak of their desire for political participation. If some commoners thought otherwise, our sources do not preserve evidence for such ideas.

Even during the heyday of the people's political involvement, participatory modes of government were not considered legitimate, and this situation is symptomatic of Zhanguo developments. For Zhanguo thinkers, unruly capital dwellers, just as unruly nobles, were a source of disorder rather than of legitimate political participation. Following Zhanguo reforms, when a territory-based, quasi-modern state replaced earlier polities, the role of capital dwellers evaporated, and the stratum as such all but disappeared from Zhanguo and subsequent history. The close association of political intervention by capital dwellers with instability and disorder during the Chunqiu age proved in retrospect to be an effective inoculation against other participatory modes of government.

CHAPTER 9

"Full Bellies, Empty Hearts"

The title of this chapter comes from the third paragraph of the *Laozi*:

> If you do not elevate the worthy, the people will not contend. If you do not esteem goods that are difficult to attain, there will be no thieves among the people. If you do not display desires, the people will not be calamitous. Therefore the orderly rule of the sage is to empty their hearts and fill their bellies, to weaken their will and strengthen their bones. He constantly causes the people be without knowledge and without desires; causes the knowledgeable to dare not [acting]. He does not act and that is all; hence everything is ruled in an orderly fashion.[1]

This statement serves as a useful departure point for a discussion of how people-oriented thought was actualized in the Warring States period. In Chapter 8 I demonstrated the ubiquity of the catchphrase "ruling for the people" from the Western Zhou through Chunqiu political discourse; below I shall analyze its impact on Zhanguo thought. What were the actual implications of this slogan? How was a ruler supposed to fulfill his obligations toward the ruled? Which demands of "the people" had to be addressed? The quoted passage suggests that the people deserved economic well-being but were supposed to be removed from political processes. Was this view representative? And if so, what were the reasons behind the opposition to having the people participate in politics? And how does this opposition correlate with the imperative to care for the people?

Tillers and Soldiers

In Chapter 8 we saw that people-oriented thought derived primarily from the peculiar conditions of the Western Zhou and Chunqiu polities, the very small-ness of which encouraged a degree of communal cohesiveness and allowed intervention of the lower strata in political processes. By the Zhanguo period, however, this situation had changed considerably. Large, territorially integrated and centralized states replaced the tiny polities of the Chunqiu age; massive conscript armies diminished the former military importance of capital dwellers; and increasing domestic stability obliterated the capital dwellers' role as kingmakers. In sharp distinction to both the preceding Chunqiu period and the subsequent imperial age, the Warring States period did not witness large-scale political action by commoners; even the very term *guo ren*, so prominent in the *Zuo zhuan*, almost disappears from Zhanguo texts.[2] We might have expected that these conditions would diminish interest in the people's political potential, but this did not happen. As I shall demonstrate, Zhanguo thinkers continuously reiterated the importance of the people for the polity, perpetuating the people-oriented tendencies of the preceding age.

First it may be useful to briefly outline the reasons for the ongoing concern for "the people" in the Zhanguo age. Three major developments may explain this. Most important was the appearance of mass infantry armies based on nearly universal conscription, which turned most of a state's male population into soldiers. Henceforth, the need to discipline these peasant conscripts and prevent their desertion became a major concern of statesmen and generals, and no thinker could ignore this issue. Proposals on how to enhance the conscripts' willingness to fight varied considerably. Some thinkers, like Mengzi and Xunzi, or authors of certain military texts, such as the *Wuzi* 吳子 and *Wei Liaozi* 尉繚子, believed that only a benevolent ruler who cared for the people's livelihood would imbue them with martial spirit; a military manuscript from Yinqueshan 銀雀山, Shandong, for instance, recommends that the ruler "love the people as a newborn baby."[3] Others, like the *Shang jun shu* authors, believed that the people could be persuaded to fight only if their individual interests and fears were addressed: high rewards for good soldiers and heavy punishments for deserters would turn cowards into brave fighters. Yet another view, most explicitly present in the *Sunzi bingfa* 孫子兵法, treats the problem as primarily military and tactical: the soldiers should be placed in "fatal terrain," "from where there is nowhere to go"—and only then they will fight to death.[4] Whatever their precise recommendations, different thinkers came to the unanimous realization that in an age of mass armies, one would not succeed militarily without paying due attention to the masses of conscripts, before and during the battle.

A second reason for the increasing concern with the people's affairs was economic. The widespread introduction of iron tools during the fourth century BCE (if not earlier) revolutionized Zhanguo agriculture, improving cultivation capabilities, increasing yields, and making it possible to turn virgin soil into farmland.[5] Leaders of the Warring States swiftly identified the economic potential of these developments and launched a series of profound economic reforms that changed the terrain, the society, and the state. Large-scale irrigation proj-

ects, wasteland reclamation, and an increase in the yields of individual households were widely recognized as crucial for the state's economic well-being,
without which no long-term military success was possible. The resulting degree
of state intervention in agricultural activities and in the life of the peasants, as
reflected in the documents found at Shuihudi and elsewhere, is truly remarkable. The state was concerned with everything, from weather conditions, to the
number and quality of iron utensils and draft animals distributed to peasant
households, to the fitness of the oxen used in agriculture, which were measured
every season, with punishment inflicted on local officials and village heads if
the oxen decreased in girth.[6] The extent and intensity of this intervention into
the life of the lower strata could not but increase the awareness of thinkers and
officials regarding to the commoners' needs.[7]

The thinkers' concern with the peasants' lives was not just a by-product
of the intensive contacts between the elite and the commoners in the inter-
ventionist Warring State, but reflected deeper problems faced by most states in
the wake of economic reforms. Massive development of wastelands and other
labor-consuming projects, such as canal construction, created occasional labor shortages, which made peasants into a most important economic—and
not just military—asset. In particular, the potential of large-scale migration of
peasants from one state to another, inflated in Mengzi's belief in commoners
"voting with their feet" against an oppressive government, was a source of major concern for power-holders.[8] Statesmen and thinkers had to consider how
to prevent negative migration balance, how to lure peasants into productive
work, how to encourage them to develop the wasteland, and how to tap their
resources without creating excessive resentment. Proposals differed considerably. Some, like Mengzi, advocated lenient government, reduced taxation, and
laissez-faire politics; others, like Shang Yang, supported proactive government
that would shape an individual household's economic behavior in accordance
with the ruler's needs; still others, like the authors of the "Qing zhong" (輕重,
Light and heavy) chapters of the *Guanzi*, proposed primarily economic means
of manipulating the people's behavior.[9] Despite their disagreements, thinkers
unanimously assigned crucial importance to the people's interaction with the
government on the economic front.

The third factor behind the increasing attention paid to commoners in
Zhanguo texts is the changed composition of the ruling elite. As discussed in
Chapter 5, new recruitment procedures and increasing social mobility allowed
a certain number of people from humble origins to join the ranks of the elite
and to enter the state apparatus. These newcomers brought with them valuable personal experience that made them particularly attentive to the people's
economic miseries. Thus aside from pragmatic concerns with the state's stabil-

ity, we cannot neglect the genuine indignation of many thinkers at the misery of commoners. The constant topic of peasants' "freezing and starving" (*dong'e* 凍餓), ubiquitous in Zhanguo texts, cannot be dismissed as pure propaganda: it evidently reflects the real empathy of members of the ruling elite for those they ruled.[10] Similar factors may stand behind the strong condemnation of wars and their devastating effects on the general populace, another common topic in contemporary writings.

This combination of objective and subjective factors explains why the people-oriented ideology continued to dominate Zhanguo discourse. Even a cursory reading of Zhanguo texts indicates a ubiquitous concern with the commoners' poverty and miserable conditions. While thinkers disagreed with regard to proper ways to ensure a decent livelihood for the masses, they uniformly demanded that the rulers address the people's needs, most prominently their welfare and personal security. To illustrate the degree of consensus on this topic I shall not pile up citations from major texts,[11] but rather focus on a thinker who is often singled out as lacking pro-people sentiments, namely, Shang Yang. While the book attributed to him, the *Shang jun shu*, contains many later additions, it is sufficiently consistent ideologically to be treated as representative of what Zheng Liangshu calls Shang Yang's "school" (*xue pai* 學派).[12]

Shang Yang appears as an unlikely candidate for a discussion of people-oriented thought. Unlike many of his rivals, he did not try to present himself as a champion of the masses; on the contrary, his book abounds with provocative statements such as "when the people are weak, the state is strong; hence the state that possesses the Way strives to weaken the people."[13] As a political practitioner, Shang Yang is renowned for his harsh treatment of the people, in particular, his advocacy of severe punishment for slight offences, his encouragement of mutual surveillance, and his establishment of mutual criminal responsibility of family members. He is similarly famous for his blatantly pro-military statements, such as his recommendation "to perform whatever the enemy is ashamed to do" and to let the people "look at war as a hungry wolf looks at meat."[14] Such pronouncements and their practical implementation in the state of Qin under Shang Yang's aegis has made many traditional and modern scholars regard this thinker as a hateful intellectual. Roger Ames, for instance, emphatically argues that "benefiting the people" is "the converse of traditional Legalist doctrine."[15] Nonetheless I think it is possible to demonstrate that on the level of both ideological commitment and the perceived practical implications of his policies, Shang Yang basically belongs to the same people-oriented tradition as Mozi, Laozi, Mengzi, and Xunzi, who are frequently identified as paragons of the people-oriented approach.

In Chapter 2 I cited Shang Yang's assertion that a state with a powerful ruler and all-penetrating law was created to benefit the people, and it is time now to explore this idea. Shang Yang believes that without a ruler, officials, and the law, the people will descend into anarchy and mutual extermination. The problem is that "while the people's nature is to seek orderly rule, their affairs are disordered."[16] The people are simply unaware of what is to their ultimate benefit, so they are unable to maintain proper rule without active government intervention. Harsh rule over them is necessary to attain sociopolitical order, without which "the rich cannot protect their possessions, while the poor cannot perform their tasks: the fields are desolated and the state is impoverished."[17] Governmental prohibitions and regulations, harsh punishments, and encouraging the people to focus on agricultural activities and to fight resolutely—all these serve the people's interest. Shang Yang summarizes:

> Therefore my theory causes the people who seek profit to get it nowhere but from tilling, and those who want to avoid disasters to escape nowhere but through warfare. Within the boundaries, each one of the people is devoted to tilling and warfare; thus they attain whatever pleases them. Hence although lands are few, grain is plenty; although the people are few, the army is strong. He who is able to implement these two within the boundaries has completed the Way of overlord and Monarch.[18]

Shang Yang's logic is clear. The people will never enjoy tranquil and affluent life until the state is rich and powerful, and the state will not attain power and full granaries unless the people are forced to till the soil and engage in war. Hence "heavy punishments and light rewards mean that the superiors love the people."[19] Similarly, Shang Yang's militarism is presented as a way to achieve universal peace: "Hence when war eradicates war, even war is acceptable; when murder eradicates murder, even murder is acceptable; when punishments eradicate punishments, even doubling punishments is acceptable."[20]

If harsh punishments are the way to personal and collective welfare, while the war is the way to peace, then, dialectically, Shang Yang's policy in general serves the same ends as those advocated by his rivals. In light of these statements, his outspoken remarks about conflicts of interest between the state and society ("the people") should be understood as pertaining to a temporary, not basic conflict. Oppressive measures are needed simply to prevent the people from harming their own best interests. In the final account, such measures serve the people:

> When a sage rules the people, he must attain their hearts; hence he is able to use force. Force generates strength; strength generates awesomeness;

awesomeness generates virtue; virtue is born out of force. The sage ruler possesses it exclusively; hence he is able to promulgate benevolence and righteousness in All under Heaven.[21]

This assertion belongs to what may well be a later layer of the *Shang jun shu* and probably reflects an attempt to accommodate its theory within "Confucian" moral discourse; but even if the terms "benevolence and righteousness" here do not reflect Shang Yang's genuine thought, the basic thrust of the argument recurs throughout the *Shang jun shu*. The thinker repeatedly stresses that his aim is not to oppress the people for the sake of the ruler but to create the favorable conditions that will allow the people to enjoy their lives. Actually, the *Shang jun shu* abounds in pronouncement about "benefiting the people" (*li min* 利民) and "loving the people" (*ai min* 愛民) to an extent unseen even in the *Mengzi*, which is widely considered a major repository of people-oriented thought. Some may dismiss these statements of Shang Yang as self-serving propaganda, but I believe this is not the case. With the probable exception of Han Feizi, Shang Yang (and the other contributors to "his" book) is less inclined to beautify his policy than any other thinker; on the contrary, he seems glad to confound his audience with cynical and controversial statements. That he ultimately chose to justify his proposals by invoking the concept of "benefiting the people" suggests at the very least the "emotive force" of people-oriented discourse in the Zhanguo age.[22] "People-bashers" like Shang Yang and "people-lovers" like Mengzi agreed on the most basic point: the people are the only true end of political action. This conviction, even before we discuss its actual impact on everyday political life, can be singled out as one of the most important peculiarities of Zhanguo political thought.

Attaining the People's Hearts

In Chapter 8 we saw that the idea of the people as the end of policy-making had already appeared in the Western Zhou texts and remained influential thereafter. The assertion that the government exists "for the people" became paradigmatic for Zhanguo thinkers. Texts of different ideological affiliations reiterate that the ruler's ultimate goal is to benefit "the people of All under Heaven." For instance, the *Shang jun shu* contains the following passage: "Hence when Yao and Shun were established in All under Heaven, this was not to personally appropriate the benefits of All under Heaven; they were established in All under Heaven for the sake of All under Heaven."[23]

The *Shang jun shu* employs the names of Yao and Shun as signifiers for proper monarchs. As the authors clarify elsewhere, such as in their narratives of the state formation, surveyed in Chapter 2, the ruler, by his very existence, benefits his subjects. These benefits, as we have seen, justify the harsh rule Shang Yang advocates and the monarchical order in general. Another staunch supporter of the ruler's authority, Shen Dao, similarly states that "the Son of Heaven is established for the sake of All under Heaven."[24] Yet while radical monarchists employed the idea that the ruler exists for the people's sake to justify central-ized monarchy, other thinkers resorted to the same idea to restrict the mon-arch's excesses. The "Gui gong" (貴公, Esteeming impartiality) chapter of the *Lüshi chunqiu* states:

> All under Heaven does not [belong to] a single man, it [belongs] to All under Heaven. The harmony of *yin* and *yang* does not prolong [the life of] a single kind, sweet dew and timely rain do not favor a single creature, the sovereign of the myriad people does not follow [whims of] a single person.[25]

The authors of this passage employ the cosmologically stipulated univer-sality of the monarch's concerns to temper the ruler's abuses, reminding the sovereign that his selfish pursuit of personal whims means forsaking his political obligations. What is remarkable for us is the ease with which "for the people" was used both to bolster the monarch's position and to criticize him. This sug-gests the almost axiomatic nature of the paradigm, for it was employed by a great variety of rival thinkers. It would not be an exaggeration to suggest that the notion of people-oriented government became as essential for Chinese political thought as the notion of monarchism; neither idea was openly ques-tioned by any known thinker.[26]

This ubiquity of the notions of "the people as foundation" and "government for the people" in Zhanguo texts has encouraged certain modern scholars to analyze these concepts through a prism of modern Western ideology, especially in the context of the idea of popular sovereignty.[27] I believe this equation is far-fetched; in Part I of this book, enough evidence was marshaled to show that the Chinese political system was intrinsically ruler-centered and that all institu-tional power was supposed to be in the monarch's hands. However, the notion of the people as the "foundation" and the end of political processes was not simply an adornment of autocracy. It served—even if only post facto—to justify rebellions and replacement of particularly inept sovereigns and as such pro-vided a peculiar focus of legitimacy independent of the monarch. At the very least, people-oriented discourse could be employed to improve the functioning of the monarchy by reminding the ruler—and other power-holders—of the legitimate needs of the lower strata. Its impact on actual policy-making should not be exaggerated, but nor can it be neglected.

Did the idea of governing "for the people" contain seeds of governing "by the people"? Were "the people" just an object of the ruler's munificence, or could they legitimately become an independent political actor? The answers to this question differ noticeably. While some scholars consider traditional Chinese attitudes about the people as axiomatically paternalistic, others assert that the people were not just supposed to benefit passively from the benevolent government, but that their views on the government's performance were exceptionally important. Indeed, certain statements by Zhanguo thinkers appear to suggest that "the people" could directly influence policy-making. And yet, as it is well known, China never developed participatory modes of government that were so prominent in the Occident. This paradox encourages certain scholars to ponder over the "paths not taken" in ancient China.[28] I believe, however, that a more careful reading of the sources and their contextualization in Zhanguo political reality may resolve this seeming paradox.

Even a cursory look at Zhanguo texts suggests that the people's political role was highly esteemed. Mengzi, for instance, claims:

> Jie and Zhou[xin] lost All under Heaven through losing the people. They lost the people through losing their hearts. There is a way to attain All under Heaven: when you attain the people, you attain All under Heaven. There is a way to attain the people: when you attain their hearts, you attain the people. There is a way to attain their hearts: gather them at what they desire, do not do whatever they detest, and that is all. The people turn to benevolence just as water flows downwards and animals head for the wilds.[29]

Mengzi's view clearly resembles that of the *Shu jing* documents, cited in Chapter 8, but it looks even more radical. While in the *Shu jing* the people's political role is conceptualized primarily through the *vox populi–vox Dei* notion, Mengzi here does not mention Heaven's Decree. Rather, to attain universal rule, an aspiring True Monarch should focus exclusively on attaining the people's hearts. The importance of the people as kingmakers and the need to "attain their hearts" is reiterated elsewhere in the *Mengzi* and in several other texts.[30] The overall political importance of the people is strongly reasserted in the *Xunzi*:

> When horses are scared of a carriage, the superior man is not tranquil in his carriage. When horses are scared of a carriage, the best is to calm them. When the people are scared of the government, the best is to be kind to them. Select the worthy and good, elevate the sincere and respectful, promote filial piety and brotherliness, care for the orphaned and widowed, sup-

port the poor and impoverished. Thus the people will be tranquil under the government; when the people are tranquil under the government, then the superior man is tranquil in his position. The tradition says: "The ruler is a boat; commoners are the water. The water can carry the boat; the water can capsize the boat." It is said about this.[31]

Xunzi echoes Mengzi in assessing that commoners (*shu ren* 庶人) are the foundation of the ruler's security. Actually, his assessment that they can "capsize the boat" implies much greater degree of rebellious activity on the part of commoners than what is testified to in Zhanguo texts. But is it possible that Xunzi's (and Mengzi's) emphasis on the people's potential for overthrowing the ruler is just a rhetorical device employed to convince the sovereign to adopt benevolent rule? To check this proposition we shall turn once again to that staunch opponent of benevolent government, Shang Yang:

> In the past, those who were able to rule All under Heaven had first to rule their people; those who were able to overcome the powerful enemy had first to overcome their people. Thus the root of overcoming the people is ruling the people, just like smelting metal or making pottery out of earth. When the foundation is not firm, then the people will be like flying creatures, like birds and beasts: who will be able to rule them? The foundation of the people is the law. Hence he who is good at orderly rule, blocks the people with the law, attaining fame and lands.[32]

The statement is unequivocal: the people are the ruler's major rivals; they are beast-like creatures who ought to be tamed by law for the sake of orderly rule. The enmity is explicit, and Shang Yang's views of the appropriate means to deal with the people are diametrically opposed to those of Mengzi and Xunzi. Yet differences aside, the three texts agree that the people are the crucial political actor; hence just like Mengzi, Shang Yang asserts that he who wants to rule All under Heaven should focus on the people's affairs first. This similarity of approach among intellectual opponents cannot be a mere coincidence: evidently the belief among Zhanguo thinkers in the people's political importance was even stronger than it was among thinkers in the previous ages.

The conviction that the people could influence the outcome of power struggles led many thinkers to express particular concern with the people's opinion, or, more precisely, with their "hearts." This is not confined to Mengzi; earlier, Confucius offered a similar opinion, saying that "without the people's trust, the state will not stand firm," and the *Laozi* suggests that the sage's political success derives from "turning the hearts of the hundred clans into his own heart."[33] Even Shang Yang, despite his low esteem of the people's moral and intellectual qualities, argues that when establishing the laws, public opinion should not be neglected:

> This is the orderly rule of the state: when [affairs] are determined by a household, you will become the Monarch; when determined by officials, you will be strong; when determined by the ruler himself, you will be weak. . . . If a criminal is invariably denounced, then the people make decisions in their hearts. When the superiors order and the people know to respond, when [law-enforcing] methods take shape in the household and are performed by the officials, then the affairs are determined by a household. The True Monarch determines prizes and punishments according to the people's hearts; the means [of law enforcement] are determined at the household level. . . . The orderly ruled state values decisions made below.[34]

This curious passage, which, as Lewis has noted, "read out of context sounds like an appeal for democracy or anarchy,"[35] shows the importance of public opinion even for a supporter of an overtly authoritarian political system. Only internalization of laws and regulations by the populace will make these regulations effective; hence Shang Yang and his intellectual followers paid considerable attention to the clarity of laws and to their universal promulgation. While in certain circumstances the *Shang jun shu* advocates taking decisive action despite public dissent, such steps are considered ad hoc expediency and not the normal way of ruling the state.[36] Just as his rivals did, Shang Yang realized the need to solicit from the population a certain degree of acceptance of policies, even if it was not outright approval.

Given this universally declared respect for the people's views, we may wonder how the thinkers intended to ensure the input of the lower strata into policy-making. It is in this regard that the ostensible paradox of Zhangguo thought becomes particularly striking. Not only did almost none of the known thinkers propose institutional solutions that would allow the people to voice their opinions on government affairs, but even modest arrangements of the Chunqiu period were largely discontinued. Although some archaizing texts mention the ruler's consultations with the people, those practices certainly do not amount to participation by commoners in the political process. For instance, the "Hong fan" (洪範, Great plan) chapter of the *Shu jing* advises the king: "When you have doubts, consult your heart, consult the officials, consult the commoners, consult milfoil and tortoise shell."[37] Yet among the five participants in "consultations," commoners are the least important, and the text thrice recommends applying the debatable policy despite their opposition. Other vestiges of "consulting the people" are mentioned in the *Zhou li* 周禮:

> The office of the minor minister of justice. He maintains the government beyond the court, gathering the myriad people to inquire [about their opinion]. First, he inquires when the capital is endangered; second, when the capital is to be moved; third, when a ruler is to be established. The positions [of the participants]: the king faces south; the Three Dukes, the heads of the provinces and the hundred clans face north; the ministers face west, the officials face east. The minor minister of justice bows to let each advance in turn and queries [their opinion]: thus the multitudes assist [the king] in attaining his will and in determining his plans.[38]

The pattern outlined in the *Zhou li* echoes historical evidence from the *Zuo zhuan*, which recorded gatherings of "the people's assembly" on occasions of capital transfer or the ruler's captivity;[39] but this apparent similarity disguises a major difference between the two texts. In the *Zhou li*, the process of consulting the "myriad people" is degraded to a position of a minor bureaucratic procedure, maintained by a petty official; its dramatic importance as attested in the *Zuo zhuan* has been abandoned, and it has become just another highly ritualized performance, far removed from actual policy-making.

In addition to these two examples, we may mention Mengzi's recommendation that the ruler solicit the opinion of capital dwellers before making significant promotions or demotions. This recommendation, discussed in Chapter 2,[40] remained an exception: Mengzi never developed it nor even raised again the issue of political activity of capital dwellers. It was Mozi who proposed what appears to be the most systematic notion of consulting the commoners. In his blueprint for the ideal state, outlined in the "Shang tong" chapters, Mozi depicts a process of routine consultation between the ruler of each administrative unit and the subject population of his unit; for example, the Son of Heaven addresses "the hundred clans of All under Heaven" saying:

> Whenever you hear of good or bad, you must report to your superiors. You must unanimously approve whatever the superiors approve, and you must unanimously disapprove whatever the superiors disapprove. When the superiors are wrong, you must admonish them, and when the inferiors are good, you must recommend them. One who conforms upward and does not ally with inferiors is rewarded by superiors and praised by inferiors. . . . One who allies with inferiors and is unable to conform upwards will be punished by the superiors and destroyed by the hundred clans.[41]

This explicit encouragement for the populace to contribute to administrative procedures is unparalleled: Mozi apparently envisioned a kind of "surveillance from below" over the office-holders, whom the people might either denounce or recommend for further promotion. This imagined popular participation within a rigidly hierarchic system of identifying with one's superiors is probably the single example of a kind of "guided democracy" in ancient Chinese thought. Needless to say, this proposition, just as Mozi's utopia in general, had a minor if any impact on the political thought and political culture of the Zhanguo and subsequent periods; at best, it constitutes a "path not taken." Moreover, even in the *Mozi*'s model, the people's political role remains marginal in comparison with the activism of the Chunqiu period capital dwellers.

Thus despite lofty pronouncements of being attentive to the "people's hearts," thinkers of the Warring States chose to diminish the possibilities of the commoners having input in policy-making. Most texts ignored the issue altogether; others, such as those surveyed above, turned it into a highly ritualized and highly irrelevant procedure. In later periods, this symbolic incorporation of commoners' views became even further devoid of practical importance. The summa of this process may be the Han dynasty arrangement, in which state officials were supposed to collect popular songs and deliver them to the monarch, for this would permit him to grasp "the people's airs" without personally having to contact the lower strata.[42]

It is time to ask now why the thinkers, who repeatedly emphasized the importance of grasping the people's needs and attaining the people's hearts, did not think of any institutionalized way of allowing the people to voice their opinions? An immediate answer would be circumstantial. As mentioned in Chapter 8, ever since the Chunqiu period, active popular participation in politics was coterminous with political turmoil. Memories of unruly capital dwellers becoming power brokers between the rulers and their rebellious ministers created strong distaste for political activism from below. Confucius succinctly summarizes this feeling when he identifies a state that possesses the Way as one in which "the commoners do not debate [government affairs]."[43] Laozi echoes him, speaking about the desirability of the people's "simplicity" (*pu* 樸). Although the *Laozi*'s dislike of "enlightening" (*ming* 明) the people is explicitly "un-Confucian," its political implications are similar to those expressed in the *Lunyu*.[44] Evidently, the thinkers' awareness of the importance of public opinion did not mean that the people should be encouraged to air their views.

Valid as it is, the political explanation for the thinkers' negative views regarding political participation by commoners is insufficient in my eyes. Even if the Chunqiu turmoil created hostility to political activism by the people, it is difficult to believe that this reason alone could have remained effective throughout the Zhanguo centuries, which witnessed not one single recorded instance of commoners taking massive political action. In my opinion deeper philosophical and social factors shaped the thinkers' dislike of commoners' political involvement. In the last section of this chapter, I shall address these factors, focusing primarily on Confucius and his followers, who frequently presented themselves as "the people's" champions, while at the same time actively discouraging the political participation of the lower strata.

Petty Men and Their Exclusion from Politics

A century ago, while assessing the "democratic potential" of ancient Chinese thought, Liang Qichao observed that the deeply hierarchical mindset of most Zhanguo thinkers was one of the major obstacles to adopting the idea of "the people's power" (*min quan* 民權).[45] This is an extremely valuable observation. Indeed, a widespread identification of the lower strata with morally impaired "petty men" (*xiao ren*) may explain the negative views of their political activism.

The strongly pronounced juxtaposition of "superior" and "petty" men is evident in the texts of so-called "Confucian" lore, from the *Lunyu* to such texts as *Mengzi, Xunzi,* or the *Zun de yi* 尊德義 from Guodian (for which see note 50 below). Although this juxtaposition is primarily ethical, both "superior" and "petty" also have explicit social connotations. In particular, the term *xiao ren* refers in the *Lunyu* and later "Confucian" writings both to persons of mean origin and to mean persons. As I shall demonstrate, throughout the Zhanguo period it had considerable semantic overlap with the terms for "commoners" (*shu ren* or *shu min* 庶民), and these groups were strongly discouraged from taking part in politics.[46]

A negative attitude toward petty men is one of the strongest features of the *Lunyu*. Petty men are those who think only of profit, particularly land; they have no understanding of righteousness; they seek conformity, not harmony; they are haughty and have no understanding of Heaven's Decree, for which reason they are reckless.[47] In a phrase that makes most modern admirers of Confucius feel uncomfortable, the Master proclaims: "Only women and petty men are difficult to nourish. When you let them close, they are unruly; when you shun them, they resent."[48]

This statement, aside from indicating Confucius's gender prejudices, is important for indicating that belonging to the category of petty men as not exclusively ethical, but in some cases inborn. It is clear from the *Lunyu* (just as it is from the *Zuo zhuan*) that a person of a noble origin who misbehave could be pejoratively labeled *xiao ren*; but was it possible for a commoner to become a *junzi*? Was *xiao ren* a transcendable category, or was it an inherent quality of people of low birth except in certain extraordinary cases? The answer is equivocal. Confucius, as is commonly known, was a great believer in education's potential to change human beings and to improve one's quality; on the individual level, therefore, he probably would not deny the possibility that any human being, or at least any male, might become a superior man. However, neither he nor any of his followers envisioned a society in which education would turn *all* the males into superior men. For many—probably for most—this category was inborn and would forever remain so. Hence Confucius is cited in the *Lunyu* as saying: "When a superior man learns of the Way, he loves others; when a petty man learns of the Way, he is easily employable."[49]

Thus learning, even if it improves the quality of a petty man, will not allow him to transcend his social category and rise to the position of a superior man. The reason for this predicament is not necessarily a bad pedigree—an issue that is never explicitly raised in the *Lunyu*—but simply the moral and intellectual impairment of commoners. This impairment is clearly indicated in another saying: "You can let the people follow [the Way], but not understand it."[50]

This statement clarifies why Confucius and his followers had a deeply embedded aversion to the people's participation in political processes. The very idea that the government should be conducted by the most able, moral, and intelligent men made contradictory the notion of sharing this responsibility with morally and intellectually impaired commoners. These are the origins of Confucian paternalism: the people deserve provision for their welfare, their interests should be of the utmost importance to the ruler, their feelings should be taken into consideration—but their direct input in decision-making is mostly undesirable. The decisively hierarchical nature of the Confucian vision is clearly outlined by Mengzi: "Some toil with their hearts, some toil with their force. Heart-toilers rule men; force-toilers are ruled by men. Those who are ruled by men, feed men; those who rule men, are fed by men—this is the common propriety of All under Heaven."[51] And again: "Without the superior men, nobody will rule the commoners; without the commoners, nobody will feed the superior men."[52]

These statements are the clearest exposition of Confucius's and his followers' sociopolitical ideal. Society is based on a separation of functions between the rulers and the ruled; and the hierarchy is both moral and social. Mengzi's first pronouncement was made in the context of polemics against Xu Xing 許行, a proponent of radical agricultural equality, who urged the rulers to till the soil to avoid exploiting the peasants. Mengzi was appalled by this supposed degradation of superior men, but his indignation is equally applicable, mutatis mutandis, to the notion of elevating commoners to the position of active participants in politics. This view is echoed in the *Xunzi*: "Hence it is said: Superior men employ virtue; petty men employ force. Force is the servant of virtue."[53]

Xunzi employs here the term "petty men" as a social category, for it is equated later in the text with "the hundred clans" (*bai xing* 百姓). Commoners as such do not deserve much respect insofar as moral and mental capabilities are concerned. Hence Mengzi made the following harsh statement: "Slight is the difference between men and beasts and birds. Commoners abandon it; superior men preserve it."[54]

This pronouncement is radical in its disdain for commoners, who, as a social category, are considered almost beast-like. Understandably, this group is not supposed to participate in political processes. Although they are the foundation of the polity and the ultimate beneficiaries of the political order, the lower strata should nevertheless be forever segregated from decision-making.

How does this deeply rooted elitism correlate with the pro-people sentiments that are so prominent in the *Mengzi* and *Xunzi*? And how does it correlate with these thinkers' frequently stated belief in the moral mutability of any human being (or at least any male), who may become a Yao or Shun or Yu? The answer, I believe, lies in distinguishing between individual and social levels of potential change. Education may alter an individual; hence Confucius's followers unanimously supported educational efforts directed at the broadest possible audience. Simultaneously, however, they realized that this potential of self-transformation for petty men is unlikely to engulf most members of the lower strata. Xunzi was explicit about this:

> Hence a petty man can become a superior man, but he is indisposed to become a superior man; a superior man can become a petty man, but he is indisposed to become a petty man. It is not impossible for petty and superior men to turn into each other, but they do not turn into each other. It is possible, but cannot be enforced on them.[55]

Xunzi's conclusion is clear. Petty men do not intend to become superior men; and because they are unwilling to transform themselves, their direct political participation is certainly unwelcome. But if this is so, how can a statesman trust the "hearts" of those impaired human beings? Xunzi and Mengzi did not address this issue. It was up to Han Feizi to point out the intrinsic contradiction between the low esteem his rival thinkers had of the people and their advocacy of being attentive to them:

> Nowadays, those who do not understand what orderly rule is say: "Attain the people's hearts." Should attaining the people's hearts bring about

orderly rule, then there would be no use for [the model ministers] Yi Yin and Guan Zhong: it would be enough just to listen to the people and that is all. Yet the people's knowledge is as useless as that of a child. Now, if a child's hair is not shaved, his stomach will ache, and if the boil is not lanced, the disease will worsen. When the child is shaved and the boil is lanced, somebody must hold him; the loving mother holds him tight, but the child still wails incessantly, as he does not know that a small pain will be greatly beneficial to him.[56]

Han Feizi shrewdly employs the reasoning of his Ru opponents to attack their people-oriented discourse. The simile of a child resembles Mengzi's beast simile, differing only in matters of emphasis. Mengzi considers commoners beast-like since they are ethically impaired; Han Feizi singles out the intellectual deficiency of commoners and hence prefers to compare them to a child. By invoking a common "Confucian" notion of parental relations between the ruler and the people, Han Feizi is able to undermine the validity of the Ru appeal to the people's hearts. Being childish and hence incompetent, the people should not be consulted; the government must work to their benefit, but should not heed their opinion. Han Feizi subsequently explains that government actions, while painful, are beneficial to the people and hence should be implemented despite the people's resentment. He concludes:

> One seeks sage and all-penetrating *shi* because the people's knowledge is considered insufficient to be guided by. In antiquity, Yu broke the way for the Yangzi and dredged the [Yellow] River, but the people gathered to throw stones at him; Zichan opened dividing lines between the fields and planted mulberries, but the Zheng people slandered him. Yu benefited All under Heaven; Zichan preserved [the state of] Zheng, but each was slandered: this clarifies that the people's knowledge is insufficient to make use of. Hence the *shi* are elevated, and the worthy and knowledgeable are sought after. To govern while expecting to match the people's [hopes] is the beginning of calamity; it is impossible to attain proper rule together with [the proponents of such views].[57]

Han Feizi supplies historical examples of the people's stupidity and short-sightedness, but then turns to a subtler argument. If the people's voices are to be heeded, then the need in meritocratic government may disappear. Han Feizi cannily addresses *shi* fears for their positions at courts, manipulating them against people-oriented discourse. His message is clear: one who relies on "the worthy and knowledgeable" persons such as Yu and Zichan has no need to seek "the people's hearts." The people should forever remain the object of policy-making; they should not become the makers of policy even indirectly, through listening to their sentiments.

Han Feizi's astute observation directs our attention toward another reason for the thinkers' unwillingness to let the people air their opinions. After all, it is precisely the self-imposed task of Zhanguo thinkers to speak on the people's behalf and in their stead. This appropriation of what Tu Wei-ming aptly defines as "the most generalisable social relevance (the sentiments of the people)"[58] by the members of the *shi* stratum was too important an asset to be yielded to the uneducated masses. It was in the best interest of the self-proclaimed champions of the people from among the educated elite to keep commoners precluded from political processes.

This suggestion may sound cynical, but it is not necessarily so. In the highly mobile society of the Warring States, those commoners with the abilities and desire to influence policy-making could join the ranks of the elite and become legitimate political players. Those who remained behind evidently lacked sufficient aspiration or talents—or so, at least, most *shi* wanted to believe. Paradoxically, then, it may be precisely because of the opening of the elite in the Zhanguo age that Chunqiu modes of commoner political participation were discontinued. In an aristocratic society a commoner, and often a *shi*, could not exercise his aspirations directly, aside from participating (and probably leading) the activities of capital dwellers. In the Warring States period, as avenues of individual advancement opened, there was no longer need to wrestle power from above. Commoners were no longer hermetically excluded from the ruling elite, and as some of them were routinely co-opted into the *shi* stratum, this may have created a kind of "popular representation" from above, which eliminated the need for active political participation from below. Yet although this arrangement worked well enough throughout the Zhanguo period, it proved inadequate under the new, imperial arrangements. Shortly after the imperial unification, collective political action by commoners was resurrected, and the results were devastating.

Epilogue: To Rebel Is Justified

When Xunzi expressed the opinion that "the [people's] water can capsize the [ruler's] boat," he could not have known that his prescience would be confirmed just twelve years after the imperial unification of 221. Shortly after the death of the First Emperor, a group of conscripts led by a mere farmhand, Chen She, rebelled in central China. Swiftly soliciting support from the rural elite,[59] Chen She tried to establish a dynasty of his own, challenging the Qin rule.

Although he and his immediate lieutenants were defeated within a few months, other groups of rebels carried on the uprising, ultimately eliminating the Qin. A new dynasty, the Han, was established under the leadership of another person of humble origin, Liu Bang (劉邦, d. 195). The first popular rebellion in Chinese history had successfully toppled the first imperial dynasty.

These well-known events became paradigmatic for later statesmen and historians. The astounding success of Chen She and his kind defied easy explanations. A generation later a leading early Han historian and political thinker, Jia Yi, was still shocked:

> Chen She came from a house that had a broken jar for its window, and where the door was held by ropes. He was a servant of peasants, an exiled among exiles. His abilities did not match even those of an average person; he lacked the worthiness of Zhongni (Confucius) and Mo Di (Mozi) or the riches of Tao Zhu and Yi Dun. He walked among soldiers and would bow and lift his head once he met colonels or captains. Heading a group of deserters, he commanded several hundred men, whom he led to attack Qin. They cut trees to make their weapons, raised bamboo poles to make their flags, and All under Heaven responded to them like an echo, gathering like clouds. Taking provisions with them, [the people] followed him like a shadow. Then bravos from east of the mountains rose together and destroyed the Qin lineage.[60]

Putting aside for the time being Jia Yi's analysis of Qin's faults, let us address the reasons for the rebellion's amazing success. The reasons are all the more important because Chen She's rebellion was not just the first instance of a massive commoner uprising in Chinese history; it also established a pattern for recurrent rebellions, which plagued the imperial dynasties from Qin and Han to Ming and Qing. Can we contextualize this rebellion within the people-oriented discourse, the contours of which we outlined above?

To answer this question, it is useful to distinguish between two major factors in the rebellion's success: its massiveness on the one hand and the active participation of the elite on the other. The reasons for its size are not always easily traceable, especially since we know regrettably little about commoners' lives under the Qin empire. Nonetheless, we can make certain assessments about the impact of unification on the peasants' lot. Above, I noted that the people-oriented thought of the Warring States period derived from a blend of genuine ideological commitment to the well-being of commoners and rational political calculations, according to which dissatisfied peasants would abscond or desert a battlefield, radically weakening the state. It is in regard to running away that unification brought about a dramatic change. As Qin ruled most of the agricultural "All under Heaven," running away from its officials was no longer a feasible option for many.[61] Furthermore, as military campaigns shifted from the life-and-death struggles of the Warring States to invading the remote outskirts of the empire, fears of massive desertions lessened. Moreover, the decrease in warfare may have radically diminished military-based career opportunities, which were one major avenue of commoner advancement into the elite in the Zhanguo age. Looking at it from this perspective, unification and the "lasting peace" it brought did not necessarily benefit the peasants, *pace* the First Emperor's lofty pronouncements.[62]

If this analysis is correct, then Chen She's rebellion appears in retrospect as a stroke of a genius. At a crucial historical junction, when the peasants had lost their former leverage with the power-holders, Chen and his followers created a new balance of power. Thereafter the ruling elite could never forget of the possibility of a violent insurrection from below. Appropriating Xunzi's insight, the anti-Qin rebel leaders had displayed remarkable "class consciousness" in the pure Marxist sense of this word.

Yet the rebellion of Chen She was not just an instance of "class struggle"; many more factors were involved in its unfolding and ultimate success. In the rebel camp, we encounter not just farmhands, vagabonds, and convicted slaves, but also village elders, local bravos, members of the former elite of the conquered Warring States, and even turncoats from among the Qin officials.[63] Needless to say, each of these groups had distinct motives for joining the rebellion, from avenging the defeat of their state by the long-hated Qin to sheer opportunism. These disparate groups never displayed solidarity beyond their immediate desire to get rid of Qin; actually, internal struggles began in the rebel camp within a few weeks of the launching of the rebellion, and it took a full six years to quell them once the Qin collapsed. But putting aside the motivations of individual rebels and of certain rebel groups, we should ask: how did it happen that so many members of the educated elite eagerly joined the rebel ranks, serving under the command of the most uncouth and—if Sima Qian can be trusted—overtly mediocre leaders, such as Chen She, Liu Bang, and their like? Among these elite members were not only former Warring States nobles, whose anti-Qin feelings are understandable, but also eminent Ru, including Confucius's descendant, Kong Jia (see p. 183), and even some of the court erudites, most notoriously Shusun Tong (叔孫通, fl. 210–190).[64] Becoming the rebels' advisors, these *shi* inaugurated a long-term pattern of elite cooperation with rebellious commoners, a cooperation that became one of the hallmarks of Chinese political culture.

This participation by the elite in the rebellious activities of the lower strata was not incidental. Rather, it reflected a centuries-long tradition that identified the people as the goal of the polity and warned the ruler of grave consequences if he forsook the people's interests. While these warnings were designed as "internal materials" for the ruling elite, once appropriated by rebellious commoners, they became a lethal weapon in their hands. Chen She's rebellion was justified not just in terms of Heaven's Decree/Mandate (a concept that was marginal during the Qin and early Han period),[65] but more basically, in terms of the guiding principles of Chinese political culture. Insofar as the Qin failed to address the needs of its subjects, its legitimacy was severely impaired, and collaboration with rebels became an acceptable political choice. While few if any elite members would have endorsed the Maoist slogan of the Cultural Revolution (1966–1976 CE)—"to rebel is justified" (*zao fan you li* 造反有理)—many of them believed that if a rebellion occurred, it was ipso facto proof of the dynasty's failure, which, in turn, severed the elite's obligations to the ruling family.

Looked at from this perspective, people-oriented discourse takes on a new dimension. In addition to allowing intellectuals to present themselves as "the people's" defenders and thereby improve their standing vis-à-vis the court, this discourse also contributed, even if inadvertently, to the most massive and persistent collective actions by commoners in human history. Recurrent rebellions were part and parcel of Chinese imperial history, becoming arguably the single most significant factor in imperial politics. Although horrific in human cost, rebellions played also a constructive role, for they both ensured an ongoing awareness on the part of the power-holders of commoners' needs and permitted readjustment of the imperial system after periods of internal stagnation. Arguably, it was the intellectual legitimation of rebellions and the active participation of the elite in them that turned disorganized acts of violence into a major political force.[66]

Yet the elite did not just provide rebels with legitimacy, Speaking in class terms, they also "entrapped" them. By joining the rebel camps, elite advisors contributed decisively toward cooptation of the rebels within the imperial political structure. The rebels were not revolutionaries; they did not intend to destroy the imperial order, but just wanted to improve their position within this order; and this potential for cooptation was shrewdly played by the elite advisors, who served as a bridge between the uncouth rebel leaders and the rules of the imperial polity. This eventual cooptation—either by granting the rebel leaders positions within the existing dynastic order, or, in case of extraordinary success, by establishing a new dynasty under the rebel leader—became possible in part because of the people-oriented discourse of the elite. This discourse created an atmosphere conducive both to elite sympathy with rebellious peasants and to peasant leaders accommodating themselves within the imperial political structure. By softening "class antagonism," the people-oriented discourse of the Zhanguo age contributed decisively to the empire's ability to withstand recurrent insurrections.[67]

This relative tolerance of the elite toward popular rebellions explains why these persistent rebellions did not become Marx's "locomotives of history," why they never turned into revolutions. Rather, as Marx's contemporary Thomas Meadows observed in the wake of the Taiping rebellion (太平, 1851–1864 CE), they became "a chief element of a national stability . . . the storm that clears and invigorates a political atmosphere."[68] Being "swallowed" by the imperial polity, rebellions did indeed become a peculiar (and very costly) readjustment system, a kind of bloody popular "election," which determined what family would rule for another dynastic cycle, corrected certain wrongs, but did not alter the foundations of the imperial polity. In the final account, this remarkable, even if unintended, success of Zhanguo intellectuals, by preparing the ideological foundations for occasional rebel cooptation into the imperial polity, became yet another contribution that ensured the empire's longevity.

The Legacy of the Warring States

If there were no contradictions in the Party and no ideological struggles to resolve them, the Party's life would come to an end.
—Mao Zedong, "On Contradictions"

The twentieth century witnessed an unprecedented upsurge of interest in the intellectual legacy of the Warring States. Academics, politicians, and occasionally even students and workers were repeatedly engulfed in controversies about the nature of ancient political thought and about its relevance (or irrelevance) to the projects of modernization, socialism, democracy, patriotism, human rights—and the other ideological agendas that intermittently dominated political discourse in China and among China-watchers abroad. At times the controversies became fierce, even grotesque—like during the infamous "Anti-Confucian" campaign of the early 1970s; at times—like under the current technocratic leadership in Beijing—they have been largely depoliticized.[1] The very depth of the emotional involvement and the participation of practicing politicians in these controversies testify to the success of Zhanguo thinkers, who still have not lost their political relevance more than twenty centuries after their time.

While modern debates over the "Hundred Schools" reflect the vitality of Zhanguo thought, the actual arguments belong mostly to contemporary ideological divisions and are often misleading insofar as the Warring States legacy per se is concerned. Ancient Chinese intellectuals—like political thinkers elsewhere—should be engaged on their own ground, in terms of their immediate goals and the adequacy of these goals to contemporaneous political context.

The political context of the Warring States dictated these thinkers' concerns. They lived in an age when the Zhou sociopolitical order had collapsed and the demand was high for solutions that would lead the Zhou ("Chinese") world toward stability and peace. Devastating warfare, endemic to the post–Western Zhou multistate system, ongoing conflicts within the ruling elite, and new developments in economics and warfare that required major administrative and military readjustments—all these determined the agenda of Zhanguo thinkers and explain the decisively political nature of their intellectual quests. This was, furthermore, an unusual age with a relatively relaxed intellectual atmosphere, when old orthodoxies had collapsed but new ones had not yet emerged, an age when few intellectual taboos remained and when competition between rival courts and existence of an interstate market of talent largely precluded state-organized ideological persecutions. It was against this background that the choices made by Zhanguo thinkers become particularly meaningful. Because these choices were the result of neither coercion nor intellectual stagnation, they have been convincing enough to influence the intellectual and political atmosphere in the Chinese world for centuries.

Among these choices, the single most important was the unanimous rejection of the multistate world of the Warring States and of dispersed political authority. It was the common conviction of the Zhanguo thinkers that only political unification of "All under Heaven" under the aegis of a single omnipotent ruler would bring the long-yearned-for peace and stability. The concept of a universal monarchy, shared by all the known thinkers—with the major exception of Zhuangzi—was the single most important outcome of Zhanguo ideological disputes. Legitimized on political, social, administrative, moral, ritual, and cosmological grounds (not necessarily in this order), the notion of monarchism decisively shaped modes of political behavior in China for more than two millennia. It became the common framework, within which political and intellectual divisions were maintained.

The second major choice made by the Zhanguo thinkers, and by extension by the educated elite as the whole, was their voluntary attachment to the state. In addition to the attraction of government service because of its emoluments and prestige, this service was also reinterpreted by mainstream thinkers—most notably Confucius and his followers—as the noblest way to self-realization. Inevitable hypocrisy, frustrations, and choruses of dissenting voices notwithstanding, this postulate of engagement in a political career became a millennia-long guideline for Chinese intellectuals. It created a situation in which possessors of the supreme moral, intellectual, and cultural authority—the Way—were also holders of political power, the most brilliant being routinely incorporated into state service. This convergence of spiritual and political authority bolstered the prestige of the state and greatly improved the quality of its ruling apparatus. Chinese emperors had at their disposal cohorts of servants who were critical but loyal, obedient but not servile, independent-minded but accepting of the basic principles of monarchic rule. This stratum of intelligent and devoted public servants navigated the Chinese empire through centuries of domestic and external challenges, ensuring its distinctive durability.

Enduring as it was, the Chinese empire certainly fell short of Zhanguo ideals.

Throughout its long history, it was plagued by conflicts and tensions, many of which reflected the intellectual uncertainties bequeathed by the Warring States thinkers to their imperial heirs. Thus the emperor was simultaneously a divinized sage and a human being whose excesses had to be controlled and whose active intervention in policy was rarely welcome. The contradiction between the official image of monarchical infallibility and the common understanding among the elite members of the hollowness of this image generated immense tension, which occasionally brought bitter conflicts between the sovereign and his officials. Lacking institutional means to restrain the emperor, thinkers had to resort to the art of persuasion, which sometimes failed to restrict the monarch's whims. But the monarchs were not undisputable beneficiaries of this situation either. Lacking sufficient intellectual authority, they routinely encountered the opposition of their ministers to their attempts at innovation and were repeatedly relegated to the position of a "living ancestor" or ritual rubber stamp. Paralyzing stalemates between the ruler and the ministers, and occasional dramatic collisions, generated disappointment and bitterness among the imperial literati.

The position of these literati reflected another irresolvable contradiction inherited from the Warring States period. Leading Zhanguo *shi* succeeded in establishing their authority as the possessors of the Way, but simultaneously their adoption of the ruler-centered political order and of the imperative of political engagement forever relegated them to a position as servants of more-often-than-not mediocre rulers. The ensuing tension between their lofty self-image and their insufficiently prestigious position at court fueled a sense of frustration—or in the harsher definition of Liu Zehua, "psychosis"—that became characteristic of the empire's "superior men."

The third tension within the imperial political structure was that between the declared high esteem for "the people" as potential kingmakers and their equally firm exclusion from political processes. Although conceptually this tension was not addressed before the introduction of Western democratic ideas in the late nineteenth century, its latent impact was considerable. Whenever the contradiction between the ostensible concern for commoners' well-being and their actual plight became untenable, the lower strata resorted to the most powerful means of readjusting the imperial system in their favor—insurrection. Although the imperial system was flexible enough to incorporate the rebels within the extant political structure, the price of these periodical "readjustments" was exceptionally high, making them a particularly negative aspect of Chinese political life during the long age of empire.

The enormous moral and material cost of these contradictions should serve as a caution against idealization of the Warring States' intellectual achievements. However, taken dialectically, in the spirit of Mao Zedong's statement in the epigraph, these contradictions and tensions may also help to explain the empire's vitality. Rigid political systems rarely survive for long periods of time, for they are unable to cope with changing circumstances. The Chinese empire, with its somewhat vague operational modes, could, and did, adjust to numerous domestic and foreign challenges. Thus, for instance, the ability of the ministers to accommodate activist monarchs, such as dynastic founders on the one hand, and minors or senile, even mentally disabled, rulers on the other; or the ability of the literati to adapt themselves to peasant emperors and to foreign conquerors—all these factors contributed to the survival of the empire. Indeed, we may consider the intrinsic contradictions of imperial political culture less as malfunctions and more as "creative tensions," to borrow Tu Wei-ming's term.[2] Insofar as these tensions generated pragmatic adaptations to changing sociopolitical landscapes and prevented ossification of the imperial system, the empire preserved much of its élan.

Chinese imperial longevity was a result of many intertwining factors, including the country's geographical context, the paucity of systematic external challenges, and the empire's great prestige in the Asian world far beyond its immediate boundaries. Yet following my thesis that this longevity owes as much to ideological as to geographical, military, or administrative factors, we may conclude that the intellectual enterprise of the thinkers of the Warring States period was impressively successful. Falling short of their promises to bring "supreme peace/evenness" (tai ping 太平), these thinkers and their imperial heirs nonetheless attained considerable stability for expanded populations, over larger territory, and for much longer periods than any comparable political system in the human history. The survival of the empire and its repeated resurrection after periods of domestic turmoil and foreign invasion brought benefits to many of its subjects, especially when judged against the terrible bloodshed of the Warring States era. From that perspective, the empire may have been considered a blessing, even though it was arguably a step backward in terms of ideological pluralism and intellectual brilliance.

Today, as the economic center of gravity of the modern world shifts back to its Asian location, and Western narratives of historical progress are increasingly questioned, blind faith in the supremacy of European sociopolitical and intellectual models gives way to more sober reflections. One is tempted, therefore, again to address the place of the Chinese empire and Chinese political culture in world history. Without either embellishing or disparaging it, we may reflect upon its strengths and weaknesses and reassess its value, not only for better understanding of the worldwide history of political ideas and political formations, but also for coping with the ever-changing political challenges of our own time.

Notes

Introduction

1. Hereafter, unless indicated otherwise, all dates are Before Common Era.

2. The term "Chinese" is anachronistic with regard to pre-imperial "China" and is used here only as a scholarly convention to designate the Zhou 周 cultural realm, the educated elite of which usually referred to themselves as the Xia 夏.

3. I adopt the term "thearch" for *di* 帝, since this neologism aptly conveys both the divine and the mundane aspects of *di*'s power.

4. For the geographical heterogeneity of China (even if we talk only of "China proper," the boundaries of which are roughly similar to those of the first imperial dynasty, the Qin), see McNeill, "China's Environmental History." China's ethnic heterogeneity is twofold. First, it always comprised groups of more or less unassimilated minorities (for the complexity of which, see, for example, Crossley, "Thinking about Ethnicity"). Second, even the so-called "Han" 漢 people appear much less homogenous than it is often imagined, and the distinctions among different subgroups of the Han may well be defined as "ethnic" ones (see, for example, Honig, *Creating Chinese Ethnicity*; Leong, *Migration and Ethnicity*).

5. For the various self-proclaimed offspring of the Roman empire, see, for example, Moreland, "The Carolingian Empire"; MacCormack, "Cuzco, Another Rome?"

6. Practical aberrations from the above model were manifold. Emperors could become hapless pawns in the hands of powerful courtiers or generals; military rule could alter the composition of the elite, while popular rebellions shattered the very foundations of the sociopolitical order. Remarkably, however, the imperial discourse and arguably the imperial ideology, at times of calamity and crisis, remained basically unchanged, which may in turn have contributed toward restoration of the "normative" principles of the empire's functioning after ages of disorder.

7. For Gramsci's notion of hegemony, see, for example, Femia, *Gramsci's Political Thought*; Adamson, *Hegemony and Revolution*.

8. For studies of the metaphysical and cosmological foundations of Chinese political thought, see, for example, Peerenboom, *Law and Morality*; Wang Aihe, *Cosmology and Political Culture*. The single least-represented topic in studies of ancient Chinese political thought is certainly that of the state-society relations in pre-imperial China.

9. The basic English "textbook" of ancient Chinese political thought is the translation of *A History of Chinese Political Thought* by Hsiao Kung-chuan (Xiao

Gongquan). This text, originally written in the mid-1940s, is fairly outdated, but it can be supplemented by two excellent textbook-level studies: Schwartz, *The World of Thought*; and Graham, *Disputers of the Tao*.

10. For the early history of the notion of a "school" or "scholastic lineage," see Csikszentmihalyi and Nylan, "Constructing Lineages"; Smith, "Sima Tan." For classical presentations of Chinese intellectual history in terms of the competing schools of thought, see, for example, Fung Yu-lan, *A History of Chinese Philosophy*; Hsiao, *A History of Chinese Political Thought*. For the ideological "modernization" of ancient Chinese thought in the early 1970s, see, for example, translated articles in the *Chinese Studies in Philosophy* in the 1970s; for an opposite, but similarly biased approach, see, for example, Rubin, *Individual and State*. The attempt to directly connect the Confucian-Legalist controversy with contemporary inner-party struggles was made by the Cultural Revolution leaders Jiang Qing (江青, 1914–1991) and Zhang Chunqiao (張春橋, 1917–2005) during a crucial meeting with scholars engaged in studies of "Legalism" on August 7, 1974 (see details in Liu Zehua, "Zhi shi guannian").

11. Liu Zehua employs the "school" labels in his textbooks (for example, *Zhongguo zhengzhi sixiang shi*), but not in his major studies, such as *Zhongguo chuantong zhengzhi sixiang fansi, Zhongguo chuantong zhengzhi siwei,* and later publications.

12. See Csikszentmihalyi and Nylan, "Constructing Lineages," 61.

13. In dating the relevant texts, I tried to outline their relative sequence, employing both assessments of other scholars and my own methodology based on lexical changes in Zhanguo writings. For my dating methodology, see Pines, "Lexical Changes"; for other studies, see the relevant footnotes. To avoid needless controversy, I have confined my study to those texts, the pre-imperial provenance of which is accepted by most scholars, leaving out some of the hotly disputed texts, such as *Wenzi* 文子, *Shizi* 尸子, *Guiguzi* 鬼谷子, and certain portions of the *Guanzi* 管子. Similarly, I have avoided focusing on those texts that may have been heavily edited in the early imperial period, such as the *Zhou li* 周禮.

14. See Boltz, "The Composite Nature," 61; Lewis, *Writing and Authority*, 58.

15. My understanding of archeological approaches, for which I am indebted to Gideon Shelach, is based on the discussion in Drennan et al., "Methods," especially 122–123.

16. Liu Xiang, in his capacity as an imperial librarian, was responsible for editing and "republishing" many important pre-imperial texts, such as the *Xunzi* 荀子, *Guanzi* 管子, and *Zhanguo ce* 戰國策. Ever since Kang Youwei (康有爲, 1858–1927), doubts have been raised with regard to possible forgery or modification of earlier texts by Liu Xiang and his son, Liu Xin (劉歆, d. 23 CE). For Kang's views, see his *Xin xue wei jing kao*; for criticism of his view, see van Ess, "The Old Text/New Text Controversy"; for the Han background of Kang's views, see Nylan, "The *chin wen/ku wen* Controversy." Modern suspicions about Liu Xiang's role as a possible "ideological unifier" of the texts have not yet been published, but they have been communicated orally at several conferences.

17. For temporal differences in the vocabulary of the texts, see Pines, "Lexical Changes." The clearest example of the Han editorial efforts is the substitution of the tabooed character *bang* (邦, the name of the Han founder, Liu Bang [劉邦, d. 195]) with the synonymous *guo* 國 (see details in Yoshimoto, "Shunjū kokujin sai kō," 582–584). Another example of Han editing is the standardization of *Shi jing* 詩經 citations in the received texts in distinction from the abundance of textual variants in the archeologically discovered manuscripts (see Kern, "The *Odes*"). However, neither Kern nor other scholars who compared received texts with their unearthed variants (Shaughnessy, *Rewriting*; Kalinowski, "La production") have discerned traits of redaction aimed at modifying the political or ideological content of the transmitted text.

18. To give just one example, judging from the relevant bibliographic aids (especially Goldin's "Ancient Chinese Civilization" and Vittinghoff's "Recent Bibliography"), the number of works published in English since the 1980s on the subject of the so-called "nominalist" (*ming jia* 名家) Gongsun Long 公孫龍 is four or five times larger than that of studies that deal with one of the greatest masterpieces of Chinese political thought, the *Shang jun shu* 商君書, attributed to Shang Yang (商鞅, d. 338). This is particularly amazing if we consider that the *Shang jun shu* is not only a much more influential work, but also a more sophisticated one, which allows for much more research than the remains of Gongsun Long's text. Significantly, while the recently published on-line *Stanford Encyclopedia of Philosophy* contains a lengthy discussion of the "school of names," neither Shang Yang, nor even such a brilliant political thinker as Han Feizi (韓非子, d. 233), is included.

19. A powerful exposition of the advantages of a contextual rather than a purely "textual" approach in studying political ideologies was made by Skinner, *The Foundations*, ix–xv.

20. Goldin, "Introduction," 3.

Chapter 1: Ritual Figureheads

1. *Zizhi tongjian* 1: 2–3. Jie 桀 and Zhouxin 紂辛 are paradigmatic "last evil rulers" of the Xia (夏, c. 2000–1600) and Shang (商, c. 1600–1046) dynasties who were overthrown respectively by Tang 湯, founder of the Shang, and King Wu 武 王 of the Zhou (周, c.1046–256); for their image, see Chapter 3. For Sima Guang's political views, see Bol, "Government, Society and State."

2. See Liang Qichao, "Zhongguo zhuanzhi," 1649.

3. Monarchism, as defined by Liu Zehua, should be distinguished from pure authoritarianism, as it refers primarily to a cultural belief in the desirability of a singular sovereign rather than to practical political arrangements that concentrate political power in the hands of a single person. For an insightful discussion about the difficulty of determining authoritarianism in China's political culture, see Bol, "Emperors."

4. For tracing ancestral cult and ritualized social gradations to the very founda-

tions of Chinese civilization, see, for example, Chang, *Art, Myth and Ritual*; Liu Li, "Ancestor Worship"; Underhill, *Craft Production*.

5. Several major studies have addressed the religious foundations of the monarch's power in China. See, for example, Zhang Rongming, *Zhongguo de guojiao;* and Okamura, *Chūgoku kodai ōken.*

6. Keightley, "The Religious Commitment," 213.

7. These regulatory functions of the Shang kings are discussed in Zhu Fenghan, *Shang Zhou*, 192–198.

8. Keightley, *Ancestral Landscape*, 103.

9. For the Western Zhou history, see Li Feng, *Landscape*; Shaughnessy, "Western Zhou." The autonomy of the regional lords was acquired gradually, as the royal control over them faded in the course of the Zhou history. Later, the two-tier power system of the Western Zhou period became a three-tier one, as by the seventh–sixth centuries BCE aristocratic lineages in most polities attained high degree of autonomy (see below in the text). The power of the heads of these lineages, however, will not be discussed here, since it never was conceptualized as legitimate and independent of the local lord but rather was seen as a by-product of the process of political disintegration. For a different view, see Zhu Ziyan, "Xian Qin."

10. For the statement that divinations should only "resolve doubts," see *Zuo*, Huan 11: 113. Already in the late Shang period the scope of the issues about which the kings divined gradually decreased (Keightley, "The Shang," 261–262), and the Zhou rulers, while initially adopting the crack-making divination practice of the Shang, soon abandoned it (see Shaughnessy, "Zhouyuan"; cf. Wang Hui, "Zhouyuan"). In the Chunqiu period, as reflected in the *Zuo zhuan* 左傳, no remnants of the ruler's exclusive prerogative to interpret divination results are traceable.

11. See Yan Yichen, *Zhoudai shizu*, 151–155; Okamura, *Chūgoku kodai ōken.*

12. For the Western Zhou ritual reform, see Falkenhausen, "Late Western Zhou Taste"; and idem, *Chinese Society*, 29–73. The hallmark of this reform was the establishment of the so-called *lie ding* 列鼎 system, according to which every noble was allowed to use a fixed number of *ding* 鼎 cauldrons and *gui* 簋 tureens during the ancestral sacrifices and in the tomb; the *ding* became the most common status-defining symbol. While none of the Zhou royal tombs have yet been excavated (excavations at the Zhou Gong Miao 周公廟 cemetery, Qishan 岐山 county, Shaanxi, did not yield unequivocal results [Xu Tianjin, "Zhou Gong Miao"]), extant texts unanimously suggest that the kings constituted a separate sumptuary category (see, for example, *Zuo*, Xi 25: 433). As for the regional lords' tombs, they are invariably graded in terms of the *lie ding* system one rank above those of contemporary nobles from the same polity: see discussions in Falkenhausen "The Waning of the Bronze Age"; Yin Qun *Huanghe*; Liang Yun, "Zhou dai."

13. During the Chunqiu period, several states (such as Jin 晉, Zheng 鄭, and Lu 魯) were ruled by a coalition of powerful noble lineages that rotated the highest state positions among themselves. The rulers, as discussed below in the text, were completely sidelined; in one instance, in the state of Lu between 517 and 510 BCE,

the nobles expelled the local lord and ruled the state in his stead. Despite their relative success during those years, nobody proposed perpetuating this situation, and after the exiled lord died, his brother was immediately enthroned.

14. For the similarity between the early Zhou cult of Heaven and ancestral cult, see Yang Tianyu, "Zhou ren"; for the identity between the supreme god of Zhou, Heaven, and Shang's Thearch (Di), see Chen Xiaofang, "Xi Zhou."

15. For the earliest claims of the Zhou kings, that they acted in Heaven's name, see, for example., the He-*zun* 何尊, cast in 1036, at the very beginning of Zhou rule (Shaughnessy, "Western Zhou," 77–78; Shirakawa, *Kinbun*, vol. 48, add. #1, 171–184). This topic recurs in most of the supposedly Western Zhou documents of the *Shu jing* and in some of the *Shi jing* odes (see, for example, Du Yong, "*Shang shu*" *Zhouchu bagao*, 204–225). For the early concept of *de* and its relation to Heaven's Decree, see Kominami, "Tenmei to toku."

16. For the appropriation of the title of *tianzi* by the Zhou kings, see Takeuchi "Seishū kinbun." For the presence of the Zhou royal ancestors in Heaven, see, for example, *Mao Shi*, "Wen Wang" 文王 16.1: 503 (Mao 235).

17. This is suggested, for instance, by Lewis, *Writing and Authority*, 355. For the weakening positions of the Zhou kings during the Chunqiu period, see Pines, *Foundations*, 110–111; for a systematic account of the royal house's history after the fall of Hao, see Ishii, *Dong-Zhou*.

18. For the detailed analysis of this inscription, see Pines, "The Question of Interpretation," 4–12.

19. This topic is discussed in Pines, "The Question of Interpretation," 12–23.

20. For the ongoing symbolic power of the kings, see Ishii, *Dong-Zhou*, 127–179. The only known attempt to appropriate the title *tianzi* was made by the notorious King Min of Qi (齊湣王, r. 300–283), but his claims were rejected even by the weakest of his neighbors, Lu and Zou 鄒 (*Zhanguo ce*, "Zhao ce 趙策 3" 20.13: 737).

21. These sporadic revivals of the kings' political power occurred throughout the entire Eastern Zhou (東周, 771–256) period. Thus while in the late Chunqiu period royal representatives were no longer invited to the interstate meetings arranged by their nominal protector and ally, the state of Jin, they resurfaced at these meetings when the interstate situation became exceptionally volatile, for example, during crises in the state of Chu 楚 in 529 and 506 (*Zuo*, Zhao 13:1353–1360 and Ding 4: 1534–1542). In the year 404, royal approval was sought by the heads of the Wei 魏, Han 韓, and Zhao 趙 lineages to confirm their de facto partition of the state of Jin. During the fourth century, the rulers of Wei and Qin tried intermittently to improve their ties with the Sons of Heaven to bolster their interstate status. Even as late as 314 the opposing sides in the turmoil that plagued the state of Yan 燕 sought the Son of Heaven's support in their bids for power or as justification of anti-Yan aggression (see the Zhongshan 中山 royal bronze inscriptions in *Cuo mu*, 379 and glosses on p. 382; Pines, "The Question of Interpretation," 20, n. 57).

22. *Lüshi chunqiu*, "Jin ting" 謹聽 13.5: 705.

23. See, for example, the assessments by Zhu Xi (朱熹, 1130–1200) in *Zhuzi yulei* 93: 2148–2149; and by Sima Guang, *Zizhi tongjian*, 1: 2–6.

24. Of the efforts to stabilize the multistate system, the most interesting, from the modern perspective, was the "interstate peace conference" of 546 (repeated in 541 BCE). For a short while, the organizers succeeded in convincing the two major powers, Jin and Chu, to cooperate in establishing a "bipolar" world headed by the leaders of these states; but within a few years this new order collapsed, thus ending all attempts to secure interstate stability and peace. See details in Kano, "Chūgoku"; and a general discussion in Pines, *Foundations*, 105–135.

25. For details on the system of hereditary allotments, see Lü Wenyu, *Zhoudai caiyi*, especially pp. 117–178; for hereditary offices see Qian Zongfan, "Xi Zhou Chunqiu," 22–26. For the comprehensive discussion about the power of Chunqiu ministerial lineages, see Zhu Fenghan, *Shang Zhou*, 525–593; cf. Tian and Zang, *Zhou Qin shehui*, 242–255; Yoshimoto, *Chūgoku sen Shin shi*, 257–288. For the ruler's authority in the Chunqiu period, see Zhao Boxiong, *Zhoudai guojia*, 276–320.

26. Yin Zhenhuan ("Cong wang wei," 19–21) identifies no less than sixty cases of murdering the ruler during the Chunqiu period, in addition to twenty-two cases of expulsion of the lord. While most of these cases were caused by succession struggles, powerful ministers usually played the decisive role in a lord's dethronement.

27. For kin- and master-centered loyalty in the Chunqiu period, see Pines, *Foundations*, 154–158, 191–197.

28. For the reliability of the *Zuo zhuan* as source for Chunqiu history, see Pines, *Foundations*, 14–39. To recapitulate, I argue that most of the data in the *Zuo zhuan* derive from its primary sources, narrative histories produced by court scribes of various Chunqiu states, and that certain embellishments notwithstanding, the text largely reflects Chunqiu period history and intellectual milieu. For different views of the *Zuo zhuan*, see Schaberg, *A Patterned Past*; Li, *The Readability of the Past*.

29. *Zuo*, Xiang 14: 1016; see also detailed discussion in Pines, *Foundations*, 139–141.

30. *Zuo*, Xiang 14: 1016.

31. *Zuo*, Xiang 14: 1016–1017. For the term *pengyou* 朋友, meaning "young brothers and sons," see Zhu Fenghan, *Shang Zhou*, 306–311.

32. For the eagerness with which Chunqiu nobles justified the ousting of Lord Zhao of Lu (魯昭公, r. 541–510) in 517, see *Zuo*, Zhao 25: 1456–1457 ; Zhao 27: 1486–1487; Zhao 32: 1519–1520; and Pines, *Foundations*, 142–146.

33. Thus the murderers of lords Li of Jin (晉厲公, 580–574), Xi of Zheng (鄭僖公, r. 570–566), and Zhuang of Qi (齊莊公, r. 553–548), just like those who ousted Lord Zhao of Lu in 517, remained unpunished and preserved their high positions despite committing what would be later considered the gravest possible crime.

34. *Zuo*, Xiang 26: 1112.

Chapter 2: Ways of Monarchism

1. See Lewis, "Warring States," 597.

2. See ibid., 597–616; Yang Kuan, *Zhanguo shi*, 188–287; Tian and Zang, *Zhou Qin shehui*.

3. Lewis, "Warring States," 603–604.

4. See Pines, "The One That Pervades the All."

5. The usage of the term *wang* in its verbal meaning ("to act as a [true] monarch"), the compound *wang zhe* 王者, the notion of the Monarch's Way (*wang dao* 王道), and similar concepts are clearly products of the mid-Zhanguo intellectual milieu. They are rare to absent in early texts, such as the *Zuo zhuan*, *Lunyu* 論語, and the core chapters of the *Mozi* 墨子, but figure prominently in the middle to late Zhanguo texts such as *Mengzi* 孟子, *Shang jun shu*, *Xunzi*, portions of the *Guanzi* 管子, and many others. The appearance of this term may indicate the thinkers' desire to distinguish between the True Monarch and a few self-proclaimed *wang* ("kings") of the Warring States.

6. These quasi-messianic expectations of the True Monarch are explicit in the *Mengzi* passage: "Once in five hundred years a True Monarch is to arise, and then there will be one who determines the destiny of the generation" (*Mengzi*, "Gongsun Chou xia" 公孫丑下 4.13: 109; see discussion of this passage on pp. 149–150).

7. See Lewis, "Warring States," 598–600; Zhao Boxiong, *Zhoudai guojia*, 244–251.

8. The dating and even the integrity of the *Lunyu* are much-contested issues (see, for example, Makeham, "The Formation of *Lunyu*"; Brooks and Brooks, *The Original Analects*; Schaberg, "Confucius as Body and Text"; Guo Yi, "*Lunyu*"). For matters in the present discussion, I largely follow Yang Bojun's 楊伯峻 assertion ("Dao yan," 26–30), according to which the bulk of the *Lunyu* sayings may have been recorded within a few generations of Confucius's disciples, and hence it predates other Zhanguo texts. However, I treat the three last chapters of the *Lunyu* (18–20) as later than the bulk of the text.

9. Certain details of the process of ritual "upgrading" by different segments of nobility at the expense of their superiors are not clear due to the incompleteness of the extant data; but this process evidently involved all segments of the nobility, although its pace and depth differed in space and time. Generally speaking, starting in the middle Chunqiu period, regional lords and the upper segment of the hereditary nobility upgraded their sumptuary privileges, particularly in terms of the status-defining *lie ding* system, while by the end of the Chunqiu period similar upgrading was carried out by the lower nobility (see Chapter 5 for further details). For a detailed discussion, see Falkenhausen, *Chinese Society*, 326–369; Yin Qun, "You Chunqiu shiqi"; see also recent updates in Cai Quanfa, "Zheng guo jisi"; Liang Yun, "Zhou dai." For textual data about ritual infractions, see Chen Shuguo, *Xian Qin lizhi*, 274–354. Importantly, the ritual system established in the early to middle Zhou period continued to function throughout the Chunqiu and early Zhanguo

periods, but constant "usurpations" of the ritual prerogatives of superiors by under-lings greatly diminished the ritual's function as a social regulator.

10. The *Zuo zhuan* discussions about ritual are summarized in Pines, *Founda-tions*, 89–104. Significantly, in a major speech in that text, a Qi statesman, Yan Ying 晏嬰, identified every social segment that would benefit from proper observation of ritual regulations, but ominously failed to mention the Son of Heaven, thus tac-itly acquiescing in the elimination of the apex of the ritual pyramid (*Zuo*, Zhao 26: 1480; Pines, "Disputers of the *Li*," 15–17).

11. For these instances, see *Lunyu*, "Ba yi" 八佾 3.1–3.2: 23–24; 3.6: 24–25; 3.22: 31.

12. *Lunyu*, "Ji shi" 季氏 16.2: 174.

13. The reference to "the retainers who hold the state's [power to issue] com-mands" evidently reflects Confucius's dissatisfaction with the usurpation of the power in the state of Lu by Yang Hu 陽虎 and his clique of retainers in 505–502.

14. *Lunyu*, "Yan Yuan" 顏淵 12.11: 128. This succinct statement allows multiple interpretations, but in any case it is clear that it disapproves of the presumptuous behavior of contemporary ministers.

15. See Yoshimoto, "Kyokurei kō."

16. *Liji*, "Qu li xia" 曲禮下 V.2: 126.

17. See ibid., V–VI.2: 105–157. Similar views in favor of the Son of Heaven's superiority are echoed in the roughly contemporary "Tan Gong" 檀弓 chapter of the *Liji* (*Liji*, "Tan Gong shang" 檀弓上 IX.3: 235–237; for the dating of this chapter, see Yoshimoto, "Dankyū kō"), and in a recently unearthed manuscript published by the Shanghai Museum, *Tianzi jian zhou* 天子建州, which may be tentatively dated to before 278 BCE.

18. *Liji*, "Qu li xia" 曲禮下 VI.2: 150.

19. The tendency toward ritual elevation of the regional lords of the Warring States is well attested in archeological data. While earlier sumptuary gradations em-phasized the continuum between the ruler's sumptuary rights and those of the aris-tocrats, by the middle Zhanguo period, this situation had changed dramatically, as is particularly visible in the gigantic burial compounds of contemporaneous rulers that completely dwarf the tombs of other elite members. See details in Falkenhau-sen, *Chinese Society*, 328–338; Zhao Huacheng, "Cong Shang Zhou."

20. I borrow the term "ritual reality" from Joachim Gentz, "The Past as a Messianic Vision," 235. The *Gongyang zhuan*, discussed by Gentz there and in his magnum opus *Das Gongyang zhuan*, parallels ritual compendia in its attitude toward the proper arrangement of the universe. The text emphasizes the rule of a universal and omnipotent Son of Heaven as the most important of the political messages al-legedly hidden by Confucius in his *Chunqiu* (春秋, *The Springs and Autumns annals*); see more in Pines, "Imagining the Empire?"

21. See, for instance, the discussion in Savage, "Archetypes."

22. *Lunyu*, "Yan Yuan" 12.19: 129; for the importance of the rulers' moral be-havior as the means to bring about the compliance of their subjects, see also "Yan

Yuan" 12.17: 129; "Zilu" 子路 13.4: 135; 13.13: 138; "Xian wen" 憲問 14.42: 159.

23. Ji Kangzi headed the Lu government between the years 492 and 468, during the reign of Lord Ai of Lu (魯哀公, r. 494–468), whom he completely sidelined. By the end of his reign Lord Ai sought support of the state of Yue 越 to oust Ji Kangzi and his allies, but the lord failed in the attempt and died in exile.

24. See *Mozi*, "Jian'ai zhong" 兼愛中 IV.15: 159–160; "Jian'ai xia" 兼愛下" IV.16: 179–180. For the dating of the so-called "core chapters" of the *Mozi*, I largely follow assertions by Wu Yujiang ("*Mozi* gepian zhenwei kao," 1027–1028), according to which these chapters may have originated within Mozi's lifetime or shortly thereafter. For possible temporal divergence among these chapters, see Maeder, "Some Observances"; Graham, *Divisions*; and Desmet, "The Growth of Compounds."

25. *Mozi*, "Shang tong shang" 尚同上 III.11: 109.

26. Ibid.

27. Ibid., III.11: 110.

28. Ibid.

29. For more about the role of Heaven in Mozi's thought, see, for example, Graham, *Disputers of the Tao*, 47–51.

30. *Mozi*, "Shang tong shang" III.11: 110–111.

31. See respectively, *Mengzi*, "Gaozi xia" 告子下 12.7: 287; "Li Lou shang" 離婁上, 7.14: 175; "Liang Hui Wang shang" 梁惠王上 1.6: 12–13. Mozi is also critical of contemporary rulers but is usually less outspoken than Mengzi (but see *Mozi*, "Fei gong shang" 非攻上 V.17: 198–199, where the rulers are identified as murderous criminals).

32. Mengzi, "Liang Hui Wang shang" 1.1: 1.

33. Ibid., 1.7: 16. The cited ode is "Si qi" 思齊 (Mao 240).

34. *Mengzi*, "Li Lou shang" 7.20: 180; cf. "Li Lou xia" 離婁下 8.5: 187.

35. The provenance of the *Laozi* is one of the most disputed issues in the history of pre-imperial texts. The discoveries of the *Laozi* fragments at the late fourth-century BCE tomb at Guodian 郭店 and of two copies of the *Laozi* in the middle second-century BCE dynasty tomb in Mawangdui 馬王堆 suggest that the text took its current form during the second half of the Warring States period, although many questions about its early history remain unanswered. See more in Liu Xiaogan, "From Bamboo Slips"; Ding Sixin, *Guodian Chu mu zhujian*, 1–85; Nie Zhongqing, *Guodian Chu jian 'Laozi'*; Shaughnessy, "The Guodian Manuscripts."

36. See *Laozi*, 66: 146; *Guodian Laozi* A: 3–4. When citing the received *Laozi*, I preserve the traditional numeration of the paragraphs and not that of the Mawangdui versions; for the Guodian texts, I refer to the number of the bundle (A, B, C for 甲、乙、丙) and supply the slips' numbers. Unless specified otherwise, I refer to the Mawangdui or Wang Bi (王弼 226–249 CE) versions, without discussing textual variants of the Guodian or later recensions.

37. See respectively *Laozi* 3: 237; 22: 340–342 (following Mawangdui versions); 57: 106 (*Guodian Laozi* A: 30–32).

38. See respectively *Laozi* 29: 377; 48: 57; 10: 265 (*Guodian Laozi* A:18–19); 66: 146 (*Guodian Laozi* A: 3–4).

39. As a ruler-oriented text, the *Laozi* differs sharply from the texts surveyed above, such as the *Lunyu, Mozi,* and *Mengzi,* each of which is predominantly (or exclusively) directed at the fellow members of the *shi* stratum, rather than at the ruler. It is for these reasons among others that I reject Tom Michael's assertion according to which the *Laozi*'s "hidden sage is not a public king" (*The Pristine Dao*, 40–50). Michael's attempt to distinguish a "pristine" and essentially nonpolitical cosmos-oriented *Laozi* from what he dubs "Confucian readings" of the text (p. 41) and his reductionist interpretation of "politics" are untenable. While the *Laozi* allows different interpretations, it is fairly clear that at least ideally the Sage is supposed to rule.

40. See, respectively, *Laozi* 75: 192; 30: 381 (*Guodian Laozi* A: 6–7); 32: 397–398 (*Guodian Laozi* A: 18–19); 37: 421 (*Guodian Laozi* A: 13–14).

41. *Laozi* 39: 8–9; the phrase in square brackets does not appear in Mawangdui versions.

42. *Laozi* 32: 398 (*Guodian Laozi* A: 18–19).

43. *Laozi* 25: 351. In the *Guodian Laozi* A: 22, the Way comes after Heaven and Earth. A few later editions (those by Fu Yi 傅弈 and Fan Yingyuan 范應元, for instance), substitute the Monarch with the less politically loaded Man (*ren* 人) (see Gao Ming's gloss in *Laozi*, 351–352). This substitution is frequently employed by those translators who prefer to see the *Laozi* as primarily apolitical (or at least amonarchical) text.

44. *Laozi* 68: 167; the Mawangdui A version omits the character "to match" (*pei* 配) before "Heaven."

45. *Guanzi*, "Mu min" I.1: 17; Rickett, *Guanzi* I: 56; I slightly modify Rickett's translation. Here and elsewhere I adopt Rickett's dating of the *Guanzi* chapters unless specified otherwise.

46. *Guanzi*, "Ban fa" II.7: 128; Rickett, *Guanzi* I: 144–145; I slightly modify Rickett's translation.

47. For different discussions of the "Nei ye" chapter, see Roth, "Psychology" and *Original Tao*; Graham, *Disputers of the Tao*, 100–105; Puett, *To Become a God*, 109–117. For the reasons I shall try to demonstrate below in the text, I disagree with Roth's dismissal of the political content of the "Nei ye"; in my eyes this text presents exactly the same blend of Dao-oriented cosmology, psychological techniques of self-cultivation, and political philosophy that Roth identified as characteristic of early "Daoist" thought (Roth, "Psychology," 606–607).

48. *Guanzi*, "Nei ye" XVI.49: 937; Rickett, *Guanzi* II: 43; cf. Roth, *Original Tao*, 58–59; Puett, *To Become a God*, 110. Roth prefers to translate the term *zheng* 正 throughout the "Nei ye" as "being aligned," referring to meditative technique (see his explanation in *Original Tao*, 4). While in many cases this translation is ac-

ceptable, I do not think it fits the above portion of the text, especially when Heaven is discussed. Moreover, Roth's translation of *zheng* as "being aligned" rather than "regular" or "correct" omits the crucial semantic layer of this term, which was clear to any Chinese reader (see also Goldin, "Review of Roth," 39–40).

49. *Guanzi*, "Nei ye" XVI.49: 937; Rickett, *Guanzi* II: 43–44; cf. Roth, *Original Tao*, 60–62; Puett, *To Become a God*, 113.

50. Roth, *Original Tao*, 116.

51. *Guanzi*, "Nei ye" XVI.49: 937; Rickett, *Guanzi* II: 44; cf. Roth 1999: 62–64; Puett, *To Become a God*, 110; Graham, *Disputers of the Tao*, 103. I concur with Roth's identification of the "one word" as Dao (1999: 117).

52. The promise that "All under Heaven" will "submit to" (*fu* 服) and obey (*ting* 聽) the adept who properly implements the techniques of "inward training" appears elsewhere in the text (*Guanzi*, "Nei ye" XVI.49: 943), further strengthening my assertion that the "Nei ye" addresses the potential ruler.

53. See, for example, "Guo ci" 國次 and "Lun" 論, *Huang Di shu* 1: 14–20 and 55–67; Yates, *The Five Lost Classics*, 56–59 and 80–87; for more about the ideology of the "Huang-Lao" texts from Mawangdui, see Peerenboom, *Law and Morality*.

54. Paraphrasing the saying of the *Laozi* 25: "Being forced to give it a name, I would call it 'Great'" (*Laozi* 25: 350). For more about the Great One (*tai yi* 太一) and its role in the *Laozi*-related cosmogony, see, for example, Allan "The Great One."

55. *Lüshi chunqiu*, "Da yue" 5.2: 256.

56. Ibid.

57. Ibid., "Ben sheng" 1.2: 20.

58. Ibid., 1.2: 21. Primarily because of this sentence I reject Puett's interpretation of this chapter as being directed at the Son of Heaven (Puett, *To Become a God*, 175–178, particularly 177).

59. For the possible origins of the genre of "Monthly Ordinances," see Yang Zhenhong, "Yue ling," 23–28.

60. *Lüshi chunqiu*, "Meng chun ji" 孟春紀 1.1: 2.

61. These warnings are included, for instance, in several of the so-called *yin-yang* 陰陽 texts unearthed in 1972 at Yinqueshan 銀雀山, Shandong (see Yates, "The Yin Yang Texts," 98–134). See also the recently published "Yan shi wu sheng" 閻氏五勝 text from Huxishan 虎溪山, Hunan, that contains similar warnings to a ruler who fails to follow the text's recommendations (Liu Lexian, "Huxishan," 67).

62. The *Shang jun shu* is a complex text that comprises what appear to be authentic writings by Shang Yang, but also many additions from later periods. See Zheng Liangshu, *Shang Yang*; Yoshinami, *Shōkun sho*; and further discussion in Chapter 9, n. 12.

63. *Shang jun shu*, "Kai sai" 開塞 II.7: 51.

64. Shang Yang's emphasis on the population growth as a source of contention, echoed later in the *Han Feizi* ("Wu du" 五蠹 XIX.49: 443), is a rare testimony to the increasing understanding of the potentially negative impact of population

pressure on social stability. The appearance of this motif in the *Shang jun shu* is doubly interesting, since the same source testifies to the underpopulation of the state of Qin in the late Zhangguo period (see *Shang jun shu*, "Lai min" 徠民 IV.15: 86–96; "Lai min" being probably the latest chapter in the *Shang jun shu*).

65. *Shang jun shu*, "Kai sai" II.7:51–52.

66. Ibid., 52.

67. Ibid., 57–58.

68. Thompson, *Shen-tzu*, "Wei de" 威德, 240–242.

69. Ibid., 235–236.

70. Ibid., "De li" 德立, 264–265.

71. See, for example, *Guanzi*, "Ba yan" 霸言 IX.23: 472; *Huang Di shu*, "Da fen" 大分 (originally named "Liu fen" 六分) 1.30–31; *Lüshi chunqiu*, "Da yue" discussed above and "Zhi yi" chapter, discussed below in the text; and Xunzi's and Han Feizi's views (for which see Chapter 4).

72. *Lüshi chunqiu*, "Shi jun" 20.1: 1321.

73. See *Xunzi*, "Wang zhi" V.9: 164–165.

74. *Lüshi chunqiu*, "Shi jun" 20.1: 1321.

75. Ibid., 1321–1322. In translating the last phrase I have relied heavily on Chen Qiyou's gloss on 1326–1327; Chen suggests reading 物 as 勿 and 章 as 旖.

76. Ibid., 1322.

77. Ibid., "Zhi yi" 執一 17.8: 1132.

78. *Shang jun shu*, "Xiu quan" 修權 III.14: 82. For the meanings of *du duan* 獨斷—exclusive decisions, see also Giele, *Imperial Decision-Making*, 21–23.

79. Creel, *Shen Pu-hai* 19: 380.

80. See, for example, *Guanzi*, "Qi chen qi zhu" 七臣七主 XVII.52: 998–999; *Xunzi*, "Wang ba" 王霸 VII.11: 223–224; *Han Feizi*, "Er bing" 二柄 II.7: 39–43.

81. *Mengzi*, "Liang Hui Wang xia" 梁惠王下 2.7: 41.

82. *Guanzi*, "Ren fa" 任法 XV.45: 909. Rickett dates this chapter to the late Zhanguo period (*Guanzi*, I: 143–144).

83. See Lewis, *Sanctioned Violence*, 53–96.

84. The "Ren fa" chapter of the *Guanzi* (XV.45: 912–913), discussed on p. 174 urges the ruler to punish by death any unauthorized action of a minister, even if its results were successful, while pardoning failures in cases where the minister strictly obeyed the ruler's command. This notion, while irrational in civil affairs, makes perfect sense in terms of military discipline (as, of course, readers of Heinrich von Kleist's *Prinz Friedrich von Homburg* know perfectly).

Chapter 3: The Search for the Ideal Ruler

1. *Mengzi*, "Liang Hui Wang shang" 1.6: 12–13.

2. See, for example, Liu Zehua, *Zhongguo chuantong zhengzhi sixiang fansi*, 154–169; Schaberg, "Remonstrance"; Zhang Fentian, *Zhongguo diwang guannian*, 520–539.

3. Special manuals were written to educate the ruler's heirs; portions of such manuals are preserved, for instance, in the chapter "Wen Wang shizi" (文王世子, "King Wen as an heir apparent") of the *Liji* (XX.8: 551–580).

4. One of the earliest and most widely cited examples of mistreatment of a remonstrating minister concerns Bigan 比干, an upright uncle of the last Shang monarch, Zhouxin, who was executed by Zhouxin to quell his admonitions. On Bigan's legend, see Zhao Ping'an, "*Qiong da yi shi*." It is possible that proliferation of the "indirect remonstrance" lore, brilliantly discussed by Schaberg in his "Playing at Critique," reflects an increasing fear of the negative consequences of remonstrating with the ruler directly.

5. *Guoyu*, "Chu yu shang" 楚語上 17.1: 483–484.

6. This comparison is doubly interesting. First, although it is pronounced in the court of Chu, which by the Zhanguo period was considered a "barbarian" state (as reflected among others in the *Guoyu*—see Pines, *Foundations*, 43–44), it expresses nevertheless a clearly "antibarbarian" sentiment. Second, unlike most Zhanguo texts, it assumes that the aliens are incapable of change and cannot be improved through proper education (cf. Pines, "Beasts or Humans"). Is it possible that a stock "barbarian" metaphor was randomly attributed by the *Guoyu* compiler to a Chu courtier without noticing an ironic dimension of this metaphor being used by a "barbarian" courtier in a conversation with a "barbarian" king?

7. *Guoyu*, "Chu yu shang" 17.1: 487.

8. For the *Guoyu*'s self-identification as a didactic device, see Pines, *Foundations*, 41–42; idem, "Speeches," 209–215.

9. The *Xunzi* explicitly states that the inept sons of Yao and Shun could not be transformed despite the superb educational abilities of their fathers (*Xunzi*, "Zheng lun" XII.18: 336–338).

10. See *Shi jing*, "Wen Wang" 文王 16.1: 205 (Mao 235); *Shang shu*, "Kang gao" 康誥 14: 205.

11. The notion of Heaven's Decree in Zhou texts was not necessarily coterminous with the idea of universal rule; occasionally it was applied to a regional lord's rule of his state or even to an individual's destiny. As a justification for the overthrow of a violent ruler, the notion of Heaven's Decree is not employed on any known occasion of internal rebellion, such as the overthrow of the Zhou kings Li (厲王, r. c. 877–841) and You (幽王, r. 781–771) or of any of the Chunqiu rulers. The only instances of dynastic death throughout the Chunqiu period were those that occurred through foreign conquest and the violent replacement of the native ruling house by the invaders.

12. *Mozi*, "Shang xian shang" 尚賢上 II.8: 67.

13. Later texts clearly distinguish between sagacity as an attribute of the ruler and worthiness as characteristic of a minister; in the *Mozi*, however, this distinction is not present in a clear form.

14. See Pines, "Disputers of Abdication," 245–248.

15. *Mozi*, "Shang xian zhong" 尚賢中 II.9: 77.

16. *Mozi*, "Tian zhi zhong" 天志中 VII.27: 303.

17. *Mozi*, "Tian zhi xia" VII.28: 320. I follow Wu Yujiang's gloss (327, n. 34) reading 賁 as the "bamboo slips" used for historical records.

18. The sentence is not clear; an alternative translation would be that ten suns appeared simultaneously in the night.

19. The nine cauldrons are the ultimate symbol of the royal power.

20. Charts from the Yellow River (*He tu* 河圖), writings from the river Luo (*Luo shu* 洛書) and the appearance of the magical animal, *chenghuang* 乘黃, became by the Zhanguo period attributes of the new Decree-bearer (see glosses in *Mozi*, 238, nn. 114–115).

21. *Mozi,* "Fei gong xia" V.19: 220–221.

22. See Graham, *Disputers of the Tao*, 293. For the absence of the abdication legend before the *Mozi*, see Pines "Disputers of Abdication," 245–248; cf. Gu Jiegang, "Shanrang chuanshuo."

23. It is commonly agreed that the Guodian texts and those published by the Shanghai Museum must have been placed in the tombs before Qin's occupation of the ancient Chu heartland in 278. Since it is highly unlikely that the texts were composed right on the eve of being put in the tomb, they may have been composed in the later half of the fourth century BCE or earlier. The following discussion of the *Tang Yu zhi Dao* and *Rong Cheng shi* is largely based on my previous studies (Pines, "Disputers of Abdication" and "Subversion Unearthed"), where I also discuss the third of the recently unearthed texts that favor abdication, the *Zi Gao*.

24. *Tang Yu zhi Dao*, slips 1–4; Li Ling, *Guodian*, 95. Additions in figure brackets stand for the tentatively reconstructed characters, which are either illegible or are missing due to a slip's damage.

25. "There is a Great Man: He rectifies himself, and the world is rectified" (*Mengzi*, "Jin xin shang" 盡心上 13.19: 308). Cf. Confucius's alleged saying: "To rectify yourself in order to pacify the hundred clans: even Yao and Shun would find it difficult" (*Lunyu* "Xian wen" 14.42: 159).

26. *Tang Yu zhi Dao*, slips 25–27.

27. A similar passage, which quite probably refers to the *Tang Yu zhi Dao*, is recorded in the *Guanzi*, where, however, the pro-abdication sentiment is strongly qualified: "[He is] benevolent, and hence does not replace the king; [he is] righteous, and hence at the age of seventy delivers the power" (*Guanzi*, "Jie"戒 X.26: 510; Rickett, *Guanzi*, 379). The *Guanzi* thus favors the abdication gesture, but opposes the minister who would not reject the offer. See also Defoort, "Mohist and Yangist Blood."

28. *Tang Yu zhi Dao*, slips 20–21.

29. See Pines, "Subversion Unearthed," 169–175.

30. *Rong Cheng shi*, slips 1–2. Hereafter I largely follow Chen Jian's ("Shangbo jian *Rong Cheng shi*") rearrangement of Li Ling's original edition (*Rong Cheng shi*).

31. *Rong Cheng shi*, slips 6–7.

32. The beginning of the slip is missing; the three characters 讓天下 ("yielded to the worthies from All under Heaven") are tentatively reconstructed on the basis of Qiu Dexiu's *Shangbo*, 257.

33. *Rong Cheng shi*, slips 9–11, 13.

34. *Rong Cheng shi*, slip 12.

35. See, for example, *Shang shu*, "Yao dian" 2: 122a, and the *Mengzi*'s passage discussed below in the text. For the importance of this topos, see Allan, *The Heir and the Sage*, 33–34.

36. *Rong Cheng shi*, slips 33–35.

37. Following Liu Jian, "*Rong Cheng shi*," 351–352, I read the disputed character 昏 as 芸, which is a loan for 昏 "muddled."

38. *Rong Cheng shi*, slips 44–45.

39. For a tentative identification of these localities, see Qiu Dexiu, *Shangbo*, 612–619.

40. Following a well-known legend of King Wen's imprisonment by Zhouxin, I translate here *chu* 出 as "to release," although nowhere does the text indicate that King Wen was initially imprisoned by Zhouxin.

41. *Rong Cheng shi*, slips 45–49.

42. A similar notion of King Wen's support of Zhouxin is mentioned in the *Lüshi chunqiu*, "Xing lun" 行論 20.6: 1389–1390, where, however, it is interpreted as sophisticated propaganda aimed at gaining popularity rather than genuine support of the ruler's undisputable legitimacy.

43. *Rong Cheng shi*, slips 49–53 recto.

44. Since the name of the text, *Rong Cheng shi* appears on the verso of the last extant slip (#53), it is unlikely that more than a few slips of the entire text are missing.

45. Asano, "*Rong Cheng shi*," 97–100.

46. *Mengzi*, "Wan Zhang shang" 萬章上 9.6: 221.

47. The *Zhanguo ce* tells of the supposed intention of Lord Xiao of Qin (秦孝公, r. 361–338) to yield the throne to his famous aide Shang Yang (*Zhanguo ce*, "Qin ce 秦策 1" 3.1: 71). The *Lüshi chunqiu* ("Bu qu" 不屈 18.6: 1196) tells of a similar gesture by King Hui of Wei (魏惠王, r. 369–319) in favor of his aide Hui Shi 惠施. Another anecdote of abdication gesture is told of King Hui's son, King Xiang (*Zhanguo ce*, "Wei ce 魏策 2" 23.4: 855).

48. Zhanguo and Han texts contain conflicting depictions of this abdication; according to some versions, the step was genuine, albeit misguided; other texts assume that the king did not expect Zizhi to accept the offer. For conflicting versions, see *Shiji* 34: 1555–1557; *Zhanguo ce*, "Yan ce 燕策 1" 29.9: 1104–1105; *Han Feizi*, "Wai chu shuo you xia" 外儲說右下 35: 338–341.

49. Zhongshan Wang Cuo-*hu* inscription in *Cuo mu*, 370. See also Pines "Disputers of Abdication," 268–271.

50. *Mengzi*, "Liang Hui Wang xia" 2.8: 42.

51. Remarkably, Mengzi justified rebellion in a putative conversation with the

reigning monarch (or so at least Mengzi's disciples want us to believe). A possible explanation for this audacity may be that King Xuan of Qi had a problematic background (his ancestors deposed the line of the legitimate lords of Qi) and he may even have been glad for Mengzi's legitimation of dynastic overthrow. Needless to say, this conjecture cannot be verified.

52. *Mengzi*, "Jin xin shang" 盡心上 13.10: 304.

53. Cited from Zhu Xi's gloss in *Sishu*, "Mengzi jizhu" 孟子集注 13:352; for similar glosses by Zhao Qi (趙岐, d. 201 C.E.) and Sun Shi (孫奭, 962–1033 CE), see *Mengzi zhengyi* 13: 2765a. This interpretation was successful enough to permit this passage to be retained in the abridged version of the *Mengzi* (*Mengzi jiewen* 7: 1006), which the Hongwu (洪武, 1368–1398) emperor purged of potentially "subversive" sayings. For further details, see Elman, *A Cultural History*, 80–81.

54. Mengzi's views of abdication have been studied by several scholars. I would single out Li Cunshan's "Fansi" as the most systematic, even if sometimes speculative, attempt to address internal contradictions in Mengzi's views of abdication and hereditary succession.

55. *Mengzi*, "Wan Zhang xia" 10.6: 245; cf. *ibid*, 10.3: 237. Elsewhere Mengzi claims that it was absolutely normal for Shun to receive All under Heaven from Yao, whose Way he shared ("Teng Wen Gong xia" 滕文公下 6.4: 145).

56. Mengzi served at the court of Qi during the latter's invasion and occupation of Yan; for his views considering Yan's turmoil, see *Mengzi* "Liang Hui wang xia" 2.10–2.11: 44–45; "Gongsun Chou xia" 公孫丑下 4.8–4.9: 99–101.

57. *Mengzi*, "Wan Zhang shang" 9.5: 219.

58. Ibid.

59. Ibid.

60. Ibid., 9.6: 221–222. Mengzi therefore tried to dismiss the notion of Qi's violent seizure of power from Yi, as mentioned in the *Rong Cheng shi* and in the *Zhushu jinian*, 2–3, to cite the earliest texts.

61. Elsewhere Mengzi, like the "Yao dian," which he cites, strongly rejects the idea that Yao abdicated in favor of Shun during Yao's lifetime and emphasizes that Shun replaced Yao only after the latter's death (*Mengzi*, "Wan Zhang shang" 9.4: 215).

62. *Mengzi*, "Wan Zhang shang" 9.6: 222.

63. Ibid.

64. See, for example, Li Cunshan, "Fansi"; Peng Bangben, "Chu jian *Tang Yu zhi Dao*."

65. See Liu Baocai, "*Tang Yu zhi Dao*."

66. For detailed discussion, see Pines, "Speeches."

67. *Shang shu*, "Yao dian" 2: 123a. The "Yao dian" was definitely created in the middle to late Zhanguo period, and it probably contains even later additions from the Qin period; see Jiang Shanguo, *Shang shu*, 140–168; Chen Mengjia, *Shang shu*, 152–163.

68. The Qianlong emperor (乾隆, 1736–1795 CE) occupied the imperial

throne for a full sixty years, reigning for another four years in the name of his son, the Jiaqing emperor (嘉慶, 1796–1820 CE). Of the pre-imperial rulers, the lengthiest reign recorded is for King Nan of Zhou (周王赧, r. 314–256). Zhao Tuo 趙佗, a former Qin general who established the kingdom of Nanyue 南越, ruled it for over seventy years from circa 210 to his death in 137.

69. See *Zhuangzi*, "Xiao yao you" 逍遙遊 1: 18; "Rang wang" 28: 744–745, 768. The same anecdotes are scattered throughout the *Lüshi chunqiu* ("Gui sheng" 貴生 2.2: 74; "Li su" 離俗 19.1: 1233–1234; Xu You's story is repeated in "Qiu ren" 求人 22.5: 1515). No text before the *Zhuangzi* mentions Xu You.

70. The earliest text to mention that "Shun had expelled Yao to Pingyang" is the now-lost *Suoyu* 瑣語, unearthed by grave robbers in 280 CE from the tomb identified as that of King Xiang of Wei (魏襄王, 318–296) (cited by Liu Zhiji [劉知幾, 661–721 CE], *Shi tong*, "Yi gu" 疑古 13.3: 384; see also Shaughnessy, *Rewriting*, 166–171). See also *Zhanguo ce*, "Yan ce 1" 29.9: 1104–1105; *Han Feizi*, "Wai chu shuo you xia" 35: 338–341; *Lüshi chunqiu*, "Bu qu" 18.6: 1196; and the discussion in Pines, "Disputers of Abdication," 285–287.

71. In the earliest portions of the *Shu jing*, such as "Jiu gao" 酒誥 or "Wu yi" 無逸, Zhouxin (usually named Shou 受) is presented as a lax and excessive ruler, who is particularly accused of heavy drinking; but there is nothing extraordinary about his misbehavior. It is only in the Zhanguo texts, beginning with the *Mozi* and the later layer of the *Shu jing* documents, like the "Mu shi" 牧誓, that the standard accusations of cruelness and debauchery are supplemented with new details, such as those outlined in the *Rong Cheng shi*. See, for example, *Shang shu*, "Mu shi" 牧誓 11: 183; *Xunzi* "Ru xiao" 儒效 IV.8: 134–136; "Yi bing" 議兵 X.15: 283; *Han Feizi*, "Yu Lao" 喻老 VII.21: 162–164; *Lüshi chunqiu*, "Xian shi" 先識 16.1: 945–946; *Zhanguo ce*, "Zhao ce 3," 20.13: 736–737. It is possible that the original "Tai shi" (泰誓, The great oath) document of the *Shu jing* (not to be confused with a forged document of the "old text" *Shu jing*, see Jiang Shanguo, *Shang shu*, 213–225) cited in the *Zuo zhuan*, *Mozi*, and *Mengzi* served as a major source for later enumerations of Zhouxin's crimes.

72. The *Tuan* 彖 commentary on the forty-ninth hexagram, Ge (革, Overturn), of the *Zhou yi* 周易 states among others: "Heaven and Earth overturn, and the four seasons are accomplished; by overturning the Decree [the kings] Tang and Wu complied with Heaven, and responded to men. Great is indeed the timeliness of "Overturn" (*Zhou yi*, 5:60c). Some scholars overemphasize this passage as justification of righteous rebellion (see, for example, Liu Xiaofeng, *Rujia geming*, 33–44). Without denying the importance of the *Zhou yi* in imperial times, I doubt that this specific commentary had a true impact on Zhanguo discourse; nor was the idea of the "inevitability" of violent "revolutions" present elsewhere outside the *Mengzi*.

73. For the detailed discussion of the nature and the dating of the "Robber Zhi" chapter, see Liao Mingchun, "Zhujian ben."

74. The struggle of Huang Di against the legendary rebel Chi You is depicted in numerous late Zhanguo sources, particularly the "Zheng luan" 正亂 chapter of

the Mawangdui Yellow Emperor's *Jing fa* (經法, *Canon: The law*) (see Yates, *Five Lost Classics*, 118–121).

75. *Zhuangzi*, "Dao Zhi" 29: 778.

76. The current text contains an additional phrase here: "King Wen was imprisoned at Youli," which is apparently a later addition (see Chen Guying's gloss 32, p. 783).

77. *Zhuangzi*, "Dao Zhi" 29: 778–779.

78. See an excellent discussion of Zhuangzi's political views in Yu Youqian, "Fandui junzhu zhuanzhi."

79. See *Zhuangzi*, "Rang wang" 28: 744–745, 768; and the discussion in Pines, "Disputers of Abdication," 284–285.

Chapter 4: An Omnipotent Rubber Stamp

1. For a recent comprehensive study of Xunzi's thought, see Sato, *The Confucian Quest for Order*; see also Goldin, *Rituals of the Way*; Liao Mingchun, *Xunzi xin tan*; Ma Jigao, *Xunxue yuanliu*; Pines "Xin jiu ronghe"; for the impact of Xunzi on the early Han thought, see Goldin, "Xunzi and Early Han Philosophy"; Han Demin, "Xunzi."

2. "In antiquity, the sages saw that human nature is bad, considering it partial, malicious, and incorrect; perverse, calamitous, and disordered. Hence they established the authority of rulers and superiors to supervise [the people]; clarified ritual and propriety to transform them; initiated laws and correctness to govern them; increased penalties and punishments to restrict them, causing All under Heaven to move through orderly government and to unify at good." (*Xunzi*, "Xing e" 性惡 XVII.23: 440).

3. For the importance of the term *fen* in Xunzi's thought, see Sato, "The Development," 27–31.

4. *Xunzi*, "Wang zhi" 王制 V.9: 165.

5. See examples in Pines, "Wu suo bu neng."

6. *Xunzi*, "Li lun" 禮論 XIII.19: 374.

7. Both the *Lunyu* and *Mengzi* stipulate the priority of family ties over political obligations (see *Lunyu*, "Zilu" 13.18: 139; *Mengzi*, "Jin xin shang" 13.35: 317). Similar views are expressed in even more radical ways in some of the Guodian documents, such as *Liu de* 六德, which stipulates priority of mourning (and, mutatis mutandis, social) obligations to the father over those due to the ruler (*Liu de*, slips 26–29; for the controversy about this passage, see Peng Lin, "Zai lun"; Wei Qipeng, "Shi *Liu de*"; Li Cunshan, "Zai shuo"). For the classicists' view, which is closer to that of Xunzi, see *Liji*, "Zengzi wen" 曾子問 XIX.7: 532–533; see also Brown's discussion in *The Politics of Mourning*, 30–32. Lai Guolong ("The Diagram," 55–56) convincingly argues that mourning obligations for the father preceded those for the ruler, and the latter may have been patterned after the former.

8. *Xunzi*, "Zhi shi" 致士 IX.14: 263.

9. *Xunzi*, "Wang zhi" V.9: 171.

10. *Xunzi*, "Junzi" XVII.24: 450.

11. For the Ru idea that "customs" are by definition deviant and partial, and should be modified, see Lewis, "Custom and Human Nature"; idem, *The Construction of Space*, 192–201.

12. *Xunzi*, "Zheng lun" XII.18: 321.

13. Ibid., 331.

14. Thus, Tan Sitong (譚嗣同, 1865–1898 CE), the major martyr of the 1898 reform movement, declared (in *Ren xue* 29: 95 and 30: 99) that Xunzi betrayed Confucius and created the concept of an imperial dictatorship, "granting the ruler the greatest and limitless power." Tan was echoed by Liang Qichao and Wu Yu (吳虞 1871–1949 CE), although these thinkers had later modified their assessments of Xunzi's legacy (see Deng Xingying, "Wu Yu"; Liao Mingchun, "Lun Xunzi de junmin," 42). For a recent reiteration of Tan's claim, see, for example, Jia Haitao, "Jianxi Xunzi."

15. *Xunzi*, "Jun Dao" 君道 VIII.12: 234.

16. *Xunzi*, "Fu guo" 富國 VI.10: 180–181.

17. *Xunzi*, "Fu guo" VI.10: 182–183. The cited ode is "Yi" 抑 (*Mao shi* 18.1:555b [Mao 256]).

18. *Xunzi*, "Zheng ming" 正名 XVI.22: 431.

19. *Xunzi*, "Chen Dao" 臣道 IX.13: 251–252; see the discussion of this passage on p. 180.

20. Following Wang Xianqian, I omit the negation 不 from the second sentence (see his gloss in *Xunzi*, 322–323).

21. *Xunzi*, "Zheng lun" XII.18: 323.

22. Ibid., 324–325.

23. This is a perfect example of what Carine Defoort calls a "vicious circle," in which only the post-factum success serves as a criterion for legitimation of the rebellion (Defoort, "Can Words Produce Order," 89–90).

24. Both atrocities are attributed to Zhouxin. Bigan was his righteous uncle, whose heart Zhouxin reportedly ordered dissected to verify whether the sage's heart had seven openings. Jizi remonstrated, but being unheeded, fled the state (see *Shiji* 3: 107–108).

25. *Xunzi*, "Zheng lun" XII.18: 325.

26. Ibid.

27. For similar views in the *Xunzi*, see "Ru xiao" 儒效 IV.8: 134–136; "Jie bi" 解蔽 XV.21: 388–389. Sima Guang's views, which echo Xunzi, are discussed at the start of Chapter 1; see also his very Xunzi-like, anti-Mengzi polemics, "Yi Meng" (疑孟, "Doubting Mengzi," in *Chuan jia ji* 73: 5–12); see also Guan Tong, "Boyi ai"; and brief discussions by Zhang Qiwei, "Yang Meng yi Xun," 22–23; Bol, *This Culture of Ours*, 234ff.

28. *Xunzi*, "Zheng lun" XII.18: 336. For more about Xunzi's rejection of the abdication doctrine, see Pines, "Disputers of Abdication," 289–291.

29. *Xunzi*, "Jun Dao" VIII.12: 234. Xunzi furthermore asserts that the ruler's benevolence is of even higher priority than his abiding by the all-important ritual norms ("Da lue" 大略 XIX.27: 488).

30. See *Xunzi*, "Zheng lun" XII.18: 336–338. Xunzi elsewhere explains that while every man is able to become a sage, "petty men" do not wish to mend their ways ("Xing e" XVII.23: 443), and, as he clarifies elsewhere ("Wang zhi" V.9: 148–149), it is possible that rulers' sons will be among the "petty men."

31. Among the most famous paragon ministers, one can mention the assistants of the Zhou dynastic founders, the Duke of Zhou (Zhou Gong 周公) and the Grand Duke Jiang (Jiang Taigong 姜大公); of later aides, the most famous is Guan Zhong, the architect of the successes of Lord Huan of Qi (齊桓公, r. 685–643). For what may be the earliest articulation of the idea that the ministerial help is crucial for the ruler's success, see Shaughnessy, "The Duke of Zhou's Retirement"; for Guan Zhong, see Rosen, "In Search of the Historical Kuan Chung."

32. Following Wang Yinzhi 王引之 (1766–1834 CE), I omit the redundant characters 之始 after the term 君子 (see his gloss in *Xunzi*, 163).

33. *Xunzi*, "Wang zhi" V.9: 163.

34. Some scholars (for example, Liao Mingchun, "Lun Xunzi de junmin guanxi," 41) assume that in the above passage Xunzi refers to a ruler (who is occasionally referred to as a *junzi* in the text, for example, "Li lun" XIII.19: 374). However, I believe that the text deals here with a "superior man" in its post-Confucius meaning of a moral person, the common usage in the *Xunzi* (for details, see Pines, "Wu suo bu neng").

35. *Xunzi*, "Jun Dao" VIII 12: 237–238.

36. Ibid., 230.

37. *Xunzi*, "Wang ba" VII.11: 223–224.

38. A recent major discussion of the principle of *wu-wei* in English is Edward Slingerland, *Effortless Action*. Slingerland focuses exclusively on *wu-wei* within the context of personal cultivation, dismissing its political connotations as "parasitic" upon, and even damaging to, the "more fundamental" aspects of the *wu-wei* as "spiritual ideal" (p. 6). This radical rejection of the political aspects of the *wu-wei* concept is based on very problematic assumptions regarding the nature and dating of several major Zhanguo texts, and in my eyes it substantially impoverishes Slingerland's discussion. Other studies that focus on political aspects of the *wu-wei* ideal often do it from the Han perspective; see, for example, Ames, *The Art of Rulership*, 28–64; Arima, "*Mu-i no chi*." For an excellent discussion of the early political usage of *wu-wei*, see Liu Zehua, *Zhongguo chuantong zhengzhi siwei*, 404–443.

39. Creel, *Shen Pu-hai* 1(9): 351–352.

40. Shen Buhai explained: "The ruler is like a torso, the minister is like an arm; the ruler is like a shout; the minister is like an echo. The ruler establishes the root, the minister maintains the twigs; the ruler orders the essentials, the minister imple-

ments the details; the ruler maintains the handles, the minister deals with the routine" (Creel, *Shen Pu-hai*, 1[4]: 346–347 ["Da ti" 大體]; see also Creel's discussion of Shen's views on pp. 59–79). Shen Dao argued: "The way of the ruler and ministers is that the minister deals with the tasks, while the ruler lacks tasks. The ruler is relaxed and joyful, while the minister is assigned a toilsome [task]. The minister exerts his knowledge and power to carry out his tasks well, while the ruler does not take part in it, observing completion and that is all: hence none of the tasks is disordered." (Thompson, *Shen-tzu*, "Min za" 民雜, 253; for Shen Dao's views, see Liu Zehua, *Zhongguo zhengzhi sixiang shi* I: 270–285).

41. For instance, on one occasion Xunzi promises that strict implementation of ritual norms will create a perfect state of affairs and "then the Son of Heaven may simply respect himself and stop [acting]" (*Xunzi*, "Wang ba" VII.11: 220–221). Elsewhere the universal quiescence is promised as the reward to the ruler who firmly upholds moral norms ("Jun Dao" VIII.12: 232). Perhaps the strongest pronouncement in favor of the ruler's quiescence appears in the "Wang ba" chapter, where Xunzi identifies activities as attributes of "an ordinary fellow" (*pifu* 匹夫) and "a servant" (*yifu* 役夫). Xunzi warns the monarch that if he intervenes in everyday affairs, he will diminish the appeal of his position to the degree that "even a slave would reject exchanging positions with the Son of Heaven" ("Wang ba" VII.11: 213).

42. *Xunzi*, "Jun Dao" VIII.12: 244.

43. *Xunzi*, "Ru xiao" IV.8: 114–117.

44. Elsewhere Xunzi again praises King Cheng's complete subservience to his minister, the Duke of Zhou: "With regard to the Duke of Zhou, King Cheng was attentive to whatever [the Duke] proposed: he knew whom to esteem!" (*Xunzi*, "Junzi" XVII.24: 452).

45. *Lao* 牢 is a sacrificial unit that comprises an ox, a sheep, and a pig.

46. *Xunzi*, "Zheng lun" XII.18: 333–336.

47. Cf. *Xunzi*, "Wang ba" VII.11: 212; "Junzi" XVII.24: 452.

48. The dating of chapters and portions of chapters in the *Xunzi* is discussed by Knoblock throughout his *Xunzi;* and in idem, "The Chronology"; see also Liao Mingchun, "Xunzi ge pian."

49. The fourth kind of ruler, the wicked monarch, does not belong to this discussion, since it is impossible to ensure a normal life under his aegis.

50. For an insightful analysis of Han Feizi's views on ruler-minister relations and his comparison with Xunzi, see Kosaki, "*Kanpishi* no *chū*"; cf. Goldin, "Han Fei's Doctrine."

51. For detailed analysis of Han Feizi's political philosophy, see Wang and Chang, *The Philosophical Foundations*; for a brief but insightful analysis of his political views as reflecting Zhanguo realities, see Yin Zhenhuan, "Cong wang wei," 21–24. In my analysis of Han Feizi's views, I do not consider two *Laozi*-related chapters ("Jie Lao" 解老 and "Yu Lao," chapters 20–21), the provenance of which are hotly disputed and which were apparently compiled by different authors (see Sarkissian,

"*Laozi*"). For different views of authenticity of Han Feizi's chapters, see Lundahl, *Han Fei Zi.*

52. Goldin, "Han Fei's Doctrine," 65.

53. *Han Feizi*, "Yang quan" 楊權 II.8: 46–47. For the detailed discussions on the theory of "forms and names" (*xing ming* 形名), see Makeham, "The Legalist Concept of *Hsing-ming.*"

54. Referring to Shun's humble position under Yao's rule before his sudden elevation, see *Han Feizi*, "Nan yi" 難一 XV.36: 349–350.

55. *Han Feizi*, "Zhong xiao" 忠孝 XX.52: 465–466.

56. *Han Feizi*, "Yang quan" II.8: 49–50.

57. The potential of a secondary city to rival the capital and become the base for a rebellion was well recognized already in the Chunqiu period, when several such rebellions happened; see, for example, the *Zuo*, Yin 1: 11–12.

58. *Han Feizi*, "Yang quan" II.8: 51.

59. During a century and a half following the demise of the ruling houses in Jin and Qi, usurpations took place only in minor states, such as Song, one of the Zhou royal principalities, and in the state of Yan during the Zizhi affair, a clear indication that Han Feizi's "rule" of ministerial treachery was actually an exception. Throughout the Zhanguo period only six rulers were murdered by their subordinates, in sharp distinction to the Chunqiu age (Yin Zhenhuan, "Cong wang wei," 21). Was Han Feizi reflecting upon Chunqiu rather than Zhanguo experience? Or was he aware of plots that never materialized and hence left no traces in the historical record?

60. See, for example, *Han Feizi*, "Ba jian" 八姦 II.8: 53–55; "Nan si" 難四 XVI.39: 382–383; "San shou" 三守 V.16: 113–114; "Bei nei" 備內 V.17: 115–117.

61. *Han Feizi*, "Nan yi" XV.36: 352

62. For Shen Buhai's views, see Creel, *Shen Pu-hai*, 59–79.

63. According to Wang Xianshen (王先慎, 1859–1922 CE), "those who gathered" refers to powerful ministers with large private retinue (gloss on pp. 36–37).

64. *Han Feizi*, "You du" 有度 II.6: 36–37.

65. *Han Feizi*, "Nan shi" 難勢 XVII.40: 392.

66. *Han Feizi*, "Da ti" 大體 VIII.29: 209.

67. Ibid., 210.

68. Possibly, orders (*ling* 令) here stand for the Decree/destiny (*ming* 命), since otherwise it is unclear whose orders the ruler is awaiting.

69. *Han Feizi*, "Zhu Dao" 主道 I.5: 26.

70. See, for example, the "Dao fa" (道法, Law of the Way) and "Lun" (論, Assessments) chapters from the *Jing fa* text from Mawangdui (*Huang Di shu*, 1–13 and 55–66; Yates, *Five Lost Classics*: 50–54 and 80–86); or the "Ren fa" chapter of the *Guanzi* (XV.45: 900–901).

71. That is, the minister will embellish the ruler's desires to entice the ruler to trust him.

72. Following Lu Wenchao (盧文弨, 1712–1799 CE), I emend 敕 to 效.

73. *Han Feizi*, "Zhu Dao" I.5: 27.

74. The "public law" (*gong fa* 公法) is to eradicate "private crookedness" (*si qu* 私曲); if the ruler abandons the law and relies on private ideas, "there will be no distinction between superiors and inferiors," argues Han Feizi ("You du" II.6: 32), implying that crookedness is not a malady of ministers only, but probably of a ruler himself. Elsewhere the ruler is urged to give up likes and dislikes ("Er bing" 二柄 II.7: 43) and to avoid granting personal favors to ministers at the expense of impartial laws ("Shi xie" 飾邪 V.19: 128–129); see also "Yong ren" 用人 VIII.27: 205–206. It is partly due to these citations that I disagree with Goldin's square identification of *gong* in the *Han Feizi* with the ruler's self-interest ("Han Fei's Doctrine," 59). Like other Zhangguo thinkers, Han Feizi believed that the ruler *should* embody the common interest (*gong*), but that he may fail to do so because he is attached to private likes and dislikes (or is misled by his crooked ministers). The difference between Han Feizi and other thinkers is that Han Feizi tries to convince the ruler that being public-minded is to be recommended purely in terms of the ruler's self-interest and not for the sake of a higher moral agenda.

75. See *Guanzi*, "Ren fa" XV.45: 900–912; "Jun chen shang" 君臣上 X.30: 545–567; *Lüshi chunqiu*, "Shen fen" 審分 17.1: 1029–1030; "Jun shou" 君守 17.2: 1049–1051; "Ren shu" 任數 17.3: 1064–1067; "Wu gong" 勿躬 17.4: 1077–1079; "Zhi du" 知度 17.5: 1091–1093; *Huang Di shu*, "Dao fa" 道法; "Guo ci" 國次; "Jun zheng" 君正; "Da fen"; "Si du" 四度 1:1–55; Creel, *Shen Pu-hai*, 346–352 ("Da ti"). Similar ideas influenced the late Zhangguo (or perhaps early Han) blueprint for the ideal monarchy, the *Zhou li* 周禮. Mark Lewis suggests that in this text "the king ... remains hidden, formless and inactive behind the visible, formed and active figures of the officials" (*Writing and Authority*, 48; for the dating of the *Zhou li*, see Peng Lin, "*Zhou li*").

76. The complexity of the *wu-wei* "trap" explains the radically different approaches concerning the place of this doctrine in the overall theory of rulership of the Zhangguo age. While some scholars (for example, Zhang Fentian, *Zhongguo diwang guannian*, 467–472) consider this as yet another manifestation of the ministers' enslavement by the ruler, others (for example, Zhang Xingjiu, "Rujia 'wu wei' sixiang") regard it as a means to constrain the monarch. A clearer distinction between overt justifications and subtle consequences of the *wu-wei* theory may be helpful to resolve the controversy.

77. The importance of Qin imperial proclamations as a source for study of Qin culture is thoroughly discussed in two brilliant studies, one by Martin Kern, *The Stele Inscriptions,* and one by Liu Zehua, *Zhongguo de Wangquanzhuyi*, 128–137. Both studies are of particular importance in defying an earlier prevalent bias according to which Qin was a "barbarous" dynasty, renowned for its destruction of culture rather than for its creation.

78. The citations are respectively from the Mt. Yi 嶧山 inscription (221 BCE; this inscription is not recorded in the *Shiji*); the Taishan 泰山 inscription (219); the

Langye 琅邪 inscription (219); the western and eastern vista of the Zhifu 之罘 inscription (218); and from the Kuaiji 會稽 inscription (c. 211). See *Shiji* 6: 243, 245, 249, 250, 261; Kern, *The Stele Inscriptions*, 14, 21, 32, 36, 39, 49.

79. The citations are respectively from the Mt. Yi, Langye, and Zhifu inscriptions (*Shiji* 6: 245, 249; Kern, *The Stele Inscriptions*, 13, 32, 36). For "stability is in unity," see *Mengzi*, "Liang Hui Wang shang" 1.6: 17–18. For the success of Qin appeal to unity, see the evidence of Jia Yi (賈誼, 200–168 BCE) (*Shiji* 6: 283).

80. Cited from the Taishan and Langye inscriptions (*Shiji* 6: 243, 245; Kern, *The Stele Inscriptions*, 22, 26, 30, 32).

81. See, respectively, the Zhifu east, Kuaiji, and Jieshi 碣石 (215) inscriptions (*Shiji* 6: 250, 261, 252; Kern, *The Stele Inscriptions*, 39, 48, 42–43).

82. See, respectively, Jieshi and Langye (twice) (*Shiji* 6: 252, 245; Kern, *The Stele Inscriptions*, 43, 27, 28). For benefiting horses and oxen, see the same inscriptions (*Shiji* 6: 245 and 252; Kern, *The Stele Inscriptions*, 33 and 42).

83. See Martynov, "Konfutsianskaia Utopiia," 25–30. Martynov discusses early Han texts, but his observation is applicable to Qin steles as well.

84. See, respectively, the Langye, Taishan, and Kuaiji inscriptions (*Shiji* 6: 245, 243, 261; Kern, *The Stele Inscriptions*, 26, 22–23, 48).

85. See, respectively, the Langye and Kuaiji inscriptions (*Shiji* 6: 245, 261; Kern, *The Stele Inscriptions*, 31, 48).

86. Taishan inscription (*Shiji* 6: 243; Kern, *The Stele Inscriptions*, 21).

87. For the importance of the titles appropriated by the August Thearch, see Liu Zehua, *Zhongguo de Wangquanzhuyi*, 131–136; cf. Zhang Fentian, *Zhongguo diwang guannian*, 170–182.

88. Taishan, Zhifu east, Kuaiji (*Shiji* 6: 243, 250, 261; Kern, *The Stele Inscriptions*, 21, 39, 47, modified).

89. This claim was reportedly made by "technical specialists" (*fang shi* 方士) at Qin's court, as an excuse for their failure to teach the emperor the art of immortality. See *Shiji* 6: 258.

90. For a good introductory discussion about the figure of the emperor under the Qin and Han dynasties, see Lewis, *The Early Chinese Empires*, 51–64. Yet *pace* Lewis (p. 2), this figure was not an imperial "innovation" but rather the apex of theoretical developments in the Warring States period, as has been demonstrated in the text.

91. For criticism of the *Shiji* "Basic Annals of the First Emperor," our major source for Qin imperial history, see, for example, Kern, *The Stele Inscriptions*, 155–163. Having this criticism in mind, we should notice that the evidence for tension between the First Emperor and his courtiers seems too overwhelming to be merely a creation of later historians, although many colorful details of Qin tyranny and atrocities may have been invented later or at least strongly inflated.

92. For the earliest attempts to summarize the reason for Qin's swift demise, see Lu Jia's (陸賈, c. 240–170) *Xin yu*, "Wu wei" 無爲 4: 62; and Jia Yi's "Discussion of Qin's faults" ("Guo Qin lun" 過秦論), *Shiji* 6: 276–284.

93. For details, see Liu Zehua, *Zhongguo de Wangquanzhuyi*, 440–449. This appropriation by the rulers of the most sacred term of pre-imperial discourse may partly explain the increasing sensitivity toward the usage of the term "sage" in nonimperial contexts, as is implied by Csikszentmihalyi, *Material Virtue*, 232–250.

94. See Martynov, "Konfutsianskaia Utopiia," 29.

95. The term "living ancestor" is employed by Ray Huang in *1587* to depict the role assigned to the Wanli emperor (萬曆, 1582–1620) by his courtiers. It resonates well with Mao Zedong's complaint that his colleagues treated him as "a dead ancestor" (that is, they respected but did not obey him, cited from Schram, *Chairman Mao*, 267). The courtiers also had an intrinsic dislike of the emperor's expressing his personal feelings, and this frequently led to awkward situations, such as the courtiers' disrupting either the emperor's relations with his living father or his mourning obligations toward his deceased ancestors. See an excellent discussion by Ebrey, "Imperial Filial Piety," for the first case; Fisher, *The Chosen One*, for the second.

Chapter 5: The Rise of the *Shi*

1. Fan Zhongyan, "Yueyang Lou ji" 岳陽樓記, in: *Fan Zhongyan quanji*, 168–169. For Fan Zhongyan's career and thought, see James Liu, "An Early Sung Reformer"; Bol, *This Culture of Ours*, 166–175.

2. The rise of the *shi* during the Zhanguo period and the intellectual implications of this has been discussed by several eminent Chinese scholars; see particularly Liu Zehua, *Xian Qin shi ren*; Yu Yingshi, *Shi yu Zhongguo wenhua*, especially 1–83; Yan Buke, *Shidafu*, especially 29–367; see also Shirley Chan, *The Confucian Shi*.

3. *Lüshi chunqiu*, "Xia xian" 下賢 15.3: 879.

4. Hsu, *Ancient China*, 34–52; 86–106.

5. For Falkenhausen's study, see his "Social Ranking in Chu Tombs" and *Chinese Society*, 370–399; for northern areas, see Yin Qun, *Huanghe*; idem, "Lun beifang zhu quyu."

6. A certain degree of upward social mobility existed in the Western Zhou period (see Li Feng, "Succession and Promotion"), but it diminished in the Chunqiu period following formation of the system of hereditary office-holding (for which see Qian Zongfan, "Xi Zhou Chunqiu"). Of the few *shi* who succeeded in making a career in the Chunqiu period, we may mention Cao Gui 曹劌, whose strategic talents allowed him to become an aide of Lord Zhuang of Lu (魯莊公, r. 693–662). Later texts depict him alternatively either as an assassin-retainer in Lord Zhuang's service (*Gongyang zhuan*, 7:2233, Zhuang 13) or as a military strategist and political advisor (see the *Zuo zhuan* and the newly unearthed *Cao Mo zhi zhen* 曹沫之陣, published by the Shanghai Museum). Another group of successful *shi* were those who joined the future Lord Wen of Jin (晉文公, r. 636–628) in his wanderings and received lucrative appointments after he ascended the throne. The very paucity of these cases indicates that the upward mobility in the Chunqiu period remained extremely limited.

7. When the *Chunqiu* reports on negative actions by the *shi*, it refers to them as "criminals" (*dao* 盜) and not by name: see the records of the turmoil in the state of Zheng (*Zuo*, Xiang 10: 973) and of Yang Hu's rebellious actions in the state of Lu (*Zuo*, Ding 8: 1562). It is worth noting that for a criminal noble to be named in the text was a humiliation, but a *shi* did not deserve even this.

8. See *Zuo*, Zhao 20: 1417; Zhao 26: 1480; and the discussion in Pines, "The Search for Stability," 28.

9. See details in Hsu, *Ancient China*, 92–105; Zhao Boxiong, *Zhoudai guojia*, 237–251. For the expansion of the administrative apparatus of the Warring States, see Lewis, "Warring States."

10. For the usage of the term *junzi* in the *Zuo zhuan*, see Pines, *Foundations*, 165–171.

11. For promoting "the upright" and "the gifted," see *Lunyu* "Wei zheng" 為政 2.19: 19; "Zilu" 13.2: 133. The *Lunyu*, however, directs the *shi* not necessarily toward serving regional lords, but rather toward serving unspecified "rulers" (*jun* 君), a term which could refer also to powerful nobles. The nobles are specifically mentioned in the text as the *shi*'s superiors, whom *shi* are supposed to serve (for example, "Wei Ling Gong" 衛靈公 15.10: 163; "Zi han" 子罕 9.16: 93).

12. Confucius's followers in the Warring States period may have decided to "update" the Master's views with regard to social mobility, turning him into a staunch supporter of the principle of "elevating the worthy." This tendency is most clear in the newly discovered text *Ji Gengzi [Kangzi] wen yu Kongzi* 季庚(康)子問於孔子, where "elevating the worthy" becomes Confucius's single most important policy recommendation.

13. For these citations, see respectively, *Lunyu*, "Li ren" 里仁 4.9: 37; "Yan Yuan" 12.20: 130; "Zilu" 13.20: 140; 13.28: 143; "Xian wen" 14.2: 145.

14. *Lunyu*, "Xian wen" 14.42: 159.

15. A *shi* also thinks of reverence when at sacrifice and of mourning when at a funeral (*Lunyu*, "Zizhang" 子張 19.1: 199).

16. *Lunyu*, "Tai Bo" 泰伯 8.7: 80.

17. *Mozi*, "Shang xian shang" 尚賢上 II.8: 66.

18. Ibid., 67.

19. Ibid., 67–68.

20. Ibid., 74.

21. *Mozi*, "Shang xian xia" II.10: 96.

22. One of the major heroes of the stories about the rulers who displayed humility when negotiating with worthy *shi* is Lord Wen of Wei (魏文侯, r. 446–396), who was indeed among the first to attract many *shi* to his court (see, for example, *Lüshi chunqiu*, "Xia xian" 下賢 15.3: 880; "Ju nan" 舉難 19.8: 1310; "Qi xian" 期賢 21.3: 1447). Many similar anecdotes about Zhanguo rulers are scattered throughout the *Zhanguo ce* and the *Shiji* (see Liu Zehua, *Xian Qin shi ren*, 104–109).

23. For the Qin system of military-based ranks, see Gao Min, "Cong *Shuihudi*"; Li Ling, "*Shang jun shu*." Social mobility in the state of Qin is vividly reflected in

the predictions of a child's future in the Qin *Almanacs* (*Ri shu* 日書) from Shui-hudi 睡虎地, Hubei, and Fangmatan 放馬灘, Gansu. The *Almanacs* offer an extraordinarily wide range of possibilities for a newborn Qin baby, from becoming a high-ranking minister (*qing* 卿), a noble (*dafu* 大夫), an official (*li* 吏), or a local bravo (*yijie* 邑傑), to, conversely, becoming a servant or (in the case of females) a concubine (*Ri Shu* yanjiu ban, "*Ri shu*"; cf. Pu Muzhou, "Shuihudi"). Shuihudi legal slips provide further details about social mobility in Qin, as, for example, in a regulation that mentions the unranked descendants of the ruling house or a statute that stipulates that a bondservant can receive an aristocratic rank in exchange for his military achievements. See *Shuihudi*, "Falü da wen" 法律答問, 137 and "Junjue lü" 軍爵律, 55; Hulsewé, *Remnants of Ch'in Law*, D164: 174 and A91: 83; for the latter case, see the discussion in Yates, "Slavery," 313.

24. For the case of Chu, see Blakeley, "King, Clan, and Courtier in Ancient Ch'u."

25. For critical remarks regarding implementations of the principle of "elevating the worthy," see, for example, *Laozi* 3: 235, *Mengzi*, "Liang Hui Wang xia" 2.7: 41; *Shang jun shu*, "Shen fa" 慎法 V.25: 136; *Han Feizi*, "Xian xue" 顯學 XIX.50: 456–461.

26. In the following discussion I am not confining myself to the term Way as such, since other terms were occasionally used for the same purpose of designing guiding social and cosmic principles (for example, *yi* 義 in the *Mozi* or *li* 禮 in the *Xunzi*). The label "Way" appears simply as the most convenient generic term of these principles, as it is employed in Graham's seminal *Disputers of the Tao*. For the semantic fields of the term Dao, see, for example, Zhang Liwen, *Zhongguo zhexue fanchou*, 40–51.

27. For different analyses of the emergence of independent intellectual authority among *shi* thinkers, see Yu Yingshi, *Shi yu Zhongguo wenhua*, 26–33; Lewis, *Writing and Authority*, 53–97; Liu Zehua, *Xian Qin shi ren*, 22–39 and 113–119.

28. An example of such a fabrication may be the "Yao dian" chapter of the *Shu jing* (see Chapter 3, n. 67, for details).

29. For Confucius's claims that he "transmits" the way of the ancients rather than "creates" anything anew, see *Lunyu*, "Shu er" 述而 7.1: 66. Mozi similarly claims that his controversial doctrines represent the true legacy of the former kings (*Mozi*, "Shang xian xia" II. 10: 97; "Jian'ai xia" 兼愛下 IV.16: 178; "Tian zhi xia" VII.28: 322). For the idea that competing thinkers invented paragon rulers of the past to use them in ideological polemics, see Gu Jiegang, "Gu shi bian"; while many of Gu's ideas have been disproved, the basic thrust of his argument remains convincing. See more about the use of historical narratives in ideological controversies in Pines, "Speeches" (where the decline in the scribes' role is discussed); Petersen, "Which Books"; Goldin, "Appeals to History."

30. The increasing willingness to overtly manipulate the past and to disregard alternative narratives is evident in many Zhanguo texts, most notably *Zhuangzi*, but also *Han Feizi* and even *Xunzi*. See more in Pines, "Speeches."

31. See Puett, *To Become a God,* for further discussion of an individual's ability to become a sage.

32. See *Lunyu,* "Weizi" 微子 18.3: 192; 18.4: 193; this chapter probably belongs to the later layer of the *Lunyu.*

33. *Mengzi,* "Gongsun Chou xia" 公孫丑下 4.2: 89.

34. See, respectively, *Mengzi,* "Liang Hui wang shang" 1.7: 17; "Teng Wen Gong xia" 6.1: 138; "Wan Zhang xia" 10.7: 248.

35. See, respectively, *Mengzi,* "Wan Zhang shang" 9.4: 215; "Teng Wen Gong xia" 6.4: 146.

36. *Mengzi,* "Teng Wen Gong xia" 6.2: 141.

37. *Mengzi,* "Wan Zhang xia" 10.8: 251.

38. Ibid., 10.4: 240.

39. For "internal" sources of moral authority in the *Mengzi,* see Brindley, "Human Agency," 206–215.

40. *Zhuangzi,* "Xiao yao you" 1: 18.

41. Ibid.

42. Ibid., 21.

43. *Xunzi,* "Fei shi'er zi" III.6: 98.

44. *Xunzi,* "Ru xiao" IV.8: 127–128. The cited poem is "He ming" 鶴鳴 (Mao 184).

45. *Xunzi,* "Ru xiao" IV.8: 117–118. For the term "Great Man," whose "brightness equals to the sun and moon, greatness fills the Eight Poles," see *Xunzi,* "Jie bi" XV.21: 397.

46. The authors of *Xunzi* and *Zhuangzi* grade the *shi* according to their proximity to the Way and reserve their panegyrics only for the best. These gradations may be indicative of the increasing heterogeneity of the *shi* stratum, as addressed above in the text. See, for example, *Zhuangzi,* "Ke yi" 刻意 15: 393; "Tianxia" 天下 33: 855; Xunzi "Bu gou" 不苟 II.3: 49–51; "Ru xiao" IV.8: 129–134. Occasionally, however, Xunzi speaks of "plain-clothed *shi* in silk-corded shoes" in terms almost identical to those used to depict the superior man and the Great Ru (see, for example, *Xunzi,* "Fu guo" VI.10: 196), which indicates his high expectations of the *shi* in general.

47. *Mozi,* "Lu wen" 魯問 XIII.49: 736.

48. Such latent expectations "to become Shun" are evident, for instance, in the *Zi Gao* manuscript published by Shanghai Museum (see Pines, "Subversion Unearthed," 161–164).

49. *Zhanguo ce,* "Qi ce 齊策 4" 11.5: 395–396. For Liuxia Ji (Liuxia Hui 柳下惠) as a model *shi,* see Chapter 6.

50. Ibid., 397.

51. Ibid.

52. For the nature of the *Zhanguo ce,* see Crump, *Intrigues,* 88–109 (cf. Goldin, "Rhetoric"); Vasil'ev, *Plany,* 33–164.

53. See, for example, *Lüshi chunqiu,* "Ai shi" 愛士 8.5: 458–460; "Zhi shi" 知士

9.3: 490–491; "Shi jie" 士節 12.2: 622–624 *et saepe*. One of the chapters ("Jie li" 介立 12.3: 627) plainly proclaims that the only reason why Lord Wen of Jin failed to become a True Monarch was his maltreatment of his devoted aide, Jie Zitui 介子推.

54. *Lüshi chunqiu*, "Shi jie" 12.2: 622–623.

55. For similar views, see also the citation at the beginning of this chapter from *Lüshi chunqiu*, "Xia xian" 15.3: 879.

56. *Lüshi chunqiu*, "Dang ran" 2.4: 96.

57. *Lüshi chunqiu*, "Xia xian" 15.3: 878. I am grateful to Wolfgang Behr for informing me of the original phonology of the characters above.

Chapter 6: To Serve or Not to Serve

1. *Mengzi*, "Teng Wen Gong xia" 6.3: 142–143.

2. *Mengzi*, "Jin xin shang" 13.20: 209. The "three joys" are family prosperity, personal integrity, and the ability to teach "outstanding talents from All under Heaven."

3. For the employment patterns of the Zhanguo *shi* and their social position, see Liu Zehua, *Xian Qin shi ren*, 1–14 and 48–101; for technical specialists (*fang shi*), see Li Ling, *Zhongguo fangshu kao*; for Zhanguo *binke*, see Shen Gang, *Qin Han shiqi de ke jieceng*, 32–50; for the assassin-retainers' biographies, see *Shiji* 86: 2515–2538.

4. Lewis, *Writing and Authority*, 72; for his general discussion, see especially 73–83.

5. See, for example, Lewis, *Writing and Authority*, 77–78.

6. In the *Construction of Space*, 86, Lewis moderates his earlier approach, acknowledging that "the great families of the Warring States were increasingly creatures of the government." Actually, we still lack evidence for a single "great family" of that age that was *independent* of "the government."

7. For Liu Zehua's study, see his *Zhongguo de Wangquanzhuyi*, 20–25; see also examples of possible *shi* landowners in his *Xian Qin shi ren*, 58–59. For early landownership in China, see Hu Fangshu, "Zhoudai gongshe"; and especially Yuan Lin, *Liang Zhou tudi zhidu*; for the earliest example of selling an inherited plot of land, see *Baoshan*, 28, slips 151–152; Wang Ying, "Cong Baoshan," 14–15. For the early Han wealthy landowners as a source of new, "societal" power, see Mao Han-kuang, "The Evolution," 74–80.

8. Active state intervention in commerce is suggested both in those texts that approve it (like the "Qing zhong" 輕重 chapters of the *Guanzi*, or, alternatively, the *Shang jun shu*), and those that disapprove of it, like *Mengzi* and *Xunzi*. Qin statutes from Shuihudi, as well as E Jun Qi 鄂君启 tallies from the state of Chu, all indicate strong surveillance of merchants; Qin even obliged them to attach the price to every object worth one cash and above (*Shuihudi*, "Jin bu lü," 金布律 37; Hulsewé, *Remnants of Ch'in Law*, A46: 53; for the E Jun Qi tallies, see Falkenhausen, "The E Jun Qi"). For the state control of and intervention in private industrial activities, see

Wagner's seminal *Iron and Steel*; see also Hong Shi, "Zhanguo Qin Han shiqi qiqi"; Wang Ying, "Cong Baoshan." For Sima Qian's biographies of merchants, see *Shiji* 129: 3256–3260.

9. See, respectively, *Mengzi*, "Gaozi xia" 告子下 12.14: 298; *Xunzi*, "Ru xiao" IV.8: 117–118. For stories about dire straits of Zhanguo *shi* outside government service, see, for example, Jing and Cai, "Shi xi Zhanguo wanqi shi"; Liu Zehua, *Xian Qin shi ren*, 61–62; for examples of rich *shi*, see Liu Zehua, *Xian Qin shi ren*, 58–59.

10. For the proliferation of the compound *buyi* in late Zhanguo texts, see Pines, "Lexical Change," 701–702. In the *Lüshi chunqiu* in particular, this term becomes a common designation of lofty *shi*.

11. *Zhanguo ce*, "Qin ce 5" 7.5: 269.

12. *Han Feizi*, "Wu du" XIX.49: 444.

13. For the ranks in Zhanguo society and their related privileges, see Liu Zehua, *Zhongguo de Wangquanzhuyi*, 25–32; Shuihudi statutes suggest legal advantages for rank holders in certain judicial procedures. These advantages may explain why even rich merchants and artisans were willing to buy rank and office (see, for example, *Han Feizi*, "Wu du" XIX.49: 455 and "Wai chu shuo zuo xia" 外儲說左下 XII.33: 301).

14. *Mozi*, "Shang xian shang" II.8: 66.

15. Ibid., 67.

16. The "vertical" (*cong* 從) alliance was a coalition of "eastern" states against Qin.

17. *Zhanguo ce*, "Qin ce 3" 5.14: 192.

18. For Fan Sui's career, see his biography in the *Shiji* 79: 2401–2418.

19. *Zhanguo ce*, "Qin ce 1" 3.2: 74–75.

20. Ibid., 75.

21. Ibid., 76.

22. *Lüshi chunqiu*, "Bo zhi" 博志 24.5: 1618.

23. Ning Yue's book in one *pian* (*Ning Yuezi* 甯越子) is recorded in the bibliographical section of the *Han shu*, but it was lost before the Sui dynasty (隋, 581–618 CE). Recently, portions of the *Ning Yuezi* were discovered in a middle-Zhanguo-period tomb, M36 from Shibancun 石板村 village, Cili 慈利 county, Hunan. For the preliminary publication of the discovery, see Zhang Chunlong, "Cili Chu jian gaishu."

24. *Lunyu,* "Li ren" 4.5: 36.

25. "Life is what I desire; righteousness is also what I desire; if I cannot obtain them together, I will abandon life and choose righteousness" (*Mengzi*, "Gaozi shang" 高子上 11.10: 265).

26. *Lunyu*, "Li ren" 4.8: 37; for the priority of the Way in a superior man's life, see *Lunyu*, "Li ren" 4.9: 37; "Wei Ling Gong" 15.32: 168.

27. See, respectively, *Lunyu*, "Zilu" 13.10: 137; "Yang Huo" 陽貨 17.5: 182 and 17.9: 183; "Zizhang" 19.25: 205.

28. See, respectively, *Lunyu,* "Wei Ling Gong" 15.20: 166, "Zi han" 9.13: 91.

29. See, for example, *Lunyu* "Ba xiao" 3.18: 30; "Xian jin" 先進 11.17: 115; "Xian wen" 14.22:153; "Wei Ling Gong" 15.10–15.11: 163–164 and 15.38: 170. In an interesting discussion, in which the disciples reveal their aspirations ("Xian jin" 11.26: 118–119), Confucius ostensibly endorses the only nonpolitical vision, that of Gongxi Hua 公西華, but even this anecdote clearly reflects the normatively political direction of the disciples' careers.

30. See *Lunyu,* "Xian wen" 14.42: 159.

31. *Lunyu,* "Zizhang" 19.13: 202; for debates about this phrase, see Su and Song, "Xue er you"; Zhang Mingqi and Bi Cheng, "Ye tan."

32. For Confucius's criticism of career-seekers, see, for example, *Lunyu,* "Yan Yuan" 12.20: 130; "Zilu" 13.20: 140.

33. Thus Confucius laments that "the Way is not implemented" and threatens to leave to the sea coast (*Lunyu,* "Gongye Chang" 公冶長 5.7: 43–44). He compares himself to a dry gourd that can be hanged but cannot be eaten ("Yang Huo" 17.7: 183), cries at despair in light of Heaven's indifference "I am finished" ("Zi han" 9.9: 89), and threatens to quit teaching, to which he has dedicated most of his life ("Yang Huo" 17.19: 187–188).

34. This message is hinted at already in the first phrase in the *Lunyu* ("Xue er" 1.1: 1), which speaks of the joy of learning and meeting friends and warns against resentment in case of nonrecognition.

35. *Lunyu,* "Xian wen" 14.1: 145.

36. *Lunyu,* "Wei Ling Gong" 15.7: 163.

37. *Lunyu,* "Tai Bo" 8.13: 82.

38. *Mengzi,* "Wan Zhang xia" 10.1: 233.

39. See *Mengzi,* "Gongsun Chou shang" 公孫丑上 3.2: 63.

40. *Mengzi,* "Gaozi xia" 12.14: 297–298.

41. For Mengzi's discussions of the former sages, see *Mengzi,* "Gongsun Chou shang" 3.2: 63 (where the superiority of Confucius is proclaimed); "Wan Zhang shang" 9.7: 225; "Wan Zhang xia" 10.1: 232–233; "Gaozi xia" 12.6: 284.

42. *Mengzi,* "Teng Wen Gong xia" 6.3: 143.

43. *Lunyu,* "Wei Ling Gong" 15.32: 168; cf. 15.38: 170.

44. See, *Mengzi,* "Gongsun Chou xia" 4.3: 92–93; "Teng Wen Gong xia" 6.4: 145–146; "Wan Zhang xia" 10.4: 239–240; 10.5: 243; 10.6: 244–245.

45. For a brief outline of Mengzi's career, see Yang Bojun's introduction in *Mengzi,* 1–3.

46. Following Yang Bojun, I read 名世 as 命世. Csikszentmihalyi (*Material Virtue,* 195, n. 65) discusses these characters, which he prefers to translate as "to give names to the age."

47. *Mengzi,* "Gongsun Chou xia" 4.13: 109. See also Csikszentmihalyi, *Material Virtue,* 195–200, for an alternative discussion of this passage.

48. *Mengzi,* "Jin xin shang" 13.1: 300.

49. Ibid., 13.4: 301.

50. For the literati incorporation of these notions, see, for example, Pankenier, "The Scholar's Frustration."

51. For studies of the *Qiong da yi shi*, see Meyer, "Structure"; Li Rui, "Guodian Chu jian *Qiong da yi shi*." Li's article contains a convenient summary of earlier studies and also of parallels to the *Qiong da yi shi* in the received texts.

52. *Qiong da yi shi*, slips 1–3; Li Ling, *Guodian*, 86.

53. *Qiong da yi shi*, slips 11–12, 15.

54. For a somewhat different analysis of *Qiong da yi shi* and of other texts that perceive of self-cultivation as a self-sustained goal, see Brindley, "Human Agency," 176–206.

55. See Vervoorn, *Men of the Cliffs*; for other important studies, see Berkowitz, *Patterns of Disengagement* (this study deals primarily with the post-Han period); Yang Huyun, *Zhongguo yinyi wenhua*. Many insightful observations about the recluses' culture are gathered in Liu Zehua, *Xian Qin shi ren*, 125–132.

56. I prefer the term "disengagement" (used by Berkowitz) to "reclusion" or "eremitism," since disengagement does not presume cutting off ties with society, as is something implied by reclusion and eremitism.

57. *Lunyu*, "Xian wen" 14.1: 145. For the Boyi and Shuqi legend, see Aat Vervoorn, "Boyi and Shuqi"; Rubin, "A Chinese Don Quixote."

58. For Zilu's criticisms of Confucius's moves, see *Lunyu*, "Yang Huo" 17.5: 182; 17.7: 183; "Yong ye" 6.28: 64.

59. See *Mengzi*, "Wan Zhang xia" 10.4: 240.

60. *Mengzi*, "Teng Wen Gong xia" 6.10: 158–159.

61. Chen Zhongzi's similarity to Boyi is supported by the account in the *Huainanzi* 淮南子 ("Silun xun" 氾論訓 13:449), according to which Chen starved himself to death to avoid eating the grains of the "calamitous age."

62. See *Mengzi*, "Teng Wen Gong xia" 6.2: 140–141; "Gaozi xia" 12.3: 293; *Xunzi*, "Bu gou" II.3: 52; cf. "Fei shi er zi" III.6: 92.

63. Chapter 18 of the *Lunyu* ("Weizi" 18.5–18.7: 193–196), probably one of the latest in this text, contains several anecdotes about Confucius's putative meetings with proud recluses who "escaped the age" (*bi shi* 避世), causing great uneasiness to the Master and to his disciples. For Xunzi's views, see below in the text.

64. The appeal of this kind of protest cannot be underestimated; it is not incidental that Xunzi considered among the achievements of the True Monarch that "there are no recluses under Heaven" (*Xunzi*, "Zheng lun" XII.18: 331). Han Feizi clearly identifies political disengagement with "negation of superiors" ("You du" II.6: 35). Eventually, in the imperial age, refusal to serve became one of the most powerful assets of dissenting intellectuals.

65. Feng Youlan (馮友蘭, 1895–1990 CE) was among the first to revive interest in Yang Zhu (see Fung, *History of Chinese Philosophy*, 133–143). In the West, this interest was spurred by A. C. Graham's provocative identification of several chapters in the *Zhuangzi* and *Lüshi chunqiu* as reflecting a "Yangist" tradition (see Graham, *Disputers of the Tao*, 53–64; for the impact of his theory, see, for example, Shun,

Mencius, 35–37; Lewis, *The Construction of Space*, 16–20). The manifold problems with this approach, which is based on a series of overtly speculative assumptions, are convincingly summarized by Goldin in his "Review of A. C. Graham." More generally, at the current stage of our knowledge any attempt to ascribe author-ship—"Yangist" or otherwise—to any single chapter of the received texts would inevitably be speculative; hence I prefer to avoid it. Moreover, nowadays, with the early provenance of the [proto-]*Laozi* and its anteriority to the [proto-]*Zhuangzi* confirmed by the Guodian discovery, it is preferable to focus on the content of these two texts, leaving aside their irresolvable authorship—at least until further archeological discoveries add new information about the history of both texts. For the renewed discussions of the *Laozi*'s provenance, see Chapter 2, n. 35; for the *Zhuangzi*, see Graham, "How Much"; Liu Xiaogan, *Classifying*.

66. *Laozi* 66: 145–149, following Wang Bi's version; *Guodian Laozi* A, slips 2–3.

67. As cited above in the text and in n. 65, it is common among Western schol-ars to ascribe concern for the body in Chinese thought to Yang Zhu and his follow-ers (see also Emerson, "Yang Chu"; Defoort, "Mohist and Yangist Blood"). Putting aside "Yangist" speculations, we should remember that the idea of protecting the body (*bao shen* 保身) was already attested in Western Zhou bronze inscriptions, where the quest for longevity was the most common topic of the so-called "auspi-cious words" (*guci* 嘏辭) (see Xu Zhongshu, "Jinwen guci," 522–548, especially 537–539). Yet there is no evidence prior to the *Laozi* of the juxtaposition of bodily preservation and a political career, and, more, generally of bodily preservation as a *political* value. It is possible that the increasing concern with the body and the self reflected a withering of the lineage-oriented mentality, but this topic deserves further exploration. For more about body-related discourse of the Zhanguo pe-riod, see Sivin, "State, Cosmos, and Body"; Lewis, *The Construction of Space*, 14–76; Brindley, "Human Agency"; McNeal, "The Body as Metaphor."

68. See, respectively, *Lunyu*, "Wei Ling Gong" 15.9: 163; *Mengzi*, "Jin xin shang" 13.42: 321.

69. *Laozi* 7: 251–252; for the earlier references, see *Laozi* (16: 302, 50: 67); see also 52: 74.

70. See *Laozi* 44: 39–40; *Guodian Laozi* A, slip 35.

71. The complexity of the text may be demonstrated by contradictory interpre-tations of the *Laozi* 13: 276–282 (*Guodian Laozi* B, slips 5–8, which can mean either "only he who esteems/loves his body more than All under Heaven apparently can be entrusted with All under Heaven," or "only he who forgets his body for the sake of All under Heaven deserves the worldly rule." See the summary of distinct views in Nie Zhongqing, *Guodian Chu jian 'Laozi,'* 267–270.

72. *Mengzi*, "Teng Wen Gong xia" 6.9: 155; and "Jin xin shang" 13.26: 313.

73. See *Lunyu* "Weizi" 18.5: 193; cf. *Zhuangzi*, "Ren jian shi" 人間事 4: 140.

74. For preserving the self as an ultimate obligation toward one's parents, see *Lunyu*, "Tai Bo" 8.3: 79; *Lüshi chunqiu*, "Xiao xing" 孝行 14.1: 732–733; *Xiao jing* 1: 49.

75. *Zhanguo ce*, "Qin ce 3" 5.18: 204.

76. For the differences between the "Inner," "Outer," and "Miscellaneous" chapters of the *Zhuangzi*, see, Graham, "How Much"; Liu Xiaogan, *Classifying*.

77. *Zhuangzi*, "Qiu shui" 秋水 17: 441.

78. *Zhuangzi*, "Ren jian shi" 4: 129.

79. "Why do All under Heaven not call you Robber Qiu, while calling me Robber Zhi?" (*Zhuangzi*, "Dao Zhi" 29: 778). Qiu is Confucius's personal name.

80. *Zhuangzi*, "Qu qie" 10: 257. This sentence is echoed also in the "Dao Zhi" chapter (29: 790) and is cited in the "Yu cong 4" (語叢, Collected sayings) section of the Guodian slips, both of which substitute "righteous *shi*" (*yi shi* 義士) for "benevolence and righteousness" (Li Ling, *Guodian*, 44, slips 8–9).

81. *Zhuangzi*, "Zai you" 在宥 11.274.

82. See *Zhuangzi*, "Wai wu" 外物 26: 705. Perhaps to counterbalance this story, the text also tells of Zhuangzi's proud rejection of service in front of his successful neighbor, whom he accuses of "draining an abscess and licking the piles" of the king of Qin in order to attain high rewards ("Lie Yukou" 列禦寇 32: 839).

83. *Lüshi chunqiu*, "Jin ting" 13.5: 705.

84. For the *Zhuangzi* "Rang wang" chapter being anterior to the *Lüshi chunqiu*, see Chao Fulin, "*Zhuangzi* 'Rang wang' pian."

85. *Zhuangzi*, "Rang wang" 28: 751.

86. *Lüshi chunqiu*, "Gui sheng" 2.2: 75.

87. *Xunzi*, "Fei shi er zi" III.6: 101.

88. Wang Niansun (王念孫, 1744–1832 CE) noticed lexical similarities between the mutual attacks in both texts: for the detailed discussion, see *Xunzi*, p. 101.

89. *Zhanguo ce*, "Qi ce 4" 118: 411.

90. See, for example, Maliavin, *Gibel' Drevnej Imperii*, 132–144. The respect for recluses remained high throughout the imperial era, despite occasional outbursts of imperial anger against those who defied the proper career pattern (Vervoorn, *Men of Caves*; Mote, "Confucian Eremitism"). It was only in the twentieth century that the situation markedly changed, and disengagement, with its ideal of passivity, was largely rejected by the modernized Chinese intelligentsia. Lu Xun (魯迅, 1881–1936 CE), brilliantly, as usual, reflected upon the hypocrisy of the "disengagement" ideal, mentioning a recluse who was fond of the *Zhuangzi*, but who simultaneously acted as a local police officer (see his "Resurrection" ["Qi si" 起死] in *Old Tales Retold*).

91. See Liu Zehua, *Zhongguo de Wangquanzhuyi*, 175–181, and passim.

Chapter 7: *Shi* and the Rulers

1. See Shaughnessy, "The Duke of Zhou"; cf. Nivison, "An Interpretation of the *Shao gao*."

2. For the altars as representatives of the collective entity of those who dwelled

in the state, see Masubuchi, *Chūgoku kodai no shakai to kokka*, 139–163; cf. Lewis, *The Construction of Space*, 147–148.

3. See more about Chunqiu views of ruler-minister relations in Pines, *Foundations*, 146–153. For the power of the ministerial lineages of the Chunqiu period, see Chapter 1, n. 25.

4. For identification of the Chunqiu ministers as "masters of the people" (*min zhi zhu* 民之主), see, for example, *Zuo*, Xuan 2: 658; Xiang 22: 1070–1071; Xiang 30: 1178–1179; Zhao 5: 1270; this designation of the ministers is absent from Zhanguo texts. For the disappearance of the notion of "loyalty to the altars" from Zhanguo texts prior to the *Xunzi*, see Pines, "Friends or Foes," 63.

5. "The superior man is not a tool" (*Lunyu*, "Wei zheng" 2.12: 17).

6. *Lunyu*, "Xian jin" 11.24: 117.

7. See *Mengzi*, "Gaozi xia" 12.6: 284. To remind readers, Tang, the founder of the Shang dynasty, had overthrown Jie, the ruler of the Xia.

8. See *Mozi*, "Geng Zhu" 耕柱 XI.46: 659; "Lu wen" XIII.49: 737–739; "Gongshu" 公輸 XIII.50: 764–765.

9. *Xunzi*, "Chen Dao" XI.13: 250; see more below in the text.

10. For Chunqiu retainers, see Zhu Fenghan, *Shang Zhou*, 531–540; Shao, "Zhoudai jiachen"; for their views of loyalty, see Pines, *Foundations*, 154–158; Suzuki, "Shunjū," 9–11. By the late Chunqiu period, the formerly lifelong contracts between a master and his retainer could no longer ensure that retainers would remain attached to their masters, which forced some nobles to resort to the religiously significant ceremony of alliance (*meng* 盟) to shore up the fidelity of their servants. Examples of such *meng* between a master and his retainers are the early fifth-century BCE Houma 侯馬 and Wenxian 溫縣 alliances (for the first, see Zhu Fenghan's discussion in *Shang Zhou*, 539; and Weld, "The Covenant Texts"; for the second, Zhao and Zhao, "Wenxian mengshu"). These efforts notwithstanding, master-retainers ties in the Zhanguo age were marked by a high degree of fluidity, as a series of anecdotes reflects; see, for example, *Shiji*, 75–78: 2351–2399.

11. *Lunyu*, "Ba yi" 3.19: 30.

12. *Zhanguo ce*, "Zhao ce 1" 18.4: 618.

13. Ibid., 617.

14. For more on the importance of "understanding" the *shi*, see, for example, *Lüshi chunqiu*, "Zhi shi" 9.3: 490–491; "Bu qin" 12.5: 640; *Zhanguo ce*, "Chu ce 楚策 4" 17.11: 589–590; *Shiji* 77: 2378–2381.

15. The importance of the friendship simile for understanding ruler-minister relations in the Warring States period is analyzed in an excellent study by Zha Changguo, "You"; cf. Pines, "Friends or Foes." The term *you* (友, "friends") was applied to ruler-minister relations already in Western Zhou texts, but then it referred primarily, if not exclusively, to relatives, particularly brothers, and not to friends (see Zhu Fenghan, *Shang Zhou*, 306–311). In the Zhanguo period, however, *you* acquired the meaning of "friends," persons who share common desires, that is, equals.

16. For detailed discussion of these texts, see Pines, "Friends or Foes," 42–49.

17. *Yu cong* 3, slip 6.

18. *Yu cong* 1, slips 78, 80, 81, 77, 82, 79. I follow Pang Pu's rearrangement ("Chu du Guodian," 9).

19. *Yu cong* 1, slip 87.

20. *Yu cong* 3, slips 1–5. See also a brief discussion of this passage in Ding Sixin, *Guodian Chumu sixiang*, 233.

21. For Lewis's remark, see *Writing and Authority*, 67; see also Mengzi's defense of the minister's right to shift allegiances below in the text. For Qin attempts to control the movement of traveling *shi*, see *Shuihudi*, "Qin lü za chao" 秦律雜抄, 80; Hulsewé, *Remnants of Ch'in Law*, C3: 104.

22. *Han Feizi*, "Nan yi" XV.36: 352.

23. *Mengzi*, "Li Lou xia" 8.3: 186.

24. *Mengzi*, "Wan Zhang xia" 10.7: 248.

25. See Martynov, "Kategoriia *de*"; cf. Onozawa, "Toku ron." Note also Mengzi's claim that "[w]hen the Way prevails under Heaven, those with smaller virtue serve those with greater virtue, the less worthy serve the worthier" (*Mengzi*, "Li Lou shang" 7.7: 168).

26. See, for example, *Lüshi chunqiu*, "Shi jie" 12.2: 622–623; "Xia xian" 15.3: 879; *Zhanguo ce*, "Yan ce 1" 29.12: 1110–1111; *Huang Di shu*, "Cheng" 乘 3: 201 (Yates, *Five Lost Classics*, 158–159).

27. *Cuo mu*, I: 341, slightly modifying Constance Cook's translation from Mattos, "Eastern Zhou," 106–107.

28. For the function of the bronze inscriptions as a means of communicating with the ancestors and a medium for expressing the donor's weltanschauung, see Falkenhausen, "Issues," 145–171.

29. For Gongmeng Yi's provocative question, see *Mozi*, "Gongmeng" 公盟 XII.48: 704. For Mengzi's reaction to a similar, albeit unspoken question (why Confucius did not possess All under Heaven), see *Mengzi*, "Wan Zhang shang" 9.6: 222. For the exclamation of Xunzi's disciples that their master "was appropriate for a position of Thearch or Monarch," see *Xunzi*, "Yao wen" 堯問 XX.32: 553.

30. The concept of *su wang* is usually associated with the *Gongyang* tradition, and it supposedly indicates Confucius's presiding over a "textual empire" (see, for example, Lewis, *Writing and Authority*, 218–238; Huang Kaiguo, "*Gongyang* xue," 76–77; Queen, "The Way of the Unadorned King"). For interesting reservations regarding common interpretations of the *su wang* topic, see van Ess, "Han dai sixiang." For the Han scholars cherishing hopes to attain political power, see Arbuckle, "Inevitable Treason."

31. To recapitulate, Su Qin initially tried to serve Qin, but later turned into the architect of an anti-Qin coalition. In addition, while serving at the court of Qi, Su Qin apparently acted as a secret agent for Qi's rival, the state of Yan. Su Qin's career is summarized by Lewis, "Warring States," 633–634; for more details, see Tang Lan, "Sima Qian," 129–136 and 145–153. The complexity of Su Qin's intrigues and the

degree of mistrust generated by his behavior is vividly depicted in the collection of his putative letters in the Mawangdui *Zhanguo zonghengjia shu*, 1–12: 21–45.

32. Among Zhanguo tragic heroes, outstanding ministers whose loyalty was not recognized by their superiors and who were, as a result, victimized, we may mention Wu Zixu, a minister at the court of Wu; a military strategist, Wu Qi (吳起, d. 381); and the semilegendary poet Qu Yuan (屈原, d. c. 278?). Sima Qian, whose personal tragedy made him particularly receptive to their stories, collected anecdotes related to these persons in chapters 65, 66, and 84 of the *Shiji*; see also Johnson, "Epic and History"; Schneider, *A Madman of Chu*. The deterioration of ruler-minister relations is elucidated by a *Zhanguo ce* anecdote, which tells that only a bad and unpopular minister could be considered loyal, as he would never usurp the ruler's power ("Dong Zhou ce" 東周策 1.11: 17).

33. These accusations are concentrated in the earlier parts of the *Shang jun shu*, such as the "Nong zhan" (農戰, Agriculture and warfare) chapter. Shang Yang warned: "The 'heroes' diligently study *Shi* and *Shu* and then follow the external forces" (*Shang jun shu*, "Nong zhan" I.3: 22; cf. "Suan di" 算地 II.6: 45–47). Other texts, such as the fragmentary *Guo Yan lun shi* (郭偃論士, Guo Yan discusses *shi*) manuscript discovered in 1972 in Yinqueshan 銀雀山, Shandong, attack peripatetic advisors as a source of slander and disorder (Yates, "Texts on the Military," 355–358).

34. Creel, *Shen Pu-hai*, 344.

35. See Shuihudi "Xiao" 效 58 and 59; Hulsewé, *Remnants of Ch'in Law*, A85: 79; A87: 81. Baoshan documents reflect stern supervision of the population records kept by low-rank officials (Weld, "Chu Law," 85–86).

36. For *Wei li zhi Dao*, see Shuihudi 167–173; an apparently similar text is the still unpublished *Zhengshi zhi chang* (政事之常, Constants of political affairs) manuscript, unearthed in 1993 from Qin tomb No. 15 at Wangjiatai 王家台, Jingzhou 荊州, Hubei (see Wang Mingqin, "Wangjiatai Qin mu," 42). The declarative—if not substantial—impact of these "Confucian" methods for the cultivation of officials is undeniable; dozens of Qin official seals commonly contain reference to such "Confucian" virtues as benevolence (*ren* 仁), sincerity (*cheng* 誠), and loyalty (*zhong* 忠) (see Wang Hui and Cheng Xuehua, *Qin wenzi*, 299–309).

37. *Guanzi*, "Ren fa" XV.45: 912–913.

38. For similar proposals, see, for example, *Han Feizi*, "You du" II.6: 34–35.

39. For Yu Rang's story, see *Shiji* 86: 2519–2521, and the discussion above in the text.

40. See p. 153 for further details about the story of Boyi and Shuqi. The putative desire of King Wu to yield All under Heaven to the righteous brothers is in all likelihood Han Feizi's exaggeration.

41. *Han Feizi*, "Jian jie shi chen" 姦劫弒臣 IV.14: 106.

42. Ibid.

43. This tragic understanding is best expressed in *Han Feizi*, "Gu fen" 孤憤 IV.11: 78–85. To remind readers, Han Feizi was slandered and killed while in Qin custody, and as a consequence, he failed to witness the triumph of his ideas.

44. *Han Feizi*, "Zhong xiao" XX.52: 468.

45. *Han Feizi*, "Xian xue" XIX.50: 459.

46. *Han Feizi*, "Wu du" XIX.49: 452.

47. For Xunzi's impact on Han political culture, see, for example, Nylan, "Confucian Piety."

48. *Xunzi*, "Ru xiao" IV.8: 117.

49. *Xunzi*, "Xiu shen" 修身 I.2: 27.

50. *Xunzi*, "Fei shi'er zi" III.6: 98.

51. See *Xunzi*, "Ru xiao" IV.8: 123.

52. *Xunzi*, "Chen Dao" IX.13: 249.

53. Ibid., 250. This statement refers specifically to the actions of Prince Wuji, for whom see below in the text.

54. *Xunzi*, "Chen Dao" IX.13: 250. For Jizi and Bigan, see Chapter 4, n. 24; for the careers of Wu Zixu, Lord Pingyuan 平原君, and Lord Xinling, see *Shiji* 65; 76; 77.

55. "The Way is a principle through which proper rule is arranged" (*Xunzi*, "Zheng ming" XVI.22: 423).

56. *Xunzi*, "Chen Dao" IX.13: 251–252. The cited poem is not a part of the current *Shi jing*.

57. *Shiji* 87: 2539.

58. See Kern, *The Stele Inscriptions*, 183–196.

59. *Shiji* 87: 2546.

60. Similar sentiments are observable in Xunzi's "Contra the Twelve Masters," Han Feizi's "Bright Learning" ("Xian xue"), and in the "All under Heaven" ("Tianxia") chapter of the *Zhuangzi* (for the possible dating of which, see Gao Heng, "Zhuangzi Tianxia pian," 457–458; Liu Xiaogan *Classifying*, 71–72).

61. *Shiji* 87: 2546.

62. For *Speeches* of the "Hundred Schools" as a historical genre, see Petersen, "Which Books?"

63. *Shiji* 87: 2546.

64. Zhifu eastern vista inscription, *Shiji* 6: 250; Kern, *The Stele Inscriptions*, 39.

65. For these regulations, see *Shuihudi*, "Jiuyuan lü" 廄苑律, 22; "Falü da wen," 128; "Jiuyuan lü," 23; Hulsewé, *Remnants of Ch'in Law* A7: 26; D130: 162–163; A8: 27; for tracing an absconded debtor to the remote southern corner of the newly established empire, the Dongting commandery 洞庭郡, see Zhang Junmin, "Qin dai de fu zhai." The heretofore published Liye 里耶 documents disclose, among other matters, how Qin officials at the district and prefecture level negotiated the appointment of two villagers to the positions of village head and postman. The report of the district bailiff to the prefect traveled three days, and the prefect's reply was given within a few hours before the document traveled back. Such rapidity of transmission and centralized control over the affairs of a remote district defy the imagination. For the translation of this correspondence, see Giele, "Signatures," 362–365.

66. The abundance of written correspondence between office-holders is certainly one of the hallmarks of Qin administration; see, for example, the explicit ban on oral reports in business cases, which had to be handled in writing only (*Shuihudi* "Nei shi za" 內史雜, 62; Hulsewé, *Remnants of Ch'in Law*, A 98: 87). For Qin cultivation of officials, see n. 36 above.

67. See Perelomov, *Imperiia Tsin'*, 66–84. The heretofore published Liye documents (such as those discussed by Giele, "Signatures," 363–364) support Perelomov's insightful assertion. For a useful, albeit not entirely flawless discussion of the Qin attempt to incorporate the *shi* within its officialdom, see Yan Buke, *Shidafu*, 224–267.

68. *Shiji* 6: 283.

69. See *Shiji* 121: 3116.

70. The establishment of the recommendation-*cum*-examination system under the Han and its impact on the composition of the elite and on the relations between the elite and the throne are discussed in Mao, "The Evolution," 81–88; Nylan, *The Five "Confucian" Classics*, 31–41. For the late imperial examination system, see an excellent discussion in Elman, *A Cultural History*.

71. The statement attributed to Confucius—"A bird can choose the tree, is it possible that a tree chooses the bird?" (*Zuo*, Ai 11: 1667)—came to stand for the freedom to choose one's master.

72. Bitter condemnations of the literati's servility were part and parcel of the intellectual modernization of China that peaked during the May Fourth Movement, 1919, and they continue to the present day (for two recent examples, see, for example, Gao and Zhu, "Cong 'zhi yu Dao'"; Ye Jianfeng, "Lun Zhanguo bai-jia"). For a more balanced discussion, which highlights the degree of the imperial literati's inferiority with regard to the throne, especially as reflected in the language of ministerial discourse, see Liu Zehua, *Zhongguo de Wangquanzhuyi*, 263–279. For similar conclusions based on an analysis of the changing mode of ritual interaction between the ministers and the ruler, see Du Jiaji, "Zhongguo gudai junchen"; Gan Huaizhen, "Zhongguo gudai junchen."

73. The much-discussed bravery and stubbornness of the late Ming literati, with their self-imposed insistence on serving the throne, may serve as an excellent illustration to this point. See, for example, Ray Huang, *1587*; Dardess, *Blood and History*; Ge Quan, *Li ming yu zhongcheng*.

Chapter 8: Ruling for the People

1. George W. Bush, Kyōto, November 16, 2005. Office of the Press Secretary, the White House. http://usinfo.state.gov/usinfo/Archive/2005/Nov/15-179929.html.

2. For Liang Qichao's views, see his *Xian Qin zhengzhi sixiang shi*, 35–44; also see his analysis of the differences between the *min ben* and *min quan* (民權, "democracy") principle on pp. 228–234. For the early modern appropriation of the

min ben concept, see Judge, "Key Words." For recent studies on the pre-Qin evolution of the *min ben* ideal, see, for example, You Huanmin, *Xian Qin minben sixiang*; Wang Baoguo, *Liang Zhou minben sixiang*; Zhou Daoji, "Woguo minben sixiang." As for the modern political implications of the *min ben* principle, approaches vary from identifying it with democracy (for example, Zhou Guitian, *Zhongguo zhengzhi zhexue*) to the diametrically opposite view, according to which it implies paternalistic "caring for the people" rather than sharing power with them (for example, Zhang Fentian, *Zhongguo diwang guannian*, 437–459; and Chapter 9, n. 27).

3. A good example of such an extensive approach is McNeal's "Acquiring the People."

4. *Mengzi*, "Jin xin xia" 14.14: 328.

5. *Mengzi*, "Wan Zhang shang" 9.5: 219. For the "Tai shi" chapter of the *Shu jing*, see Chapter 3, n. 71. A very similar citation appears in the "Gao Yao mo" (皋陶謨, Plans of Gao Yao) chapter of the "authentic" ("new script") *Shu jing* (4: 139c). This chapter was probably composed in the late Chunqiu or early Zhanguo period (see Jiang Shanguo, *Shang shu*, 169–172).

6. *Zuo*, Xiang 31: 1184.

7. *Shu jing*, "Kang gao" 康誥 14: 203c.

8. The references in the summary above are to the "Duo fang" 多方, "Shao gao" 召誥, "Wu yi" 無逸, "Kang gao," and "Zi cai" 梓材 documents.

9. For various estimates regarding the dating of the Western Zhou documents of the *Shu jing*, see, for example Chen Mengjia, *Shang shu*; Jiang Shanguo, *Shang shu*, Du Yong, *"Shang shu" Zhouchu bagao*; Kryukov, *Tekst i Ritual*, 296–326; Vogelsang, "Inscriptions and Proclamations." The two latter studies are particularly radical in doubting the date of even the earliest Western Zhou documents of the *Shu jing*, and while their results are far from decisive, they suffice to dictate utmost caution when dealing with the *Shu jing* as a source for historical realities of the early Zhou age.

10. See, for instance, late Western Zhou odes such as "Jie Nan shan" 節南山, "Zheng yue" 正月, and "Shi yue zhi jiao" 十月之交 (*Mao shi* 12.1: 440–12.2: 448, Mao 191–193), which lament the people's plight. The Mu-*gui* 牧簋 inscription mentions an appointment made specifically to hinder local officials from abusing the "multiple people" (*shu min* 庶民), which indicates that caring for "the people" was indeed part of the Zhou political discourse (see *Yin Zhou jinwen* 8.4343; Shirakawa, *Kinbun* 19.104: 360; and the discussion in Li Feng, "Succession and Promotion," 19–20).

11. *Mengzi*, "Liang Hui Wang xia" 2.3: 31. This phrase was incorporated in the forged "Tai shi" document.

12. The political context of Western Zhou people-oriented thought is explored by McNeal, "Acquiring the People," 51–77.

13. In addition to these usages, Qiu Xigui suggests that when deities/Heaven are concerned, "the people" may refer to all human beings, the ruler and the ruled

alike (see his "Bin Gong-*xu*," 68). An interesting attempt to systematize the meaning of the terms *ren* (人 man) and *min* was made by Gassman, "Understanding Ancient Chinese Society." Gassman's sociological division of these terms, with *min* confined to the lower strata, is not entirely convincing, however; not only it can be refuted by careful reading of some of Gassman's sources, such as the *Chunqiu* annals, but, more generally, the very expectation of terminological precision in political parlance is largely untenable.

14. *Mao shi*, "Sheng min" 生民, 17.1: 528a (Mao 245).

15. See *Mao shi*, "Mian" 綿 16.2: 509b (Mao 237); "Zheng min" 烝民 18.3: 568a (Mao 260); "Si wen" 思文 19.2: 590a (Mao 275).

16. During the Western Zhou period, the Zhou (Ji 姬) clan became too large to maintain reasonable cohesiveness and so fragmented into independent lineages, most of which headed autonomous polities. For the kinship structure of the Western Zhou period, see Zhu Fenghan, *Shang Zhou*, 242–449.

17. This simile is first attested in the "Nan shan you tai" 南山有臺 and "Jiong zhuo" 泂酌 odes of the *Shi jing* (*Mao shi*, 10.1: 419c and 17.3: 544a, Mao 172 and 251 respectively).

18. I omit the *Guoyu* from my discussion of the Chunqiu period because this text underwent significant ideological editing in the Zhanguo period (see Pines, "Speeches," 209–215). For people-oriented ideology in the *Zuo zhuan*, see, for example, Zheng Junhua, "Lun *Zuo zhuan* de min ben sixiang."

19. *Zuo*, Huan 6: 111–112.

20. For the concept of the people as masters of the deities, see, for example, the *Zuo*, Zhuang 10: 182–183; Zhuang 32: 251–253; Xi 5: 309–310; Xi 19: 382. See further discussions in Pines, *Foundations*, 70–84; Liu Jiahe, "*Zuo zhuan*."

21. Tian Changwu and Zang Zhifei estimate that in the early Chunqiu period, even large capital cities comprised no more than 3,000 families (see their *Zhou Qin shehui*, 178 and a general discussion on pp. 167–183; see also Lewis, *The Construction of Space*, 139–140; for a more cautious analysis, see Chen Shen, "Early Urbanization"). To exemplify the tiny size of contemporary polities, suffice it to mention that after their disastrous defeat by the Di 狄 tribesmen in 660, only 730 "men and women" of the state of Wei 衛 remained alive (*Zuo*, Min 2: 266). However terrible the massacre by the Di, the original population of the Wei capital was probably no larger than a few thousand people.

22. Many scholars in China and Japan have addressed the nature of *guo ren*; of these studies I rely primarily on those by Yoshimoto, "Shunjū kokujin kō" and "Shunjū kokujin sai kō" (see also his *Chūgoku sen Shin shi*, 207–256); Tian and Zang, *Zhou Qin shehui*, 43–53; Cai Feng, "Guoren de shuxing"; Chao Fulin, "Lun Zhou dai guoren." See also the recent discussion by Lewis, *Construction of Space*, 136–150.

23. For the role of infantry in Chunqiu warfare, see Kolb, *Die Infanterie im alten China*, 167–260.

24. See *Zuo*, Min 2: 265–266; Xi 19: 384–385; Zhuang 27: 236. For difficulties of maintaining martial spirit of capital dwellers, see also Kolb, *Die Infanterie im alten China*, 235–240.

25. *Zuo*, Cheng 16: 881. The cited poem is the "Si wen" hymn, which refers to Hou Ji (*Mao shi* 19.2:590a [Mao 275]).

26. See *Guoyu* "Zhou yu 周語 1" 1.3–5: 10–15 for details.

27. See for example, *Zuo*, Xi 28: 452; Wen 7: 556–558; Wen 18: 633; Cheng 15: 874–875; Xiang 10: 979–981; Xiang 19: 1050; Xiang 27: 1137; Xiang 30: 1176; Xiang 31: 1189 *et saepe*.

28. For the government's efforts to attract commoner support, see, for example, *Zuo*, Cheng 2: 807; Cheng 16: 906. For the examples of scheming ministers cited, see, respectively *Zuo*, Wen 16: 620–622; Xiang 29: 1157–1158; Zhao 3: 1234–1236; Zhao 26: 1480.

29. See, for example, *Zuo*, Xi 28: 452; Wen 18: 643; Cheng 13: 867; Cheng 15: 876; Xiang 15: 1022; Zhao 7: 1292; Zhao 22: 1434; Ding 8: 1566.

30. See, for example, *Zuo*, Xi 15: 360; Xi 18: 378; Xi 28: 469; Xiang 30: 1176; Zhao 20: 1412; Ding 8: 1566; Ai 1: 1607.

31. For the supposition that capital dwellers were citizens rather than subjects, see Tian and Zang, *Zhou Qin shehui*, 51. Employment of the city-state model to depict Chunqiu polities began with Miyzaki Ichisada, "Shina jōkaku," and was adopted by many scholars in China and Japan, see, for example, Kaizuka Shigeki, "Shunjū jidai no toshi kokka"; Du Zhengsheng, *Zhoudai chengbang*; Lin Ganquan, "Cong *Zuo zhuan* kan"; for a brief analysis of this equation, see also Yates, "The City State." Some scholars go further in comparing the putative Chunqiu city-states with Greek *poleis*, looking for common political patterns among them. See, for example, Rubin, "Narodnoe Sobranie" and "Tzu-Ch'an"; Ri Zhi, "Cong *Chun qiu*"; and more recently Lewis, *Construction of Space*, 136–150; for a systematic response to these views, see Lü Shaogang, "Zhongguo gudai"; Zhao Boxiong, *Zhoudai guojia*, 321–331; Pines, "Bodies," 174–181.

32. For brief summaries of Zichan's activities, see Rubin, "Tzu-Ch'an"; Zhang Hengshou, "Lun Zichan de zhengzhi gaige"; Pines, "The Search for Stability," 31–42; Martin, "Le Cas Zichan."

33. *Zuo*, Xiang 31: 1192.

34. *Zuo*, Zhao 4: 1254. The cited poem is not a part of the current *Shi jing* collection.

35. See, for example, *Zuo*, Xiang 30: 1182; for Zichan's attentiveness to public opinion, see *Zuo*, Zhao 7: 1291–1293; for his pursuit of his own course despite public resentment, see *Zuo*, Zhao 18: 1394; Zhao 19: 1405.

36. *Zuo*, Xiang 14: 1017–1018.

37. For the role of blind musicians as preservers of the semihistorical-semi-legendary past, see Hawkes, "The Heirs of Gao-Yang." A similar picture of overall participation in remonstrance activities is presented in the *Guoyu*, "Zhou yu 1" 1.3: 11–13.

Chapter 9: "Full Bellies, Empty Hearts"

1. *Laozi* 3: 235–239, following the Mawangdui versions.

2. In the *Zuo zhuan* alone, the term *guo ren* is mentioned in sixty-seven passages, while in all the major Zhanguo texts together, including the ritual compendia and the *Gongyang* and *Guliang* commentaries of the *Chunqiu*, it is mentioned in only forty-seven passages (of which five are in the *Mengzi*, six in the *Liji* and *Zhanguo ce*, and fourteen in the *Lüshi chunqiu*—mostly when this text cites the *Zuo zhuan*). Only the *Mengzi* occasionally refers to the capital dwellers as significant political actors (see *Mengzi*, "Liang Hui Wang xia" 2.7: 41, cited on pp. 51–52).

3. *Yinqueshan*, "Shou fa shou ling deng shi san pian" 守法守令等十三篇 2, slip 829, p. 133. For other texts, see, for example, *Mengzi* "Liang Hui Wang xia" 2.12: 47; *Xunzi*, "Yi bing" 議兵 X.15: 265–290; *Wei Liaozi*, "Zhan wei" 戰威 4: 18–19; *Wuzi*, "Tu guo" 圖國 1: 36–37 (Sawyer, *The Seven Military Classics*, 248 and 207). See also Lewis, *Sanctioned Violence*, 128–133.

4. See *Shang jun shu*, "Yi yan" 壹言 III.8: 60; "Jin ling" 靳令 III.13: 78–79; *Wu Sunzi*, "Jiu di" 九地 11.106–109 (Sawyer, *The Seven Military Classics*, 178–179).

5. For the importance of iron in the Zhanguo economy, see Wagner's seminal *Iron and Steel*. See also Bai Yunxiang, *Xian Qin Liang Han tieqi*.

6. See *Shuihudi*, "Tian lü" 田律, "Jiuyuan lü," 19–23; Hulsewé, *Remnants of Ch'in Law*, A1–8: 21–27.

7. This understanding of the economic conditions of the lower strata is vividly clear in such divergent texts as *Mengzi*, *Shang jun shu*, *Guanzi,* and the *Lüshi chunqiu,* among others.

8. The locus classicus of this concern with the people's migration is *Mengzi*, "Liang Hui Wang shang" 1.3:5; the idea that the people may vote with their feet recurs throughout the *Mengzi* (for example, "Liang Hui Wang shang" 1.6: 13; 1.7: 17; *et saepe*). The importance of migration is reflected in many other texts, such as the "Lai min" chapter of the *Shang jun shu* (IV.15: 86–96; this chapter was composed, according to the events it mentions, ca. 250). The precise scale of this migration—legal and illegal—is impossible to verify, but Stephen Sage (*Ancient Sichuan*, 134–136) suggests, for example, that "dozens to hundreds thousands" of Qin settlers arrived in the Sichuan area during the century of Qin rule there. Qin legal documents record numerous cases of absconders, who "left the country" (*chu bang* 出邦), and the option of "fleeing" (*wang* 亡) is vividly present in Qin *Almanacs* (*Ri shu* 日書) as well (see also Shi Weiqing, "Lun Qin").

9. For the detailed discussion of these distinct approaches, see Wu Baosan, *Xian Qin jingji sixiang*.

10. See, for example, *Mozi*, "Fei gong zhong" V.18: 202; "Jie yong shang" 節用上 VI.20: 242; *Laozi* 75: 192; 30: 381 (*Guodian Laozi* A: 6–7); 31: 387–396 (*Guodian Laozi* C:6–10); *Mengzi*, "Liang Hui Wang xia" 2.12: 47; "Li Lou shang" 7.14: 175; *Xunzi*, "Fu guo" VI.10: 182–183; *Yanzi chunqiu*, 1.5: 13.

11. For detailed survey of people-oriented political proposals, see You Huan-

min, *Xian Qin minben sixiang*; Wang Baoguo, *Liang Zhou minben sixiang*; McNeal, "Acquiring the People."

12. For different opinions regarding the dating of the *Shang jun shu* and of its individual chapters, see Zheng Liangshu, *Shang Yang*; Yoshinami, *Shōkun sho*; cf. Zhang Jue's notes in *Shang jun shu quanyi*. Portions of the book are highly likely to be original Shang Yang's memoranda, as they include the first person pronoun *chen* (臣, "subject, minister"), which is rare in Zhanguo texts. Similarities in content and style of most (albeit not all) chapters had been noted by Schwartz, *The World of Thought*, 331.

13. *Shang jun shu*, "Ruo min" 弱民 V.20: 121; cf. "Shuo min" 說民 II.5: 36.

14. *Shang jun shu*, "Qu qiang" I.4: 27 and "Hua ce" IV.18: 108.

15. Ames, *The Art of Rulership*, 153 and the discussion on 153–164. This negative assessment of Shang Yang is traceable to the early Han period, if not earlier; significantly, Shang Yang is one of the very few personages in Sima Qian's *Shiji* whose biography ends with the overtly negative assessment by the historian (*Shiji* 68: 2237). For another relatively recent example of harsh sentiments against Shang Yang, see, for example, Rubin, *Individual and State*, 55–88.

16. *Shang jun shu*, "Shuo min" II.5: 37.

17. *Shang jun shu*, "Suan di" II.6: 49.

18. *Shang jun shu*, "Shen fa" V.25: 139.

19. *Shang jun shu*, "Qu qiang" I.4: 30.

20. *Shang jun shu*, "Hua ce" IV.18: 107; see also "Jin ling" III.13: 81.

21. *Shang jun shu*, "Jin ling" III.13: 82. A very similar saying appears also in "Shuo min" II.5: 38.

22. The concept of the "emotive meaning" of ethical terms was developed by Stevenson in "Persuasive Definitions" and introduced into Sinology by Carine Defoort in "Is There Such a Thing as Chinese Philosophy?"

23. *Shang jun shu*, "Xiu quan" III.14: 84.

24. Thompson, *Shen-tzu*, "Wei de," 240. For the evolutionary theories of the state formation by Shang Yang and his followers, see *Shang jun shu*, "Kai sai" II.7: 51–52; "Hua ce" IV.18: 106–107; "Jun chen" 君臣 V.23: 129–130; see also Chapter 2 for further discussion.

25. *Lüshi chunqiu*, "Gui gong" 貴公 1.4: 44.

26. Thus Mozi argued that "the Supreme Thearch, spirits and deities established the capital and placed their leaders . . . to increase benefits and eradicate troubles of the myriad people, to enrich the poor and multiple the few, to secure the endangered and to order the chaotic" (*Mozi*, "Shang tong zhong" III.12: 119–120). Xunzi similarly claimed "Heaven did not give birth to the people for the ruler's sake; it establishes the ruler for the people's sake" ("Da lue" XIX.27: 504). See also *Mengzi*, "Jin xin xia" 14.14: 328; cf. *Zuo*, Xiang 14: 1016.

27. For the attempts to find seeds of China's supposedly indigenous democratic ideas in the concept of "the people as foundation," see, for example, Murthy, "The Democratic Potential"; Sor-hoon Tan, *Confucian Democracy*, 132–156; Enbao

Wang and Titunik, "Democracy"; Nuyen, "Confucianism." Most scholars of ancient Chinese political thought are reluctant to endorse these hasty equations; see, for example, Zhang Fentian, "Lun 'li jun wei min'"; cf. Li Xiantang, "Lun Rujia minben sixiang"; Xing Lin, "Minben sixiang."

28. A good example of the "paths not taken" approach is Hui, *War and State Formation*.

29. *Mengzi*, "Li Lou shang" 7.9: 171.

30. For the people as potential kingmakers, see Chapter 3 (especially the sections on the *Rong Cheng shi* and *Mengzi*). For "attaining the people's hearts," see also *Guanzi*, "Xiao kuang" 小匡 VIII.20: 411; *Lüshi chunqiu*, "Shun min" 順民 9.2: 479.

31. *Xunzi*, "Wang zhi" V.9: 152

32. *Shang jun shu*, "Hua ce" IV.18: 107.

33. See *Lunyu* 12.7: 125; *Laozi* 49: 58.

34. *Shang jun shu*, "Shuo min" II.5: 40. I borrow the translation of 器 as "law-enforcing method" from Lewis (*Sanctioned Violence*, 93).

35. Lewis, *Sanctioned Violence*, 93.

36. In a putative discussion, which supposedly convinced Shang Yang's patron, Lord Xiao of Qin (秦孝公, r. 361–338), to adopt a reform course, Shang Yang emphatically argued that the people's opinion should not be taken into consideration: "You cannot contemplate the beginnings with the people, but can enjoy the results together with them" (*Shang jun shu*, "Geng fa" 更法 I.1: 2)

37. *Shang shu*, "Hong fan" 洪範 12: 191a. The "Hong fan" was probably created in the middle Zhanguo period, although its provenance is still debatable (see Nylan, *The Shifting Center*).

38. *Zhou li*, "Xiao sikou" 小司寇 35: 873. In translating 弊 as "determining" (斷), I follow the gloss by Du You (杜佑, 735–812 CE) in *Tong dian* 75: 2040.

39. See, for example, *Zuo*, Xi 15: 360; Ai 1: 1607.

40. See *Mengzi*, "Liang Hui Wang xia" 2.7: 41; and the discussion on pp. 51–52. Another archaizing text that pretends to reconstruct the function of the people's assembly is the "Pan Geng" 盤庚 chapter of the *Shu jing*, which presents a speech supposedly made by the Shang king Pan Geng to convince his people to agree for the capital relocation (*Shu jing*, "Pan Geng" 9: 168–173).

41. *Mozi*, "Shang tong shang" III.11: 110.

42. For the establishment of the office of song collectors in the Han period, and its ritual background, see Kern, "The Poetry of Han Historiography," 33–35.

43. *Lunyu*, "Ji shi" 16.2: 174.

44. See *Laozi*, 65: 140–141, 57: 106–107 (*Guodian Laozi* A: 32). The idea of the people's simplicity became especially attractive to the so-called Legalist thinkers, and it figures particularly prominently in the *Shang jun shu* (for example, "Nong zhan" I.3: 20); *Guanzi*, "Qi chen qi zhu" XVII.52: 981–982; *Han Feizi*, "Da ti" IX.29: 210.

45. Liang Qichao, *Xian Qin zhengzhi sixiang*, 242–243.

46. For a good analysis of the usage of the term *xiao ren* in the *Lunyu* and of its overt social connotations, see Li Xiaoying, "*Lunyu* zhong de 'xiao ren.'"

47. See *Lunyu*, "Wei zheng" 14: 17; "Yan Yuan" 12.16: 129; "Zilu" 13.23: 141; 13.25–26: 143.

48. *Lunyu*, "Yang Huo" 17.25: 191. For controversies around this saying, and the attempts to interpret it in a less gender-biased way, see, for example, Li Chenyang, "Introduction," 3–4; Goldin, "The View of Women," 139–140.

49. *Lunyu*, "Yang Huo" 17.4: 181.

50. 民可使由之, 不可使知之。*Lunyu*, "Tai Bo" 8.9: 81. This statement was so embarrassing from the perspective of modern ideas of equality that many scholars, most notably Liang Qichao (*Xian Qin zhengzhi sixiang*, 232), tried to reinterpret it by adding commas: 民可, 使由之;不可, 使知之。("When the people are able, let them follow [the Way], when they are unable, let them understand it"). This curious attempt to dismember an ancient sentence for the sake of modern political ideals was crushed recently with the discovery of the *Zun de yi* text from Guodian, which cites this sentence in a way that does not permit the proposed dismemberment (民可使道之, 而不可使知之。*Zun de yi*, slips 21–22; see also Pang Pu, "Shi you shi zhi." See a fierce discussion about this passage in "Confucius's on-line forum" http://www.tomedu.com/ydbbs/dispbbs.asp?BoardID=8&ID=11633&page=1.

51. *Mengzi*, "Teng Wen Gong shang" 5.4: 124.

52. Ibid., 118–119. For "commoners" Mengzi uses here the term *ye ren* 野人, literally, the "people of the fields," originally a designation of the subjugated population beyond the capital walls.

53. *Xunzi*, "Fu guo" VI.10: 182. See also Xunzi, "Jie bi" XV.21: 399, for further elaboration about the need to uphold the sociopolitical hierarchy.

54. *Mengzi*, "Li Lou xia" 8.19: 191. For more about the distinctions Mengzi draws between men and beasts, see Peterson, "The Grounds of Mencius' Argument." The use of the beast simile for impaired humans—either commoners or aliens—is frequent in Zhanguo thought; for example, Xunzi identifies the petty men's behavior as "beast-like" (*Xunzi*, "Rong ru" 榮辱 II.4: 61); see also Pines, "Beasts or Humans," 62–69.

55. *Xunzi*, "Xing'e" XVII.23: 443.

56. *Han Feizi*, "Xian xue" XIX.50: 445–446.

57. Ibid., 446.

58. See Tu Wei-ming, "The Structure and Function of the Confucian Intellectual," 20.

59. Immediately after occupying the regional capital, Chen 陳, Chen She gathered "village elders and local bravos" (*Shiji* 48: 1952), who approved of his plans. This local rural elite became an important source of support for the rebels, although its role has rarely been noted by later historians, with the major exception of Perelomov, *Imperiia Tsin'*, 66–84.

60. *Shiji* 48: 1964–1665; I modify Watson's translation (*Records*, 80). Tao Zhu

and Yi Dun were fabulously rich merchants; "east of the mountains" hints at the states of the former anti-Qin coalition.

61. Of course, one could run into the woods to join a bandit gang, which eventually supplied much of the manpower for Chen She and other rebels; but this choice differs markedly from the Zhanguo option of crossing the boundaries in search of normal agricultural life. For Qin's surveillance over "internal absconders," as reflected in the Liye materials, see Zhang Junmin, "Qin dai de fu zhai."

62. For the First Emperor's self-propaganda, see pp. 108–109. Qin waged wars along the northern and southern frontiers, where desertion was not an immediate option for a conscript; while the scope of this warfare was considerable, it probably permitted less social mobility than the endless struggles of the Warring States had. Social mobility was very much a source of concern for Chen She and his followers. If we are to believe Sima Qian, when Chen She was enticing his soldiers to rebel, he promised: "We shall die, but attain great Name. Kings, lords, generals and chancellors—are they sown?" (*Shiji* 48: 1952, Chen She means that many kings and lords are self-made).

63. This heterogeneity of the rebel camp caused Jack Dull to question the identification of the rebellion as a "peasant" movement (see his "Anti-Qin Rebels"). I think, however, that Dull grossly overstates his case, ignoring entirely the mass nature of the rebellion (see also comments by Esherick, "Symposium," 283).

64. For Shusun Tong's biography, see *Shiji* 99: 2720–2726.

65. It is worth remembering that neither Qin imperial proclamations nor the rebels' propaganda addressed the issue of Heaven's Decree (see also Loewe, "The Authority of the Emperors").

66. A comprehensive discussion of popular rebellions and their role in Chinese political culture is still lacking, for interest in this topic has subsided both in the West (where popular movements are studied primarily from the religious angle) and in China itself (where the "class struggle" discourse has disappeared from academic publications after dominating historical studies during Mao's years). For some preliminary insights, see Esherick, "Symposium" and Crowell, "Social Unrest."

67. For the degree of the rebel cooptation into Chinese imperial culture, see, for example, Aubine, "The Rebirth of Chinese Rule." It is worth remembering that some of the most murderous rebels in Chinese (if not in human) history, such as Huang Chao (黃巢, d. 884 CE) and Li Zicheng (李自成, 1606–1645 CE), acted very much within the boundaries of the imperial political culture, at times being offered positions by the imperial government and establishing (with limited success) quasi-imperial bureaucratic systems. See more in Levy, *Biography of Huang Ch'ao*; Parsons, *The Peasant Rebellions*.

68. For revolutions as "locomotives of history," see Marx, "The Class Struggles in France," 122. For Meadows's views, see his *The Chinese and Their Rebellions*, 27.

Meadows remarked: "*Of all the nations that attained a certain degree of civilization, the Chinese are the least revolutionary and the most rebellious*" (25, italics in original).

The Legacy of the Warring States

1. For the "Anti-Confucian" (more precisely, "criticize Lin [Biao 林彪, 1907–1971], criticize Confucius" [*pi Lin pi Kong* 批林批孔] campaign), see Louie, *Critiques of Confucius*, 97–136; Perelomov, *Konfutsij*, 372–386. During the campaign, thousands of teams of students and workers were required to write essays criticizing Confucius and extolling "Legalist" thinkers such as Shang Yang.

2. See Tu, "The Creative Tension between *Jen* and *Li*."

Bibliography

Pre-1850 Texts and Epigraphic Sources, by Titles

Baoshan Chu jian 包山楚簡. Published by Hubei sheng Jingsha tielu kaogu dui 湖北省荊沙鐵路考古隊. Beijing: Wenwu, 1991.

Boshu Laozi jiaozhu 帛書老子校注. Compiled and annotated by Gao Ming 高明. Beijing: Zhonghua shuju, 1996.

Cao Mo zhi zhen 曹沫之陣. Transcribed and annotated by Li Ling 李零. In *Shanghai bowuguan cang Zhanguo Chu zhushu*, vol. 4 (2004), 239–285.

Chuan jia ji 傳家集. By Sima Guang 司馬光. Rpt. in *Siku quanshu* 四庫全書 (electronic edition).

Chunqiu fanlu yizheng 春秋繁露義證. Compiled by Su Yu 蘇輿. Beijing: Zhonghua shuju, 1992.

Chunqiu Gongyang zhuan zhushu 春秋公羊傳注疏. Annotated by He Xiu 何休 and Xu Yan 徐彥. In *Shisanjing zhushu*, vol. 2, 2189–2355.

Chunqiu Zuo zhuan zhu 春秋左傳注. Annotated by Yang Bojun 楊伯峻. Beijing: Zhonghua shuju, 1981.

Cuo mu: Zhanguo Zhongshan guo guowang zhi mu 䂂墓—戰國中山國國王之墓. Published by Hebei Sheng wenwu yanjiu suo 河北省文物研究所. Beijing: Wenwu, 1995.

Da Dai Liji jiegu 大戴禮記解詁. Compiled by Wang Pinzhen 王聘珍. Beijing: Zhonghua shuju, 1992.

Fan Zhongyan quanji 范仲淹全集. Compiled by Fan Nengjun 范能濬, collated by Xue Zhengxing 薛正興. Nanjing: Fenghuang chubanshe, 2004.

Gongyang zhuan. See *Chunqiu Gongyang zhuan*.

Guanzi jiaozhu 管子校注. Compiled by Li Xiangfeng 黎翔鳳. Beijing: Zhonghua shuju, 2004.

Guben Zhushu jinian jizheng 古本竹書紀年輯證. Edited by Fang Shiming 方詩銘, Wang Xiuling 王修齡. Shanghai: Guji chubanshe, 1980.

Guodian Chu mu zhujian 郭店楚墓竹簡. Published by Jingmenshi Bowuguan 荊門市博物館. Beijing: Wenwu, 1998.

Guodian Laozi. In *Guodian Chu mu zhujian,* 109–122.

Guoyu jijie 國語集解. Compiled by Xu Yuangao 徐元誥. Beijing: Zhonghua shuju, 2002.

Han Feizi jijie 韓非子集解. Compiled by Wang Xianshen 王先慎. Beijing: Zhonghua shuju, 1998.

Han shu 漢書. By Ban Gu 班固 et al. Annotated by Yan Shigu 顏師古. Beijing: Zhonghua shuju, 1997.

Huainanzi 淮南子. *Huainan honglie jijie* 淮南鴻烈集解. Compiled by Liu Wendian 劉文典, collated by Feng Yi 馮逸 and Qiao Hua 喬華. Beijing: Zhonghua shuju, 1997.

Huang Di shu. See *Mawangdui Han mu boshu.*

Ji Gengzi [Kangzi] wen yu Kongzi 季庚(康)子問於孔子. Transcribed and annotated by Pu Maozuo 濮茅左. In *Shanghai bowuguan cang Zhanguo Chu zhushu*, vol. 5 (2006), 193–235.

Laozi. See *Boshu Laozi.*

Liji jijie 禮記集解. Compiled by Sun Xidan 孫希旦. Beijing: Zhonghua shuju, 1995.

Liji zhengyi 禮記正義. Annotated by Zheng Xuan 鄭玄 and Kong Yingda 孔穎達. In *Shisanjing zhushu*, vol. 2, 1222–1696.

Liu de 六德. In *Guodian Chu mu zhujian*, 187–190.

Lunyu yizhu 論語譯注. Annotated by Yang Bojun 楊伯峻. Beijing: Zhonghua shuju, 1992.

Lüshi chunqiu jiaoshi 呂氏春秋校釋. Compiled and annotated by Chen Qiyou 陳奇猷. Shanghai: Xuelin, 1990.

Mao shi zhengyi 毛詩正義. Annotated by Zheng Xuan 鄭玄 and Kong Yingda 孔穎達. In *Shisanjing zhushu*, vol. 1, 259–629.

Mawangdui Han mu boshu "Huang Di shu" jianzheng 馬王堆漢墓帛書《黃帝書》箋證. Compiled, transcribed, and annotated by Wei Qipeng 魏啓鵬. Beijing: Zhonghua shuju, 2004.

Mengzi. See *Mengzi yizhu.*

Mengzi jiewen 孟子節文. Compiled by Liu Sanwu 劉三五. Rpt. in *Beijing tushuguan guji zhenben congkan* 北京圖書館古籍珍本叢刊, vol. 1, 955–1016. Beijing: Shumu, 1988.

Mengzi yizhu 孟子譯注. Annotated by Yang Bojun 楊伯峻. Beijing: Zhonghua shuju, 1992.

Mengzi zhengyi 孟子正義. Annotated by Zhao Qi 趙岐 and Sun Shi 孫奭. In *Shisanjing zhushu*, vol. 2, 2659–2728.

Mozi jiaozhu 墨子校注. Compiled and annotated by Wu Yujiang 吳毓江. Beijing: Zhonghua shuju, 1994.

Qiong da yi shi 窮達以時. In *Guodian Chu mu zhujian*, 143–146.

Rong Cheng shi 容成氏. Transcribed and annotated by Li Ling 李零. In *Shanghai bowuguan cang Zhanguo Chu zhushu*, vol. 2 (2002), 247–292.

Shanghai bowuguan cang Zhanguo Chu zhushu 上海博物館藏戰國楚竹書. Edited by Ma Chengyuan 馬承源. 6 vols. Shanghai: Guji chubanshe, 2000–2007.

Shang jun shu zhuizhi 商君書錐指. Annotated by Jiang Lihong 蔣禮鴻. Beijing: Zhonghua shuju, 1996.

Shang shu zhengyi 尚書正義. Annotated by Kong Yingda 孔穎達. In *Shisanjing zhushu*, vol. 1, 109–258.

Shi jing. See *Mao shi.*

Shiji 史記. By Sima Qian 司馬遷 et al. Annotated by Zhang Shoujie 張守節, Sima Zhen 司馬貞, and Pei Yin 裴駰. Beijing: Zhonghua shuju, 1997.

Shisanjing zhushu 十三經注疏. Compiled by Ruan Yuan 阮元. Beijing: Zhonghua shuju, 1991.

Shi tong tong shi 史通通釋. By Liu Zhiji 劉知幾. Annotated by Pu Qilong 浦起龍. Taibei: Liren shuju, 1993.

Shuihudi Qin mu zhujian 睡虎地秦墓竹簡. Published by Shuihudi Qin mu zhujian zhengli xiaozu 睡虎地秦墓竹簡整理小組. Beijing: Wenwu, 2001.

Shu jing 書經. See *Shang shu*.

Sishu zhangju ji zhu 四書章句集注. Annotated by Zhu Xi 朱熹. Beijing: Zhonghua shuju, 2001.

Tang Yu zhi Dao 唐虞之道. In *Guodian Chu mu zhujian*, 157–158.

Tianzi jian zhou 天子建州. Annotated by Cao Jinyan 曹錦炎. In *Shanghai bowuguan cang Zhanguo Chu zhushu*, vol. 6 (2007), 307–338.

Tong dian 通典. Compiled by Du You 杜佑. Annotated and collated by Wang Wenjin 王文錦 et al. Beijing: Zhonghua shuju, 1988.

Wei Liaozi 尉繚子. In Liu Dianjue (Lau, Dim-cheuk) 劉殿爵, comp. *Bing shu si zhong (Sunzi, Wei Liao zi, Wuzi, Sima fa) zhuzi suoyin* 兵書四種 (孫子, 尉繚子, 吳子, 司馬法)逐字索引, 15–35. Xianggang (Hong Kong): Shangwu, 1992.

Wu Sunzi fawei 吳孫子發微. Annotated and discussed by Li Ling 立零. Beijing: Zhonghua shuju, 1997.

Wuzi 吳子. In Liu Dianjue (Lau, Dim-cheuk) 劉殿爵, comp. *Bing shu si zhong (Sunzi, Wei Liao zi, Wuzi, Sima fa) zhuzi suoyin* 兵書四種 (孫子, 尉繚子, 吳子, 司馬法)逐字索引, 36–44. Xianggang (Hong Kong): Shangwu, 1992.

Xiao jing yizhu 孝經譯注. Annotated by Hu Pingsheng 胡平生. Beijing: Zhonghua shuju, 1996.

Xin yu jiaozhu 新語校注. Compiled by Wang Liqi 王利器. Beijing: Zhonghua shuju, 1996.

Xunzi jijie 荀子集解. Compiled by Wang Xianqian 王先謙. Beijing: Zhonghua shuju, 1992.

Yanzi chunqiu jishi 晏子春秋集釋. Collated by Wu Zeyu 吳則虞. Beijing: Zhonghua shuju, 1962.

Yinqueshan Han mu zhujian 銀雀山漢墓竹簡. Edited by Yinqueshan Han mu zhujian zhenli xiaozu 銀雀山漢墓竹簡整理小組. Vol. 1. Beijing: Wenwu, 1985.

Yin Zhou jinwen jicheng yinde 殷周金文集成引得. Compiled by Zhang Yachu 張亞初. Beijing: Zhonghua shuju, 2001.

Yu cong 語叢. In *Guodian Chu mu zhujian*, 191–219.

Zhanguo ce zhushi 戰國策注釋. Annotated by He Jianzhang 何建章. Beijing: Zhonghua shuju, 1991.

Zhanguo zonghengjia shu 戰國縱橫家書. In *Mawangdui Han mu boshu (san)* 馬王堆漢墓帛書 (三), ed. Mawangdui Han mu boshu zhengli xiaozu 馬王堆漢墓帛書整理小組, 21–84. Beijing: Wenwu, 1983.

Zhou li zhushu 周禮注疏. Annotated by Zheng Xuan 鄭玄 and Jia Gongyan 賈公彥. In *Shisanjing zhushu* 十三經注疏, vol. 1, 631–940.

Zhou yi zhengyi 周易正義. Annotated by Wang Bi 王弼 and Kong Yingda 孔穎達. In *Shisanjing zhushu*, vol. 1, 5–108.

Zhuangzi jinzhu jinyi 莊子今注今譯. Annotated by Chen Guying 陳鼓應. Beijing: Zhonghua shuju, 1994.

Zhushu jinian 竹書紀年. See *Guben Zhushu jinian*.

Zhuzi yulei 朱子語類. Compiled by Li Jingde 黎靖德, collated by Wang Xingxian 王星賢. Beijing: Zhonghua shuju, 1986.

Zi Gao 子羔. Transcribed and annotated by Ma Chengyuan 馬承源. In *Shanghai bowuguan cang Zhanguo Chu zhushu*, vol. 2 (2002), 179–199.

Zizhi tongjian 資治通鑑. By Sima Guang 司馬光. Annotated by Hu Sanxing 胡三省. Beijing: Zhonghua shuju, 1992.

Zun de yi 尊德義. In *Guodian Chu mu zhujian*, 171–175.

Zuo. See *Chunqiu Zuo zhuan*.

Secondary Works

Adamson, Walter L. *Hegemony and Revolution: A Study of Antonio Gramsci's Political and Cultural Theory*. Berkeley: University of California Press, 1980.

Allan, Sarah. "The Great One, Water, and the *Laozi*: New Light from Guodian." *T'oung Pao* 89, no. 4–5 (2003): 237–285.

———. *The Heir and the Sage: Dynastic Legend in Early China*. San Francisco: Chinese Materials Center, 1981.

Ames, Roger T. *The Art of Rulership: A Study of Ancient Chinese Political Thought*. Albany: State University of New York Press, 1994.

Arbuckle, Gary. "Inevitable Treason: Dong Zhongshu's Theory of Historical Cycles and Early Attempts to Invalidate the Han Mandate." *Journal of the American Oriental Society* 115, no. 4 (1995): 585–597.

Arima Takuya 有馬卓也. " 'Mu-i no chi' no riron ko-u"「無爲の治」の理論構造. *Kyūshu Chūgoku gakkai-hō* 九州中國學會報 27 (1989): 21–41 and 29 (1991): 1–21.

Asano Yūichi 淺野裕一. "*Rong Cheng shi* de shanrang yu fangfa"《容成氏》的禪讓與放伐. In his *Zhanguo Chujian yanjiu* 戰國楚簡研究, trans. Sato Masayuki 佐藤將之, 85–112. Taibei: Wanjuan lou, 2004.

Aubin, Françoise. "The Rebirth of Chinese Rule in Times of Trouble: North China in the Early Thirteenth Century." In *Foundations and Limits of State Power in China*, ed. Stewart Schram, 113–146. Hong Kong: The Chinese University Press, 1987.

Bai Yunxiang 白雲翔. *Xian Qin Liang Han tieqi de kaoguxue yanjiu* 先秦兩漢鐵器的考古學研究. Beijing: Kexue chubanshe, 2005.

Berkowitz, Alan. *Patterns of Disengagement: The Practice and Portrayal of Reclusion in Early Medieval China*. Stanford: Stanford University Press, 2000.

Blakeley, Barry B. "King, Clan, and Courtier in Ancient Ch'u." *Asia Major* (third series) 5, no. 2 (1992): 1–39.

Bol, Peter K. "Emperors Can Claim Antiquity Too: Emperorship and Autocracy under the New Policies." In *Emperor Huizong and Late Northern Song China: The Politics of Culture and the Culture of Politics*, eds. Patricia B. Ebrey and Maggie Bickford, 173–205. Cambridge, MA: Harvard University Asia Center, 2006.

———. "Government, Society and State: On the Political Visions of Ssu-ma Kuang and Wang An-shih." In *Ordering the World: Approaches to State and Society in Sung Dynasty China*, eds. Robert P. Hymes and Conrad Schirokauer, 128–192. Berkeley: University of California Press, 1993.

———. *"This Culture of Ours": Intellectual Transitions in T'ang and Sung China*. Stanford: Stanford University Press, 1992.

Boltz, William G. "The Composite Nature of Early Chinese Texts." In *Text and Ritual in Early China*, ed. Martin Kern, 50–78. Seattle: University of Washington Press, 2005.

Brindley, Erica. "Human Agency and the Development of Self-Cultivation Ideologies in the Warring States." PhD dissertation, Princeton University, 2002.

Brooks, E. Bruce, and A. Taeko Brooks. *The Original Analects: Sayings of Confucius and His Successors*. New York: Columbia University Press, 1998.

Brown, Miranda. *The Politics of Mourning in Early China*. Albany: State University of New York Press, 2007.

Cai Feng 蔡鋒. "Guoren de shuxing ji qi huodong dui Chunqiu shiqi guizu zhengzhi de yingxiang" 國人屬性及其活動對春秋時期貴族政治的影響. *Beijing daxue xuebao (zhexue shehui kexue ban)* 北京大學學報 (哲學社會科學版) 3 (1997): 113–121.

Cai Quanfa 蔡全法. "Zheng guo jisi yizhi ji qingtong liqi yanjiu" 鄭國祭祀遺址及青銅禮器研究. *Wenwu* 10 (2005): 75–79, 96.

Chan, Shirley. *The Confucian Shi, Official Service, and the Confucian Analects*. Lewiston, NY: Edwin Mellen, 2004.

Chang, Kwang-Chih. *Art, Myth, and Ritual: The Path to Political Authority in Ancient China*. Cambridge, MA: Harvard University Press, 1983.

Chao Fulin 晁福林. "Lun Zhou dai guoren yu shumin shehui shenfen de bianhua" 論周代國人與庶民社會身份的變化. *Renwen zazhi* 人文雜誌 3 (2000): 98–105.

———. "*Zhuangzi* 'Rang wang' pian xingzhi tanlun" 《莊子·讓王》篇性質探論. *Xuexi yu tansuo* 學習與探索 2 (2002): 114–119.

Chen Jian 陳劍. "Shangbo jian *Rong Cheng shi* de zhujian pinhe yu pianlian wenti xiaoyi" 上博簡《容成氏》的竹簡拼合與編連問題小議. In *Shangbo guan cang Zhanguo Chu zhushu yanjiu xubian* 上博舘藏戰國楚竹書研究續編, eds. Shanghai daxue gudai wenming yanjiu zhongxin 上海大學古代文明研究中心 and Qinghua daxue sixiang wenhua yanjiu suo 清華大學思想文化研究所. 327–334. Shanghai: Shanghai shudian, 2004.

Chen Mengjia 陳夢家. *Shang shu tonglun* 尚書通論. Beijing: Zhonghua shuju, 1985.

Chen Shen. "Early Urbanization in the Eastern Zhou in China (720–221 B.C.): An Archeological Overview." *Antiquity* 68 (1994): 22–44.

Chen Shuguo 陳戍國. *Xian Qin lizhi yanjiu* 先秦禮制研究. Changsha: Hunan jiaoyu, 1991.

Chen Xiaofang 陳筱芳. "Xi Zhou Tian Di xinyang de tedian" 西周天帝信仰的特點. *Shixue yuekan* 史學月刊 5 (2005): 27–32.

Creel, Herrlee G. *Shen Pu-hai: A Chinese Political Philosopher of the Fourth Century B.C.* Chicago: University of Chicago Press, 1974.

Crossley, Pamela. "Thinking about Ethnicity in Early Modern China." *Late Imperial China* 11, no. 1 (1990): 1–34.

Crowell, William G. "Social Unrest and Rebellion in Jiangnan during the Six Dynasties." *Modern China* 9, no. 3 (1983): 319–354.

Crump, James I., Jr. *Intrigues: Studies of the Chan-kuo Ts'e.* Ann Arbor: University of Michigan Press, 1964.

Csikszentmihalyi, Mark. *Material Virtue: Ethics and the Body in Early China.* Leiden: Brill, 2004.

———, and Nylan, Michael. "Constructing Lineages and Inventing Traditions through Exemplary Figures in Early China." *T'oung Pao* 89, nos. 1–3 (2003): 59–99.

Dardess, John W. *Blood and History in China: The Donglin Faction and Its Repression, 1620–1627.* Honolulu: University of Hawai'i Press, 2002.

Defoort, Carine. "Can Words Produce Order? Regicide in the Confucian Tradition." *Cultural Dynamics* 12, no. 1 (2000): 85–109.

———. "Is There Such a Thing as Chinese Philosophy? Arguments of an Implicit Debate." *Philosophy East and West* 51, no. 3 (2003): 393–413.

———. "Mohist and Yangist Blood in Confucian Flesh: The Middle Position of '唐虞之道 (Tang Yu zhi Dao)'?" *The Bulletin of the Museum of Far Eastern Antiquities* 76 (2004).

Deng Xingying 鄧星盈. "Wu Yu dui Xunzi de pingshuo" 吳虞對荀子的評說. *Gansu shehui kexue* 甘肅社會科學 6 (1994): 8–11.

Desmet, Karen. "The Growth of Compounds in the Core Chapters of the *Mozi*." *Oriens Extremus* 45 (2005–2006): 99–118.

Ding Sixin 丁四新. *Guodian Chu mu zhujian sixiang yanjiu* 郭店楚墓竹簡思想研究. Beijing: Dongfang chubanshe, 2000.

Drennan, Robert D., Teng Mingyu, Christian E. Peterson, Gideon Shelach, Gregory G. Indrisano, Zhu Yanping, Katheryn M. Linduff, Guo Zhizhong, and Manuel A. Román-Lacayo. "Methods for Archeological Settlement Study." In *Regional Archaeology in Eastern Inner Mongolia: A Methodological Exploration*, ed. Chifeng International Collaborative Archaeological Project, 122–151. Beijing: Kexue chubanshe, 2003.

Du Jiaji 杜家驥. "Zhongguo gudai junchen zhi li yanbian kaolun" 中國古代君臣之禮演變考論. In *Zhongguo shehui lishi pinglun* 中國社會歷史評論, ed. Zhang Guogang 張國剛, vol. 1, 255–269. Tianjin: Tianjin guji chubanshe, 1999.

Du Yong 杜勇. *"Shang shu" Zhouchu bagao yanjiu* 《尚書》周初八誥研究. Beijing: Zhongguo shehui kexue, 1988.

Du Zhengsheng 杜正勝. *Zhoudai chengbang* 周代城邦. Taibei: Lianjing, 1979.

Dull, Jack L. "Anti-Qin Rebels: No Peasant Leaders Here." *Modern China* 9, no. 3 (1983): 285–318.

Ebrey, Patricia. "Imperial Filial Piety as a Political Problem." In *Filial Piety in Chinese Thought and History*, eds. Alan K. L. Chan and Sor-hoon Tan, 122–140. London: Routledge Curzon, 2004.

Elman, Benjamin A. *A Cultural History of Civil Examinations in Late Imperial China.* Berkeley: University of California Press, 2000.

Emerson, John. "Yang Chu's Discovery of the Body." *Philosophy East and West* 46, no. 4 (1996): 533–566.

Esherick, Joseph W. "Symposium on Peasant Rebellions: Some Introductory Comments." *Modern China* 9, no. 3 (1983): 275–284.

Ess, Hans van. "Han dai sixiang shi shang de 'su wang' wenti" 漢代思想史上的"素王"問題. In *Qin Han sixiang wenhua yanjiu* 秦漢思想文化研究, eds. Xiong Tieji 熊鐵基 and Zhao Guohua 趙國華, 173–179. Taiyuan: Xiwang chubanshe, 2005.

———. "The Old Text/New Text Controversy: Has the Twentieth Century Got It Wrong?" *T'oung Pao* 80, nos. 1–3 (1994): 146–70.

Falkenhausen, Lothar von. *Chinese Society in the Age of Confucius (1050–250 BC): The Archeological Evidence.* Los Angeles: Cotsen Institute of Archaeology at UCLA, 2006.

———. "The E Jun Qi Metal Tallies: Inscribed Texts and Ritual Contexts." In *Text and Ritual in Early China*, ed. Martin Kern, 79–123. Seattle: University of Washington Press, 2005.

———. "Issues in Western Zhou Studies: A Review Article." *Early China* 18 (1993): 139–226.

———. "Late Western Zhou Taste." *Études Chinoises* 18, nos. 1–2 (2000): 143–178.

———. "Social Ranking in Chu Tombs: The Mortuary Background of the Warring States Manuscript Finds." *Monumenta Serica* 51 (2003): 439–526.

———. "The Waning of the Bronze Age: Material Culture and Social Developments, 770–481 B.C." In *The Cambridge History of Ancient China*, eds. Michael Loewe and Edward L. Shaughnessy, 352–544. Cambridge: Cambridge University Press, 1999.

Femia, Joseph V. *Gramsci's Political Thought: Hegemony, Consciousness, and the Revolutionary Process.* Oxford: Clarendon Press, 1981.

Fisher, Carney T. *The Chosen One: Succession and Adoption in the Court of Ming Shizong.* Boston: Allen & Unwin, 1990.

Fung Yu-lan (Feng Youlan 馮友蘭). *A History of Chinese Philosophy.* Translated by Derk Bodde. Vol. 1. Peiping (Beijing): Henry Vetch, 1937.

Gan Huaizhen 干懷真. "Zhongguo gudai junchen de jingli jiqi jingdian quanshi" 中國古代君臣間的敬禮及其經典詮釋. *Taida lishi xuebao* 臺大歷史學報 31 (2003): 45–75.

Gao Heng 高亨. "Zhuangzi Tianxia pian qianzheng" 莊子天下篇箋證. In his *Wen shi shulin* 文史述林, 457–523. Beijing, Zhonghua shuju, 1980.

Gao Min 高敏. "Cong *Shuihudi Qin jian* kan Qin de cijue zhidu" 從《睡虎地秦簡》看秦的賜爵制度. Rpt. in his *Shuihudi Qin jian chu tan* 睡虎地秦簡初探, 123–134. Taibei: Wanjuan lou, 2000.

Gao Weihao 高偉浩, and Zhu Xiaohong 朱曉鴻. "Cong 'zhi yu Dao' dao 'cong yu wang'—shanggu shi feng shanbian yi pie" 從"志於道"到"從於王"—上古士風嬗變 一瞥. *Henan jidian gaodeng zhuanke xuebao* 河南機電高等專科學校學報 10, no. 1 (2002): 74–76.

Gassman, Robert H. "Understanding Ancient Chinese Society: Approaches to *Ren* 人 and *Min* 民." *Journal of the American Oriental Society* 120, no. 3 (2000): 348–359.

Ge Quan 葛荃. *Li ming yu zhongcheng: Shi ren zhengzhi jingshen de dianxing fenxi* 立命與忠誠: 士人政治精神的典型分析. Hangzhou: Zhejiang renmin chubanshe, 2000.

Gentz, Joachim. *Das Gongyang zhuan: Auslegung und Kanoniesierung der Frühlings und Herbstannalen (Chunqiu)*. Wiesbaden: Harrassowitz Verlag, 2001.

———. "The Past as a Messianic Vision: Historical Thought and Strategies of Sacralization in the Early *Gongyang* Tradition." In *Historical Truth, Historical Criticism and Ideology: Chinese Historiography and Historical Culture from a New Comparative Perspective*, eds. Helwig Schmidt-Glintzer, Achim Mittag, and Jörn Rüsen, 227–254. Leiden: Brill, 2005.

Giele, Enno. *Imperial Decision-Making and Communication in Early China: A Study of Cai Yong's Duduan*. Wiesbaden: Harrasowitz Verlag, 2006.

———. "Signatures of 'Scribes' in Early Imperial China." *Asiatische Studien/Études Asiatique* 59, no. 1 (2005): 353–387.

Goldin Paul R., compiler. "Ancient Chinese Civilization: Bibliography of Materials in Western Languages." http://paulrgoldin.com/db3/00258/paulrgoldin .com/_download/AncientChineseCivilizationBibliography.pdf.

———. "Appeals to History in Early Chinese Philosophy and Rhetoric." *Journal of Chinese Philosophy* (forthcoming).

———. "Han Fei's Doctrine of Self-Interest." In his *After Confucius: Studies in Early Chinese Philosophy,* 58–65. Honolulu: University of Hawai'i Press, 2005.

———. "Introduction: Toward a Thick Description of Chinese Philosophy." In his *After Confucius: Studies in Early Chinese Philosophy,* 1–18. Honolulu: University of Hawai'i Press, 2005.

———. "Review of A. C. Graham, tr. *Chuang-tzŭ: The Inner Chapters* and of Harold D. Roth, ed. *A Companion to Angus C. Graham's 'Chuang tzu.'*" *Early China* 28 (2003): 201–214.

———. "Review of Harold D. Roth, *Original Tao.*" *Sino-Platonic Papers* 98 (2000): 100–108.

———. "Rhetoric and Machination in *Stratagems of the Warring States.*" In his *After Confucius: Studies in Early Chinese Philosophy,* 76–89. Honolulu: University of Hawai'i Press, 2005.

———. *Rituals of the Way: The Philosophy of Xunzi.* Chicago: Open Court, 1999.

———. "The View of Women in Early Confucianism." In *The Sage and the Second Sex: Confucianism, Ethics, and Gender,* ed. Li Chenyang, 133–162. Chicago: Open Court, 2000.

———. "Xunzi and Early Han Philosophy." *Harvard Journal of Asiatic Studies* 67, no. 1 (2007): 135–166.

Graham, Angus C. *Disputers of the Tao: Philosophical Argument in Ancient China.* La Salle, IL: Open Court, 1989.

———. *Divisions in Early Mohism Reflected in the Core Chapters of Mo-tzu.* Singapore: The Institute of East Asian Philosophies, 1985.

———. "How Much of *Chuang Tzu* Did Chuang Tzu Write?" In his *Studies in Chinese Philosophy and Philosophical Literature,* 282–321. Singapore: Institute of East Asian Philosophies, 1986.

Gu Jiegang 顧頡剛. "*Gu shi bian* di yi ce zi xu" 古史辨第一冊自序. Rpt. in *Gu Jiegang gu shi lunwenji,* 顧頡剛古史論文集, ed. by Pian Yuqian 駢宇騫, vol. 1, 1–100. Beijing: Zhonghua shuju, 1988.

———. "Shanrang chuanshuo qi yu Mojia kao" 禪讓傳說起於墨家考. Rpt. in *Gu Jiegang gu shi lunwenji* 顧頡剛古史論文集, ed. by Pian Yuqian 駢宇騫, vol. 1, 295–369. Beijing: Zhonghua shuju, 1988.

Guan Tong 関桐. "Boyi ai, Liuxia Hui bu gong – du Sima Guang 'Yi Meng' zhaji zhi yi" 伯夷隘, 柳下惠不恭—讀司馬光《疑孟》札記之一. *Guanzi xuekan* 管子學刊 2 (2005): 110–120.

Guo Yi 郭沂. "*Lunyu, Lunyu* lei wenxian, Kongzi shiliao – cong Guodian jian tan qi"《論語》、《論語》類文獻、孔子史料—從郭店簡談起. http://www.bamboosilk.org/Wssf/Guoyi6-01.htm.

Han Demin 韓德民. "Xunzi 'jun Dao' lilun zai Han dai de zhankai" 荀子"君道"理論在漢代的展開. In *Guoji Ruxue yanjiu* 國際儒學研究, ed. Guoji Ruxue lianhe hui 國際儒學聯合會, 276–331. Beijing: Guoji wenhua chubanshe, 2001.

Hawkes, David. "The Heirs of Gao-Yang." *T'oung Pao* 69 (1983): 1–23.

Hong Shi 洪石. "Zhanguo Qin Han shiqi qiqi de shengchan yu guanli" 戰國秦漢時期漆器的生產與管理. *Kaogu xuebao* 考古學報 4 (2005): 381–410.

Honig, Emily. *Creating Chinese Ethnicity: Subei People in Shanghai, 1850–1980.* New Haven: Yale University Press, 1992.

Hsiao Kung-Chuan (Xiao Gongquan 蕭公權). *A History of Chinese Political Thought* Volume One: *From the Beginnings to the Sixth Century A.D.,* trans. Frederick W. Mote. Princeton: Princeton University Press, 1979.

Hsu Cho-yun. *Ancient China in Transition*. Stanford: Stanford University Press, 1965.

Hu Fangshu 胡方恕. "Zhoudai gongshe suoyouzhi xia de guizu siyou tudi" 周代公社所有制下的貴族私有土地. *Zhongguo gudaishi luncong* 中國古代史論叢 3 (1981): 64–96.

Huang Kaiguo 黃開國. "Gongyang xue de Kongzi gai zhi shuo"《公羊》學的孔子改制說. *Qilu xuekan* 齊魯學刊 3 (2004): 76–80.

Huang, Ray (Huang Renyu 黃仁宇). *1587: A Year of No Significance*. New Haven: Yale University Press, 1981.

Hui, Victoria Tin-Bor. *War and State Formation in Ancient China and Early Modern Europe*. Cambridge: Cambridge University Press, 2005.

Hulsewé, A. F. P. *Remnants of Ch'in Law: An Annotated Translation of the Ch'in Legal and Administrative Rules of the 3rd Century B.C. Discovered in Yün-meng Prefecture, Hu-pei Province, in 1975*. Leiden: Brill, 1985.

Ishii Kōmei 石井宏明. *Dong-Zhou wangchao yanjiu* 東周王朝研究. Beijing: Zhongyang minzu daxue, 1999.

Jia Haitao 賈海濤. "Jianxi Xunzi dui junzhu ducai zhuanzhi 'helixing' de lunzheng" 簡析荀子對君主獨裁專制政治"合理性"的論證. *Fuyang shiyuan xuebao (sheke ban)* 阜陽師院學報(社科版) 2 (1997): 19–24.

Jiang Shanguo 蔣善國. *Shang shu zongshu* 尚書綜述. Shanghai: Guji chubanshe, 1988.

Jing Hongyan 景紅艷, and Cai Jingbo 蔡靜波. "Shi xi Zhanguo wanqi shi de lu li sixiang" 試析戰國晚期士的祿利思想. *Jinyang xuekan* 晉陽學刊 1 (2005): 72–75.

Johnson, David. "Epic and History in Early China: The Matter of Wu Tzu-Hsü." *Journal of Asian Studies* 40, no. 2 (1981): 255–271.

Judge, Joan. "Key Words in the Late Qing Reform Discourse: Classical and Contemporary Sources of Authority." *Indiana East Asian Working Papers Series on Language and Politics in Modern China*. Winter 1994. http://www.indiana.edu/~easc/resources/working_paper/noframe_5_all.htm#N_23.

Kaizuka Shigeki 貝塚茂樹. "Shunjū jidai no toshi kokka" 春秋時代の都市國家. In *Kaizuka Shigeki chosakushū* 貝塚茂樹著作集, vol. 1, *Chūgoku no kodai kokka* 春中國の古代國家, 255–382. Tōkyō: Chūō Kōronsha, 1976.

Kalinowski, Marc. "La production des manuscrits dans la chine ancienne: Une approche codicologique de la bibliothèque funéraire de Mawangdui." *Asiatische Studien/Études Asiatiques* 59, no. 1 (2005): 131–168.

Kang Youwei 康有為. *Xin xue wei jing kao* 新學偽經考, collated by Zhu Weijing 朱維錚 and Liao Mei 廖梅. Xianggang (Hong Kong): Sanlian shudian, 1998.

Kano Osamu 河野收. "Chūgoku kodai no aru hibusō heiwa undō" 中國古代 或非武裝平和運動. *Gunji shigaku* 軍事史學 13, no. 4 (1978): 64–74.

Keightley, David N. *The Ancestral Landscape: Time, Space, and Community in Late Shang China (ca. 1200–1045 B.C.)*. Berkeley: Institute of East Asian Studies, 2000.

————. "The Religious Commitment: Shang Theology and the Genesis of Chinese Political Culture." *History of Religions* 17, nos. 3–4 (1978): 211–224.

————. "The Shang: China's First Historical Dynasty." In *The Cambridge History of Ancient China*, eds. Michael Loewe and Edward L. Shaughnessy, 232–291. Cambridge: Cambridge University Press, 1999.

Kern, Martin. "The *Odes* in Excavated Manuscripts." In *Text and Ritual in Early China*, ed. Martin Kern, 149–193. Seattle: University of Washington Press, 2005.

————. "The Poetry of Han Historiography." *Early Medieval China* 10–11, no. 1 (2004): 23–65.

————. *The Stele Inscriptions of Ch'in Shih-huang: Text and Ritual in Early Chinese Imperial Representation.* New Haven: American Oriental Society, 2000.

Knoblock, John H. "The Chronology of Xunzi's Works." *Early China* 8 (1982–1983): 29–52.

————. *Xunzi: A Translation and Study of the Complete Works.* 3 vols. Stanford: Stanford University Press, 1988–1994.

Kolb, Raimund T. *Die Infanterie im alten China: Ein Beitrag zur Militärgeschichte der Vor-Zhan-Guo-Zeit.* Mainz am Rhein: Philipp von Zabern, 1991.

Kominami Ichirō 小南一郎. "Tenmei to toku" 天命と德. *Tōhō gakuhō* 東方學報 64 (1992): 1–59.

Kosaki Tomonori 小崎智則. "*Kanpishi* no *chū* ni tsuite" 《韓非子》の「忠」につ いて. *Nagoya daigaku Chūgoku testugaku ronshū* 4 (2005): 25–38.

Kryukov, Vassilij M. *Tekst i Ritual: Opyt Interpretatsii Drevnekitaiskoj Epigrafiki Epokhi In'-Chzhou.* Moscow: Pamiatniki Istoricheskoj Mysli, 2000.

Lai Guolong. "The Diagram of the Mourning System from Mawangdui." *Early China* 28 (2003): 43–99.

Leong Sow-Theng. *Migration and Ethnicity in Chinese History: Hakkas, Pengmin, and Their Neighbors.* Ed. Tim Wright. Stanford: Stanford University Press, 1997.

Levy, Howard S., trans. and annotator. *Biography of Huang Ch'ao.* Berkeley: University of California Press, 1955.

Lewis, Mark E. *The Construction of Space in Early China.* Albany: State University of New York Press, 2006.

————. "Custom and Human Nature in Early China." *Philosophy East and West* 53, no. 3 (2003): 308–322.

————. *The Early Chinese Empires: Qin and Han.* Cambridge, MA: Harvard University Press, 2007.

————. *Sanctioned Violence in Early China.* Albany: State University of New York Press, 1990.

————. "Warring States: Political History." In *The Cambridge History of Ancient China*, eds. Michael Loewe and Edward L. Shaughnessy, 587–650. Cambridge: Cambridge University Press, 1999.

————. *Writing and Authority in Early China.* Albany: State University Press of New York, 1999.

Li Chenyang. "Introduction: Can Confucianism Come to Terms with Feminism?" In his *The Sage and the Second Sex: Confucianism, Ethics, and Gender*, 1–22. Chicago: Open Court, 2000.

Li Cunshan 李存山. "Fansi jing shi guanxi: Cong 'Qi gong Yi' shuo qi" 反思經史關係：從"啓攻益"說起. *Zhongguo shehui kexue* 中國社會科學 3 (2003): 75–85.

———. "Zai shuo 'wei fu jue jun'" 再説"為父絕君." *Zhejiang shehui kexue* 浙江社會科學 5 (2005): 93–98.

Li Feng. *Landscape and Power in Ea... ...risis and Fall of the Western Zhou 1045–771 BC*. Cambridge: C... ...sity Press, 2006.

———. "Succession and Promotion: Elite ...ity during the Western Zhou." *Monumenta Serica* 52 (2000): 1–35.

Li Ling 李零. *Guodian Chujian jiaodu ji* 郭店楚簡校讀記. Rev. ed. Beijing: Beijing daxue chubanshe, 2002.

———. "*Shang jun shu* zhong de tudi renkou zhengce yu jue zhi" 《商君書》中的土地人口政策與爵制. *Guji zhengli yu yanjiu* 古籍整理與研究 6 (1991): 26–30.

———. *Zhongguo fangshu kao* 中國方術考. Beijing: Dongfang chubanshe, 2001.

Li Rui 李銳. "Guodian Chu jian *Qiong da yi shi* zai kao" 郭店楚簡窮達以時再考. *Xin chutu wenxian yu gudai wenming yanjiu* 新出土文獻與古代文明研究, eds. Xie Weiyang 謝維揚 and Zhu Yuanqing 朱淵清, 268–278. Shanghai: Shanghai daxue chubanshe, 2004.

Li Wai-yee. *The Readability of the Past in Early Chinese Historiography*. Cambridge, MA: Harvard University Asia Center, 2007.

Li Xiantang 李憲堂. "Lun Rujia minben sixiang de zhuanzhizhuyi shizhi" 論儒家民本思想的專制主義實質. *Lishi jiaoxue* 歷史教學 5 (2003): 21–25.

Li Xiaoying 李曉英. "*Lunyu* zhong de 'xiao ren' bianxi" 《論語》中的"小人"辨析. *Jiangnan xueyuan xuebao* 江南學院學報 15, no. 1 (March 2000): 29–31.

Liang Qichao 梁啟超. *Xian Qin zhengzhi sixiang shi* 先秦政治思想史. Beijing: Dongfang, 1996.

———. "Zhongguo zhuanzhi zhengzhi jinhua shi lun" 中國專制政治進化史論. In his *Yin bing shi wenji dianjiao* 飲冰室文集點校, collated by Wu Song 吳松 et al., vol. 3, 1649–1667. Kunming: Yunnan jiaoyu chubanshe, 2003.

Liang Yun 梁云. "Zhou dai yong ding zhidu de dongxi chabie" 周代用鼎制度東西差別. *Kaogu yu wenwu* 考古與文物 3 (2005): 49–59.

Liao Mingchun 廖名春. "Lun Xunzi de junmin guanxi shuo" 論荀子的君民關係說. *Zhongguo wenhua yanjiu* 中國文化研究 16 (1997): 41–44.

———. "Xunzi ge pian xiezuo niandai kao" 《荀子》各篇寫作年代考. In his *Zhongguo xueshu shi xin zheng* 中國學術史新證, 535–546. Chengdu: Sichuan daxue chubanshe, 2005.

———. *Xunzi xin tan* 荀子新探. Taibei: Wenjin chubanshe, 1994.

———. "Zhujian ben 'Zhuangzi~Dao Zhi' pian tanyuan" 竹簡本《莊子·盜跖》

篇探源. Rpt. in his *Chutu jianbo congkao* 出土簡帛叢考, 196–216. Wuhan: Hubei jiaoyu chubanshe, 2004. Originally published in *Wenshi* 文史 45 [1998], 49–60.

Lin Ganquan 林甘泉. "Cong *Zuo zhuan* kan Zhongguo gudai chengbang de zhengzhi tizhi" 從《左傳》看中國古代城邦的政治體制. *Zhongguo shehui kexueyuan yanjiusheng yuan xuebao* 中國社會科學院研究生院學報 6 (1998): 20–29.

Liu Baocai 劉寶才. "*Tang Yu zhi Dao* de lishi yu linian—jianlun Zhanguo zhongqi de shanrang sichao"《唐虞之道》的歷史與理念—兼論戰國中期的禪讓思潮. *Renwen zazhi* 人文雜誌 3 (2000): 106–110.

Liu, James, T. C. (Liu Zijian 劉子健). "An Early Sung Reformer: Fan Chung-yen." In *Chinese Thought and Institutions*, ed. John K. Fairbank, 105–131. Chicago: Chicago University Press, 1957.

Liu Jiahe 劉家和. "*Zuo zhuan* zhong de renben sixiang yu minben sixiang" 左傳中的人本思想與民本思想. *Lishi yanjiu* 歷史研究 6 (1995): 3–13.

Liu Jian 劉劍. "*Rong Cheng shi* shi du yi ze"《容成氏》釋讀一則. In *Shangbo guan cang Zhanguo Chu zhushu yanjiu xubian* 上博舘藏戰國楚竹書研究續編, eds. Shanghai daxue gudai wenming yanjiu zhongxin 上海大學古代文明研究中心 and Qinghua daxue sixiang wenhua yanjiu suo 清華大學思想文化研究所, 351–352. Shanghai: Shanghai shudian, 2004.

Liu Lexian 劉樂賢. "Huxishan Han jian 'Yan shi wu sheng' ji xiangguan wenti" 虎溪山漢簡〈閻氏五勝〉及相關問題 *Wenwu* 文物 7 (2003): 66–70.

Liu Li. "Ancestor Worship: An Archaeological Investigation of Ritual Activities in Neolithic North China." *Journal of East Asian Archaeology* 2, nos. 2–1 (2000): 129–164.

Liu Xiaofeng 劉小楓. *Rujia geming jingshen yuanliu kao* 儒家革命精神源流考. Shanghai: Sanlian shudian, 2000.

Liu Xiaogan. *Classifying the Zhuangzi Chapters*. Trans. William E. Savage. Michigan Monographs in Chinese Studies 65. Ann Arbor: Center for Chinese Studies, University of Michigan, 1994.

———. "From Bamboo Slips to Received Versions: Common Features in the Transformation of the *Laozi*." *Harvard Journal of Asiatic Studies* 63, no. 2 (2003): 337–382.

Liu Zehua 劉澤華. *Xian Qin shi ren yu shehui* 先秦士人與社會. Rev. ed. Tianjin: Tianjin renmin chubanshe, 2004.

———. "Zhi shi guannian yu fangfa jingyan suotan" 治史觀念與方法經驗瑣談 (unpublished paper).

———. *Zhongguo chuantong zhengzhi siwei* 中國傳統政治思維. Changchun: Jilin jiaoyu, 1991.

———. *Zhongguo chuantong zhengzhi sixiang fansi* 中國傳統政治思想反思. Beijing: Sanlian, 1987.

———. *Zhongguo de Wangquanzhuyi* 中國的王權主義. Shanghai: Renmin chubanshe, 2000.

————, ed. *Zhongguo zhengzhi sixiang shi* 中國政治思想史. 3 vols. Hangzhou: Zhejiang renmin chubanshe, 1996.

Loewe, Michael. "The Authority of the Emperors of Ch'in and Han." Rpt. in his *Divination, Mythology and Monarchy in Han China,* 85–111. Cambridge: University of Cambridge Press, 1994.

Louie, Kam. *Critiques of Confucius in Contemporary China.* New York: St. Martin's Press, 1980.

Lü Shaogang 呂紹綱. "Zhongguo gudai bu cunzai chengbang zhidu – jian yu Ri Zhi tongzhi shangque" 中國古代不存在城邦制度—兼與日知同志商榷. *Zhongguo shi yanjiu* 中國史研究 4 (1983): 91–105.

Lü Wenyu 呂文鬱. *Zhoudai caiyi zhidu* 周代的采邑制度. Enlarged ed. Beijing: Shehui kexue wenxian chubanshe, 2006.

Lundahl, Bertil. *Han Fei Zi: The Man and the Work.* Stockholm: Institute of Oriental Languages, Stockholm University, 1992.

Ma Jigao 馬積高. *Xunxue yuanliu* 荀學源流. Shanghai: Guji chubanshe, 2000.

MacCormack, Sabine. "Cuzco, Another Rome?" In *Empires: Perspectives from Archaeology and History*, eds. Susan E. Alcock et al., 419–435. Cambridge: Cambridge University Press, 2001.

Maeder, Erik W. "Some Observances on the Composition of the 'Core Chapters' of the *Mozi*." *Early China* 17 (1992): 27–82.

Makeham, John. "The Formation of *Lunyu* as a Book." *Monumenta Serica* 44 (1996): 1–24.

————. "The Legalist Concept of *Hsing-ming*: An Example of the Contribution of Archeological Evidence to the Re-Interpretation of Transmitted Texts." *Monumenta Serica* 39 (1990–1991): 87–114.

Maliavin, Vladimir V. *Gibel' Drevnej Imperii.* Moscow: Nauka, 1983.

Mao Han-kuang. "The Evolution in the Nature of the Medieval Genteel Families." In *State and Society in Early Medieval China,* ed. Albert Dien, 73–109. Stanford: Stanford University Press, 1990.

Martin, François. "Le Cas Zichan: Entre Légistes et Confuanistes." In *En suivant la Voie royale: Mélanges offerts en hommage à Léon Vandermeersch*, compiled by Jacques Gernet and Marc Kalinowski, with the collaboration of Jean-Pierre Diény, 69–83. Paris: École française d'Extrême-Orient, 1997.

Martynov, Aleksandr S. "Kategoriia *de* – sintez 'poriadka' i 'zhizni.'" In *Ot Magicheskoi Sily k Moral'nomy Imperativu: Kategoriia De v Kitajskoj Kul'ture*, eds. L. N. Borokh and A. I. Kobzev, 36–75. Moscow: Izdatel'skaia firma 'Vostochnaia Literatura' RAN, 1998.

————. "Konfutsianskaia Utopiia v Drevnosti i Srednevekov'e." In *Kitajskie Sotsial'nye Utopii*, eds. L. P. Deliusin and L. N. Borokh, 10–57. Moscow: Nauka, 1987.

Marx, Karl. "The Class Struggles in France, 1848 to 1850" (1850). Rpt. *Collected Works of Karl Marx and Frederick Engels*, vol. 10, 45–145. London: Lawrence and Wishart, 1978.

Masubuchi Tatsuo 增淵龍夫. *Chūgoku kodai no shakai to kokka* 中國古代の社會と國家. Tōkyō: Kōbun, 1963.

Mattos, Gilbert L. "Eastern Zhou Bronze Inscriptions." In *New Sources of Early Chinese History: An Introduction to the Reading of Inscriptions and Manuscripts*, ed. Edward L. Shaughnessy, 85–124. Berkeley: The Society for the Study of Early China and The Institute of East Asian Studies, University of California, 1997.

McNeal, Robin P. "Acquiring the People: Social Organization, Mobilization, and Discourse on the Civil and the Martial in Ancient China." PhD dissertation, University of Washington, 2000.

———. "The Body as Metaphor for the Civil and Martial Components of Empire in *Yi Zhou shu*, Chapter 32: With an Excursion on the Composition and Structure of the *Yi Zhou shu*." *Journal of the American Oriental Society* 122, no. 1 (2002): 46–60.

McNeill, John R. "China's Environmental History in World Perspective" In *Sediments of Time: Environment and Society in Chinese History*, eds. Mark Elvin and Liu Ts'ui-jung, 31–49. Cambridge: Cambridge University Press, 1998.

Meadows, Thomas T. *The Chinese and Their Rebellions, Viewed in Connection with Their National Philosophy, Ethics, Legislation, and Administration* (1856). Rpt. Stanford: Academic Reprints, 1953.

Meyer, Dirk. "Structure as a Means of Persuasion as Seen in the Manuscript *Qiong Da Yi Shi* 窮達以時 From Tomb One, Guodian." *Oriens Extremus* 45 (2005–2006): 179–210.

Michael, Thomas. *The Pristine Dao: Metaphysics in Early Daoist Discourse*. Albany: State University of New York Press, 2005.

Miyazaki Ichisada 宮崎一定. "Shina jōkaku no kigen isetsu" 支那城郭の起源異説. *Rekishi to chiri* 歴史と地理 32, no. 3 (1933): 187–203.

Moreland, John. "The Carolingian Empire: Rome Reborn?" In *Empires: Perspectives from Archaeology and History*, eds. Susan E. Alcock et al., 392–418. Cambridge: Cambridge University Press, 2001.

Mote, Frederick. "Confucian Eremitism in the Yüan Period." In *The Confucian Persuasion*, ed. Arthur F. Wright, 202–240. Stanford: Stanford University Press, 1960.

Murthy, Viren. "The Democratic Potential of Confucian Minben Thought." *Asian Philosophy* 10, no. 1 (2000): 33–47.

Nie Zhongqing 聶中慶. *Guodian Chu jian 'Laozi' yanjiu* 郭店楚簡老子研究. Beijing: Zhonghua shuju, 2004.

Nivison, David S. "An Interpretation of the *Shao gao*." *Early China* 20 (1995): 177–194.

Nuyen, A. T. "Confucianism, the Idea of *Min-pen*, and Democracy." *Copenhagen Journal of Asian Studies* 14 (2000): 130–151.

Nylan, Michael. "The *Chin Wen/ku Wen* Controversy in Han Times." *T'oung Pao* 80, no. 1–3 (1994): 83–145.

———. "Confucian Piety and Individualism in Han China." *Journal of the American Oriental Society* 116, no. 1 (1996): 1–27.

———. *The Five "Confucian" Classics*. New Haven: Yale University Press, 2001.

———. *The Shifting Center: The Original "Great Plan" and Later Readings*. Sankt Augustin: Institut Monumenta Serica and Nettetal: Steyler Verlag, 1992.

Okamura Hidenori 岡村秀典. *Chūgoku kodai ōken to saishi* 中國古代王權と祭祀. Tōkyō: Gakuseisha, 2005.

Onozawa Seiichi 小野澤精一. "Toku ron" 德論. In *Chūgoku bunka sōsho 2: Shisō gairon* 中國文化叢書 2: 思想概論, ed. Akatsuka Kiyoshi 赤塚忠 et al., 151–184. Tōkyō: Taishukan shoten, 1968.

Pang Pu 龐朴. "Chu du Guodian Chujian" 初讀郭店楚簡. *Lishi yanjiu* 歷史研究 4 (1998): 5–10.

———. "'Shi you shi zhi' jie'" "使由使知"解. *Wenshi zhishi* 文史知識 9 (1999): 31–36.

Pankenier, David W. "'The Scholar's Frustration' Reconsidered: Melancholia or Credo?" *Journal of the American Oriental Society* 110, no. 3 (1990): 434–459.

Parsons, James B. *The Peasant Rebellions of the Late Ming Dynasty*. Tucson: University of Arizona Press, 1970.

Peerenboom, Randall P. *Law and Morality in Ancient China: The Silk Manuscripts of Huang-Lao*. Albany: State University of New York Press, 1993.

Peng Bangben 彭邦本. "Chu jian *Tang Yu zhi Dao* chu tan" 楚簡《唐虞之道》初探. In *Guodian Chujian guoji xueshu yantao hui lunwenji* 郭店楚簡國際學術研討會論文集, ed. Wuhan daxue Zhongguo wenhua yanjiuyuan 武漢大學中國文化研究院, 261–272. Wuhan: Hubei renmin chubanshe, 2000.

Peng Lin 彭林. "Zai lun Guodian jian *Liu de* 'wei fu jue jun' ji xiangguan wenti" 再論郭店簡《六德》"為父絕君"及相關問題. *Zhongguo zhexue shi* 中國哲學史 2 (2001): 97–102.

———. *"Zhou li" zhuti sixiang yu chengshu niandai yanjiu*《周禮》主題思想與成書年代研究. Beijing: Zhongguo shehui kexue chubanshe 1991.

Perelomov, Leonard S. *Imperiia Tsin': Pervoe Tsentralizovannoe Gosudarstvo v Kitae*. Moscow: Nauka, 1961.

———. *Konfutsij: Zhizn', Ucheniie, Sud'ba*. Moscow: Nauka, 1993.

Petersen, Jens Østergård. "Which Books Did the First Emperor of Ch'in Burn? On the Meaning of *Pai Chia* in Early Chinese Sources." *Monumenta Serica* 43 (1995): 1–52.

Peterson, Willard J. "The Grounds of Mencius' Argument," *Philosophy East and West* 29, no. 3 (1979): 307–321.

Pines, Yuri. "Beasts or Humans: Pre-Imperial Origins of Sino-Barbarian Dichotomy." In *Mongols, Turks and Others*, eds. Reuven Amitai and Michal Biran, 59–102. Leiden: Brill, 2004.

———. "Bodies, Lineages, Citizens, and Regions: A Review of Mark Edward Lewis' *The Construction of Space in Early China*." *Early China* 30 (2005): 155–188.

———. "Disputers of Abdication: Zhanguo Egalita‌‌‌‌‌nd the Sovereign's Power." *T'oung Pao* 91, nos. 4–5 (2005): 243–300

———. "Disputers of the *Li*: Breakthroughs in the Co‌‌‌of Ritual in Preimperial China." *Asia Major* (third series) 13, no. 1 (2000): 1–41.

———. *Foundations of Confucian Thought: Intellectual Life in the Chunqiu Period, 722–453 B.C.E.* Honolulu: University of Hawai'i Press, 2002.

———. "Friends or Foes: Changing Concepts of Ruler-Minister Relations and the Notion of Loyalty in Pre-Imperial China." *Monumenta Serica* 50 (2002): 35–74.

———. "Imagining the Empire? Concepts of 'Primeval Unity' in Pre-imperial Historiographic Tradition." In *Concepts of Empire in Ancient China and Rome: An Intercultural Comparison*, eds. Achim Mittag and Fritz-Heiner Muetschler, 65–87. Oxford: Oxford University Press, 2008.

———. "Lexical Changes in Zhanguo Texts." *Journal of the American Oriental Society* 122, no. 4 (2002): 691–705.

———. "'The One That Pervades the All' in Ancient Chinese Political Thought: Origins of the 'Great Unity' Paradigm." *T'oung Pao* 86, nos. 4–5 (2000): 280–324.

———. "The Question of Interpretation: Qin History in Light of New Epigraphic Sources." *Early China* 29 (2004): 1–44.

———. "The Search for Stability: Late Ch'un-ch'iu Thinkers." *Asia Major* (third series) 10 (1997): 1–47.

———. "Speeches and the Question of Authenticity in Ancient Chinese Historical Records." In *Historical Truth, Historical Criticism and Ideology: Chinese Historiography and Historical Culture from a New Coparative Perspective*, eds. Helwig Schmidt-Glintzer, Achim Mittag, and Jörn Rüsen, 195–224. Leiden: Brill, 2005.

———. "Subversion Unearthed: Criticism of Hereditary Succession in the Newly Discovered Manuscripts." *Oriens Extremus* 45 (2005–2006): 159–178.

——— (You Rui 尤銳). "Wu suo bu neng er wu suo wei: Xunzi duiyu wangquanzhuyi de tiaozheng" 無所不能而無所為：荀子對於王權主義的調整. (unpublished ms.).

———. "Xin jiu de ronghe: Xunzi dui Chunqiu sixiang chuantong de chongxin quanshi" 新舊的融合：荀子對春秋思想傳統的重新詮釋, *Guoli zhengzhi daxue xuebao* 國立政治大學哲學學報 11 (2003): 137–183.

Pu Muzhou (Poo Mu-chou) 蒲慕州. "Shuihudi Qin jian *Ri shu* de shijie" 睡虎地秦簡《日書》的世界. *Zhongyang yanjiuyuan lishi yuyan yanjiusuo jikan* 中央研究院歷史語言研究所集刊 62, no. 4 (1993): 623–675.

Puett, Michael J. *To Become a God: Cosmology, Sacrifice, and Self-Divinization in Early China.* Cambridge, MA: London: Cambridge University Press, 2002.

Qian Zongfan 錢宗範. "Xi Zhou Chunqiu shidai de shilu shiguan zhidu ji qi pohuai" 西周春秋時代的世祿世官制度及其破壞. *Zhongguoshi yanjiu* 中國史研究 3 (1989): 20–30.

Qiu Dexiu 邱德修. *Shangbo Chu jian 'Rong Cheng shi' zhuyi kaozheng* 上博楚簡《容成氏》注譯考證. Taibei: Taiwan Guji, 2003.

Qiu Xigui 裘錫圭. "Bin Gong-*xu* mingwen kaoshi" 豳公盨銘文考釋. In his *Zhongguo chutu gu wenxian shi jiang* 中國出土古文獻十講, 46–77. Shanghai: Fudan daxue chubanshe, 2004.

Queen, Sarah A. "The Way of the Unadorned King: The Politics of Tung Chung-shu's Hermeneutics." In *Classics and Interpretations: The Hermeneutic Traditions in Chinese Culture*, ed. Tu Ching-i, 173–193. New Brunswick, NJ: Transaction Publishers, 2000.

Ri Shu yanjiu ban 日書研究班. "*Ri shu*: Qin guo shehui de yi mian jingzi" 日書：秦國社會的一面鏡子. In *Qin jian Ri shu jishi* 秦簡日書集釋, ed. Wu Xiao-qiang 吳小強, 291–311. Changsha: Yuelu, 2000.

Ri Zhi 日知. "Cong *Chun qiu* cheng ren zhi li zai lun Yazhou gudai minzhu zheng-zhi" 從《春秋》稱人之例再論亞洲古代民主政治. *Lishi yanjiu* 歷史研究 3 (1981): 3–17.

Rickett, Allyn W. *Guanzi: Political, Economic, and Philosophical Essays from Early China*. 2 vols. Princeton: Princeton Library of Asian Translations, 1985–1998.

Rosen, Sydney. "In Search of the Historical Kuan Chung." *Journal of Asian Studies* 35, no. 3 (1976): 431–440.

Roth, Harold D. *Original Tao: Inward Training and the Foundations of Taoist Mysticism*. New York: Columbia University Press, 1999.

———. "Psychology and Self-Cultivation in Early Taoistic Thought." *Harvard Journal of Asiatic Studies* 51, no. 2 (1991): 599–650.

Rubin, Vitaly [Vitalij] A. "A Chinese Don Quixote: Changing Attitudes to Po-i's Image." In *Confucianism: The Dynamics of Tradition*, ed. Irene Eber, 155–184. New York: Macmillan, 1986.

———. *Individual and State in Ancient China: Essays on Four Chinese Philosophers*. Trans. Steven I. Levine. New York: Columbia University Press, 1976.

———. "Narodnoe Sobranie v Drevnem Kitae v VII–V vv. do n.e." *Vestnik Drevnej Istorii* 4 (1960): 22–40.

———. "Tzu-Ch'an and the City-State of Ancient China." *T'oung Pao* 52 (1965): 8–34.

Sage, Steven F. *Ancient Sichuan and the Unification of China*. Albany: State University of New York Press, 1992.

Sarkissian, Hagop. "*Laozi*: Re-visiting Two Early Commentaries in the *Hanfeizi*." MA thesis, University of Toronto, 2001.

Sato, Masayuki. *The Confucian Quest for Order: The Origin and Formation of the Political Thought of Xun Zi*. Leiden: Brill, 2003.

———. "The Development of Pre-Qin Conceptual Terms and Their Incorporation into Xunzi's Thought." In *Linked Faiths: Essays on Chinese Religions and Traditional Culture in Honor of Kristofer Schipper*, eds. Jan A. M. de Meyer and Peter M. Engelfriet, 18–40. Leiden: Brill, 2000.

Savage, William D. "Archetypes, Model Emulation and the Confucian Gentleman." *Early China* 17 (1992): 1–25.

Sawyer, Ralph D., tr. *The Seven Military Classics of Ancient China*. Boulder, CO: Westview, 1993.

Schaberg, David C. "Confucius as Body and Text: On the Generation of Knowledge in Warring States and Han Anecdotal Literature." Paper presented at the conference "Text and Ritual in Early China." Princeton, October 2000 (unpublished).

———. *A Patterned Past: Form and Thought in Early Chinese Historiography*. Cambridge, MA: Harvard University Asia Center, 2001.

———. "Playing at Critique: Indirect Remonstrance and Formation of *Shi* Identity." In *Text and Ritual in Early China*, ed. Martin Kern, 194–225. Seattle: University of Washington Press, 2005.

———. "Remonstrance in Eastern Zhou Historiography." *Early China* 22 (1997): 133–179.

Schneider, Laurence A. *A Madman of Chu: The Chinese Myth of Loyalty and Dissent*. Berkeley: University of California Press, 1980.

Schram, Stuart, ed. *Chairman Mao Talks to the People; Talks and Letters: 1956–1971*. Trans. John Chinnery and Tieyun. New York, Pantheon Books, 1975.

Schwartz, Benjamin I. *The World of Thought in Ancient China*. Cambridge, MA: Harvard University Press, 1985.

Shaughnessy, Edward L. "The Duke of Zhou's Retirement in the East and the Beginnings of the Minister-Monarch Debate in Chinese Political Philosophy." *Early China* 18 (1993): 41–72.

———. "The Guodian Manuscripts and Their Place in Twentieth-Century Historiography on the *Laozi*." *Harvard Journal of Asiatic Studies* 65, no. 2 (2005): 414–457.

———. *Rewriting Early Chinese Texts*. Albany: State University New York Press, 2006.

———. "Western Zhou Bronze Inscriptions." In his *New Sources of Early Chinese History: An Introduction to the Reading of Inscriptions and Manuscripts*, 57–84. Berkeley: The Society for the Study of Early China and the Institute of East Asian Studies, University of California, 1997.

———. "Zhouyuan Oracle-Bone Inscriptions: Entering the Research Stage?" *Early China*, 11–12 (1985–1987): 146–163.

Shao Weiguo 邵維國. "Zhoudai jiachen zhi shulun" 周代家臣制述論. *Zhongguoshi yanjiu* 中國史研究 3 (1999): 39–50

Shen Gang 沈剛. *Qin Han shiqi de ke jieceng yanjiu* 秦漢時期的客階層研究. Changchun: Jilin wenshi chubanshe, 2003.

Shi Weiqing 施偉青. "Lun Qin zi Shang Yang bianfa hou de taowang xianxiang" 論秦自商鞅變法後的逃亡現象. *Zhongguo shehui jingji shi yanjiu* 中國社會經濟史研究 2 (2004): 39–46.

Shirakawa Shizuka 白川靜. *Kinbun tsūshaku* 金文通釋. 56 vols. Kōbe: Hakutsuru bijutsukan, 1962–1984.

Shun Kwong-loi. *Mencius and Early Chinese Thought*. Stanford: Stanford University Press, 1997.

Sivin, Nathan. "State, Cosmos, and Body in the Last Three Centuries B.C." *Harvard Journal of Asiatic Studies* 55, no. 1 (1995): 5–37.

Skinner, Quentin. *The Foundations of Modern Political Thought*. Volume One: *The Renaissance*. Cambridge: Cambridge University Press, 1992.

Slingerland, Edward. *Effortless Action: Wu-wei as Conceptual Metaphor and Spiritual Ideal in Early China*. Oxford: Oxford University Press, 2003.

Smith, Kidder. "Sima Tan and the Invention of Daoism, 'Legalism,' *et cetera*." *Journal of Asian Studies* 62, no. 1 (2003): 129–156.

Stanford Encyclopedia of Philosophy. http://plato.stanford.edu/contents.html#1.

Stevenson, Charles L. "Persuasive Definitions." *Mind* 47 (1938): 331–350.

Su Baorong 蘇寶榮, and Song Yongpei 宋永培. "'Xue er you ze shi' ying zuo he jie?" "學而優則仕" 應作何解? *Hebei shifan daxue xuebao* 河北師範大學學報 3 (1983): 77–79

Suzuki Yoshikazu 鈴木喜一. "Shunjū jidai no kunshin ronri" 春秋時代の君臣倫理. *Nihon Chōgoku gakkaihō* 日本中國學會報 34 (1982): 1–16.

Takeuchi Yasuhiro 內竹康浩. "Seishū kinbun uchi no 'tenshi' ni tsuite" 西周金文中の《天子》について. In *Ronshū: Chūgoku kodai no moji to bunka* 論集：中國古代の文字と文化, 105–130. Tōkyō: Kyūko shoin, 1999.

Tan Sitong 譚嗣同. *Ren xue* 仁學, annotated by Wu Hailan 吳海兰. Beijing: Huaxia chubanshe, 2002.

Tan, Sor-hoon. *Confucian Democracy: A Deweyan Reconstruction*. Albany: State University of New York Press, 2003.

Tang Lan 唐蘭. "Sima Qian suo mei you jianguo de zhengui shiliao – Changsha Mawangdui boshu *Zhanguo congjengjia shu* 司馬遷所沒有見過的珍貴史料—長沙馬王堆帛書《戰國縱橫家書》. In *Zhanguo conghengjia shu* 戰國縱橫家書, ed. Mawangdui Hanmu boshu zhengli xiaozu 馬王堆漢墓帛書整理小組, 123–153. Beijing: Wenwu, 1976.

Thompson, P. M. *The Shen-tzu Fragments*. Oxford: Oxford University Press, 1979.

Tian Changwu 田昌五, and Zang Zhifei 臧知非. *Zhou Qin shehui jiegou yanjiu* 周秦社會結構研究. Xian: Xibei daxue chubanshe, 1996.

Tu Wei-ming (Du Weiming 杜維明). "The Creative Tension between *Jen* and *Li*." *Philosophy East and West* 18, nos. 1-2 (1968): 29–39.

———. "The Structure and Function of the Confucian Intellectual in Ancient China." In his *Way, Learning and Politics: Essays on the Confucian Intellectual*, 13–28. Albany: State University of New York Press, 1993.

Underhill, Anne P. *Craft Production and Social Change in Northern China*. New York: Kluwer Academic/Plenum Publishers, 2002.

Vasil'ev, Kim V. *Plany Srazhaiushchikhsia Tsarstv (Issledovaniia i Perevody)*. Moscow: Nauka, 1968.

Vervoorn, Aat. "Boyi and Shuqi: Worthy Men of Old?" *Papers in Far Eastern History* 29 (1983): 1–22.

———. *Men of the Cliffs and Caves: The Development of the Chinese Eremitic Tradition to the End of the Han Dynasty*. Hong Kong: Chinese University Press, 1990.

Vittinghoff, Helmolt. "Recent Bibliography in Classical Chinese Philosophy." *Journal of Chinese Philosophy* 28, nos. 1–2 (2001).

Vogelsang, Kai. "Inscriptions and Proclamations: On the Authenticity of the 'Gao' Chapters in the *Book of Documents*." *Bulletin of the Museum of Far Eastern Antiquities* 74 (2002): 138–209.

Wagner, Donald B. *Iron and Steel in Ancient China*. Leiden: Brill, 1993.

Wang Aihe. *Cosmology and Political Culture in Early China*. Cambridge: Cambridge University Press, 2000.

Wang Baoguo 王保國. *Liang Zhou minben sixiang yanjiu* 兩周民本思想研究. Beijing: Xueyuan chubanshe, 2004.

Wang, Enbao, and Regina F. Titunik. "Democracy in the Theory and Practice of *Minben*." In *China and Democracy: The Prospect for a Democratic China*, ed. Zhao Suisheng, 73–88. New York: Routledge, 2000.

Wang, Hsiao-po, and Leo S. Chang. *The Philosophical Foundations of Han Fei's Political Theory*. Honolulu: University of Hawai'i Press, 1986.

Wang Hui 王暉. "Zhouyuan jiagu shuxing yu Shang Zhou zhi ji ji li de bianhua" 周遠甲骨屬性與商周之際祭禮的變化. In his *Guwenzi yu Shang Zhou shi xinzheng* 古文字與商周史新證, 15–41. Beijing: Zhonghua shuju, 2003.

Wang Hui 王輝, and Cheng Xuehua 程學華. *Qin wenzi jizheng* 秦文字集證. Taibei: Yinwen, 1999.

Wang Mingqin 王明欽. "Wangjiatai Qin mu zhujian gaishu" 王家台秦墓竹簡概述. In *Xin chu jianbo yanjiu* 新出簡帛研究, eds. Sarah Allan (Ailan 艾蘭) and Xing Wen 邢文, 26–49. Beijing: Wenwu, 2004.

Wang Ying 王穎. "Cong Baoshan Chu jian kan Zhanguo zhong wan qi Chu guo de shehui jingji" 從包山楚簡看戰國中晚期楚國的社會經濟. *Zhongguo shehui jingji shi yanjiu* 中國社會經濟史研究 3 (2004): 14–17.

Watson, Burton, trans. *Records of the Grand Historian*. Vol. 3: *Qin Dynasty*. Hong Kong: Chinese University of Hong Kong, 1993.

Wei Qipeng 魏啓鵬. "Shi *Liu de* 'wei fu jue jun'" 釋《六德》"為父絕君." *Zhongguo zhexue shi* 中國哲學史 2 (2001): 103–106.

Weld, Susan R. "Chu Law in Action: Legal Documents from Tomb 2 at Baoshan." In *Defining Chu*, eds. Constance A. Cook and John S. Major, 77–97. Honolulu: University of Hawai'i Press, 1999.

———. "The Covenant Texts at Houma and Wenxian." In *New Sources of Early Chinese History: An Introduction to Reading Inscriptions and Manuscripts*, ed. Edward L. Shaughnessy, 120–160. Berkeley: Society for Study of Early China, 1997.

Wu Baosan 巫寶三. *Xian Qin jingji sixiang shi* 先秦經濟思想史. Beijing: Shehui kexue chubanshe, 1996.

Wu Yujiang 吳毓江. "*Mozi* gepian zhenwei kao" 墨子各篇真偽考. In *Mozi jiao-zhu* 墨子校注, compiled and annotated by Wu Yujiang, 1025–1055. Beijing: Zhonghua shuju, 1994.

Xing Lin 邢琳. "Minben sixiang yu Zhongguo gudai zhuanzhizhuyi" 民本思想與中國古代專制主義. *Xuchang xueyuan xuebao* 許昌學院學報 24, no. 4 (2005): 8–11.

Xu Tianjin 徐天進. "Zhou Gong Miao yizhi de kaogu suo huo ji suo si" 周公廟遺址的考古所獲及所思 *Wenwu* 8 (2006): 55–62.

Xu Zhongshu 徐仲舒. "Jinwen guci shili" 金文嘏辭釋例 (1936). Rpt. in his *Xu Zhongshu lishi lunwen xuanji* 徐仲舒歷史論文選輯. 502–564. Beijing: Zhong-hua shuju, 1998.

Yan Buke 閻步克. *Shidafu zhengzhi yansheng shi gao* 士大夫政治演生史稿. 3rd ed. Beijing: Beijing daxue, 2003.

Yan Yichen 嚴毅沉. *Zhoudai shizu zhidu* 周代氏族制度. Harbin: Heilongjiang renmin chubanshe, 2001.

Yang Bojun 楊伯峻. "Dao yan" 導言. In *Lunyu yizhu* 論語譯注, annotated by Yang Bojun, 1–37. Beijing: Zhonghua shuju, 1991.

Yang Huyun 楊胡雲. *Zhongguo yinyi wenhua* 中國隱逸文化. Kunming: Yunnan daxue chubanshe, 2004.

Yang Kuan 楊寬. *Zhanguo shi* 戰國史. Rev. ed. Shanghai: Renmin chubanshe, 1998.

Yang Tianyu 楊天宇. "Zhou ren ji tian yi zu pei kao" 周人祭天以祖配考. *Shixue yuekan* 史學月刊 5 (2005): 24–26.

Yang Zhenhong 楊振紅. "Yue ling yu Qin Han zhengzhi zai tantao – jian lun yue ling yuanliu" 月令與秦漢政治再探討—兼論月令源流. *Lishi yanjiu* 歷史研究 3 (2004): 17–38.

Yates, Robin D. S. "The City State in Ancient China." In *The Archaeology of City-States: Cross-Cultural Approaches*, eds. Deborah L. Nichols and Thomas H. Charlton, 71–90. Washington, DC: Smithsonian, 1997.

———, trans. *The Five Lost Classics: Tao, Huang-Lao and Yin-Yang in Han China.* New York: Ballantine Books, 1997.

———. "Slavery in Early China: A Socio-Cultural Approach." *Journal of East Asian Archaeology* 3, nos. 1–2 (2001): 283–331.

———. "Texts on the Military and Government from Yinqueshan: Introductions and Preliminary Transcriptions." In *Xin chu jianbo yanjiu* 新出簡帛研究, eds. Sarah Allan (Ailan 艾蘭) and Xing Wen 邢文, 334–387. Beijing: Wenwu, 2004.

———. "The Yin Yang Texts from Yinqueshan: An Introduction and Partial Re-construction, with Notes on their Significance in Relation to Huang-Lao Daoism." *Early China* 19 (1994): 74–144.

Ye Jianfeng 葉劍鋒. "Lun Zhanguo baijia zhengming dui zhuanzhizhuyi de fuhua zuoyong ji qi lishi yingxiang" 論戰國百家爭鳴對專制主義的孵化作用及其歷史影響. *Hubei sheng shehuizhuyi xueyuan xuebao* 湖北省社會主義學院學報 4 (2004): 68–70.

Yin Qun 印群. *Huanghe zhongxiayou diqu de Dong Zhou muzang zhidu* 黃河中下游地區的東周墓葬制度. Beijing: Shehui kexue chubanshe, 2001.

———. "Lun beifang zhu quyu de Chunqiu Zhanguo mu" 論北方諸區域的春秋戰國墓. In his *Xian Qin kaogu tanwei* 先秦考古探微, 109–286. Beijing: Renmin ribao chubanshe, 2004.

———. "You Chunqiu shiqi Zhongyuan diqu suizang tong liqi zuhe kan dangshi guizu diwei zhi bianqian" 由春秋時期中原地區隨葬銅禮器組合看當時貴族地位之變遷. In his *Xian Qin kaogu tanwei* 先秦考古探微, 94–102. Beijing: Renmin ribao chubanshe, 2004.

Yin Zhenhuan 尹振環. "Cong wang wei jicheng he shi jun kan junzhu zhuanzhi lilun de zhubu xingcheng" 從王位繼承和弒君看君主專制理論的逐步形成. *Zhongguoshi yanjiu* 4 (1987): 17–24.

Yoshimoto Michimasa 吉本道雅. *Chūgoku sen Shin shi no kenkyū* 中國先秦史の研究. Kyōto: Kyōto University Press, 2005.

———. "Dankyū kō" 檀弓考. *Kodai bunka* 古代文化 44. no. 2 (1992): 38–46.

———. "Kyokurei kō" 曲禮考. In *Chūgoku kodai reisei kenkyū* 中國古代禮制研究, ed. Kominami Ichirō 小南一郎, 117–163. Kyōto: Kyōto University Press, 1995.

———. "Shunjū kokujin kō" 春秋國人考 *Shirin* 69, no. 5 (1986): 631–670.

———. "Shunjū kokujin sai kō" 春秋國人再考. *Ritsumeikan bungaku* 立命館文學 578 (2003): 581–592 http://www.ritsumei.ac.jp/acd/cg/lt/rb/578pdf/yoshimot.pdf.

Yoshinami Takashi 好并隆司. *Shōkun sho kenkyū* 商君書研究. Hiroshima: Keisuisha, 1992.

You Huanmin 游喚民. *Xian Qin minben sixiang yanjiu* 先秦民本思想研究. Changsha: Hunan daxue chubanshe, 1991.

Yu Yingshi 余英時. *Shi yu Zhongguo wenhua* 士與中國文化. Shanghai: Shanghai renmin chubanshe, 1987.

Yu Youqian 虞友謙. "Fandui junzhu zhuanzhi de sixiang xianqu – *Zhuangzi* wu jun lun sixiang chu tan" 反對君主專制的思想先驅—《莊子》無君論思想初探. *Fudan xuebao (shehui kexue ban)* 復旦學報（社會科學版）3 (1982): 82–88.

Yuan Lin 袁林. *Liang Zhou tudi zhidu xin lun* 兩周土地制度新論. Changchun: Dongbei shifan daxue chubanshe, 2000.

Zha Changguo 查昌國. "You yu liang Zhou junchen guanxi de yanbian" 友與兩周君臣關系的演變. *Lishi yanjiu* 歷史研究 5 (1998): 94–109.

Zhang Chunlong 張春龍. "Cili Chu jian gaishu" 慈利楚簡概述. In *Xin chu jianbo yanjiu* 新出簡帛研究, eds. Sarah Allan (Ailan 艾蘭) and Xing Wen 邢文, 4–11. Beijing: Wenwu, 2004.

Zhang Fentian 張分田. "Lun 'li jun wei min' zai minben sixiang tixi zhong de lilun diwei" 論"立君為民"在民本思想體系中的理論地位. *Tianjin shifan daxue xuebao (shehui kexue ban)* 天津示範大學學報(社會科學版）2 (2005): 1–7.

———. *Zhongguo diwang guannian—shehui pubian yishi zhong de 'zun jun—zui jun' wenhua fanshi* 中國帝王觀念—社會普遍意識中的"尊君—罪君"文化範式. Beijing: Zhongguo renmin daxue chubanshe, 2004.

Zhang Hengshou 張恒壽. "Lun Zichan de zhengzhi gaige he tiandao, minben sixiang" 論子產的政治改革和天道、民本思想. In his *Zhongguo shehui yu sixiang wenhua* 中國社會與思想文化, 139–169. Beijing: Renmin chubanshe, 1989.

Zhang Jue 張覺, annotator. *Shang jun shu quanyi* 商君書全譯. Guiyang: Guizhou renmin chubanshe, 1993.

Zhang Junmin 張俊民. "Qin dai de fu zhai fangshi – du *Xiangxi Liye Qin dai jian du xuanshi*" 秦代的付債方式—讀《相西里耶秦代簡牘選釋》. *Shaanxi lishi bowuguan guankan* 陝西歷史博物館館刊 10 (2003): 288–292.

Zhang Liwen 張立文. *Zhongguo zhexue fanchou fazhan shi (Tian Dao pian)* 中國哲學範疇發展史（天道篇）. Taibei: Wunan tushu chuban gongsi, 1996.

Zhang Mingqi 張鳴岐, and Bi Cheng 畢誠. "Ye tan 'xue er you ze shi'" 也談"學而優則仕". *Huadong shifan daxue xuebao* 華東師範大學學報 2 (1985): 43–46.

Zhang Qiwei 張奇偉. "Yang Meng yi Xun yu shijia de pinglun" 揚孟抑旬與史家的評論. *Shixue shi yanjiu* 史學史研究 4 (2001): 19–25.

Zhang Rongming 張榮明. *Zhongguo de guojiao: Cong shang gu dao Dong Han* 中國的國教—從上古到東漢. Beijing: Zhongguo shehui kexue chubanshe, 2001.

Zhang Xingjiu 張星久. "Rujia 'wu wei' sixiang de zhengzhi neihan yu shengcheng jizhi – jian lun 'Rujia ziyouzhuyi' wenti" 儒家"無爲"思想的政治内涵與生成機制—兼論儒家"自由主義"問題. *Zhengzhixue yanjiu* 政治學研究 2 (2000): 74–87.

Zhao Boxiong 趙伯雄. *Zhoudai guojia xingtai yanjiu* 周代國家形態研究. Changsha: Hunan jiaoyu, 1990.

Zhao Huacheng 趙化成. "Cong Shang Zhou 'jizhong gong mu zhi' dao Qin Han 'duli lingyuan zhi' de yanhua guiji" 從商周"集中公墓制"到秦漢"獨立陵園制"的演化軌跡. *Wenwu* 文物 7 (2006): 41–48.

Zhao Ping'an 趙平安. "*Qiong da yi shi* di jiu hao jian kaolun—jian ji xian Qin Liang Han wenxian zhong Bigan gushi de yanbian" 《窮達以時》第九號簡考論—兼及先秦兩漢文獻中比干故事的衍變, *Guji zhengli yanjiu xuekan* 古籍整理研究學刊 2 (2002): 18–21.

Zhao Shigang 趙世綱, and Zhao Li 趙莉. "Wenxian mengshu de lishuo yanjiu" 溫縣盟書的歷朔研究. In *Xin chu jianbo yanjiu* 新出簡帛研究, eds. Sarah Allan (Ailan 艾蘭) and Xing Wen 邢文, 197–205. Beijing: Wenwu, 2004.

Zheng Junhua 鄭君華. "Lun *Zuo zhuan* de min ben sixiang" 論左傳的民本思想. *Zhongguo zhexue* 中國哲學 10 (1983): 19–38.

Zheng Liangshu 鄭良樹. *Shang Yang ji qi xuepai* 商鞅及其學派. Shanghai: Guji chubanshe, 1989.

Zhou Daoji 周道濟. *Woguo minben sixiang de fenxi yu tantao* 我國民本思想的分析 與探討.Taibei: Zhongyang yanjiuyuan sanminzhuyi yanjiusuo, 1977.

Zhou Guitian 周桂鈿, ed. *Zhongguo zhengzhi zhexue*. Shijiazhuang: Hebei renmin chubanshe, 2001.

Zhu Fenghan 朱鳳瀚. *Shang Zhou jiazu xingtai yanjiu* 商周家族形態研究.Tianjin: Guji chubanshe, 1990.

Zhu Ziyan 朱子彦. "Xian Qin Qin Han shiqi de liang zhong junzhu guan" 先秦 秦漢時期的兩重君主觀. *Shixue yuekan* 史學月刊 2 (2004): 19–23.

Index

About the Author

Yuri Pines is a Michael W. Lipson Professor of Chineses Studies at the Hebrew University of Jerusalem. His earlier publications include *Foundations of Confucian Thought: Intellectual Life in the Chunqiu Period, 722–453 B.C.E.* (University of Hawai'i Press, 2002).